THE POLITICAL CONSEQUENCES
OF THINKING

SUNY Series in
Political Theory: Contemporary Issues
Philip Green, editor

THE POLITICAL CONSEQUENCES OF THINKING

Gender and Judaism in the Work of Hannah Arendt

Jennifer Ring

STATE UNIVERSITY OF NEW YORK PRESS

Published by
State University of New York Press, Albany

© 1997 State University of New York

All rights reserved

Printed in the United States of America

No part of this book may be used or reproduced in any manner whatsoever without written permission. No part of this book may be stored in a retrieval system or transmitted in any form or by any means including electronic, electrostatic, magnetic tape, mechanical, photocopying, recording, or otherwise without the prior permission in writing of the publisher.

For information, address State University of New York Press, State University Plaza, Albany, N.Y. 12246

Production by Marilyn P. Semerad
Marketing by Hannah J. Hazen

Library of Congress Cataloging-in-Publication Data

Ring, Jennifer, 1948–
  The political consequences of thinking : gender and Judaism in the work of Hannah Arendt / Jennifer Ring.
    p. cm. — (SUNY series in political theory. Contemporary issues)
  Includes bibliographical references and index.
  ISBN 0-7914-3483-4 (alk. paper).
  1. Arendt, Hannah. Eichmann in Jerusalem. 2. Holocaust, Jewish (1939–1945)—Influence. 3. World War, 1939–1945—Jews—Rescue––Palestine. 4. Holocaust, Jewish (1939–1945)—Public opinion.
  5. Public opinion—Israel. 6. Israel—Politics and government.
  7. Jews—New York (State)—New York—Politics and government.
  8. Arendt, Hannah. Jews as pariah. I. Title. II. Series.
D804.3.R54   1997
940.53'18—dc21   96-47278
                                                                  CIP

10 9 8 7 6 5 4 3 2 1

*For Norman, JoJo, and Lilly
with all my love*

CONTENTS

Acknowledgments	xi
Chapter 1 Introduction	1
Hannah Arendt, Judaism, and Gender	1
Identity Politics and Multiculturalism	4
Assimilation and Gender	6
Race and Gender	9
The Context of Feminist Theory	13
Structure and Organization of the Book	18
Chapter 2 The Politics of the *Eichmann* Controversy	21
Arendt and *Eichmann in Jerusalem*	21
The Controversy	26
Chapter 3 Israel and the Holocaust	43
The Dawning of Reality	46
The Structure of Discomfort	50
Attempts at Rescue	57
Israeli Attitudes Toward the Holocaust Victims	71
Postwar Negotiations with Germany	75
The "Kastner Trial"	80
The Trial of Adolf Eichmann	84
Chapter 4 The New York Intellectuals and *Eichmann in Jerusalem*	91
The New York Intellectuals and Judaism	91
The New York Intellectuals and the Holocaust	98
Postwar Politics and the New Yorkers	101
The New York Intellectuals and Hannah Arendt	103

Chapter 5	Race, Gender and Judaism:	
	The *Eichmann* Controversy as Case Study	109
	Nazis and Sexuality	112
	Racism, Sexism, and Jewish Masculinity	119
	Assimilation as Gendered:	
	The *Partisan Review* Crowd Revisited	131
	Jewish Women	139
	The *Eichmann* Controversy, Gender, and Judaism	150
Chapter 6	Transition	157
	Thinking about *Eichmann*	157
	The Political Consequences of Thinking	164
	Arendt as Jewish Gadfly	166
Chapter 7	Biblical and Rabbinic Approaches to Thinking	173
	Thinking Like a Jew	173
	The Bible	177
	Talmud	179
	Midrash	185
	The Middle Ages	186
	Mysticism	187
	Jewish Historical Consciousness	188
Chapter 8	Greek and Hebrew: The Structure of Thinking	195
	The Structure of Hebrew Thought Compared to Greek	196
	Rabbinic Thought	201
	Scaffolding	205
Chapter 9	Toward Understanding Arendt as a Jewish Thinker	213
	A Jewish Soul in a German Scholar	213
	The Political Trouble with Philosophy	220
	Warm-Up Exercise: An Impressionistic Reading of "Truth and Politics"	225

Chapter 10 The Pariah and Parvenu in *Thinking* 231
  Seeing and Hearing 231
  Classical and Jewish Orthodoxy 238
  Socrates as Pariah 242
  The Wordly Results of Thinking 247

Chapter 11 Jewish Themes in Political
    Action and History 255
  Judaism and the Space for Political Action 255
  Judaism and Arendt's Concept of History 263
  Community in Dark Times 270

Chapter 12 Conclusion 275
  Judaism 275
  Gender 284

Appendix Reviews of Raul Hilberg's
    The Destruction of the European Jews 289

Notes 297

Selected Bibliography 337

Index 349

ACKNOWLEDGMENTS

My deepest gratitude is reserved for my husband, Norman Jacobson, and our daughters, Johanna and Lillian. Their love and support sustains me always, most recently through a few difficult years. I am awed by their adaptability, lust for adventure, and cheerfulness, which allowed me to believe in this project and myself, even when little else was certain.

Tsipora Peskin reminded me that when a Jew writes for one person she writes for the world, and shared with me her personal insights about Israel during the post-Holocaust years.

Clay Morgan of SUNY Press and Series Editor Philip Green greeted this project with energy and enthusiasm after reading an early excerpt. Their support and editorial advice, along with the gratifying responses of the reviewers who read the manuscript for SUNY Press, ensured its timely completion.

I am also grateful for the support of my small family of friends who continue to read my work and to set an example of scholarly excellence and integrity: Elisabeth Young-Bruehl, Arlene Saxonhouse, Eugene Victor Wolfenstein, Michael Rogin, Hanna Pitkin, Mary Dietz, Joan Burton, Rabbi Judy Shanks, and my mother, Frances Ring. Thanks also to Peggy Spaugh for help with the final manuscript preparation, and to Pat Hull at U.C. Berkeley for stepping in at the last minute to extricate the manuscript from a computer that threatened to eat it. Her patience and tenacity ensured the book's safe arrival at press as well as the preservation of my sanity.

I wrote this book out of the deepest respect for the memory of Hannah Arendt, accompanied by my sense of her energy. I hope it is true to her spirit.

I also acknowledge the following editors/publishers for allowing me to reproduce materials:

Excerpts from THE LIFE OF THE MIND by Hannah Arendt, copyright © 1978 by Harcourt Brace & Company, reprinted by permission of the publisher.

Excerpts from THE BLUE AND YELLOW STARS OF DAVID by Dina Porat, Cambridge, Mass., reprinted by permission of the publisher: Harvard University Press, copyright © 1990 by the President and Fellows of Harvard College.

Excerpts from George L. Mosse, NATIONALISM AND SEXUALITY: MIDDLE-CLASS MORALITY AND SEXUAL NORMS IN MODERN EUROPE, copyright © 1985 by George L. Mosse. (Madison: The University of Wisconsin Press) reprinted by permission of The University of Wisconsin Press.

Excerpts from Paul Breines, TOUGH JEWS: POLITICAL FANTASIES AND THE MORAL DILEMMA OF AMERICAN JEWRY, 1990. New York: Basic Books reprinted by permission of Harper Collins Publishers.

Excerpts from Margaret Canovan, HANNAH ARENDT: A REINTERPRETATION OF HER POLITICAL THOUGHT reprinted with the permission of Cambridge University Press.

Excerpts from HEBREW THOUGHT COMPARED WITH GREEK by Thorleif Boman, copyright © 1960 SCM Press used by permission of Westminster John Knox Press.

Excerpts from BACK TO THE SOURCES reprinted with the permission of Simon & Schuster from BACK TO THE SOURCES by Barry Holtz, copyright © 1984 by Barry W. Holtz.

Excerpts from Amos Funkenstein, PERCEPTIONS OF JEWISH HISTORY, copyright © 1993, Berkeley: University of California Press reprinted by permission of The Regents of the University of California.

Excerpts from Yehuda Bauer, JEWS FOR SALE? NAZI-JEWISH NEGOTIATIONS, 1933-1945, copyright © 1994, New Haven: Yale University Press reprinted by permission of Yale University Press.

Excerpts from Hannah Arendt, THE HUMAN CONDITION, 1958. Chicago: The University of Chicago Press reprinted by permission of The University of Chicago Press.

Excerpts from THE SEVENTH MILLION, by Tom Segev. Translation, copyright © 1993 by Haim Watzman. Reprinted by permission of Hill and Wang, a division of Farrar, Strauss and Giroux, Inc.

H.R.Trevor-Roper's review of THE DESTRUCTION OF THE EUROPEAN JEWS by Raul Hilberg is reprinted from COMMENTARY, April, 1962, by permission; all rights reserved.

Excerpts from BETWEEN PAST AND FUTURE by Hannah Arendt. Copyright 1954, 1956, 1957, 1958, 1960, 1961 by Hannah Arendt. Used by permission of Viking Penguin, a division of Penguin Books USA, Inc.

Oscar Handlin, for permission to reprint excerpts from his review of Raul Hilberg's book THE DESTRUCTION OF THE EUROPEAN JEWS, from *American Journal of Sociology* 68, 1 (July 1962).

CHAPTER 1

Introduction

HANNAH ARENDT, JUDAISM, AND GENDER

This is another book about Hannah Arendt. The perspective that justifies its writing is deceptively simple, but I have nowhere read it before. My thesis is that Hannah Arendt was a Jewish woman, two facts about her identity which affected the content of her scholarship and the way her work has been received. That Jewishness and gender may have colored both her intellectual work and its reception has been neither acknowledged nor accepted. This is not to say that there has not been scholarly work done concerning both Arendt's gender and religion.[1] The point of this book is to consider the impact of her Jewish identity specifically on her *intellectual* work, and her gender on her work's *reception*.

My underlying agenda is to make it intellectually respectable to be a Jewish woman. This may not sound revolutionary: there have been many Jewish women intellectuals. Jews are, at least according to stereotype, a scholarly people, and so it is not surprising that Jewish women would be among the prominent intellectuals. But as I argue in chapter 5, this impression is false. While there have been a few prominent Jewish women scholars—for the most part writers and political activists—their numbers have been infinitesimal in comparison with the preponderance of Jewish male scholars. In addition, the prominence, which is to say, respectability, of the women results from the fact that their work can be divorced from Jewish scholarship per se. The old assimilationist adage, "A Man on the Street; A Jew at Home" applies also to public Jewish women. Until very recently, perhaps just a generation or two of Jewish feminists, Jewish women have earned public respect because their work was *not* intellectually Jewish. It has been either political—socialist or Zionist, and adhering to a male-defined party line—or literary and artistic, but not explicitly Jewish.

To claim that Jewish women scholars are respected *despite* their Jewishness, or that Hannah Arendt's life has been dichotomized into Jewish activist and German scholar may appear extravagant. Nobody, including Hannah Arendt, has denied that she was Jewish, or that her Judaism had a profound influence on her life. With regard to gender, feminists have studied and written about its impact on her life and work. My point of departure is subtle, but fundamental: I believe Arendt's "Jewishness" affected the content and structure of her scholarship, and that her "femaleness" affected the way her work was received, especially with regard to her most controversial work, *Eichmann in Jerusalem*. Arendt's "Jewishness" is usually discussed only in relation to her specifically Jewish political writings, which were composed early in her career, during the time of her flight from the Holocaust and arrival in New York. Her Jewishness has also been discussed in relation to the first book-length manuscript she wrote after her doctoral dissertation, *Rahel Varnhagen: The Life of a Jewish Woman*. It certainly makes sense to discuss Arendt's Jewishness in relation to her most explicitly Jewish writings. But it also serves the purpose of segregating her most respected scholarship from her Jewishness, as though her cultural identity should have no influence whatsoever upon her most influential work. I will not spend much time in this volume on either her Jewish political writings, or on *Rahel Varnhagen*.[2] Indeed, I confess to an unfashionable disinterest in *Rahel Varnhagen*—I have read it several times, and simply find it less compelling than Arendt's other work. I am in pretty good company in this opinion. Karl Jaspers, while encouraging Arendt to publish the volume, found it a "loveless" treatment of Varnhagen. "This work still seems to me to be your own working through of the basic question of Jewish existence, and in it you use Rahel's reality as a guide to help you achieve clarity and liberation for yourself.... Rahel seems to have wakened neither your interest nor your love.... No *picture of Rahel* herself emerges but only, so to speak, a picture of events that chose this individual as their vehicle.... Your view of Rahel is, I feel, loveless."[3] Arendt used Jaspers' criticism as justification for her insistence that she did not want to publish the book: "Regardless of what I will have to say here in response to your letter, our agreement remains in force: I won't publish the book."[4] This is not to say that the work an author does *not* want to publish might not prove an elucidating avenue toward understanding her work; only to state at the outset, that I leave analysis of *Varnhagen* to others more interested in probing it.

The themes addressed in both *Rahel Varnhagen* and Arendt's Jewish political writings *are* important to my work here, but I will not approach them directly. Instead, I focus upon the writing presumed to be free of Jewish influence. Arendt's central Jewish concepts, for which I will look in the least obvious sources, are the pariah and parvenu, the outsider and the assimilationist. I will seek their presence in what is usually regarded as Arendt's most "ethnic free" work: *The Human Condition* and *Thinking*, the first volume of *The Life of the Mind*. The logic is that while it is not difficult to find Jewish themes in Arendt's most explicitly Jewish writings, if there is also evidence of the influence of Judaism on even her most "universal" or "objective" works in political theory, we stand to learn something about the role Judaism played throughout her work, and can better understand her as an integrated person. She was a Jewish woman scholar, rather than an activist Jew early in her life, a classical scholar interested in political action early in her scholarly career and in thinking only later on, and a woman only when she baked pastries or offered culinary advice to Gertrud Jaspers.[5] By extension, we stand to learn something about the influence of race and ethnicity on scholarship.

IDENTITY POLITICS AND MULTICULTURALISM

From this standpoint, then, the book is a case study in identity politics and cultural pluralism. What influence, if any, does cultural identity have upon creative work? The question is central to our time, and freighted with significance. Hannah Arendt and a host of serious scholars deny the impact of her Jewish identity upon her intellectual work. By nearly unanimous agreement, the major influences on Arendt's *scholarship* are taken to be Kant, Heidegger, Jaspers, Socrates, Aristotle, and perhaps Augustine. By nearly equally unanimous agreement, the central influence on her *political* convictions are regarded as the rise of totalitarianism in Europe, the Holocaust, and the political refuge Arendt found in the United States. Anti-Semitism is linked to totalitarianism, and her Jewish interest in preventing its recurrence is acknowledged to have had an impact on her political outlook, at least to the extent of shaping her sometimes idealistic faith in democracy, her belief in the importance of statehood and national identity, and her disdain for arrivistes and social climbing parvenus. To suggest, however, that there may exist some "Jewish" influence upon her scholarship is taken as smacking of racist essentialism.

Such resistance to considering the influence of Judaism on Arendt's scholarly life itself strikes me as a form of anti-Semitism. The assumption that one's life experiences as an African American, a Spanish American, an Asian American, or Native American may influence the way one reads, thinks, responds politically, and writes, is the foundation of the multicultural project in American academic life: a perspective I regard as completely legitimate. While I do not believe the claims of multiculturalism should be used as an excuse to ignore the important works of the Western tradition, neither do I believe that those "classics" comprise the exclusive essence of an education, nor that an education that overlooks race, ethnicity, and gender can be complete. But cultural blindness on the part of both Western European cultural chauvinists *and* advocates of a multicultural approach have overlooked Judaism as a part of identity politics and the multicultural dialogue. Defenders of the "Western tradition" regard Judaism as parochial, while defenders of multicultural progressivism regard it as conservative and "white." It has been left to Jewish feminists to argue that neither side has it right: Judaism is neither "white" nor "male," neither conservative nor "ethnically correct," implying inherently progressive politics. Part of my project here is to explore the influence of Judaism upon creative work, as one might explore the influence of any other cultural identity upon one's scholarly or artistic perspective.

Raising the question of the influence of Jewish identity upon Arendt's (or any Jewish scholar's) work raises a host of questions pertaining to multiculturalism itself. I will focus on two major issues: (1) the trade-off between parochialism and racial exclusivity, on the one hand, and assimilation on the other; and (2) the intersection of racism and sexism as components of the mechanism of oppression.

How does membership in an ethnic, religious, racial, cultural, or gender group affect one's creativity or scholarly product? Some forms of creativity are expressive, make no pretense at "objectivity," and thus the influence of race or ethnicity is not regarded as "undermining" of excellence. Still, there is a "Western tradition" in art and music that privileges certain forms of expression as "the canon," as defining greatness. Kant's aesthetic and moral philosophy assumes a noumenal essence of beauty and goodness with no acknowledgment that our ability to "recognize" excellence may very well be culturally determined. On the other hand, what is the relationship between "folk art," for example, and "fine art"? Does the terminology itself reflect cultural bias? Or are there valid standards of evaluation that may be undermined by a glib deference to cultural relativism?

The issue that concerns me is in a way even more complex, since it has to do not with creative or artistic expression but with the nature of philosophical or ethical "truth." Here the name of the game is "universalism" or "objectivity." To be interested in truth, or in thinking, but not in objectivity is regarded as a contradiction in terms. The assumption is that "Jewish truth" cannot differ from "Christian truth." Truth and thinking transcend particularity. It might be argued that Arendt's project in *The Life of the Mind* was to articulate a method for thinking that would not defer to a monolithic and static conception of "Truth." Was that project culturally determined? Is the conception of thinking she sought to articulate, with its dialogical method and insistence on lack of closure, more compatible with a "Jewish" conception of "truth" than, for example, a Christian European conception? Is there a way to discuss the cultural determinants of her project without reducing both Judaism and Christianity to stereotypes and oversimplifications? Jews adhere to a monotheistic, profoundly acorporeal image of God, while Christianity adheres to a Trinitarian view of God and believes in Jesus as the incarnation of God: both corporeal and visible. Does that affect either the Jewish or Christian conception of truth? These are just the most obvious differences that surface when one thinks of comparing Christian and Jewish philosophy. Obviously, Christianity and Judaism are more complex than can be reduced to even the simplest formulae such as these. But does that complexity make it impossible to address the role of religious background upon a philosopher's approach to truth?

On top of this complexity is the question of whether religion, conceived more broadly as cultural heritage, has an effect upon intellectuals who are not particularly religious. Arendt was unquestionably Jewish; indeed, being Jewish in a time and place of anti-Semitic genocide determined the course of her life and work. But she was by nobody's account a religious person. So what does it mean to identify her as "Jewish" in relation to her scholarly work?

ASSIMILATION AND GENDER

Hannah Arendt wrote powerfully on the dangers of assimilation, of her disrespect for parvenus, for those Jews who sought to escape their Jewishness, who thought they could be "A Man in the Street and a Jew at Home." She regarded them as social climbers, arrivistes, "inauthentic"—and by no means benign. Their betrayal of themselves through escape from Judaism fed anti-Semitism. However, when it came to her intellectual life, I shall argue, Arendt herself sought to assimilate to the respectability of the classical tradition: standards of truth and excellence defined by Greek, Roman, Christian, and Western European (particularly German) influences. Thus while she proudly laid claim to her classical scholarly background, she did not perceive that claim as assimilationist. She wrote to Gershom Scholem in 1963, in response to his criticism of *Eichmann in Jerusalem*, in which he accused her of being "from the German Left," "I am not one of the 'intellectuals who came from the German Left. . . .' I came late to an understanding of Marx's importance because I was interested neither in history nor in politics when I was young. If I can be said to 'have come from anywhere,' it is from the tradition of German philosophy." In the same letter Arendt also identified herself as a Jew, "as a matter of course": "Well, in this sense I do not 'love' the Jews, nor do I 'believe' in them; I merely belong to them as a matter of course, beyond dispute or argument."[6] The two nonintegrated aspects of her identity are experienced unproblematically. She saw herself as a German philosopher and a Jew, but in separate aspects of her life.

If Arendt herself saw no problem in keeping the main parts of her identity separate, on what grounds, then, can I suggest that she was a Jewish woman parvenu in a Christian male intellectual world? Does identifying a Jewish strain in Arendt's scholarship when she identified herself only as a European-educated scholar betray arrogance and detachment on my part? Am I suggesting that she suffered from "false consciousness," performing a crude sort of psychological reductionism, pretending to be able to probe Hannah Arendt's unconscious? I do not intend to stand in judgment of Hannah Arendt's relationship to her Judaism, but to use her to explore the temptations of assimilation, and the limitations of exclusionism, in myself, as another Jewish woman scholar, and by implication in all of us who consider ourselves outsiders.

Whether I succeed in striking the proper tone—respectful, neither arrogant nor overly deferential—is of course left to the judgment of the reader.

These questions are complicated by the fact that assimilation itself is a term in need of definition. It is unlikely that assimilation is a one-way street, with "dominant society" defining the terms to which newcomers or outsiders must conform. Chances are there is some mutuality of influence. The cultural standards to which Jews sought to conform in Europe and the United States were not monolithic and static but, like everything else, responsive to historical and economic influences, including the arrival of newcomers into their midst. When we discuss assimilation as embodying the dangers of loss of culture, when orthodox Jews, for example, fear that any mingling with the goyim will result in contamination and loss of Judaism, we assume that assimilation demands relinquishment of a culture conceived in static terms, a molding of the community of outsiders to the dominant culture, also perceived in static terms. Surely this is an extreme and somewhat distorted picture.

Still, a more moderate fear of loss of identity through assimilation continues to characterize every ethnic group seeking to enter an existing society. On the one hand, there is the desire to fit, to participate in the advantages and privileges available from society. Beyond the instrumental advantages, there exist inherent benefits to experiencing more of the world: parochialism is by definition limiting. It may offer security, but can also be experienced as confining, suffocating. On the other hand, no group is so filled with self-loathing that it welcomes its own dissolution into another group. One "assimilates" at the risk of losing authenticity and self-knowledge. The completely assimilated person may possess less of him or herself than the unassimilated outsider.

Adding to the complications of assimilation is a fact that has been largely neglected by scholars: assimilation is gendered. The pathways toward assimilation for men and women are different. Men are often expected to be assimilated first and more fully. The definition of assimilation often presumes that the group to be assimilated are men. The primary model of Jewish assimilation in Western Europe and the United States is male; women were given the task of preserving, to the extent possible, Judaism in the home. This is discussed in chapter 5.[7]

With regard to Hannah Arendt, I shall argue that she retained her disdain for social assimilationism, but was oblivious to the dangers of scholarly assimilation. But there is a complicating factor: her vulnerability to the Greek and Christian standards of Western European scholarship was, I believe, shaped by her gender. Jewish male intellectuals may also be susceptible to the belief that Jewish scholarship is parochial in a manner antithetical to the pursuit of "classical" truth or "objectivity." However, scholarship is such a dearly held cultural priority for Jewish men that becoming a secular European or American scholar, rather than a more traditional Talmudic scholar, was one of the acceptable paths of Jewish male assimilation. No such path was open to Jewish women.

A Jewish woman scholar was, to begin with, never a scholar of Judaism. For a modern woman to choose a scholarly life was itself a break with Jewish tradition, and so it is possible to see that Arendt was never aware of the "choice" of being either a Jewish or an assimilated scholar. If she were to be a scholar, she *had* to be a European "universalist" scholar, which makes it more comprehensible that she would have neglected Jewish sources in her intellectual work. Still, I will raise the questions, in chapters 9, 10, and 11, of the tenacious, if sometimes unconscious, influence of her Jewish heritage upon the content of her work. I will attribute to Arendt's "Jewish soul" questions raised as she sought to articulate a worldly way of thinking available to all people, not just experts. And I will argue that Arendt the German-educated scholar could not respond adequately to the questions raised by her Jewish soul. The discord between her Jewish self and her German scholarly persona accounts for a lack of resolution in her final intellectual project.

RACE AND GENDER

Also addressed in this volume: the relationship between race, or ethnicity, and gender in the modern world. The first part of the book is a discussion of the response to Arendt's most controversial work, *Eichmann in Jerusalem*. I argue that the rage directed at her report in *The New Yorker* and its subsequent publication as a book was excessive, reflecting something deeper than rationally based objections to her observations and conclusions. The vitriolic nature of the response from prominent Jews in the United States and Israel was affected by the fact that Arendt was a Jewish woman, the only Jewish woman with a public following to speak out against the entirely male leadership of the European and Israeli Jewish communities during the Holocaust. Holocaust survivors, Israeli Zionists, and American Jewish intellectuals had very little in common, and few points of agreement on anything having to do with the Holocaust. In effect, they were all prepared to accuse the other groups of cowardice, incompetence, and failure to respond adequately and appropriately to the Nazi menace. But they reached an uncharacteristic consensus on what they considered the inappropriateness of Arendt's response, which in part accused the Jewish leadership of cowardice, incompetence, and failure to respond adequately and appropriately to the Nazi menace.

The book opens with a detailed account of the response to Arendt's *Eichmann*, and works its way to a systematic analysis of gender as a determining dimension, in chapter 5. In brief, my argument is that Jewish men in America, Europe, and Israel had different but related reasons to feel "unmanned," in a specifically sexual way, by the Holocaust. But the Holocaust was the culmination of at least a century of anti-Semitic racism, in which Jews were accused of being sexually debased, with Jewish men labeled "feminine" and Jewish women "masculine." George Mosse's superb study of the relationship between nationalism, racism, sexism, and homophobia is discussed in some detail in this context.[8] Implicit in Mosse's analysis is the interdependence of racism and sexism. Racism is an extension of nationalism, with sexism a central component of the mechanism of racial prejudice. It was no accident that Jews were associated with "abnormal" sexuality, albeit in a hailstorm of contradictions: Jewish men were effeminate, had homosexual proclivities, and were also lascivious, lusting after gentile women. By labeling them "Other" sexually, the Nazis sought to provoke enough fear to "justify" their plan to annihilate the Jews.

Nazi genocide may have been the extreme example of the convergence of racism, sexism, and homophobia. However, sexist imagery is a part of every form of racism. The pertinent correlate for contemporary Americans is the history of anti-black racism in the United States. Prevailing racist stereotypes of African American men also present them as sexual predators, libidinous, violent, out of control. Simultaneously, opponents of racism claim black men have been "emasculated" by a history of slavery and racist oppression. While racists and progressives argue over the nature of black male sexual identity, black women disappear from the dialogue, the focus of nobody's concern about either racist or sexist oppression. Black feminists have argued that a more accurate reading of African American history is that black women have been "masculinized," turned into work animals and idealized as towers of strength, regarded as sexual, which is to say sexually available to any man with the inclination, but not feminine—a trait reserved for white women in American society. Bell hooks argues that African men, while enslaved by Americans, were encouraged to dominate their own women, and fell into the trap of imitating white patriarchal customs, a form of "identification with the oppressor" that continues the cycle of racial and sexual oppression in America today.[9]

The black feminist argument holds for all racially oppressed groups, including Jews. A European Christian model of masculinity has been sold to men throughout at least the Western world, perhaps all of the world that has been colonialized or fallen under control of European imperialism. The sexual "ideal" of aggressive, combative, domineering masculinity has served to keep both racial and sexual hierarchies in place. One form this oppression takes is that women of racial or cultural minorities who publicly object to domination from the men of their own group run the risk of being accused of "race betrayal" by their communities. Hannah Arendt did not speak out publicly on issues that could in any way be defined as "feminist." But she did publicly criticize Jewish "patriarchs," the Jewish male leaders of the mid-twentieth century. That these men were the intended victims not only of Nazi genocide, but of worldwide consensus on their lack of masculinity—a stereotype that may have arisen as recently as with the rise of nationalism, or may go back as far as the rabbinic age—made her criticism unbearable to much of the Jewish community after the Holocaust. The Jewish response, and especially the response of the Jewish leadership in America and Israel to Arendt's outspokenness, was suitably crazed.

I risk arousing similar objections to my argument in this book, that Jewish women have a problem not only with anti-Semites, but with certain Jewish patriarchal attitudes. In chapter 5 I discuss the "problem" of the contemporary generation of Jewish male scholars who are attuned to feminist issues with insight, conviction, and sophistication. The problem is, with so many helpful Jewish men in the community, on what grounds can I criticize their resistance, as well as the resistance of many of their feminist friends and colleagues, to seeing the links between anti-Semitism and *Jewish* silencing of Jewish women who break ranks with prevailing scholarly norms? Anti-Semitism not only victimizes Jews with its sexual slander: the accusation that Jewish men are (horrors!) feminine. Anti-Semitic sexism, and by extension any racist sexism, works because Jewish men act in collusion with it when they silence and dominate Jewish women in the name of not embarrassing the Jews. They tacitly accept the anti-Semitic image that Jewish men are effeminate if they "allow" their women a public and critical voice.

Hannah Arendt spoke out publicly and critically about Jewish leadership during the Holocaust and was accused of betraying the Jewish people. Anita Hill was publicly critical of a prominent black man and was accused of betraying the African American community. But that is another issue. Men who regard themselves as Jewish feminists should look at their own needs when they participate in setting the Jewish feminist agenda: presentation of themselves as unimaginably understanding men effectively silences female criticism yet again, this time by co-opting it. These men might take a turn at just listening.

So, of course, might the Jewish men who are not feminists, and who believe that any criticism, especially public, from a Jewish woman is unforgivable. So, too, should non-Jewish members of cultural minorities who, in upholding male domination, inadvertently strengthen its correlate, racial dominance, by silencing the women of their own communities.[10]

THE CONTEXT OF FEMINIST THEORY

A methodological note is important here, and so is locating this work in the context of Feminist Theory. I have written elsewhere, and more extensively, on the subject of epistemology and feminist theory, and will not digress on that subject at any length here.[11] Still, two things should be noted: (1) many of the aspects of my argument in this volume are not amenable to the conventional standards of positivist, empirical proof, and (2) there exists extensive literature dicussing the hidden gender biases in so-called objective, empirical scientific studies.

The argument about race betrayal is a good example of the inappropriateness of conventional empirical evidence. Women who provoke the charge of "race betrayal," such as Anita Hill when she came forward with accusations of sexual misconduct against Justice Clarence Thomas, or Hannah Arendt, when she came forward with criticism of the European Jewish leadership during the Holocaust, are unlikely to be directly accused of making the *men* of the race look bad. Nobody is about to say, "The dignity of Jewish (or African American or Hispanic or Asian American) men is more important than, and indeed incompatible with, publicly expressed female criticism of any sort!" We are beyond the point of saying directly, "Be Silent, Woman!" along with Sophocles, or Aristotle quoting Sophocles in his *Politics*: "A modest silence is a woman's crown." I believe something similar to that sentiment is still pervasive, but it will no longer be stated directly, anymore than racist sentiments, especially among the intelligentsia, are expressed as explicitly as they were thirty or forty years ago. More likely, instead of saying, "The dignity of Jewish (or African American, or Hispanic or Asian American) *men* must be protected," the statement is phrased, "The dignity of the Jewish *people* is at stake here!" never acknowledging that the particular ethnic group is being defined exclusively by its men. As black feminists know, when the question arises, as it has from time to time throughout history, of whose needs should take precedence "Blacks or Women?" Black women disappear from the discourse. The 1869 Congressional decision to give black men the vote was referred to as "The Negroes' Hour" (although Angela Davis, in *Women, Race and Class*, believes it should more accurately have been referred to as "The Hour of the Republican Party"), thoroughly overlooking the exclusion of black, as well as white and other, women from the enfranchisement.

One aspect of the difficulty of "proving" that gender influences a controversy, is that public display of female anger is taboo. The taboo itself is hidden, perhaps because even acknowledging women's anger, unless it is in the service of sexual devotion to a man, is so frightening that we cannot face it long enough to perceive the prohibition against it.[12] When women's anger *is* acknowledged, it is tamed by the modifier "irrational." She is not righteously angry, as a strong, intelligent man might be: she is crazy. As bell hooks notes, "Madness, not just physical abuse, was the punishment for too much talk if you were female."[13]

Thus I will not be able to point to an instance of one of Hannah Arendt's critics during the *Eichmann* controversy stating directly: "Underlying my objection to what Arendt wrote is that I can't abide women's critical anger directed at respected public men." The response of Arendt's critics, both during the 1960s and today, has more often been: "Gender had absolutely nothing to do with what was offensive about *Eichmann in Jerusalem*. The criticism stemmed from the fact that she betrayed the Jewish community, and it made no difference whatsoever that she was a woman making the argument."

There is abundant feminist literature on the difficulty of "seeing," or finding evidence for gender bias in the world, as well as on the engenderment of public discourse. In *Talking*

Back: Thinking Feminist, Thinking Black, for example, bell hooks discusses the pervasive, and cross-cultural penchant for silencing women. She refers to young girls' habit of keeping diaries as symptomatic of "the fear of exposure, the fear that one's deepest emotions and innermost thoughts will be dismissed as mere nonsense . . . holding and hiding speech." With regard more specifically to adult women's public voices, hooks notes "For many women, it is not a simple task to talk about men or to consider writing about men. Within patriarchal society, silence has been for women a gesture of submission and complicity, especially silence about men. Women have faithfully kept male secrets, have passionately refused to speak on the subject of men."[14]

Carol Gilligan's *In A Different Voice* (1982) is a widely respected discussion of the unacknowledged engenderedness of scholarly discourse.[15] Gilligan analyzes hidden male biases in the well-respected studies on moral reasoning of Harvard psychologist Lawrence Kohlberg. Kohlberg and his associates developed a scale of ranked hierarchies of complexity of moral thinking. Gilligan demonstrates that the scale assumes a male perspective, ranking the girls who participated in the studies at a "lower" level of reasoning than the boys, yet not perceiving that the test results reflected a gender bias that remained unexplored and unaccounted for. The overall "higher" scores achieved by the boys were assumed to have been objectively merited. Male moral reasoning, at least as exemplified by our culture, involves the capacity to "individuate," to create distance between the self and the moral problem, and the capacity to think abstractly, in terms of impersonal rights. An alternative, which Gilligan argues is more characteristic of girls and women, and which was considered by Kohlberg to be less sophisticated than the boys' abstract reasoning, is the ability to become involved, to reason in terms of responsibility to another person rather than abstract rights. Since in our culture the ability to reason abstractly, to differentiate oneself from others, is defined as adulthood itself, the males studied by Kohlberg appeared more advanced, not only in terms of their ability to think through a moral dilemma, but also in terms of basic "maturity." The girls of the test, and women in general, were perceived as more childlike, unable to differentiate between themselves and another human being.

An unbiased perspective would have taken into account not "natural" diffences in males and females, but sufficiently different cultural experiences to account for alternative models of adulthood, *not* ranked hierarchically. Whatever the flaws of Gilligan's study, it was a pathbreaking work in articulating the invisibility of male bias uncritically accepted as "objective" and showered in scholarly respectibility.

On a more abstract level, Catharine MacKinnon, in a number of works, discusses gender politics and male bias at the very core of the concept of objectivity. "The male epistemological stance, which corresponds to the world it creates, is objectivity: the ostensibly uninvolved stance, the view from a distance and from no particular perspective apparently transparent to its reality. It does not comprehend its own perspectivity, does not recognize what it sees as subjective like itself.... What is objectively known corresponds to the world and can be verified by pointing to it (as science does) because the world itself is controlled from the same point of view"[16] The penchant to regard objectivity as the icon of truth is itself gendered, and not recognized as such. Many aspects of women's experience cannot be identified by pointing to them.

MacKinnon is well supported by feminist philosophers of science and knowledge. Prevailing public sentiment may regard the "truths" of "hard" science—physics, for example—as simply unarguable. But there remain issues, addressed by Sandra Harding, Evelyn Fox Keller, Anne Fausto-Sterling, and others, about how the questions that have come to define physics became paradigmatic in the first place. Who sets the agenda for the priorities in scientific inquiry? Why is the physical world defined as more "real" than the less tangible worlds of culture and expression? How is it that the methodologies of the physical and biological sciences are more highly respected than the methodologies of the humanities and the arts? That is, the entitlement and privileging of a given epistemology (empiricism, positivism) is *itself* culturally determined, and gendered by virtue of the gender of the majority of its practitioners. Harding remarks, "I have been suggesting reasons for reevaluating the assumption that physics should be the paradigm of scientific knowledge seeking. If physics ought not to have this status, then feminists need not 'prove' that Newton's laws of mechanics, or Einstein's relativity theory are value laden in order to make the case that the science we have is suffused with . . . gender."[17]

Feminist theorists have also identified hitherto unrecognized male biases in even the most progressive or radical social theories. Consider Nancy Hartsock's critique of traditional Marxist theory in her essay "The Feminist Standpoint"[18] The "standpoint position" as defined by Hartsock is not simply an "interested" position, but also an engaged one. This is obviously antithetical to the "scientific" neutrality or objectivity preferred by conventional scientists of all stripes, but also a departure from the "engagement" of Marx's "scientific socialism," his historical materialist stance. For while dialectical materialism does acknowledge the limits of positivist objectivism, it is also characterized by the conceit that it embodies the "one true" stance toward history. In contrast, Hartsock suggests, "A specifically feminist historical materialism might . . . enable us to expand the Marxian account to include all human activity rather than focussing on activity more characteristic of males in capitalism" (158). The difference between this and the stance that presumes its own objectivity is that "The concept of a standpoint structures epistemology in a particular way. Rather than a simple dualism, it posits a duality of levels of reality" (160).

Thus I am hardly the first theorist to argue for the engenderedness of a public controversy that has not before been seen as gendered. I suggest not that gender is the *only* lens through which to view the *Eichmann* controversy and its reception, but that it is a plausible and powerful interpretation, giving us insight into how gender works, and making sense of an otherwise somewhat mysterious hostility toward Arendt. In this sense, I would argue, along with the psychologists, that the total denial of the role played by gender in the controversy is suspect, and may point to an important dimension of resistance to seeing gender as pervasively at work as it is in the world. In my discussion of the *Eichmann* controversy, and Arendt's scholarship written in its aftermath, I do not "apply" feminist theory in an overt way. Rather, my working assumptions are feminist in that I believe that many things, including public discourse, are gendered while not acknowledged to be, and I look for that dimension in the details that underlay manifest social data.

STRUCTURE AND ORGANIZATION OF THE BOOK

Having insisted that Hannah Arendt was one woman, a Jewish scholar, educated in the German classical tradition but encountering life experiences that imposed both her Jewishness and her gender upon her scholarly life, I now confess that the book I have written is divided into two parts, one dealing with the Jewish politics of the controversy over *Eichmann in Jerusalem* and the other dealing with Arendt's intellectual project that grew out of the controversy. While I do not intend this division to signal my acquiescence to dividing Arendt into a Jewish political writer and a European philosophical scholar, I intend the discussion as a careful examination of what happened to turn the response to *Eichmann* into the trauma that it was for Arendt, and how the unexpected force of criticism resulted in her efforts to expand upon her claim that the absence of thinking is sufficient to create political catastrophes. The themes that unite the political controversy and the scholarly project are Judaism and gender.

The first part of the book, on the *Eichmann* controversy, considers both Jewish and gender politics. Jewish politics are considered from the standpoint of the Israeli response to *Eichmann*, as well as the response of the New York Jewish intellectuals who led the American attack on Arendt. The Eichmann trial was a loaded political issue in Israel, the focal point of a decades-long battle between Labor Zionists and Conservative Zionists in the Yishuv, over the proper relationship between Israel and Germany before, during, and after the Holocaust. Tied in with this was the complicated history of attitudes toward Diaspora Jews. David Ben Gurion and the Mapai party had a particular stake in claiming responsibility for capturing and prosecuting Eichmann, since they had borne the brunt of conservative criticism that their pragmatic political stance had amounted to collaboration with the Nazis. They also had a particular stake in Hannah Arendt not reminding the world of the Israeli political battles that had preceded Eichmann's capture. They sought to prosecute Eichmann in the name of World Jewry, not the Labor Zionist party.

The New York Intellectuals, assimilationists who had reason to be embarrassed by their avoidance of their Jewish identities throughout their lives, including during the Holocaust, and who had recently undergone a remarkable political odyssey from socialism to conservatism, also had a stake in not being reminded of their less than satisfactory response to European Jews during the Holocaust. There thus existed related but not identical reasons for prominent Jews in Israel and America to have been upset by Arendt's report. What brought the two sides together was the gender dimension, the relationship between anti-Semitic racism and sexism, discussed in detail in chapter 5.

The second part of the book is the discussion of Jewish themes in Arendt's "non-Jewish" writings: the essays dealing with the nature of truth and community from *Between Past and Future* and *Men in Dark Times*, and *Thinking*, in which she systematically attempts to find in the history of philosophy, and articulate for worldly use, an approach to thinking that would be applicable to worldly concerns, firmer than "opinion," less monolithic than "Truth," open-ended and dialogical, and available to all people, not just "professional thinkers" and philosophers. My argument is that the sort of thinking she sought closely resembles a rabbinic style, although she was unaware of that fact. Arendt was thus more of a Jewish thinker than she knew or acknowledged, and less than she needed to be to successfully accomplish her purpose in *The Life of the Mind*.

In order to make my case convincingly, I need to present a coherent description of "Jewish thinking," which I offer in chapters 7 and 8. Chapter 7 deals with the history of Jewish thought from Biblical and Talmudic times, to modern conceptions of the meaning of history to Jews; chapter 8 is a structural and epistemological analysis of Jewish thinking, incorporating a comparison of Greek and Hebrew thought, from the standpoint of Thorlief Boman's classic monograph, and Max Kadushin's traditional Jewish discussion of the structure of rabbinic thought, as well as a discussion of contemporary scholarship on the characteristics of rabbinic thinking. In the final three chapters, I attempt to apply the accumulated discussion of the nature of Jewish thinking to Arendt's quest in *Thinking*, culminating in her presentation of Socrates, and finally to the concept of political action and public space in *The Human Condition* and *Between Past and Future*.

The effort thus, is to determine how the female and Jewish aspects of Hannah Arendt's existence exerted influence upon her work and its reception, without reducing her in any way to a prefabricated, cookie-cutter image of a "Jewish Woman." Along the way, we should learn something about the impact of identity politics on intellectual life with its presumption to be above it all.

CHAPTER 2

The Politics of the *Eichmann* Controversy

ARENDT AND *EICHMANN IN JERUSALEM*

That *Eichmann in Jerusalem* represents a critical turning point in Arendt's life and work is widely acknowledged. The controversy greeting its publication is infamous, and was profoundly disturbing to Arendt. Her biographer believes it scarred and shortened her life, as she felt misunderstood, betrayed, and abandoned by old friends and colleagues. In terms of Arendt's own appraisal, as well as her commentators, *Eichmann in Jerusalem* was a work that presented her with the project that lasted until the end of her life. As Elisabeth Young-Bruehl reports: "The controversy precipitated by Hannah Arendt's series in the *New Yorker* raged for nearly three years, and it continues to simmer even now when the book made from the articles is in its twentieth reprinting. Almost every study of the Holocaust published since 1963 has explicitly or implicitly acknowledged the controversy and the fierce emotions that flowed through it." Young-Bruehl also attributes the book with prompting Arendt "to write her political morals.... What she aimed at was a political Critique of Judgment."[1] It has been obvious from Arendt's notes, in nearly everything she wrote after *Eichmann in Jerusalem*, that Eichmann impressed upon her the importance of articulating a worldly way of thinking in order to prevent the recurrence of thoughtless evil. From "Truth and Politics": "This essay was caused by the so-called controversy after the publication of *Eichmann in Jerusalem*."[2] From "Thinking and Moral Considerations": "To talk about thinking seems to me so presumptuous that I feel I owe you a justification. Some years ago, reporting on the trial of Eichmann in Jerusalem, I spoke of 'the banality of evil' and meant with this no theory or doctrine, but something quite factual, the phenomenon of evil deeds, committed on a gigantic scale, which would not be traced to any particularity of wickedness, pathology, or ideological conviction in the doer, whose only personal distinction was perhaps extraordinary shallowness."[3] From *The Life of the Mind*: "Actually, my preoccupation with mental activities has two rather different origins. The immediate impulse came from my attending the Eichmann trial in Jerusalem . . . the only notable characteristic . . . in his [Eichmann's] behavior . . . was not stupidity but *thoughtlessness*. . . . Could the activity of thinking as such, the habit of examining . . . be among the conditions that make men abstain from evil-doing or even actually 'condition' them against it?"[4]

Two dimensions of Arendt's *Eichmann* argument have upset or offended a primarily Jewish audience of her contemporaries.[5] First, was her argument that Eichmann was no monster, harbored no extreme anti-Semitic views, but was nonetheless capable of sending hundreds of thousands of Jews to their deaths. What appalled her was how such evil could be visited upon the world in the absence of explicit evil intent. Not the willful desire to murder, but the thoughtless, almost passive desire to please his superiors, to perform well on the job, is what accounted for the destruction of innocent life. In arguing that evil can be committed thoughtlessly, Arendt threatened and offended many intelligent people who regard themselves as thinking beings and good people. Arendt implied that all might be vulnerable to failure to think. This assertion is unpleasant enough, but her association of the absence of thinking with the capacity for mass murder was too profoundly upsetting for many people to bear.

Claiming that Eichmann was not so exceptional, but in fact dangerously "ordinary" was much more disturbing than acquiescing in his exceptionality. Those of us who would like to believe that we are not exceptionally bad might have a more difficult time accepting that we don't always think, if abstaining from thinking is enough to create catastrophes. Indeed, the people who think most are the ones most likely to be upset by such a theory. It is the good people who could not believe that Eichmann might not have been unusually bad, and it was precisely those good people in whom Hannah Arendt placed her hope for the future. Arendt notes that the Jerusalem judges did not believe Eichmann when he said he did not hate Jews, because "they were too good, and perhaps also too conscious of the very foundations of their profession, to admit that an average 'normal' person, neither feeble-minded nor indoctrinated nor cynical, could be perfectly incapable of telling right from wrong" (*Eichmann* 26).

A second dimension of her argument that aroused anger was Arendt's contention that the Jewish leadership's desire to keep their community together led them to negotiate with the Nazis and may actually have contributed to the slaughter of Jews. By so doing, the Jewish leadership tacitly accepted the insane Nazi fiction about the Jews instead of rejecting all premises of Nazi ideology. The Jewish leadership, in her terms, should have preceded from a state of mind that denied that there even *was* a "Jewish Problem." The Jews had a *Nazi* problem, and needed to save themselves as expediently as possible. She claimed that the Jewish leaders were drawn into accepting Nazi premises and responding to them as though they were rational. Many Jews took offense at statements such as:

> In the matter of cooperation, there was no distinction between the highly assimilated Jewish communities of Central and Western Europe and the Yiddish-speaking masses of the East. In Amsterdam as in Warsaw, in Berlin as in Budapest, Jewish officials could be trusted to compile the lists of persons and of their property, to secure money from the deportees to defray the expenses of their deportation and extermination, to keep track of vacated apartments, to supply police forces to help seize Jews and apartments, and to get them on trains, until, as a last gesture, they handed over the assets of the Jewish community in good order for final confiscation.[6]

The two aspects of her argument are not entirely separable. The belief that Arendt meant that Eichmann, as opposed to his actions, was not exceptionally evil seemed to be the other side of the coin from the implication that the Jewish leadership had not behaved in an exceptionally virtuous manner. Arendt argued that Eichmann did not need to have been a demon for his acts to have been demonic, and that the Jewish leaders were not entirely and universally innocent victims. Both sides of the argument hurt, and the hurt was amplified because few of her readers noticed that she made a distinction between Jewish leaders and the Jewish "masses." She seemed to be saying only that the Nazis weren't so bad and the Jews weren't so good.

The subtitle of the book, "A Report on the Banality of Evil" was regarded as a reflection of nihilism, of a belief that there is no such thing as evil. Arendt countered this misinterpretation of the title with the statement that evil *does* exist in the world, and that the task is to understand how to prevent its occurrence on such a massive scale. She consistently refused the solace of doctrines, ideologies, or even catch phrases. She reiterated, regarding the "banality of evil": "Behind that phrase, I held no thesis or doctrine, although I was dimly aware of the fact that it went counter to our tradition of thought—literary, theological, or philosophic—about the phenomenon of evil" (*Thinking* 3). But she does challenge the unquestioned assumption that evil deeds are perpetrated only by evil people, and many were unwilling to let that statement go.

Prominent Jews charged Arendt with airing dirty linen in public: if she had complaints against Jewish behavior during the Holocaust, she should have taken them up in a private manner within the Jewish community itself. From one perspective, Arendt was accused of a colossal lack of good taste, or judgment. I believe that she did not wish to indict the Jewish people as a whole, but had grave doubts about the judgment of the Jewish *leadership* of Europe. She mentions Leo Baeck specifically in this regard, which was received as a betrayal bordering on heresy. Barnouw notes, in her excellent chapter on the *Eichmann* controversy, "Arendt does not say so explicitly;

but the implications are clear and they are deeply disturbing—more so than the fact that there will always be selfish, cruel men and women among every people, and that situations of extreme stress bring out the worst as well as the best in a person. The implications were disquieting because they suggested that the Jewish leaders, too, caught in the totalitarian system, suffered from an impaired moral faculty."[7] Arendt was concerned that the leaders had misled their followers by failing to treat them as adults and encouraging them to think for themselves. Instead the Jewish masses had been treated like children by their own leaders, who had themselves fallen victim to the insanity of the environment created by the Nazis. "The whole truth was that if the Jewish people had really been unorganized and leaderless, there would have been chaos and plenty of misery but the total number of victims would hardly have been between four and a half and six million people" (*Eichmann* 125).[8]

In contrast to what I believe was Arendt's differentiation between the Jewish leaders and masses, Barnouw and others argue that while she did not intend to indict the Jewish masses, she believed nobody escaped responsibility for the events of the Holocaust:

> The truly provocative element of Arendt's analysis was her insistence that the questions posed by the Eichmann trial had to be dealt with in the context of modern political experience and that Israel should conduct itself—in conducting the trial of Eichmann—as a modern, secular state among other states. In doubting the wisdom of the leaders and, above all, the wisdom of the victims in following them so blindly, Arendt implicitly measured them against a possibly different kind of behavior described by political speech and action.... Arendt attempted to show that it was in the nature of this particular crime against humanity that the distinction between criminal and victim was not always clear. [Gershom] Scholem simply rejected this attempt with the comment, "What perversity!"[9]

This is not the only time in her life that Arendt was thought to have been too critical of the "good guys," when she may only have been criticizing the leadership of the "good guys" and not the followers.[10] But even if Arendt believed that the

Jewish leadership in Europe during the Holocaust had acted unwisely, she makes it clear that the real blame lies with the Nazis and nobody else. "I have dwelt on this chapter of the story, which the Jerusalem trial failed to put before the eyes of the world in its true dimensions, because it offers the most striking insight into the totality of the moral collapse *the Nazis caused* (emph. mine) in respectable European society—not only in Germany but in almost all countries, not only among the persecutors but also among the victims" (*Eichmann* 125–26).

Likewise, she makes clear early in the volume that the Jews did not have the option of organized resistance. In this, Jaspers disagreed with her, and she ultimately was more precise in defining the nature of resistance, admitting that there had indeed been resistance of different sorts.[11] She had no alternative plan of action for the Jews. In response to the question put continually before the Jews by the court in Jerusalem, "Why did you not resist?" Arendt states, "The court received no answer to this cruel and silly question, but one could easily have found an answer had he permitted his imagination to dwell for a few minutes on the fate of those Dutch Jews who in 1941, in the old Jewish quarter of Amsterdam, dared to attack a German security police detachment. Four hundred and thirty Jews were arrested in reprisal and they were literally tortured to death.... There exist many things considerably worse than death, and the S.S. saw to it that none of them was ever very far from their victims' minds and imagination" (*Eichmann* 12). Her argument in *Eichmann* is that a nearly universal failure to think on the part of both oppressors and victims allowed the destruction of the Jews to proceed.

THE CONTROVERSY

In the United States, the controversy over *Eichmann* centered on a series of articles and reviews of the book in *Partisan Review* in 1963, additional articles in *Commentary*, *The New Republic*, and *Dissent*, forums and meetings "all over New York," where "the 'collective psychoanalysis' went on ... "[12] including a forum sponsored by *Dissent*. The general profile of the controversy is sufficiently well documented that I need not take up space with it here.[13] I shall review here only the substance of the objections expressed by some of Arendt's most prominent critics and defenders as a groundwork for my argument that Arendt naively misjudged both her audience and how she was perceived. The most vicious attacks were written by Lionel Abel and Norman Podhoretz. Marie Syrkin wrote a sharply critical but thought-provoking essay. Arendt was defended by her friends Mary McCarthy and Dwight Macdonald, both of whom were then attacked by Abel in an escalation of nastiness. Daniel Bell wrote a balanced and thoughtful review of her book that was appreciative but ultimately critical of her stance. Gershom Scholem expressed deep offense and disappointment in rather paternalistic terms.

Norman Podhoretz wrote an exceptionally nasty review in *Commentary*.[14] He accused Arendt of "scholarly pretensions," quoted Raul Hilberg's *The Destruction of the European Jews* approvingly against Arendt when her argument is actually very similar to Hilberg's and in fact relies upon Hilberg's data.[15] Podhoretz writes, "Miss Arendt's sources are for the most part secondary ones (she relies especially on Raul Hilberg's *The Destruction of the European Jews*) and her manipulation of evidence is at all times visibly tendentious" (202). We shall see this pattern in many of Arendt's critics: Hilberg is applauded for his scholarship while Arendt, who makes a similar argument (discussed in detail in the following chapter) is excoriated for betraying the Jews, and for relying on Hilberg's "superior" scholarship to do it.

Podhoretz seemed intent upon symbolizing exactly the sort of close-mindedness that Arendt worried about in *Eichmann* and her later work on thinking and the absence of it:

> Murderers with the power to murder descended upon a defenseless people and murdered a large part of it. What else is there to say? ... For uninteresting though it may be to say so, no person could have joined the Nazi party, let alone the S.S. who was not at the very least a vicious anti-Semite; to believe otherwise is to learn nothing about the nature of anti-Semitism. (205–206)

He concludes with rigid high-handedness: "But the truth is—*must* be—that the Jews under Hitler acted as men will act when they are set upon by murderers, no better and no worse: the Final Solution reveals nothing about the victims, except that they were moral beings and hopelessly vulnerable in their powerlessness" (208). Period. End of discussion.

Lionel Abel's essay in *Partisan Review*[16] was described by Dwight Macdonald as "solemnly foolish," apparently for its pompous and patronizing style, and its startlingly obvious contradictions, which were elegantly exposed by Mary McCarthy and Dwight Macdonald. The two major contradictions that undermine the effectiveness of Abel's criticism are that he used Raul Hilberg against Arendt, when as he knows, Arendt relied upon Hilberg's data, and when Hilberg is even more strident than Arendt on the same "offensive" points.[17] Abel, several months later, recanted his appreciation of Hilberg at the *Dissent* forum, where he is reported to have "pounded the speaker's table in outrage" over Hilberg's remarks, "lamented that he had ever admired Hilberg's scholarship and then made a passionate attack on Arendt's work, culminating with the bizarre opinion that Arendt had been rightly called by some unnamed friend of Abel's 'the Rosa Luxemburg of nothingness.'"[18] Abel finished his performance by screaming at Alfred Kazin, when he rose to defend Arendt, "Who asked you to come up here? Who asked for your opinion?"[19]

Nonetheless, in his *Partisan* article earlier in the Spring, Abel cited Hilberg against Arendt, stating for example that "Miss Arendt's" analysis makes a mystery of the reason for the existence of the *Judenrate* where "Raul Hilberg makes [it] perfectly clear."[20] Abel implied that Arendt is more adamant about the destructive role of the *Judenrate* than was Hilberg.

Abel also accused Arendt of contradicting her earlier work on *Totalitarianism*, while at the same time dismissing the accuracy of that earlier work. "Every point Miss Arendt maintained in her book on totalitarianism she would today have to retract and deny in order to seriously criticize the decisions made by the leaders of the Jewish councils between 1941 and 1944" (227–28). For good measure Abel added, "But no state can be as powerful as Miss Arendt thought 'the Totalitarian State' to be" (229). We shall discover that Abel and his colleagues had a profound stake in defending *The Origins of Totalitarianism* against any later development of Arendt's thought that appeared to contradict the premises of the earlier work. (See discussion in chapter 4, pp. 103–108.)

Mary McCarthy attempted to untangle Abel's logic with the question "Supposing Abel is right and there is a contradiction between the earlier book and the present one, what would it prove? That she was right then and wrong now or vice versa? His triumphant tone seems to announce that she was wrong both times, which is impossible, at least in the terms in which he states her arguments."[21] After a noble effort, McCarthy despairs, "As the reader can see, the attempt to correct Abel on one point at once brings up another and leads, if one will let it, into a maze. It is like arguing with a hydra" (94). McCarthy and the other participants in this "debate" were chastised by *Partisan Review* editor William Phillips for trying to score debaters' points against one another on an issue of such moral magnitude.[22]

Abel, Gershom Scholem, and Marie Syrkin were so overwrought by Arendt's book that they interpreted Arendt's reference to Eichmann as a "convert to Zionism" as a serious statement, rather than the irony she intended. The offending passages are on pages 40–42, where Arendt refers to Eichmann's "idealism," and his sudden enthusiasm for reading about Zionism, when he was given the responsibility for deporting Jews. Arendt notes:

> Eichmann's account during the police examination of how he was introduced into the new department—distorted, of course, but not wholly devoid of truth—oddly recalls this fool's paradise. The first thing that happened was that his new boss ... required him to read Theodor Herzl's *Der Judenstaat*, the famous Zionist classic, which converted Eichmann promptly and forever to Zionism. This seems to have been the first serious book he ever read and it made a lasting impression on him. (*Eichmann in Jerusalem* 40)

Abel observed, "For quite obviously, a man in charge of the extermination of all European Jewry could hardly have been committed 'forever' to the Zionist ideology" (221). McCarthy is astonished: "How could Abel have missed the irony in Miss

Arendt's account of this 'conversion'?" (87). Dwight Macdonald agreed that missing Arendt's irony took some willful blindness, although he noted, ironically himself, "She uses irony, for instance, a dangerous device if the reader from stupidity or calculation, insists on reading it straight (In this case, I'd call it calculated stupidity)" (PR 31:2, 268). "Mr. Abel is solemnly foolish, as usual: 'Now Miss Arendt's effort to present Eichmann as a convinced adherent of the Zionist ideology is, as Marie Syrkin has shown, completely unconvincing. For quite obviously a man in charge of the extermination of all European Jewry could hardly have been committed 'forever' to the Zionist ideology.' Obviously. One might even expect Miss Arendt to see *that*" (268).

Abel's one potentially relevant point is that Arendt made neither a political nor a moral argument in *Eichmann*, but an aesthetic one. By this he meant that her concern was primarily that the European Jews should have "chosen" to die resisting the Nazis, rather than to be slaughtered passively. The imputation was that Arendt wished for the European Jews a prettier death. Daniel Bell, although himself critical of Arendt, referred to this interpretation as "cruel." It was certainly not what Arendt was writing about although, ironically, it was an issue among some Zionists in Israel.[23]

Abel's *Partisan Review* piece is an example of the extremes to which the attack on Arendt went. It is more instructive to focus on the balanced if critical discussions that raise serious issues. Daniel Bell, Dwight Macdonald, Gershom Scholem, and Marie Syrkin offer food for thought.

Gershom Scholem, in his well-known letter to Arendt of 23 June 1963 (reproduced in Ron Feldman's *The Jew as Pariah: Jewish Identity and Politics in the Modern Age*), reminds Arendt:

> There is the question thrown at us by the new youth of Israel: Why did they allow themselves to be slaughtered? As a question, it seems to me to have profound justification; and I see no readily formulated answer to it. At each decisive juncture, however, your book speaks only of the *weakness* of the Jewish stance in the world. I am ready enough to admit that weakness; but you put such emphasis upon it that, in my view, your account ceases to be objective and acquires overtones of

malice. The problem, I have admitted, is real enough. Why, then, should your book leave one with so strong a sensation of bitterness and shame—not for the compilation, but for the compiler?... It is that heartless, frequently almost sneering and malicious tone with which these matters, touching the very quick of our life, are treated in your book to which I take exception.[24]

Scholem goes on to accuse Arendt of lacking what in the Jewish tradition is called *Ahavath Israel*, "Love of the Jewish People," and chastises her for showing no circumspection in the presentation of her argument: "A discussion such as is attempted in your book would seem to me to require—you will forgive my mode of expression—the most old-fashioned, the most circumspect, the most exacting treatment possible—precisely because of the feelings aroused by this matter.... I regard you wholly as a daughter of our people, and in no other way. Thus I have little sympathy with that tone—well expressed by the English word 'flippancy' which you employ so often in the course of your book. To the matter of which you speak, it is unimaginably inappropriate." Like a father berating his daughter for speaking to him publicly with lack of respect, worse, for embarrassing the family in front of strangers, he continues, "To speak of all this, however, in so wholly inappropriate a tone—to the benefit of those Germans in condemning whom your book rises to greater eloquence than in mourning the fate of your own people—this is not the way to approach the scene of that tragedy."[25]

Arendt responded to Scholem with a respectful but wounded letter. After protesting that she was not, as Scholem had claimed, a member of the German Left, after insisting that one cannot love anything as abstract as "a people" or any sort of collectivity, she remarked, "Well, in this sense I do not 'love' the Jews, nor do I 'believe' in them; I merely belong to them as a matter of course beyond dispute or argument." She also insisted to Scholem in what amounted to an eloquent and prescient attack upon "political correctness" that he was upset because her views are unconventional: "How you could believe that my book was 'a mockery of Zionism' would be a complete mystery to me, if I did not know that many people in Zionist circles have become incapable of listening to opinions or arguments which are off the beaten track and not consonant with their ideology. There are exceptions, and a Zionist friend of mine remarked in all innocence that the book, the last chapter in particular... was very pro-Israel—as indeed it is. What confuses you is that my arguments and my approach are different from what you are used to: in other words, the trouble is that I am independent."[26]

Most telling for our immediate purposes, however, is her statement: "This grief ['that wrong done by my own people naturally grieves me more than wrong done by other peoples'], however, in my opinion is not for display, even if it should be the innermost motive for certain actions or attitudes. Generally speaking, the role of the 'heart' in politics seems to me altogether questionable."[27]

Scholem was responding to her passage on Eichmann's "Zionism" with his chastisement, "I wish to say only that your description of Eichmann as a 'convert to Zionism' could only come from somebody who had a profound dislike of everything to do with Zionism. These passages in your book I find quite impossible to take seriously. They amount to a mockery of Zionism; and I am forced to the conclusion that this was, indeed, your intention."[28] Arendt retorted, with obvious exasperation, "Public opinion, especially when it has been carefully manipulated, as in this case, is a very powerful thing. Thus, I never made Eichmann out to be a 'Zionist.' If you missed the irony of the sentence—which was plainly in *oratio obliqua*, reporting Eichmann's own words—I really can't help it. I can only assure you that none of the dozens of readers who read the book before publication had ever any doubt about the matter."[29]

Marie Syrkin's critical review, "Miss Arendt Surveys the Holocaust" (*Jewish Frontier* [May 1963]) is a thoughtful, very critical analysis, which Arendt apparently respected, and regarded as "loyal opposition." Syrkin also believed that Arendt indicted the victims and exonerated the Nazis. "The smear technique works both ways. Not only are Nazi concentration schemes labeled as 'Zionist' by the author, but all the agonizing efforts of the Zionists to save whomever they could from Germany before it was too late are described by Miss Arendt as cheery collaboration with the Nazis" (8). As evidence for these accusations, Syrkin offered not much more than Arendt's now famous "Offending Quotation" brought out again and again by all Arendt's critics. Arendt had written:

> But the whole truth was that there existed Jewish community organizations and Jewish party and welfare associations on both the local and the international level. Wherever Jews lived, there were recognized Jewish leaders and these leaders, almost without exception, cooperated in one way or another, for one reason or another, with the Nazis. The whole truth was that if the Jewish people had really been unorganized and leaderless there would have been chaos and plenty of misery but the total number of victims would hardly have been between five and six million. (Syrkin 7)

Syrkin, like Abel (at least before he became disenchanted with Hilberg at the meeting in New York), admired Hilberg's book, and used it against Arendt.[30] But unlike Abel, Syrkin did raise some troubling questions about what she considered to be Arendt's selective use of the data. She accused Arendt of possessing an "ability to disregard whatever does not suit her thesis," and of ignorance, "not in the sense of a lack of knowledge (who would question Miss Arendt's erudition?) but a wilful ignoring of the obviously pertinent which would invalidate her basic position" (14). Syrkin is stinging when she notes "What does Miss Arendt suggest as an alternative to 'selection'? Should the Palestinians merely have announced: 'Run pell-mell to the ships and let the fastest board!'?" (9).

With regard to her accusation that Arendt judged people who faced impossible choices, Syrkin poignantly observed, "In every process of 'selection,' life for one meant death for another. In a sense everyone who escaped from Hitler, as in all escapes from disaster where the possibilities of rescue are limited, took the place of another, if only by being one of an immigration quota. The implications of guilt and innocence become incalculable and few are morally entitled to pass judgment" (12). In sum, Syrkin echoes what Scholem believed, that Arendt was insufficiently identified with the Jewish people.

What is at the root of the shortcomings of Miss Arendt's trial of the trial is *her* view of Jewish history, a view commonly held by assimilationists of the Council for Judaism stripe, on the one hand, and radicals of the old school on the other. In this view every affirmation of Jewish national awareness is culpable and to be strictured either as multiple loyalty or treason to a larger international idea. That is why a Jewish intellectual of Miss Arendt's caliber is able not only to distort the facts but—more important—to fail so signally in sympathy and imagination. (14)

The irony here is that if Arendt had indeed been as critical of the European Jewish masses as her critics accused her of being, she would have had plenty of support among the Israelis—both the leadership and the masses. In the following chapter I shall consider in detail the complexities of the Israeli attitudes toward the Holocaust. There had always been loathing from the conservative Zionists toward any negotiations with the Nazis before and during the war, or the Germans afterwards. The *Judenrate* had always been the object of the disdain of the Conservative Zionists in Palestine, who suspected them of "collaborating" with the Nazis. But even among the more moderate Labor Zionists, including Ben Gurion, the Mapai party, and the masses of left-leaning secular Zionists in Israel, there was ample evidence of ambivalence, and occasionally, real disrespect for the European Jewish victims and their leaders who had lacked the foresight to emigrate to Israel. The "official" attitude toward the *Judenrate* and the Holocaust victims was, in the years after the war, responsive to Israeli party politics, as we shall see.[31]

The question of whether Arendt "should" have written a report on Eichmann that self-consciously represented a Jewish perspective thus became the intellectual core of the controversy. Mary McCarthy noted a certain basic division in the response to Arendt's book, between Jews and gentiles: the Jews were much more critical of Arendt than the non-Jews. There was, in turn, objection to McCarthy's observation, and although certainly the dichotomy was not hard and fast, to deny that Jewish and gentile responses differed reflects an affected "color blindness," fashionable perhaps in the early sixties, where the deeper significance of cultural and racial differences were all but denied. The Jewish and gentile responses to Arendt *did* differ. It seemed easier for the gentiles to give her the benefit of the doubt, to understand that she was not a "Self-Hating Jewess" who wrote a "Pro-Eichmann Series."[32] Macdonald notes the racism and the sexism implicit in the title with the remark that he had not seen the term *Jewess* in print "since those fascist sheets in the thirties" (262).

I shall conclude my review of the controversy over *Eichmann in Jerusalem* with Daniel Bell's argument that Arendt should have written from a more tribal Jewish, rather than a universalist perspective, and Dwight MacDonald's response. Bell refers to two historic versions of justice: one tribal and retributive; the other more disinterested, "rooted in the natural law, which demands of men penalties for the disruption of the moral order itself."[33] Arendt chose to write about justice of the second sort, where some insisted that her judgment would have benefited from a stronger tribal perspective. Bell's concluding section, "The Parochial and the Universal," compares the Jewish perspective and Arendt's perspective, which he respects in the abstract, but believes was misguided in its particular context.

> For the Israelis, Nazism was one of the long procession of brutalities committed within the tradition of anti-Semitism. For Miss Arendt the Nazi crimes, the rationalized murder of entire populations, is the beginning of a new set of fearful possibilities in human history. In short, Miss Arendt insisted that the Israelis, in trying Eichmann in a Jewish court and on specifically Jewish issues, missed a crucial point of modern history. Moreover, by kidnaping Eichmann in Argentina and thus extending the territorial principle of seizure beyond its borders, a precedent was created for the breakdown of international law whereby in the future, for example, an African state could kidnap a segregationist leader in America and try him in Ghana or Guinea for crimes against the black people. For her, the Israeli mistake was to be parochial at a time when the problem of mass murder had become universal. (427–28)

This reading is fair and appreciative, although Bell questions whether it is the most appropriate stance under the circumstances. "It is this tension between the parochial and the universal that explains the furious emotions over Miss Arendt's book.... The agony of Miss Arendt's book is precisely that she takes her stand so unyieldingly on the side of disinterested justice, and that she judges both Nazi and Jew. But abstract justice, as the Talmudic wisdom knew, is sometimes too 'strong' a yardstick to judge the world" (428).

He closes with a story from the Talmudic Haggadah, probably included to ground his argument for a Jewish perspective in the Jewish text. The story is touching, but reveals more than Bell intended. The story is called the "Alphabet of Creation," which clearly inspired the title of his review. It describes all the letters of the alphabet competing for the honor of being the first letter of the Torah. The story, which is intended for children, concerns a rabbi and the young boy to whom he asks the question: "Why did God begin the world with the letter 'B'?" (Note the indistinguishability between the beginning of the *world* and the beginning of the *word*, in Hebrew thought. *Bereshit* is Hebrew for "In the Beginning," which of course, opens the Bible. The answer to the boy's question is that "B" is also the first letter of the word *baruch*, or blessed.) What Bell fails to notice is that the Talmudic story, presumably intended to bring Arendt "back" to her Jewish roots, was in all likelihood not available to Arendt. It was part of the exclusively male culture of the Talmud and Torah. Few Jewish girls would have had access to it in the early twentieth century, or the centuries of its existence prior to the twentieth century.[34] It was not a part of Arendt's intellectual or cultural heritage because she was not a Jewish male.

Macdonald took up the "objective v. tribal" justice issue raised by Daniel Bell, but he regarded Arendt's attempt to take the universalist perspective as admirable. "It is an interesting, and depressing historical exercise to imagine what the reactions would have been to a book like this in the thirties, when all of us, from Miss McCarthy to Mr. Abel, despised national and racial feelings and were hot for truth, justice, and other universals. The suggestion that certain people and institutions should be exempt from criticism would have embarrassed everybody (except the Stalinists)" (PR 31:2 268). MacDonald continued,"I think Mr. Bell and Mr. Scholem have made explicit, because their intention was understanding rather than polemics, the concealed, perhaps even unconscious, assumption that explains the violence of the Jewish attacks on Miss Arendt's book. Both reproach her because she lacks a special feeling in favor of her fellow Jews" (269).

Macdonald concluded with a plea for maintaining the universalist perspective:

> I am not Jewish, but if I were I hope I would not agree with Mr. Bell that "in this situation, one's identity as a Jew... is relevant," if it means applying a different ("weaker") yardstick to Jews. A yardstick is not a yardstick if it is more or less than three feet long, and justice is not justice unless it is universalistic. I am old-fashioned enough (as of the thirties) to still find these favored, special, exceptional categories of race or nation morally suspect and intellectually confusing. And so I take heart in a book like *Eichmann in Jerusalem*. (269)

The most responsible voices in this debate seem to me to be those of Bell, Macdonald, Syrkin, and Scholem. But as represented by these thinkers, the argument for the specifically Jewish perspective is, in my opinion, not as persuasive—at least not in the abstract—as the argument that Arendt's desire for a universal standard is commendable. That is, the arguments from Bell, Scholem, and Syrkin, the responsible voices claiming she should have written from a more self-consciously Jewish standpoint, seem disingenuous. Macdonald's point is well taken: these same scholars would most likely decline to make their point universal, recommending that all scholarship be written from a particular standpoint. The call for Jewish loyalty is special pleading.

But contrary to their own professional advocacy of "scholarly objectivity," her critics' insistence that Arendt argue from a more "tribal" perspective has become emblematic of the multicultural issues so central to contemporary academic life. The debate in academia about whether the demand for a "universal" or "objective" approach to thinking, along with the privileging of the Western European "canon," reveals only the hegemony of Western European men, is at heart a debate about the nature and possibility of "Truth" in scholarship. A Jewish standpoint is usually neglected by advocates of cultural pluralism—a point I shall address in due course. But the argument for including the work of African Americans, Asian Americans, Hispanics, women, gays and lesbians, and so forth in undergraduate college curricula represents an effort to question the objectivity and universality available to the white Western males who have until very recently represented "the canon" in nearly every field of scholarly pursuit, and echoes the controversy over *Eichmann in Jerusalem*.

The inclusion of "the Other" and a questioning of the centrality of the white male perspective is an intellectual quest with which I am in sympathy. Indeed, it seems to me that the best chance we have for balanced (which is not to say "objective") perspectives on major ethical issues is to become thoroughly aware of our own standpoint and how it may be influenced by ethnicity, gender, and so forth. By understanding our own ethnic and gendered "biases" we stand a chance of being compassionate and understanding about the biases of others. Philosophically, I regard this position as dialectical: thorough and self-conscious immersion in "particularity" of perspective is the means of gaining access to a more "universal" perspective.

Since I hold doubts about the possibility of objectivity, it is puzzling to find myself drawn to Arendt's defenders in the *Eichmann* matter, who argue for the validity of her quest for an "objective" understanding of justice. Why am I compassionate about her lack of acknowledgment of the influence of gender and Jewishness upon her intellectual work and its reception? One reason is certainly my disdain for the self-proclaimed ethical purity of her detractors: the demand for a "Jewish" perspective from men who had built their careers on their ability to be "cosmopolitan" or universal thinkers is disengenuous to the point of being hypocritical, as I discuss in chapters 4 and 5. Yet approval of the "objectivity" of a "universal" perspective from Arendt's supporters goes against the grain of what I believe about the undeniable influence of specific culture. My hunch is that all concerned—Arendt, her defenders, and her critics—were engaged in a massive act of denial, the critics demanding that she support a Jewish perspective, her friends arguing that she stick to her universal human quest, all of them thoroughly overlooking the fact that she was a Jewish woman, which may have affected both what she argued, and how her argument was received.

In the latter part of this volume, I explore in detail, the ways in which Arendt's Jewishness *did* influence her scholarly work, a phenomenon that has gone unrecognized by Arendt herself as well as students of her work. With regard to the specific critical response to *Eichmann in Jerusalem*, it is the importance of her gender that has been unacknowledged. The prevailing argument is that objections to her work had nothing to do with gender, but rather were appropriately focused upon the substance of her work. The controversy had nothing to do with whether a woman or a man had made the charges she did. Arendt was treated no differently than any other critic of Jewish behavior during the Holocaust. Raul Hilberg is cited for comparative purposes: he was also severely criticized for making much the same argument in his monumental study, *The Destruction of the European Jews*.[35] More importantly, her tone was offensive: snide, cynical, irreverent, and inappropriate for addressing a tragedy of the scope of the Holocaust. She was thus justly chastised for her aloof and even disrespectful tone. That "inappropriate" tone, as well as the offensive substance of her argument, reflect an ambivalent attitude toward her own Jewishness. What is offensive about *Eichmann in Jerusalem* is the "Jewish self-hatred" that it reflects—which has nothing to do with her being a woman. Arendt's involvement with Heidegger is an example of this "Jewish self-hatred," which is what underlay the fury of the reaction of the Jewish community.

All of these arguments will be addressed in due course. At least one can be quickly dispensed with here. Hilberg was *not* attacked with anywhere near the vehemence that Arendt was, and indeed, the reviews of his book, *The Destruction of the European Jews*, in which he makes even more extensive excoriations of the Jewish leadership than Arendt, indicate that he was treated with respect, even in the most critical reviews. In spite of the fact that he lacked the flambouyant public persona of Arendt, was not a scholar with an international reputation (the result of Arendt's *Origins of Totalitarianism*), did not publish his report in the widely read *New Yorker*, and hence was less significant as a target of critical attention, his scholarship was taken seriously, and he was never accused of betraying the Jewish community, or of exhibiting "Jewish self-hatred."[36]

Arendt was accused, by a primarily Jewish chorus of objectors, of having been disloyal to the Jewish people in publishing her report. Gender was not even an acknowledged concept during the height of the controversy in the early 1960s, and its role in the response to *Eichmann* is just as vociferously denied today by some.[37]

In a sense, Arendt was the victim of double jeopardy: the two aspects of her identity are mutually exclusive. The Jewish perspective has traditionally been a male perspective, and the Jewish male perspective has also not been regarded as "universal," or even "objective," unless the Jewish aspect of the male is overlooked. A new generation of scholars writes less critically about Arendt and *Eichmann in Jerusalem*, focusing, as we have seen, on *Eichmann* as the book that motivated Arendt to try to bridge the gap between her earlier concern with action and her later preoccupation with the life of the mind. However, the recent writings on *Eichmann in Jerusalem* still fail to take into account the role of gender on the work's reception, while also overlooking the specifically Jewish dimension to the controversy.

Although the younger generation is not incensed, as the generation of Arendt's peers had been, at what they regarded as a betrayal of her own people, contemporary scholars tend to separate Hannah Arendt the brilliant and original political theorist from Hannah Arendt the Jewish woman, the refugee from the Holocaust, the woman whose very life had been threatened and altered by the biological fact that she had been born Jewish. Arendt herself may have contributed to this bifurcation of her work into political and philosophical. In her more political writings up to and including *Eichmann in Jerusalem*, she unabashedly claims her Jewish identity. Being a Jew constitutes a part of how she looks at the political world. I am thinking of writings collected in Ron Feldman's *The Jew as Pariah, Eichmann in Jerusalem*, some of the essays in *Men in Dark Times*, and in a different tone, *Rahel Varnhagen*. In her explicitly Jewish political writings she is engaged, combative, arguing over the desirability of courses of action that have direct impact on the world and specifically on the Jewish people. She is a Jew in public. But she keeps this Jewishness separate from her life as a philosopher and political theorist. In *The Human Condition, On Revolution, The Life of the Mind*, and her essays written during that period, in *Between Past and Future* and elsewhere, she courts the possibility of philosophical "universality," with her focus on Greek, German, and Christian thinkers. Contemporary scholars have responded to Arendt by considering the influence on her work of Plato, Socrates, Aristotle, Augustine, Duns Scotus, Vico, Kant, Heidegger, and Jaspers. To raise the possibility that her Jewish, let alone her female, identity might have influenced her scholarly as well as her political writings amounts to a minor heresy: an apparent diminution of Arendt's status as a thinker.[38]

If Arendt can be split into a Jewish political writer and a "universal" (read: Western classicist) philosopher or theorist, how tempting it must be to divide her work into an "early" and a "late" Arendt: the Arendt preoccupied with action and the Arendt preoccupied with thinking, the Arendt with "pre-1971" and "post-1971" ideas about judgment. Since I suggested in the introduction that Arendt's work is of a piece, that the same woman wrote the early and the late stuff, it seems incumbent upon me to argue for the unity of Hannah Arendt's soul: she was a Jewish woman, a classical scholar, a German refugee, and ultimately an American academic. But the developments of her life that contributed to her identity as a scholar do not completely replace its foundation in gender and Jewish identity. As Freud argues in *Civilization and Its Discontents*, the layers of the past are buried beneath the present, much like the architectural ruins of Roman civilization underlay the city that is contemporary Rome.[39]

In the beginning, Arendt was Jewish and female. She never denied either aspect of herself, but, like her followers, publicly claimed the Jewish part only in relation to her specifically Jewish and usually political writings. The female part seems to have been regarded as completely private—"merely biological"—carrying no impact for her intellectual work at all. In Arendt's own terms, Arendt the philosopher was not affected by Arendt the Jew or Arendt the woman.[40]

Meanwhile, *Eichmann in Jerusalem* has become an intellectual challenge, its Jewish content all but forgotten. Arendt and her students prefer to confine her Jewishness to her Jewish political writings. I believe if we allow Hannah Arendt to be one whole human being, the Jewish woman along with the classical scholar, we may have access to solving the inconvenient mysteries created by the dichotomies that have been associated with her work. The specifically Jewish content of the trial has become lost in the concern with Hannah Arendt's relationships, intellectual or otherwise, with Kant, Heidegger, Camus, postmodern thought, the structure of narrative, and a dozen other fashionable concerns. This is not to disparage Arendt's provocativeness as a thinker, and as a scholar who anticipated many of the concerns of our age. But without understanding Arendt as a woman and a Jew, studying her thought in relation to the writings of non-Jewish men is bound to be abstract. The younger generation of scholars ignore the impact of her gender and her Jewish identity upon her scholarship, and in spite of their appreciation of her work, her most outspoken critics, the ones who accused her of betraying her own people, go unanswered.

In the chapters that follow, the controversy over *Eichmann in Jerusalem* will be studied from the perspectives of Judaism and gender.

CHAPTER 3

Israel and the Holocaust

The furor over *Eichmann in Jerusalem* seems disproportionate to the arguments advanced in the book, which were not particularly original. Raul Hilberg's three-volume, thousand-page opus, *The Destruction of the European Jews* had advanced similar arguments even more stridently. Arendt, however, was attacked for many reasons by the "New York Intellectuals," including the charge that she had "stolen" data and arguments from Hilberg, while Hilberg, initially anyway, was not criticized with anywhere near the vehemence as was Arendt. In fact, his book was fairly well received, and reviewed widely and respectfully. In Israel, by contrast, both Hilberg and Arendt were suppressed.[1] *Eichmann* thus touched off different Jewish nerves in Israel and in the United States, and the ferocity with which Arendt was attacked reflected the difference. The issue upon which Israeli and American Jews shared a tacit agreement was the gender dimension, which I shall discuss in due course. If what Arendt wrote was "nervy," it was even more jolting because she was a woman. The furor over *Eichmann* reflected the politics of both Judaism and gender, topics to which we turn in this and the following chapters.

Now to argue that the *Eichmann* controversy reflects Jewish politics is not very surprising: it touched upon *the* Jewish issue. But some explanation is called for to explain the disproportionate vitriol of the controversy. In a recent book, *The Seventh Million: The Israelis and the Holocaust*,[2] Tom Segev reports that Hannah Arendt believed both that Ben Gurion himself had demanded that *Eichmann in Jerusalem* be banned in Israel, and that the book was simply not important enough to warrant such fury.

> Its nonpublication in Hebrew rankled Arendt, but the book itself, she said, was less important than people thought. She had written it in anger at what she saw as Israel's attempt to exploit the Eichmann trial for political purposes. She told me that, were she to write it again, she would write it differently. Its subtitle, *A Report on the Banality of Evil*, was blown out of proportion, she argued. Then she added, with the biting irony that characterized her, that *Eichmann in Jerusalem* could at most serve as a guide to reporters on how to cover a historical trial.[3]

Alexander Bloom, in his history of the New York Intellectuals, concurs that the furor created by Arendt's book was extraordinary. "Hannah Arendt's work occasioned fireworks rarely seen in New York Intellectual circles.... Arendt's book provoked a hailstorm of criticism and enormous debate, well beyond mere political discussion."[4] He reports that the symposium sponsored by *Dissent* was described by Norman Podhoretz as "a kind of protest meeting against the book," and that Alfred Kazin, who also had reservations about Arendt's book, nonetheless rose to her defense at that meeting because he was her close friend and "My defense of her was personal.... I was outraged by the mob spirit" (Bloom 330; see also, this volume, chapter 4, pp. 100, 101). Why such extraordinary fury?

The Israeli attitude toward the Holocaust is not a simple matter, and Arendt's outspokenness, which only reflected debates that had been raging in Israel for years, was embarrassing in the sense that she exposed the debate to non-Israelis, airing dirty linen. Israel preferred to present a united front to the non-Zionist world. Party politics were not for the eyes of the *goyim*, nor for American Jews either. Nonetheless, if Arendt was victimized in a manner that other scholars—most notably Hilberg—was not, some attempt at explanation is warranted.

Israel and the Holocaust   45

In this chapter I shall consider the Zionist and Israeli politics that may have influenced the meaning of the Eichmann trial and the response to Arendt's report. I draw from three recent studies about Israel and the Holocaust: Tom Segev's *The Seventh Million: The Israelis and the Holocaust* (Hill and Wang, 1993); Dina Porat's *The Blue and Yellow Stars of David: The Zionist Leadership in Palestine and the Holocaust, 1939–1945* (Harvard, 1990); and Yehuda Bauer's *Jews for Sale: Nazi-Jewish Negotiations, 1933–1945* (Yale, 1994).

The early Zionist stance toward the Holocaust is far from simple loyalty to the Jewish people, far from Scholem's *Ahaveth Israel*. Comparing the three accounts provides a range of interpretations of the issues that confronted Jews in Palestine during the Holocaust. From our privileged historical standpoint of the present, the Holocaust may seem so unequivocally demonic that extraordinary action should have been obviously mandated to the entire world, and most certainly to the Jewish leadership in Palestine. As Dina Porat observes, "Jews who have grown up in Israel find it extremely difficult to understand why the Yishuv never launched any unconditional, extraordinary action—outside the rules of the game—some preemptive operation commensurate with the pain and the rage" (Porat 262). The reality of the time was murkier, dominated by the diabolical paradox that the more unprecedented and inhuman the deeds carried out by the Nazis, the more difficult it was for "ordinary" people to absorb, accept and defend against them.

The response of Palestinian Jews to the Holocaust, and the Israeli attitude toward both the Holocaust and their own response to it was (and is) not static.[5] Trying to describe it is tantamount to describing a river during a natural disaster: what was all movement to begin with, although contained within banks, becomes volatile, dangerous, and unpredictable, as it responds to a deluge, a rock slide, fallen timber, and so forth. The course of the river itself is liable to change. So there is no definitive "Israeli response" or "Zionist response" to the Holocaust: the response was always in process, developing through out and during the aftermath of the catastrophe.

But since my argument is that the role of the Eichmann trial, and the Israeli response to Arendt, was affected by Israel's attitude toward the Holocaust and their role during it, it becomes important to identify both the reality of actions taken by the Yishuv in response to the Holocaust and the Israeli reading of their own actions. Nothing Jews in Palestine could have done would have been adequate to stem the tide of disaster, and this sense of frustration and powerlessness gave rise to post-hoc guilt and discomfort. But apart from the fact that nothing would have worked, allegations that Zionists were ambivalent about rescue efforts and ambivalent about the victims and survivors must themselves be considered. The despair over failed efforts when everything has been tried is one thing; guilt over Zionist inaction or disdain for the Holocaust victims is something else, and potentially more explosive. Dina Porat notes, "Today, there are two lapses in particular that disturb Jews: the time gap between events in Europe and the response to them, and the attitude gap between the nature of the Holocaust and the response of the Yishuv" (Porat 261). What were the circumstances that gave rise to these lapses?

THE DAWNING OF REALITY

Porat identifies the date when the reality of systematic Nazi extermination of the Jews was "officially" acknowledged as 17 December 1942. On that date, Anthony Eden read a statement in Parliament which was carried in newspapers throughout the world, on behalf of the Allied governments, making public their awareness of the German mobilization to annihilate the Jewish people. From that point, "the point at which the extermination was officially recognized for what it was" (Porat 52), denial of the reality was no longer publicly possible, even though the details were so horrifying that people both in the Yishuv and throughout the civilized world, continued—perhaps to their credit—to respond with incredulity.

> The Holocaust was an acute deviation from the collective experience of humanity. Even in the history of such long-suffering people as the Jews, it was unprecedented and, therefore, unthinkable. People who managed to crawl out of mass graves

and return to the remnants of their communities encountered total disbelief.... People had difficulty in believing their own eyes, and today survivors find it difficult to believe their own memories. (Porat 44)

Yehuda Bauer echoes Porat's perspective with the plea that "We must differentiate between information and its internalization, or 'knowledge'; and in this case there is absolutely no proof that information on planned mass murder, as opposed to pogrom-like shootings and other persecutions was received during the early months of deportation. Internalization—that is, acceptance of information as correct and thinking in accordance with that information and later possibly action—is a complicated process" (Bauer 72). Bauer places the date of "internalization," or acceptance of the information about Nazi genocide in the fall of 1942, or perhaps "even later than that."

But as with any horrible truth with which one must come to terms, there is rarely a moment of unequivocal acceptance, of recognition where the fog lifts and one sees with dazzling clarity what has really been going on: the fog continues to roll back in. As in psychotherapy or psychoanalysis, the most difficult truths are approached slowly and cautiously, denied, crept up on again, and often denied again and again, until they are slowly integrated into one's perspective on reality in a form that does not destroy the patient. One protects oneself from what one cannot absorb.

There is plenty to indicate that Jewish recognition of the Nazi plan to annihilate them was approached and denied throughout the war. Certainly before December 1943 there had been reports from "reliable sources"—eye witnesses and refugees—that were available but not believed. And certainly after 1943, and well into 1944, leaders of the Yishuv continued to be incredulous, needing to be told again and again that it was really happening. There is evidence that the impulse to deny continued well into the postwar period, and that not until the Eichmann trial itself was an effort made to teach the Israeli public, collectively, in terms that would be accepted once and for all and integrated into Israeli civic culture, about the reality of the Holocaust.

Porat tells us that from September of 1942 on, before Eden's announcement, "Information concerning the methodical extermination of the Jews of Europe... reached Palestine." Yet, "Leaders of the Yishuv... received the news with disbelief. Stories of death factories and commercial use of the dead seemed even more incredible than previous stories about the monstrous methods employed in mass killing, and had the effect of further discrediting the previous information" (Porat 30). And at the other end of events, in May of 1944, Rabbi Michael Dov-Beer Weissmandel, who was in hiding near the Slovokian-Hungarian border, sent a letter to Geneva addressed to free-world Jews, in which he detailed the horrors of Auschwitz, and concluded with anguish,

> And you, our brethren, the People of Israel, in all the free countries... how can you keep silent about this murder.... You are cruel, you are murderers—for this cruel silence of yours, for your lack of action.... We beg and plead and demand of you to take action immediately.... Our brethren, People of Israel, have you gone mad? Don't you know what hell we are living in? (Porat 216)

Even after denial was no longer "officially" possible, most of the world remained paralyzed in the face of the magnitude of the Nazi evil. The Jews in the killing zones and elsewhere were most affected by the paralysis and inaction, both their own and that of the rest of the world.

To prevent misunderstanding of the discussion that follows, let me state my belief that in spite of decisions that might appear questionable from one perspective or another, the Zionist leadership in Palestine faced an utterly impossible situation. The situation was *created by the Nazis*, and second guessing or judging the "choices" made by the Jewish leadership must be seen in that context. The leaders of the Yishuv lacked sufficient power to save most of the Disapora Jews, or to prevent the Nazi catastrophe from occurring. They comprised a tiny group of people, in terms of the scale of national populations, with literally no political power. Britain controlled Palestine and stood in greater need of Arab oil than anything the Jews could offer. While the Allied powers—specifically Great Britain and the United States—professed humanitarian horror at what they knew of the Nazis extermination policies and tactics, their willingness to jeopardize international political priorities in order to actually save European Jews was minimal. With regard to rescue by political negotiation, ransom, or direct military strikes in the form of parachuting resistance fighters into occupied Europe, or executing bombing raids on the death camps, Allied response was sluggish and burdened by political red tape at best; negligent to the point of being lethal, at worst.

For example, a United States state department official reported to Moshe Shertok, foreign representative of the Yishuv, in April of 1943, that Hitler could not be approached with a plea to release Jews because, as Anthony Eden had already said, it was "'beneath our dignity,' and 'it will not help; Hitler will not release anyone.' Furthermore, 'if he does release hundreds of thousands or a million Jews—what shall we do with them, where shall we take them?'" (quoted in Porat 141). Shertok could not respond that the Yishuv was willing to absorb any Jews the Allies would assist in rescuing because Britain had, in 1939, issued the famous "White Paper" limiting the purchase of land by Jews, and restricted Jewish immigration to Palestine over the next five years to a total of 75,000. After 1944, Jewish immigration would be subject to Arab consent. Great Britain could not afford to alienate Arab interests, and Porat concludes, "As far as the Allies were concerned, Weizmann, Ben Gurion, and Shertok were a tolerated annoyance, ceaselessly pressing, appealing, and demanding despite the war and all the difficulties it involved. In short, the Yishuv's position was even weaker than it had been before the war" (255).[6]

Thus in a world that appeared either indifferent or murderous, Zionist leaders could do very little to save European Jewry. The overwhelming reality of being a Jew anywhere in the world during Hitler's reign was *impotence*. But recognition of one's impotence is no defense against guilt, over one's inability to respond to evil, or guilt about whatever one has failed to accomplish. Zionist impotence gave rise to Israeli guilt, which in turn dominated the politics of the Eichmann trial, and took the form of rage at Arendt's report.

THE STRUCTURE OF DISCOMFORT

The lines along which the political factions in the Yishuv divided over the appropriate response to the Holocaust resembled party or factional divisions in any nation or community, except that the stakes were dire. In a "lose-lose game," tragedy was the likely outcome no matter what action was taken. This contributed, perhaps, to even more bitter factional in-fighting than in a conventional political situation. Jewish politics in the Yishuv divided along lines represented by the more pragmatic approach of the dominant Labor Zionist (Mapai) party, and the purer "moralist" approach of the Orthodox religious Jews in Palestine. Secular political Zionists differed profoundly from the religious fundamentalists. Additionally, political Zionists were themselves divided along a more conventional political spectrum. Although the Zionist party was predominantly socialist, there was increasing opposition from "Revisionists"—centrist, more conservative Zionists, who often during the crisis sided with Agudat Yisrael, the orthodox religious group which was not Zionist at all.

Mapai, the socialist Zionist party, controlled about 50 percent of all the institutions in the Yishuv, and 75 percent of the workers' union. Its various committees discussed and largely determined, though unofficially, the policy of the Yishuv. Still there were political struggles with Revisionists on the right and with the more radical parties and groups within the labor movement on the left (Porat 11). At the other extreme was Agudat Yisrael, the ultraorthodox, anti-Zionist party, which refused to be included in the Yishuv's institutional framework (Porat 7).

Lining up on the side of Mapai but forming independent organizations, were the Jewish Agency Executive (JAE), the operative organ of the World Zionist Organization, and the Histadrut, or General Federation of Jewish Workers in Palestine. The JAE, Mapai, and Histadrut comprised the three wings of Palestinian Zionism. "The Histadrut gave Mapai its broad socioeconomic base and the Agency its political power" (Porat 11). The head of Histadrut was David Remez, of the JAE, Yitzhak Gruenbaum, and of the Mapai, David Ben Gurion.

Other important actors in this often feuding group of Zionist leaders were Eliyahu Dobkin, head of the Histadrut immigration department, and co-head, with Meyer Schapira, of the JAE's immigration department, Moshe Shertok (later Sharett), head of the JAE's political department, and Chaim Weizmann, president of the World Zionist Organization.

The divisive issues echoed Jewish responses to persecution from the beginning of Jewish history: the "heroic" stance of armed resistance to the death, versus the more passive stance of compromise in an effort to survive. Obviously, during the Holocaust neither stance "worked": Jews were killed when they fought back and killed when they did not. The debate in the Yishuv took place along a continuum which at one end argued for heroic and direct military intervention, no matter how suicidal, and at the other, political negotiations with the Nazis and the Allied powers for the rescue of however many Jews it was possible to rescue. The more orthodox religious Jews and the Revisionists leaned toward "heroic" intervention, while the secular Zionists leaned toward the more complex and morally troublesome pragmatic stance.

In Nazi-occupied Europe, the question that confronted the trapped Jews was how to maximize whatever slim chance of survival there might be. At the center of the effort was the resistance leadership, who were predominantly European Zionists. Should the young leaders, when the futility of their work in their European communities became apparent, save themselves by taking up the offer of escape to Israel, or should they die with the people they had lived with and struggled to save? The European Zionists overwhelmingly chose to stay and die with their friends and families, offering what last-minute solace they could, rather than abandoning their communities for the sake of the future of Zionism. To the Zionists in Israel, this stance seemed passive, weak, and politically irresponsible. The horrible truth was that the Zionist enterprise in Israel would most certainly fail if there were no European Jews left alive to populate the new Jewish state, hence there was no "correct" answer to the question of whether it was better for the leadership of the European resisters to die in Europe or escape to Israel. Jews in the Yishuv at first believed that dying with their communities constituted Diaspora weakness and "passivity." But from the standpoint of the young European Zionists, the less "heroic" and less morally tolerable stance would have been saving themselves and letting their communities perish in the Holocaust.

In Israel the debate among Zionists concerned whether to devote attention to the urgent needs of building a Jewish state or to spend scarce resources attempting to rescue whatever they could of the "remnant" of European Jews. Once again, there was no "correct" answer: neglecting the needs of building a Jewish state left the European Jews with no place to escape to, while failing to respond to the perishing millions threatened to leave a Jewish homeland bereft of a population. The ultraorthodox Jews, represented by Agudat Yisrael, made the most extreme arguments for a morally pure stance: act to save the Jews of the Diaspora at all costs, spare nothing to intervene on behalf of Diaspora Jews, but under no circumstances think of negotiating with the Germans.

Ultimately, neither stance "worked" in the sense of providing an effective guide to action. As Dina Porat succinctly remarks, "Their achievements were minute in proportion to the Holocaust" (136). Ben Gurion himself sadly observed, "It would be impossible to say that our work met with even a small measure of success" (in Segev 89). Segev provides the statistics to confirm the validity of Ben Gurion's observation:

> There had been about nine million Jews in Europe on the eve of the war; about six million were killed, leaving three million alive. Most of them were saved by Germany's defeat in the war. Some were spared thanks to help they received from various governments and organizations such as the Joint Distribution Committee and from thousands of good-hearted people in almost every country—the 'righteous gentiles.' There were dramatic rescue operations such as the flight across the Pyrenees from France to Spain and the convoys of Jews that sailed from Denmark to Sweden. Only a few survivors owed their lives to the efforts of the Zionist movement. (Segev 96)

It was the failed Zionist efforts that haunted the Israelis during the Eichmann trial, and which I believe had an impact upon the Israeli response to Arendt's book. The specifics of Zionist awareness about the Holocaust and the rescue operations attempted become important in enabling us to assess Israeli attitudes toward the adequacy or inadequacy of their response.

Porat argues that while information was available to leaders in the Yishuv before 1942, it was simply not comprehended fully or taken seriously. "Mass murders" were still thought of in terms of "hundreds" of deaths, Yishuv leaders still believed that "the sufferings of the Jews were incidental to the German occupation" (Porat 22), and "the gap between what was actually happening and what the Yishuv perceived to be happening had become abysmal" (Porat 20).

In February of 1942, the *SS Struma*, a leaky old boat packed with 770 Jewish refugees, was refused entry into Palestine, under terms of the British "White Paper." The immigrants had hoisted a sign pleading "Save Us," but the boat was turned back into the open sea. It sank, drowning all aboard except one. There was outrage among the Israelis that took the form of fury at Britain, but we may understand the rage was also about the increasing awareness of the powerlessness of the Yishuv. Porat observes, "This incident illustrated not only the gravity of the situation in Europe, but also the Yishuv's helplessness" (24).

Still, newspapers in the Yishuv continued to be cautious in their reporting of events in Europe, and regardless of political affiliation, warned their readers that reports of extermination by methods other than shooting were probably exaggerated. Throughout 1942, increasingly detailed and accurate news of methodical Nazi extermination of Jews continued to be greeted with incredulity. All of the Jewish leaders—Gruenbaum, Ben Gurion, Dobkin, and others, participated in this disbelief. A refugee from Poland, Ya'acov Kurtz, reported, "People did not believe me. They said I was exaggerating. I was interrogated as if I were a criminal trying to put something over on people. They asked me how I could know what was happening in some place while I was locked into a ghetto" (Porat 36–37). When Dobkin asked a woman who had escaped from the same ghetto as Kurtz whether she was perhaps exaggerating, she slapped his face and left the room.

> Even Dobkin, who devoted a lot of time and energy to dealing with the news, was incapable of accepting forms of human brutality for which he had no existing frame of reference. It was especially hard to believe that the first to be murdered were always children, the elderly, and the infirm. "I admit," Shertok cabled to London in November, "that had I not heard it myself from people who had been there, I would not have believed it." Ben Gurion expressed a similar feeling. (Porat 37)

Even after 17 December 1942, when the extermination was officially acknowledged as a verified fact, "very little changed in the way in which the news was received and processed in Palestine" (41). Both Porat and Segev report an initial public response to the news, but after a few months, "After the spring of 1943... less time and space were devoted to it. Like the disaster that befell Polish Jewry with the outbreak of the war, the extermination ceased to command special attention once the details had become familiar" (Porat 41). Segev reports, "'We read, we sigh, and go on,' wrote a Jewish Agency leader. 'Everyone knows that they should get emotional over news of the Holocaust, Katznelson said. Everyone knows that the situation is horrible, but people have trouble understanding those stories as part of their personal experience'" (Segev 77). For the second half of 1943 onward the Holocaust was, in the words of Segev, "no big news" (Segev 76).

The Yishuv felt removed from events, and believed in 1943 that they still lacked an accurate and comprehensive picture of the situation. As late as 1944, more than a year later, Ben Gurion told the JAE that 'we don't know what the real situation in Poland is'" (Porat 41). Porat, referring to contemporary Israel, describes "the issue of the Yishuv's organized public reaction to the annihilation of European Jewry" as "still an open wound." In Palestine, daily life continued, "scarcely affected by the war." Indeed, economic growth was accelerated by the war as the British army placed large local orders, soldiers passing through spent money in Palestine, construction boomed, business was conducted, and "there were even celebrations" (Porat 62–63).

Meanwhile when in mid-May of 1944, 430,000 Hungarian Jews were sent to Auschwitz, "the Yishuv stood by helplessly, stunned at the rate of the transports, the efficiency of the extermination apparatus, and the number of victims" (Porat 62).

It was not a matter of a blanket denial of reality on the part of the Yishuv leaders, but rather a combination of incredulity and helplessness. The frustration and feeling of impotence manifested itself in the form of bickering and in-fighting among people who were essentially allies: the JAE, Histadrut, and Mapai. In mid-1943, "the JAE was sharply criticized for its lack of real initiative, its failure to conduct a thorough discussion of the task of Zionism in such times, and its failure to allocate money for large-scale rescue operations" (Porat 75). JAE head Gruenbaum stated publicly that allocating resources in the Yishuv should take precedence over rescue operations, which he regarded at the time as futile.[7] A Joint Rescue Committee was constituted in order to coordinate efforts among the various organizations in the Yishuv. But instead of rising above factional splits, it fell into the cracks between the organizations, which included an increasingly wide crevice between Ben Gurion of the Mapai, and Gruenbaum of the JAE. Both men regularly overlooked the rescue committee's suggestions, in part to the extent that each believed it reflected the ideas of the other. Ben Gurion's power base was the Labor movement, and the pioneering settlement movement, in which he had been active for almost three decades. Gruenbaum belonged to the centrist General Zionist party, had come to Israel from Poland only in 1933, and was cut off from his Polish power base. Ben Gurion despised parliamentary mannerisms and hyperbole and faulted Gruenbaum for his penchant for them. Porat reports that "people who worked closely with both were unequivocal in their view that 'Ben Gurion could not stand Gruenbaum'" (Porat 70).

In contrast to Gruenbaum, Ben Gurion believed the rescue of the European Jews was important morally as well as financially. "It is not merely a question of helping the Jews of Europe; it is raising the stature of Palestine and the Zionist funds. The fact that Palestinian Jewry has taken the lead in rescue operations is an important Zionist asset," he claimed (Porat 85). This is the pragmatic perspective of a profoundly political man. Ben Gurion was also reluctant to alienate the British or Americans by insisting on the more aggressive rescue operations suggested by some. When he advocated approaching the American Joint Distribution Committee for help financing possible rescue operations, the JDC and the Israeli JAE became embattled over who actually represented world Jewry, what the division of labor between the organizations should be, whence money from rescue operations should come and, when it was clear that the Americans had more money than the Israelis, who should be in charge of the rescue effort. Additional strains in the already tense relationship between Ben Gurion and Gruenbaum resulted when Ben Gurion sought assistance from the JDC, the very outfit that challenged Gruenbaum's claim to leadership of the world's Zionists. The JAE and the JDC quarreled about who would represent Diaspora Jewry before European and international authorities and who would get credit for the rescue efforts. The stakes were not insignificant: "Zionists and non-Zionists were competing for the support of Jews during the war and—not less important—afterward" (Porat 99).

Meanwhile, the Histadrut was now openly critical of the JAE for what it regarded as its inaction over rescue efforts—which may not have been so inappropriate a stance, since the JAE under Gruenbaum continued to insist that it was not the body responsible for rescue, even though it claimed to represent Zionism in the world. Many people agreed with them, and the Histadrut took the initiative for rescue from the Yishuv. The JAE was forced to follow its lead in order to save face. Porat sums up the delicate political situation:

> Most critics . . . were wary of diminishing the Zionist budget or of eating into funds for defense. Nor did they want an open confrontation with the JAE which they considered to be the supreme political authority, entrusted with carrying out Zionist policy. The result was that the harshest critics of the JAE became its propelling force.[The Histadrut] did the Zionist movement and Zionist Executive a great service—by taking the initiative and forcing the Agency Executive to follow suit, the Histadrut Executive saved the Agency's honor. (Porat 93)

Relations between the JAE and the Central Committee of the Mapai continued to be strained, undoubtedly because Ben Gurion and Gruenbaum hated each other. "The feeling was widespread that there was no real dialogue between the Central committee and the JAE on such crucial issues as the Holocaust and rescue. The Mapai representatives in the JAE, especially Ben Gurion, were not sharing their information and calculations with the top echelon of their party" (157). A prolonged effort to rescue 29,000 children from the Holocaust fell through, which was a deep disappointment to Ben Gurion. The trouble was really lack of international support, and the plans foundered on technical details over safe passage for the children. Parents in Europe were still not convinced that annihilation was immanent, and refused to put their children on unsafe boats. But getting trainloads of Jewish children across borders in Europe to Israel would have called for international political wizardry. And there had also been bitter, and as it turned out futile, quarreling among Jewish leaders in the Yishuv over what sort of education the children would receive: Zionist or Orthodox religious? In the end, the children never arrived and the point of debate was moot, but it was not the only time that the parties became embattled over what sort of Jews to rescue from the Holocaust, or of what to do with them afterwards. There was a "party key," used by all of the leaders at different times, targeting for rescue Jews of political persuasion compatible with whomever thought they were making decisions at the time.[8]

In spite of both domestic and international division among the Jews, the attempts at rescue took many forms, from direct military intervention, to negotiating with the Nazis. The issue that returned to haunt the Mapai and the JAE was whether negotiating with the Nazis for release of Jews—whether children or adults—was in keeping with the Jewish tradition of survival, or was tantamount to dealing with the devil.

ATTEMPTS AT RESCUE

Attempts at rescue stumbled along, hindered by disbelief over the nature of the Holocaust, political bickering and lack of funding, and occasional serious moral debates over the trade-offs between survival and resistance. Contemporary sources differ about the whole-heartedness of the rescue efforts. Of the three scholars we refer to here, Tom Segev is the most skeptical, believing that Palestinian Jews were never fully committed to rescue, and indeed, did not do everything they could have done to intervene on behalf of Jews trapped in the Holocaust. He emphasizes a deep Zionist ambivalence toward Diaspora Jews: almost as though the Holocaust was what you could expect if you were foolish enough to believe it was possible for Jews to live in European society, away from a Jewish homeland. And indeed there were, as we shall see, profound cultural differences between the Jews who survived the Holocaust and immigrated to Palestine and the Jews of the Yishuv. Dina Porat and Yehuda Bauer focus more on the efforts that *were* made by the Palestinian Jews on behalf of the Europeans.

But even Dina Porat, whose work is the most balanced and subtle of the three, betrays the seams that showed through the rescue efforts. Although she chronicles at length the various efforts to save European Jews, which included political negotiations with Allies and Neutral countries, ransom plans, and plans for direct military intervention, she also admits that

> The total amount spent for rescue (from the Yishuv) in 1943 was about 320,000 pounds (the equivalent of about $8.6 million in 1989). The Jewish National Fund spent more than three times as much that year for reforestation and land purchase, as did the Jewish Agency for its own range of activities in Palestine. The MRF spent 500,000 pounds for defense purposes and for the support of soldiers' families. (87)

Bauer clearly would like to present the Jews of the Yishuv as unequivocally in favor of rescue. He is disdainful of Segev's book, referring to it as "a very cleverly written 'liberal' historical revisionist thesis" (Bauer 82, fn.60). He argues that Jews began to act as soon as they were aware of the Holocaust, and that the activists were indeed heroes: "Yet heroes they all are. Their attempts to save Jews involved tremendous self-sacrifice, courage and devotion" (Bauer 259). For their efforts they were greeted with misunderstanding and ingratitude, the result, Bauer states, of frustration at the inevitable failure of their attempts. "The wrath and frustration of the Jewish people finally turned against itself. Ever since the Holocaust, an increasing number of books and articles have accused the Jewish wartime leadership of failing to rescue, of negotiating with the enemy, of pandering to hostile 'Allies'" (Bauer 258).

However, in spite of his intentions, Bauer's book also reveals moments of ambivalence as well as powerlessness on the part of Jews in the Yishuv. He claims, for instance, that "It is fairly clear now that Ben Gurion received detailed information the moment it became available. He appears to have grasped fully the implications of the Nazi murder plans; and, contrary to established views, he became extremely active in promoting approaches to the Allies to persuade them to intervene in favor of European Jews" (Bauer 82). Yet a few pages later, Ben Gurion sounds more like a pragmatic politician than an idealistic hero: "It seems fairly clear that Schwartz, Ben Gurion, Shertok, and even Mayer sent [ransom money to the Allies] not because they believed that such a rescue was practical but because they did not want to be accused after the war of missing an opportunity to rescue Jews, even if the scheme was very doubtful" (Bauer 90). Ben Gurion himself did not believe that claiming ignorance of Nazi genocide was an excuse for inaction. He remarked, "No one needed official announcements to know that Hitler had intended to exterminate the Jews—it was all in *Mein Kampf*" (Segev 79). Yet as we have seen, acceptance of that knowledge was slow to spread, and the capacity of the Yishuv to respond to it was hampered by reluctance to accept the truth, battles over what should be done, as well as the capacity to execute plans.

Here we shall concentrate on the three most dramatic, and most problematic, rescue attempts: (a) the early negotiations with the Nazis for the release of Jews, called "Haavara," or transfer; (b) the effort to send paratroopers from the Yishuv behind Nazi lines into occupied territory, to help with resistance efforts; and (c) the infamous "Trucks for Blood" deal, where in the midst of the Holocaust, efforts were made to trade 10,000 trucks for a number of Jews.

Haavara

As early as the 1930s, Palestinian Zionists had negotiated with the Nazis under what was referred to as *haavara* ("transfer" in Hebrew). The Hebrew term was used in the German documents to refer to the negotiations between Zionists and Nazis to transfer selected Jews to the Jewish homeland. Segev notes, "The *haavara* ("transfer") agreement—the Hebrew term was used in the Nazi documents as well—was based on the complementary interests of the German government and the Zionist movement: the Nazis wanted the Jews out of Germany; the Zionists wanted them to come to Palestine. But there was no such mutuality of interests between the Zionists and German Jewry. Most German Jews would have preferred to stay in their country" (Segev 20). The agreement was possible only when German Zionists began to respond to Hitler and the anti-Semitism he whipped up. But this early recognition of anti-Semitism was still a long way from anticipating the full horror of the Holocaust.

Bauer notes:

> German Zionists saw the rise of Nazism as consistent with their pessimistic view of gentile society. Nobody foresaw the Holocaust; and although the Zionist dream of emigrating to Palestine remained theoretical before 1933—the number of German Jews who emigrated there was very small—the realization now spread that the revocation of Jewish emancipation in Germany was final and that Jews would have to emigrate. (Bauer 7)

Zionists in Palestine were interested in encouraging migration from Germany—especially of Jews with some capital to invest in the homeland. This was attractive to the German Jews only after they became were worried that the Nazis might confiscate their property.

In the early 1930s the British also looked favorably upon increasing immigration to Palestine, if it meant a transfer of capital as well, and if jobs could be found for the immigrants. Non-Zionist and anti-Zionist Jews outside Germany also wanted Germans and German Jews to reach some agreement since an increase of anti-Semitism there might provoke a flood of immigrants to their countries, and increase anti-Semitism there. Meanwhile, Zionists in Palestine sought a slow, orderly exodus from Germany, in order to avoid social and economic dislocations, and to help build the homeland. Bauer observes, "The obvious answer for both, but especially for the Zionists, was to negotiate with the Nazis. The Nazis wanted to get rid of the Jews, didn't they? And the Zionists wanted to absorb them gradually in Palestine, as moneyed settlers, not impoverished refugees.... The result was negotiations over the orderly exit of Jews with capital from Germany" (Bauer 8). The Jewish Agency became involved in trying to convince the Nazi government to "permit the export of Jewish capital in a way that would be attractive to the Germans" (Bauer 10).

But it was not so simple. Jewish agencies throughout the world began to respond in protest to the anti-Semitism of the newly ensconced Nazi government, and the weapon of choice was the threat of a worldwide Jewish boycott of German goods. The boycott undoubtedly would not have been effective: in spite of anti-Semitic fantasies, Jews simply did not have enough economic power to make a dent on international politics.[9] But the threat apparently had some impact on the Nazis, precisely because of their anti-Semitic paranoia: they were convinced that a Jewish boycott could be organized and would be effective, because there was a Jewish conspiracy controlling world finance. The threat of a boycott thus, ironically, prompted the Nazis to cooperate with the Zionist negotiators for Haavara — and touched off a bitter debate among Jews about whether Zionists should be negotiating with Nazis at all, for anything, under any circumstances. The boycott, at this stage, was the more militant response to growing Nazi power. The American Jewish Congress, chaired by Rabbi Stephen Wise, had come out in favor of a boycott, although Wise had been reluctant, and many of the wealthier Jewish merchants in America had also been resistant. Popular sentiment in the United States and in Israel supported the boycott. Haavara was objected to by Wise and the "mainstream Zionists" of America, on the one hand, and the right-wing Revisionist Zionists in Palestine on the other. The advocates of boycott argued that "Ha'avarah was an agreement with enemies of the Jewish people, that every effort should be made to topple the Nazi government through an economic boycott, and that the masses of the Jewish people were prepared to fight the Nazis even if the official leadership of the Zionist movement was not" (Bauer 11).

The debate over Haavara reflected an age-old debate among Jews about tactics for survival: compromise morally by meeting the enemy on his own terms, and enhance chances for survival; or choose isolation, militant resistance when possible, maintain moral purity, but risk slaughter at the hands of the invariably more powerful enemy. The choice, in terms of Jewish history, is between the Maccabees or "Jeremiah the Prophet, for example."[10]

Finding any common ground with the Germans both during and after the Holocaust thus "led to collective soul searching among the Jews in Palestine and to a crisis of identity. Who are we, they asked—humans, Jews, or Zionists?" (Segev 28). Some argued "that there was no reason not to negotiate with Adolf Hitler to save German Jews and bring them to Palestine; after all, Moses had had no qualms about negotiating with Pharaoh to take the children of Israel out of Egypt" (Segev 29). The negotiations with Nazi Germany also included selecting the best "human material" from among the Jews, to bring to Palestine. "The labor Zionists who dominated the agency believed that a new society needed to be created.... In parceling out the immigration certificates, they... gave preference to those who could play a role in their program for building the country. They preferred healthy young Zionists, ideally with agricultural training or at least a willingness to work on the land" (Segev 42).

This was the position of the JAE, or labor Zionists; the orthodox Jews in Palestine, as well as the Revisionist (conservative) Zionists regarded any negotiations with the Nazis as an abomination. In any event, the possibility of negotiations came only *before* the extermination program was put into effect, while far too many German Jews still believed it was possible to remain in Germany. At that stage, many German Jews were simply not interested in immigrating to Palestine, a stance that fed later Israeli disdain for many of the survivors who reached the Holy Land only when it was no longer a matter of choice. This, in turn, complicated relations between survivors and Sabras with sometimes tragic consequences.

Bauer, who has profound disagreements with Segev on a number of issues, indirectly confirms Segev's reading. He shows that the Gestapo, and especially Eichmann, were helpful in arranging for the "transfer" of Jews even *after* the Kristallnacht, "which was intended to push the Jews into a helter-skelter flight from the Reich." That is, Bauer confirms that Jews were reluctant to leave Germany before they were sure they had to, rather than constituting a ready and willing body of potential Zionists, held against their will in Germany by Nazis. He thus avoids the issue of Jewish-Nazi negotiations with the rejoinder that it cannot properly be called "negotiations."

> We can hardly talk of Nazi-Jewish negotiations in this context; the cooperation was between persecutor, who at that stage wanted to rid himself of the victim, and the representatives of the groups of victims, who were trying to escape his clutches.... There was, on one side, brutal direct pressure ... and, on the other side, the desperate efforts of Jewish groups and their leaders to escape from a trap—they were caught between the Nazis, an inhuman British policy, neutral indifference, and a powerless Jewish-Zionist leadership. (Bauer 53–54)

While Bauer's effort to demonstrate how the Yishuv was not really "negotiating" with Nazis is to present the Jewish leadership as in no way morally compromised by their choice, his information does confirm what will later be important for Segev's argument: that most of the German Jews did *not* want to emigrate to Palestine, were not Zionists, and came late and under duress, causing deep tensions between European refugees and Palestinian Zionists, and aggravating the sense of guilt among the Yishuv that perhaps they had not done everything they might have for the Holocaust victims.

Military Intervention

There were two major attempts at military rescue: one involved bombing the killing centers, the other sending paratroopers from the Yishuv to offer moral support and assistance to the resistors in Hungary and Poland. With regard to the idea of bombing

Auschwitz, it was Gruenbaum's turn to take the initiative. In late May of 1944, the Jewish Agency offices in Jerusalem were contacted, and Moshe Shertok was asked to approach the Allied governments with the request to bomb railway stations leading from Hungary to Poland, in order stop the transport of the Jews to the killing centers. Gruenbaum took it upon himself to approach the American consul general in Jerusalem, Lowell C. Pinkerton, on his own initiative, before meeting with the JAE a week or so later. To his surprise, both the JAE and David Ben Gurion objected to bombing any places where there might be Jews. It was apparent that neither Ben Gurion nor the JAE were aware of the fact the Auschwitz and Birkenau were not labor camps, but extermination installations. When, a month or so later, refugees reached Palestine and made a full report on Auschwitz, there was a more unified Zionist effort to persuade the Allies to bomb the killing centers.

Although the strategic value to the Allies might be open to debate, the symbolic value to the Jews was not:

> Its main value would be its long-range influence. It would demonstrate that the Allies had declared direct war on the Nazi extermination; it would discredit German propaganda claiming that the Allies were actually satisfied with the killing of Jews; it would remove once and for all any doubts still lingering in Allied circles about the authenticity of the information about the mass murder; it would give weight to the threats of retaliation against the murderers and thus serve as a deterrent; and, finally, it might create domestic pressure in Germany against the continued extermination. (Porat 217)

The bombing never took place, and Porat notes with disgust, "Although Churchill and Eden agreed to the bombing—and it was one of the few plans, if not the only one, that Eden apparently agreed to—they did not exert any real pressure on their subordinates to carry it out. There is no way to avoid the conclusion that the Allies did not bomb Auschwitz because they were simply indifferent to the fate of the Jews" (Porat 219).

The effort to drop resistance fighters behind Nazi lines by parachute would undoubtedly have served an even more dubious strategic purpose, and there is divided opinion about its symbolic value. Reports of horrors in the ghettoes were reaching the Yishuv, and in late 1942, Moshe Shertok approached British intelligence in Cairo with the request for assistance in training one thousand Zionist commandos and sponsoring a parachute drop into Poland. The commandos would cross into Hungary to help with the resistance movement there. The British, who did not want a large group of paratroopers in the Yishuv trained by themselves, with the potential to act against them after the war, agreed to a much more modest plan. It resulted in thirty-two paratroopers making the mission in mid-1944. Of the thirty-two, twelve were captured, seven were executed, and the rest returned to tell the tale.

The training program was a strain on all concerned because the Israeli commandos had "informal attitudes" compared to the demands of the British army officers who were training them. The British believed the Zionists were exploiting the program for their own political purposes (which may not have been so far from the truth, although the relevance of that observation is questionable) and the volunteers made it clear that they regarded their duty to the Jewish people as more important than their military obligations to the Allies. "Most of them had refused to pledge allegiance to the British army or wear its uniform even though their chances of survival were clearly much better if they were captured wearing British uniforms" (Porat 223).

The parachutists did not receive specific operational guidelines from either the British or the Zionist leaders, partly because the situation in Europe was so volatile that it was impossible to give specific instructions, and partly because the goals of the mission were obviously symbolic. Dobkin told two of the volunteers, "If you deliver greetings from Palestine to the Diaspora, you will have fulfilled your mission" (Porat 226). Segev reports that when, before the mission, the volunteers asked for operational instructions from the Yishuv leaders, "Ben Gurion told them to make sure 'that the Jewish people recognize the Land of Israel as their land and fortress' so that after the war they would come by the thousands. Eliahu Golomb, a leader of the Haganah, Mapai, and Histradrut, and "unofficial defense minister in the prestate decades" (Porat 310), told them that the goal was "to show the Jewish people how to 'stand proud.' One Jewish Agency official told them to bring the 'Messiah' to the Jews of the Exile; Golda Meir just wept" (Segev 87).

Segev also claims that while they may have been sent off on a glorious mission as a symbol of Zionist spirit, they were received with incredulity by the Eastern Europeans. It looked a little too much like a political gambit, a public relations ploy on the part of the Zionists, which may have actually jeopardized the work of the resistance movement in Eastern Europe. Egon Rott, a Jewish rebel leader in Slovokia, berated them: "'Really, why did you come? Did you think this was a child's game here? You wanted to be heroes? ... You came here to play soldiers. ... Didn't you think of the responsibility you were giving us? Until now we were responsible only for our own lives, but now you are weighing on our consciences.' He told them to get on the first flight out and return to the Holy Land" (Segev 88).

But Dina Porat offers a different perspective. She believes that the paratroopers could have served a much more important purpose if they had not waited for training and authorization from the British, but had just gone, the way resistance fighters always go: "Why did the Yishuv send no emissaries in the way the movements of Europe sent their own emissaries—from one ghetto to the next, independently, without the support of outside bodies, Jewish or non-Jewish?" (Porat 228). This surely would have been less dramatic than dropping from the skies into Europe, and lends some credence to those who believe that the Zionists were exploiting a dramatic gesture, rather than effectively getting involved in the European resistance. But the young volunteers themselves were surely idealists, even if their leaders were more jaded. "The parachutists were from the same mold as the youth who fought in the ghettos, who crossed borders, who took care of orphans and forged documents. They happened to have immigrated to Palestine earlier than their European counterparts, but they came from the same background ... to many Jews in Europe they represented the spirit of the Yishuv, and as such they helped renew faith in Palestine and Zionism during the Holocaust" (Porat 228).

Hannah Senesh, one of the parachutists who was captured when she crossed the border into Hungary, tortured for five months and finally killed, became a heroine for Jews in the Diaspora and in Israel, and lent some credibility to the argument that a concern for Zionism in Palestine was compatible with concern for Jews of the Diaspora. She urged her comrades who were reluctant to cross into Hungary, "We did not come here 'on condition,' that we would cross the border only if everything was assured beforehand . . . we have to act without calculations or unnecessary deliberations. We must not be late. If Hitler succeeds in annihilating all the Jews of Europe, there is no future for us in Palestine, either" (Porat 227). Still, Porat wonders, "Why did no one leave Geneva, Istanbul, or Sweden on foot to serve as 'a gesture, a sign, a hand extended as a token of sharing our fate'?" (228).

From Segev and Porat we derive dramatically different interpretations of the rescue effort. Was it a cynical political gesture, or a gesture that was symbolically important, even if inadequately or half-heartedly executed? Either way, the conclusion was the same: the efforts of the Zionists were perceived, by themselves as well as others, as inadequate.

Trucks for Blood

Perhaps the most infamous rescue effort of all was the ill-fated "Trucks for Blood" venture, which sealed the fate of Rudolf Kastner in Israel, and by extension determined the political significance of the Eichmann trial for Ben Gurion and the Mapai. If Kastner had not been involved in negotiating with Nazis over this deal, the Eichmann trial most certainly would have been conducted differently, Hannah Arendt would probably have written a different report of the trial, which would, perhaps, have been received differently. The Israeli political context for the trial of Adolf Eichmann in Jerusalem was, from a certain perspective, a dramatic sequel to a trial involving Rudolf Kastner in 1954.

Rudolf Kastner was a Hungarian Jew, a lawyer and a journalist, who had been a Zionist functionary in Budapest associated with Mapai (Ben Gurion's party). After the war he emigrated to Israel, worked in the Ministry of Commerce and Industry, and held ambitions for a seat in the Knesset. While in Hungary during the war, he had headed the Hungarian

Rescue Committee, which had involved negotiating with Eichmann.

The "Trucks for Blood" deal was apparently Eichmann's brainchild, and it involved from the Jewish side, Hungarians Rudolf Kastner and Joel Brand, and in Palestine, Gruenbaum and the JAE. Joel Brand, born in 1906 in Hungary, was educated in Germany, where his family had moved. He later became a Communist agent, working for the Comintern as a sailor, and a middle-rank Communist functionary until he was arrested when the Nazis came to power. He was released in 1934, returned to Hungary, and became a Zionist, joining the labor-Zionists there, which was also the party Kastner had joined. Bauer tells us "He tried to train for emigration to Palestine, but he was not of the stuff that pioneers are made: he had a restless nature, loved the city, with its cafes and bars, and was known to drink." When Kastner came to Budapest he met Brand, and apparently found in him a kindred spirit. Although Brand was an adventurer, and Kastner a much more respectable political functionary, the two became friends. Bauer notes, "From a Hungarian Jewish point of view, people like Kastner and Brand were marginal—they were totally unknown in the community, and they were foreigners.... In addition, they were Zionists" (Bauer 152).

In mid-April of 1944, not long after the Nazis had occupied Hungary, Eichmann approached Brand with an offer to release one million Jews for 10,000 trucks, and other items: eighty tons of coffee, twenty tons of tea, twenty tons of cocoa, and two million bars of soap. Eichmann would release 100 Jews for each truck delivered. The proposal was delivered to Brand, who gave it to Venia Pomerantz in Istanbul, who presented it, concealed in a tube of shaving cream, to the JAE in Jerusalem. He did not tell the Jerusalem group that the response to the proposal in Istanbul had been "a desire to get up and cry 'All lies!' A deceptive, villainous proposal" (Porat 189). The JAE's response was not so different: they had spent years trying to negotiate with Eichmann to ransom Jews. In their experience, the usual outcome was that Eichmann's subordinates took their money, and sent the victims to their deaths. But Kastner's response was "Was there anything else left for us to do? Did anyone suggest other, better rescue possibilities?" (Porat 190).

But there simply were not the 10,000 trucks, as well as the other goods, in Israel. Segev cites Ben Gurion's succinct explanation for the failure of the Plan: "Where were we going to get ten thousand trucks?" The Allies had to be approached to help come up with the goods. Ben Gurion was convinced that nothing would happen without Allied assistance. Predictably, Gruenbaum and Ben Gurion differed: Gruenbaum believed that the Allies would not go along with it, since it involved transferring goods to the Germans that would strengthen their war effort. "Gruenbaum...was certain that the British would simply obstruct the whole matter as they had other plans. Ben Gurion and Kaplan, however, were convinced that, without the Allies' cooperation, as Ben Gurion said, 'we will not be able to move'" (Porat 191). Most of the others agreed with Ben Gurion, and the Allies were approached. Porat believes that "acting alone, Britain would have rejected the German proposal outright on its own merits. But because its overall policy required cooperation with the United States to check Soviet expansion in Eastern Europe, it had to show willingness to accommodate any American interest in saving Jews, especially on the eve of presidential elections in the United States" (Porat 196).

The negotiations bogged down in international intrigue and bureaucratic red tape. Gruenbaum suggested that negotiations continue only on the condition that the deportations to the death camps be stopped, and observed that he had been right in objecting to disclosing the details to the British—by the time the Allied governments were ready to negotiate, there would be no Jews left in Hungary to negotiate about. But it was also true that Eichmann made it clear that the Germans were not prepared to allow the rescued Jews to emigrate to Palestine. He did not want to anger the Arabs by contributing to a strong Jewish Palestine, and he told Brand and Kastner that "because Nazis believed Judaism to be a malignant disease, they wanted the Jews spread through the Allied territories—including Spain, North Africa, and North America—in order to contaminate the enemy" (Porat 197).

During the course of the negotiations, when he realized that neither the Jews nor the Allies trusted his proposal, Eichmann offered as a "good faith" gesture to release a number of Jews, to be picked by Kastner (Brand was being detained in Istanbul by the Nazis at the time), placed on a train, and guaranteed safe passage to Switzerland. Kastner agreed—which is what ultimately brought his downfall in Israel—and 1,684 persons were put on a train that became known as Noah's Ark. It was later referred to in Israel as "The VIP train." Kastner put his own family on the train, as well as many people from his native village in Hungary. He was later accused in Israel of saving his own family at the expense of other innocent victims. Bauer argues that this is an unjust accusation. Kastner put his family on the train at great risk, since nobody trusted that the Nazis would not simply send the trainload to Auschwitz, after holding it hostage to the negotiations.

> The gamble was a tremendous one, and to convince others that it was worth the try, Kastner put his own family in the train. As Hansi Brand [Joel's wife] said in her testimony at the Eichmann trial in Jerusalem: "If he [Kastner] put his own children [on the train], perhaps these people really will be brought to a neutral country. That made me calm, because I hoped that these people, whom we persuaded with such difficulty to get on the train, would be brought to freedom despite everything." (Bauer 198)

That Kastner had trouble convincing people to get on the train suggests that people in Hungary still did not believe in the immanence of deportation to the killing centers. Kastner was accused, at his trial in Israel, of deceiving the people by not informing them of their impending doom at Nazi hands. Bauer insists that everybody in Hungary already knew: after all this was 1944. "To the question that was asked in 1954 of Kastner—Why did you not warn the Jews?—The first answer was that most of them already had the information, and the second answer should have been, Yes, a serious attempt was made, and it failed. People did not want to listen. But Kastner, unaccountably, did not say this in 1954" (Bauer 159). 1954 refers to the date when Kastner was first accused of being a Nazi collaborator by Malchiel Gruenwald, the man he would sue unsuccessfully for libel.

There were several moments when Kastner did not choose to attempt to justify his actions for the benefit of his accusers, with grave consequences for himself. None of the sources I have consulted on this matter believe that Kastner was guilty of anything except doing his best to save whatever Jews he could, and failing, and then failing to "explain" his failure. It seems understandable that he would have felt weary and pessimistic about his chances of being understood in Israel in 1960. His trials were yet another tragedy of the Holocaust. We shall return shortly to a fuller consideration of the trial of Rudolf Kastner as a political prelude to the Eichmann trial, after pausing to outline the political climate surrounding it.

ISRAELI ATTITUDES TOWARD THE HOLOCAUST VICTIMS

Political debates in Israel over response to the Holocaust continued through the postwar period, and centered upon the same two dimensions that were troublesome during the war: (a) what contact, if any, Israel should have with Germany, and (b) what the attitude of Zionist Jews should be toward the victims/survivors of the Holocaust, many of whom turned up on Israel's collective doorstep. The politics of postwar negotiations with Germany echo precisely the political lines that had earlier been drawn in negotiations with the Nazis over Haavara. The Mapai and Ben Gurion, the dominant labor Zionist party and its pragmatic political leader, believed that Israel could not afford an isolationist stance, and must join the international community of nations. The Mapai began negotiations with the German government over needed goods—some of them military—and over reparations and restitution for the victims of the Holocaust living in Israel. Political conservatives and orthodox Jews in Israel opposed any contact with Germany, and sought to avoid any moral compromise that would derive from contact with the nation that had allowed the slaughter of six million Jews to proceed. Their sense of outrage was appropriate, but not practical for the survival of Israel as a state. The attitude toward the victims and survivors of the Holocaust was enormously complicated. The complexity is apparent in Porat's discussion of the Israeli response to the European resistance leaders' choice to die with their communities at the hands of the Nazis, rather than allow themselves to be rescued by the Israelis for the sake of Zionism. Porat suggests that Israeli Zionists mistook this stance for weakness or cowardice, for preferring "the life of a beaten dog to death with honor," as Yitzhak Gruenbaum remarked in 1942.[11] Segev argues that this was *the* operative stance in Israel toward the Holocaust. Porat believes there was recognition and later remorse for its harshness. For example, in 1944 a conversation took place in Palestine between David Remez and Chaika Klinger, of the Hungarian underground. She was explaining the importance of the resistance leaders' refusing Israeli rescue, which had been construed by the Israelis as passivity and disloyalty to Zionism. She told Remez,

> "The pioneering vanguard of a people without the people is of no value. If rescue is the order of the day, then the entire people has to be rescued. If destruction is—then the pioneers will be destroyed, too." Turning to David Remez, who apparently was in tears, she said, "Now is not the time or place to lament the fate of the movement. Our people in the movement went the right way—the only way they could have gone—though tragic and terrible." Remez replied, "I am weeping because we were too late, really late." (Porat 242)

The European youth movement members believed that they had been profoundly misunderstood by the Yishuv, and Eliyahu Dobkin conceded, "I am not sure that we can really understand the depth of their tragedy" (Porat 242). Porat remarks that as time passed, and more information arrived on conditions in Europe, Palestinian respect for the European Jews grew. She goes so far as to refer to "the Yishuv's newfound respect for European Jewry," although she admits that it had little impact on immigration policy, which continued to use "the political key" of giving preference to veteran Zionists and their families for immigration permits (Porat 245).

Segev believes that the Zionist attitude toward the Holocaust Jews was more unequivocally disdainful. Holocaust victims represented a threat to the Zionist self-image of strength and militancy. The threat cut close to the bone, as many of the Zionists had themselves emigrated to Palestine from Eastern Europe, or were the children of Eastern European immigrants. Reasons for the decision to leave Europe for Israel were not necessarily the visionary idealism Zionists would have preferred as a characteristic of all the Jewish pioneers: often the "voluntary" arrivals in Palestine were fleeing anti-Semitic regimes before Hitler came to power. The distinction between the Diaspora Jews now being slaughtered, and those who had escaped, was too subtle to be psychologically satisfying.

Crediting oneself for having had the foresight to flee before the Nazis arrived at one's doorstep doesn't amount to much of a buffer from the discomfort of seeing yourself in the Holocaust victims. One gets the feeling that the Zionists in Israel needed to find a handle for distinguishing themselves from the victims they had almost become. Segev suggests that the public attitude of the Zionists during the latter years of the war vascilated between mourning for the victims before they were dead, and being disdainful of the weakness of European Jewry. "There was no clearer, more grotesque, even macabre expression of the tendency to think of the Holocaust in the past tense: while the Yishuv discussed the most appropriate way to memorialize them, most of the victims were still alive" (104). And alternatively: "Negation of the Exile took the form of a deep contempt, and even disgust, for Jewish life in the Diaspora, particularly in Eastern Europe, which was characterized as degenerate, degraded, humiliating, and morally corrupt. In their tragedy, Diaspora Jews seemed even more repellent" (109). We shall consider the full implications of Segev's interpretation in chapter 5, on Gender and Judaism, where we consider the possibility that Zionists regarded themselves as masculine (on a European Christian model) and hence "superior" to the "feminine" Jews of the Diaspora.

When the European survivors began arriving in the Yishuv they were compared to Israeli youth, who, having undergone no comparable trauma, seemed (and were) strong and healthy by contrast. One teacher rationalized the essays of his students, which lacked compassion for Israeli Holocaust survivors with the observation, "Our youth are proud and upright in stance and spirit. They believe in their strength and know its value. They love freedom, desire space and liberty, and will not tolerate humiliation or repression." Segev wryly adds, "This was the 'new man' that socialist Zionism had prophesied" (109). The tragedy of the Israelis during the Holocaust is that in spite of their virile stance, their unwillingness to identify with European Jews assured them of the very ineffectiveness they sought to avoid. "The New Jews standing tall in Palestine, did just what the persecuted Jews of the Exile had always done, and were as powerless as they had been . . . the Zionist Jewish community in Palestine comes out looking just like any other Jewish community in the world. Only their better fortune and their hubris distinguished them from their brothers" (Segev 110).

Israelis—perhaps understandably—found the survivors' stories debilitating, depressing, and often simply unbelievable. Survivors, equally understandably, needed to talk, but soon gave up. Holocaust survivors, especially the children, were often so damaged by the experience that emotional adjustment to everyday life was an unrealistic goal. Segev tells of a girl who survived Bergen Belsen and was sent to Sweden to convalesce. "There she saw life proceeding, as if nothing had happened: boys and girls her age, healthy and properly dressed, went to school. This threw her into shock again." She recuperated somewhat and was sent to Israel. Her "integration" into a series of Kibbutzim was unsuccessful, and ultimately she married another survivor and moved to an apartment in a small town. She became a well-known author of children's literature and had two daughters. "She writes in Hebrew but has never lost her Polish accent: always something of an outsider, always a Holocaust survivor" (Segev 157). This, obviously, was one of the "success" stories.

The problem was at least as much symbolic as it was material. "The Sabra represented a national ideal, and the Holocaust survivor its reverse," Segev writes. "Each new arrival was a reminder that the Zionist movement had been defeated in the Holocaust.... The Zionist movement had been helpless. Not only did the Yishuv not come to the rescue, but it now found itself in a position where its existence and future depended on the willingness of the Holocaust survivors to settle in the country and fortify its army against the Arab threat" (181). Joel Palgi, one of the paratroopers who had been on the Holocaust rescue mission with Hannah Senesh, had tried, upon his return to Palestine, to report what he had seen in Europe. He wrote, "No one was interested in accounts of Jewish suffering. They wanted a different story, about the few who had fought like lions.... I realized that we were ashamed of those who were tortured, shot, burned. There is a kind of general agreement that the Holocaust dead were worthless people. Unconsciously, we have accepted the Nazi view that the Jews were subhuman" (Segev 183). This observation is confirmed by a cruel but widespread Israeli slang usage: the word *sabon*, or soap, came to be used to refer to Holocaust survivors in Israel.

POSTWAR NEGOTIATIONS WITH GERMANY

Zionist ambivalence toward the Holocaust victims manifested itself in the form of postwar Israeli party politics. In the 1950s Ben Gurion was Prime Minister and the issue was negotiation with the (West) German government to accept restitution and compensation for property lost to Holocaust survivors living in Israel. There was also the issue of trade arrangements with Germany of economic benefit to Israel. A boycott of Germany was regarded by some as the high moral ground. But the survival of Israel as a state, and its aspirations for recognition as part of the international community, would be hurt by shunning all communication with Germany. The United States and other countries were endeavoring to bring Germany back into the family of nations and Israel was trying to establish an international position against the efforts of Arab countries to isolate the Jewish state.

Some of the survivors living in Israel sought to reestablish ties with the old country. "Twelve years of Nazi rule had not expunged the memories of childhood and youth" (Segev 197). An enraged isolation that prevented Israel from achieving political stability, and survivors from facing their past, might not be the most advisable path politically, economically, or emotionally. Besides, it involved the implicit indictment of *all* Germans, which constituted a form of racism, in spite of the reality of German responsibility for Jewish genocide. Some Germans—notably West German Chancellor Konrad Adenauer—expressed responsibility, remorse and a willingness to negotiate restitution for the millions of dollars worth of Jewish property illegally seized by the Nazis. On 27 September 1951, Adenauer made an historic declaration in the Bundestag in Bonn, which included the statement: "Unspeakable crimes have been committed in the name of the German people, calling for moral and material indemnity, both with regard to the individual harm done to the Jews and with regard to the Jewish property for which no legitimate claimants still exist" (Segev 202).

The agreement under consideration between Israel and Germany was for reparations, and concerned only the property of German Jews seized by Germans. But it was easily misconstrued to mean that the Germans were willing to pay money for the blood of the Jews they had murdered, in the belief that they could "make things right." Centrist and right-wing political leaders in Israel emphasized that interpretation. In the debate that ensued in the Knesset, Elimelech Rimalt of the centrist General Zionist party told the members of the question put to him by his young son over the German reparations: "My little son came to me and asked, 'How much will we get for Grandma and Grandpa?'" (Segev 215). Both his parents had been murdered in the Holocaust, Rimalt added, as he pressed for refusal of the German offer.

The party lines drawn over reparations reflected the same divisions in Israeli politics that had surfaced in the debates over how to respond to the Nazis. Labor Zionists in the Mapai were opposed by the Orthodox Right, and by the centrist revisionist Zionists, who had by now formed their own party, Herut, under the leadership of Menachim Begin. Begin led the most vociferous opposition to Ben Gurion and the "Mapai-Nazi Blood Market." When Ben Gurion delivered a speech in support of the agreement with Germany, in which the Prime Minister argued, "Let not the murderers of our nation also be its heirs," Begin stormed out and led a protest demonstration back to the Knesset. The demonstration turned violent, and the Knesset was forced to adjourn, its members escaping the building under police protection. Demonstrators struggled with the police and many arrests were made, which gave rise among the protestors to accusations that Ben Gurion and his party were no better than Nazi Stormtroopers.

Several days later, Begin addressed the Knesset and made it clear that he would go to extreme measures to prevent negotiations with Germany:

> Nations worthy of the name have gone to the barricades for lesser matters... we, who saw our fathers dragged to the gas chambers; we who heard the clatter of the death trains;... we before whose eyes the elderly mother was murdered in the hospital... shall we fear risking our lives to prevent negotiations with our parents' murderers?... We are prepared to do anything, anything to prevent this disgrace to Israel. (Segev 219–20)

Begin was suspended for three months for threatening violence. The Knesset voted in favor of accepting German restitution for the illegally seized property of Holocaust survivors. The vote was sixty-one to fifty, with five abstentions, and four absentees.

There were profound differences between the experience of the Holocaust survivors, and the needs of the Israeli politicians who now competed for control over the institutionalization of the memory of the Holocaust. Although there were many survivors in the Herut party, Begin was distorting the truth when he presented himself as one of them. While he had been born in Poland, and while his parents had been killed by the Nazis, he had emigrated to Palestine as a youth, before he was endangered. He did not, as he often implied in his speeches, witness his parents' deaths. While his histrionics may not have been an exaggeration of the sufferings of many, they did not describe his own experiences, and failed to express the subjectivity of many of the victims, who were indifferent to Begin's efforts. In the early 1950s the survivors experienced the Holocaust as

> first and foremost a part of the individual biographies of its survivors; it was their personal catastrophe. Begin did not understand this. He may have been ahead of his time; years later the Holocaust did indeed develop into a sort of civic national religion. But in the early 1950's the memory of the Holocaust was sharp and fresh, and begin's operatic anti-German rhetoric never succeeded in expressing the force of personal suffering or touching the depths of individual tragedy. For this reason the survivors had little difficulty ignoring what he demanded of them and accepting their share of the compensation money. The money changed nothing within them, nor was it particularly relevant to their identity as survivors; at most it allowed them to buy larger apartments (Segev 226).

The Holocaust, at this stage in Israel's history, was a political football, with the various political parties vying for access to the creation of a "civic national religion." The danger in this is that the Holocaust was appropriated and exploited for political purposes, while the reality of the survivors was often overlooked.

Not surprisingly, the German administrative apparatus set up for restitution proved nearly as inhuman as the killing apparatus had, as Holocaust survivors attempted to establish, in German, the exact extent of their damages. This required finding witnesses who had also survived, to testify to the veracity of claims about one's residence before one was dragged from it, the contents of one's home before it was seized, the expenses incurred in the flight from Germany, if flight had been possible, or witnesses to one's specific treatment by Nazis in the death camps, if flight had been impossible. The greater a victim's personal losses, in terms of family members, friends, and neighbors, the more difficult it became to establish the validity of one's claim to lost property. Consider the following two German responses to claims:

> We have taken note of your claim that, when you arrived at the camp, you said that you were older, in order to save yourself from the extermination of the children, but your vita indicates that you were in fact 18 months older and as a result it is not clear to us why you had to give a false date when you registered at the camp. (Segev 246).

or,

> We have taken note of your claim that the injury to your spinal cord was caused in Buchenwald camp, when an SS officer whose name you did not mention, because you allegedly do not recall it, kicked you with his boot and allegedly also stomped on you. But it appears from your curriculum vitae that in 1951 you enlisted in the Israel Defense Forces. We therefore request that you produce for our examination a copy of your army medical file, translated... since if you were found fit for military service, it may be that the damage to your spinal cord was not severe or may have resulted from your army service. (Segev 247)

The bureaucratic language and mind set reflected distance from emotional reality and the "logic" of the technician in the face of the human suffering it was causing. In this respect, it was an accurate reflection of the situation during the period of Nazi hegemony in Germany as described by Hannah Arendt. Survivors were interrogated and the conditions of their survival doubted by the German bureaucracy.

But compounding that stance, Israeli neighbors often regarded the survivors' very existence as suspicious evidence that they had not resisted the Nazis, and had survived at the expense of their neighbors. Hansi Brand, Joel Brand's widow, who was living in Israel, was often questioned by her neighbors for her husband's alleged failure to save Jews, with the contradictory imputations that he either collaborated with Nazis or did not *successfully* collaborate with the Nazis.

> Those people who knew her story always asked why she and her husband had not done anything against the Nazis early on. And they always, always asked her how she had been saved, until she began to feel that she had to apologize for living. The stories she and her husband told competed with the stories of the Warsaw ghetto uprising, she said, and could not win. they had only fought for their lives, not to be heroes.

80   The Political Consequences of Thinking

The country wanted heroes. The Brands could only offer a story of survival. (Segev 271)

An additional irony is that while the payments extracted from Germany were being touted by Ben Gurion's party as a victory, a demonstration of the effectiveness of the Zionists and the protective role played by Israel, many of the claims for restitution on the part of the German refugees were based upon damages incurred because they had been forced to leave Germany for Israel, which they never would have done had it not been for the Nazis (Segev 244).

THE "KASTNER TRIAL"

We now return to the final chapter of Rudolf Kastner's story, which set the political stage for the trial of Adolf Eichmann in Jerusalem. In 1950, Israel passed a "Nazi Collaborators Law," which called for the prosecution of any person suspected of collaborating with the Nazis. The atmosphere that gave rise to it was such that survivors in Israel who believed they recognized faces of *Judenrate* members had taken to accusing them on the spot, publicly, often inciting vigilante-style violence. In 1946, the Israeli newspaper *Haaretz* reported that at an intersection in Tel Aviv, an agitated crowd had surrounded a young man, while several people beat him on the head, shouting "Murderer!" "Gestapo!" "'The man stood there, white-faced, and then tried to escape,' the reporter wrote" (Segev 259). He had been accused of being a Jewish policeman in the ghetto at Auschwitz. The "Kastner Trial" (which was really the Gruenwald trial) became a symbol for the anger at Jewish officials during the Holocaust.

In 1954 Rudolf Kastner was publicly accused of being a Nazi collaborator by an old, and rather eccentric, Hungarian Jewish refugee named Malchial Gruenwald, who claimed in a pamphlet he wrote and distributed to various public officials, that Kastner was guilty of violating the Nazi Collaborators Law. In fact, since he had been such a prominent figure in negotiating with the Nazis in Hungary, Kastner had already been investigated in 1950 when the law first passed. He was not found guilty of any infringement. Kastner tried to ignore Gruenwald, but it soon became apparent that his political career depended upon his response. He sued Gruenwald for libel. At the trial, Gruenwald's defense attorney, Shmuel M. Tamir, managed to put Kastner on the defensive, turning the trial into a show against all Jews who had "collaborated" with the Nazis. In essence, this was a trial of the *Judenrate*, by political opponents of Ben Gurion and the Mapai. The *Judenrate*'s willingness to cooperate with Nazis was implicitly being compared to Ben Gurion and the Mapai, who had been negotiating with Germans since the war's end. The atmosphere was of almost moblike hostility in Israel to anyone associated with the *Judenrate*. That the political consequences for Ben Gurion were enormous, creating a need for him to recoup his losses with the Eichmann trial, is evidenced by the fact that he was forced to resign after the Kastner trial—although he was returned to power by a narrow margin in the ensuing election. Yehuda Bauer believes that the Kastner trial "was the beginning of the end for center-left governance in Israel. . . . The 1977 swing in favor of the rightist Likud party was in some degree due to the Kastner Affair" (Bauer 3).

During his opening testimony, Kastner appeared calm and confident of his own innocence. "Kastner spoke quietly, believably, convinced he had done right. He came across as a bold man who saved the lives of hundreds in his community, perhaps thousands. He seemed more a tragic hero than a scoundrel. When he concluded his testimony, Justice Halevy suggested to Gruenwald that he retract his accusations. Gruenwald refused, and the cross-examination by defense attorney Shmuel M. Tamir began" (Segev 266). Kastner became defensive when Tamir pressed him on some apparent discrepancies in his testimony. Then Tamir moved in for the kill: to make Kastner the symbol of all prominent European Jews who had negotiated with the Nazis in any way. Politically, the effort was also to reopen the debate about Ben Gurion's negotiations with Germany over restitution.

> [Tamir] presented the following thesis to the court: Kastner knew the Nazis intended to exterminate Hungarian Jewry but kept the information from the members of his community. Had he but warned them in time, they might have been able

> to flee to Romania or organize armed resistance. Since they did not know what awaited them, they boarded death trains without resistance. (Segev 271)

As previously noted, this seems to have been be a gross distortion of what actually happened in Hungary. It is likely that people feared getting on Kastner's train because they were aware of and feared murderous Nazi treachery. Yet, remaining where they were, refusing to board the Noah's Ark train indicates that they may not have been convinced that their deportation to the death camps was immanent . . . or it just may be one more example of the absence of choices open to the Jews. It should also be noted that Tamir's statement is identical to the argument Arendt was accused by her critics of "heartlessly" making. It was exploited by her Israeli and New York detractors as evidence of her disloyalty to the Jews. It was argued that she had unjustly judged the *Judenrate*. At the Kastner trial, the same argument used to condemn Arendt was put forward by the *conservatives*, who believed the *Judenrate*, Kastner, the Mapai had betrayed the Jewish people by dealing with the Germans.

Gruenwald was found not guilty of most of the libel charges filed against him. Israeli political parties and newspapers made the most of it. Huge headlines announced the verdict, and newspapers devoted entire pages to it. They made much of the judge's claim that in dealing with Eichmann, Kastner had "sold his soul to the devil." *Herut* (Begin's party's newspaper) ran Kastner's picture with the caption, "Eichmann's partner," and all of the factions in Israel took advantage of the situation to make what political capital they could.

> The Communist *Kol Haam* said the negotiations between Kastner and Eichmann reflected the Nazi collaboration of the entire Zionist movement, as if there had never been a Hitler-Stalin pact. The religious parties saw Kastner as a representative of secular Zionism, as if there had been no observant Jews in the Judenrats. The leftist opposition parties Mapam and Ahdut Haavodah now identified themselves with the ghetto rebels, though during the Holocaust their people had been Mapai's partners in running the yishuv under the British. (Segev 285–86)

The Mapai was accused of having a "ghetto" mentality, compromising rather than taking a more militant stance, leading without any feeling for the homeland, devoid of spiritual independence. It was portrayed as at odds with the spirit and life of the new nation, the growing Land of Israel, "of the generation that had established the state with its blood and that would preserve it in the face of the trials of tomorrow" (Segev 286). The Mapai press was "paralyzed, trapped. It did not, of course, want to acknowledge that the judge was right, but neither did it want to attack the verdict, lest it give the impression that the party was thus defending its own interests" (Segev 286).

Kastner appealed the verdict, and two and a half years later the Supreme Court quashed the sentence, and justified most of Kastner's acts. But the legal vindication came too late for Kastner: several months before the decision was handed down, on 3 March 1957, while returning home from work late at night, Kastner was shot and killed in front of his home.[12]

There are several points made clear by this event. First, the issue of Jewish collaboration with the Nazis was nothing new in Israel. Hannah Arendt was certainly not the first to mention it publicly, although she was perhaps the first prominent person, and certainly the first woman, to write about it for a non-Israeli audience. "Collaboration" was a volatile public issue, raising profound moral questions, as well as being exploited for political purposes. Secondly, Ben Gurion "lost" the "Kastner trial" even though he tried to keep a safe distance from the affair.[13] Tamir went out of his way to associate Kastner with the Mapai, and to draw associations between Jews who negotiated with the Nazis during the Holocaust and Ben Gurion's willingness to resume relations with Germany after the war. Several years before the trial, Tamir had published an article in *Herut* in which he accused Ben Gurion of "'direct partnership' in the extermination of the Jews of Europe and establishment of relations with West Germany," and referred to him as the "Minister of Treason and Minister of Abomination" (Segev 266).

In the appeal, which cleared Kastner, Supreme Court Justice Zalman Heshin noted that while Jewish history has had its share of rebels, martyrs, and heroes, there is also another tradition in Judaism, of surviving and saving what could be saved: "Jeremiah the prophet, for example, preached surrender to the enemy and an alliance with him, while Rabbi Yohanan Ben Zakkai chose to save what could be saved in a time of trouble. Despite this, no one accused them of selling their souls to the devil" (quoted in Segev 307). The question tormenting the Jews was the same, whether about Haavara before, ransom during, or restitution after the Holocaust: did dealing with Germans during and after the Holocaust reflect weakness, rather than the more strident stance Israel associated with strength?

Ben Gurion, in spite of distancing himself from the Kastner affair, disbanded his government and called an election. He retained his position as Prime Minister, although his party lost five seats in the Knesset. He then became involved in yet another controversial set of negotiations with the Germans to purchase two submarines for self-defense against Nassar and the Arabs, who were threatening to annihilate Israel. He was forced to resign yet again, and was once again returned to power. But as this second resignation and reconstitution of his government took place, Ben Gurion knew he held one ace in the hole for clearing himself of association with Kastner and the suspicion that he was "soft on Germans": Mossad (Israeli Secret Service) agents had just informed him that they would be bringing him Adolf Eichmann.

THE TRIAL OF ADOLF EICHMANN

From its inception, then, the Eichmann trial was an intensely political event. There was the obviously illegal move of kidnaping Eichmann from Argentina, which undermined the moral credibility of Israel as representative of all Jewish victims, and threatened to set a dangerous international legal precedent. There was also the question of whether Israel had the "right" to try a German for crimes against the Jews. Arendt was not alone in suggesting that an international trial of Eichmann for crimes against humanity might have been more instructive to the world, although she and others acquiesced in the face of the impracticality of that suggestion. Nahum Goldman, president of the World Zionist Organization, suggested an international trial, as did several (non-Israeli) newspapers. Martin Buber agreed, commenting in a news magazine interview, "I do not think the victim should be the judge as well" (in Segev 329).

Ben Gurion and Goldman disagreed with each other in an exchange of open letters. Ben Gurion contended that Goldman's suggestion was an affront to Israel's sovereignty, and insisted that Israel was the only nation qualified to judge unprecedented crimes against the Jewish people. "'The Holocaust that the Nazis wreaked on the Jewish people is not like other attrocities that the Nazis committed in the world', Ben Gurion wrote to Goldman, 'but a unique episode that has no equal, an attempt to totally destroy the Jewish people, which Hitler and his helpers did not dare try with another nation. It is the particular duty of the State of Israel, the Jewish people's only sovereign entity, to recount this episode in its full magnitude and horror'" (Segev 329).

As high-minded as this may sound, the trial served partisan Mapai purposes, as well as coming at a moment when national spirit in Israel was beginning to flag. There were ethnic tensions, and riots in various quarters in Israel. Israel was losing its sense of (Ashkenazic) unity, and its sense of historical mission. Young Israelis felt no connection with the Holocaust and its survivors, and for the first time in its brief history, the flush of its energetic origins was wearing off. In claiming the trial of Adolf Eichmann for Israel, and placing it on the public stage, Ben Gurion had two goals: to remind the countries of the world that "the Holocaust obligated them to support the only Jewish state on earth." And secondly to "impress the lesson of the Holocaust on the people of Israel" (Segev 327).

There were also the pressing needs of Ben Gurion's own party, which had been on the defensive in the wake of both its stance on relations with Germany and the Kastner affair:

> The Eichmann trial would also enable Mapai to reassert its control over the heritage of the Holocaust, which it had lost to Herut and the parties of the left. The trial was meant, there-

fore, to expunge the historical guilt that had been attached to the Mapai leadership since the Kastner trial; it was to prove that—despite the ties with Germany, despite the reparations agreements and the arms deals—the Ben Gurion administration was not insensitive to the Holocaust (Segev 328).

Indeed, no one had to drum up interest in the Eichmann trial. When the announcement was made that Eichmann was in Israeli custody, the entire nation was riveted to every word about the upcoming trial.

Attorney General Gideon Hausner was faced with a decision about whether to limit the charges to Eichmann's actual deeds, or to let the trial grow into a large, public expose of the Holocaust in general. Hausner had more than enough documentation to convict Eichmann for his own part in arranging the slaughter of hundreds of thousands of Jews: "Even a fraction of them would have been enough to convict him ten times over" (Segev 338). However, with the advice and approval of Ben Gurion, Hausner decided to "shock the heart," beyond simply carrying out a legal mission. "I wanted people in Israel and the world to come closer, through the trial, to this great catastrophe" (Segev 338). So he invited witnesses to testify, and the number who came forth amounted to a national catharsis. In fact, the trial did succeed in ensconcing the Holocaust in the consciousness of the world, as well as Israeli youth, and succeeded in creating a "civic national religion" in Israel, ensuring that the Holocaust would not be lost to history. It also may well have served and as emotional catharsis for the Holocaust victims living in Israel, as they could finally, publicly, and with the blessings of the government of Israel, tell their stories to their Israeli neighbors.

The political capital made by the trial, and the moral compromises of all concerned, seem inevitable in any world less than perfect. They pale in the shadow of the hell that the Nazis actually imposed upon the world, and with which the Israelis and the Holocaust survivors were attempting to come to terms.

In letting the trial develop into an expose of the entire extermination campaign, Hausner, with Ben Gurion's blessing, presented all Holocaust victims as Zionists, which was patently untrue. Many of the victims perished precisely because they were *not* Zionists, and had remained in Europe until it was too late to escape to Israel or anywhere else. The irony is that the Israeli prosecution went out of its way to present the victims of the Holocaust in precisely the manner in which they had been incapable of treating them as arrivals in Israel. Instead of the usual contrast between the European victims and stalwart Israelis, who surely would have fought to the death rather than allowed themselves to be led to slaughter, Hausner now portrayed the Holocaust victims themselves as brave resisters. Exaggerated polarization still dominated the scenario painted by the prosecution in the Eichmann trial, only now the "weak and degenerate Jews" were played by the *Judenrate*—like Kastner—who had been attacked by the Israeli conservatives, and defended by Mapai. Now Mapai assumed a stance resembling that of the conservatives, castigating the *Judenrate* as representing the "spiritual degeneracy and the Jewish submissiveness of the Exile," while defending the bravery of the victims and survivors (Segev 360).

Arendt's argument that the *Judenrate* contributed to the slaughter by participating in Nazi logic thus, ironically, paralleled the *conservative*, more militantly Zionist argument. Now, however, she was accused of being anti-Semitic by Ben Gurion and others who sought to distance themselves from the accusation that they had been too conciliatory toward the Germans. Her criticism of exaggerated polarizations of good and evil obscured efforts to draw political lines clearly. She was *also*, by implication, critical of the Zionists, who had not always been so ready to define the European Jews as made of the same brave stuff as themselves. It is evident that while Arendt may have offended many in Israel, she would have run afoul of Ben Gurion and the Mapai most dramatically. They stood most to gain politically from maintaining control of the meaning of the Eichmann trial, and they would have felt most betrayed by *both* aspects of her criticism: of the *Judenrate*, *and* of the Zionists.

In the final analysis, Arendt's *Eichmann in Jerusalem* was explosive in Israel because it exposed to the world uncomfortable political conflicts that the Israelis preferred to keep to themselves. In particular, it was embarrassing to David Ben Gurion and the Mapai party, because Arendt took a similar stand on the *Judenrate* as his opponents had in the Kastner affair. This may also have seemed to imply criticism about his political negotiations with Germany after the war. However, it is unlikely that Arendt held that position, an isolationism consistent with conservative Israeli politics. Rather, she offended simply because she refused to polarize concerned parties into victims and villains, or heroes and victims, or martyrs and villains. Mapai, which had actually had a history of pragmatic politics, rather than indulging in polarizing extremism, had been forced into a defensive stance by the right-wingers, and were themselves indulging in the terminology of good and evil they had resisted in the past. The Mapai "party line" during the Eichmann trial was that the Jews were entirely innocent as human beings as well as victims, and that all the Nazis were equally evil. The association of European Jewish victims with Zionists was disingenuous and inaccurate. Israelis had been contrasting the European Jews with themselves; now they argued for their similarity, in contrast with both the Nazis and the *Judenrate.*

Arendt's arguments were embarrassing, simply because she did not write for the benefit of Israeli politics: she sought, self-consciously, to erode the tendency to view even the politics of the Holocaust in terms of good and evil. Israeli neglect of the Holocaust victims, and the difficulties experienced between the Sabras and the survivors, were also a sore spot inflamed by Arendt's unwillingness to paint a prettier picture of the Zionist stance. Still, I believe that she was clear about the fact that it was the *Nazis* who were solely responsible for creating the impossible situation, which forced decisions that no people should have to make. She did not imply any shared guilt for the death camps: they were entirely the doings of the Nazis. She only lamented that the choices forced upon Jews and others throughout the world were impossible, and that the responses to the

Nazis had been invariably ineffective and unsatisfactory, both morally and politically.

The Israelis had not behaved like angels, and Arendt had not expected them to. Nonetheless, after the war, when they were attempting to present to the world a somewhat sanitized version of their actual response to the Holocaust, her insights were received as disloyalty, whereas her hope had been that the world could learn some truly valuable lessons from the tragedy.

CHAPTER 4

The New York Intellectuals and *Eichmann in Jerusalem*

THE NEW YORK INTELLECTUALS AND JUDAISM

Meanwhile back in New York, Arendt's critics in the Jewish Intellectual Community had their own reasons to be embarrassed by *Eichmann in Jerusalem*. Her critics among the editors of the *Partisan Review* and *Commentary* shared a similar history, a similar attitude toward their Judaism, and considerable guilt over their stance toward the Holocaust.

The original editors of the *Partisan Review* were either children of Eastern European Jewish immigrants, or immigrants themselves, having come to the United States as children. Although sons of Eastern European poverty, their attitudes closely resembled those of the more elite generation of educated German and Viennese Jews of the Weimar era.[1] They minimized the importance of their Jewishness, and emphasized an adherence to *Bildung*, a belief in enlightened rationalism that transcended national or cultural borders. They sought to break out of the Jewish immigrant ghetto, leave Jewish identity behind, and forge a new identity in terms of Western culture.

Their self-consciously internationalist stance is captured in the term they used to describe their perspective: *Cosmopolitanism*. Cosmopolitanism was accompanied by the insistence that they were "genetically... only partly or questionably Jewish."[2] Terry Cooney notes, "Jewishness as an idea and sentiment played no significant role in their expectations.... In the 30s... it was precisely the idea of discarding the past, breaking away from families, traditions and memories which excited the intellectuals. They meant to declare themselves citizens of the world" (Cooney 31).

Sometime after World War II, they embraced a conservative, anti-Communist stance. Scholars are divided about whether the new conservatism was part of a belated, post-Holocaust identification with Israel, or whether their disenchantment with Stalin was the beginning of an estrangement from communism and organized radical politics that led them not only to react conservatively but to seek the comfort of another identity. They had always been "alienated"—whether from Judaism or mainstream American life—but needed the solace of a group identity to ease the pain of that alienation. Judaism was available as an identity for them: indeed, the Jewish community had been waiting for their young men to grow up and return to their senses, and their Jewishness.

Cooney argues that their "cosmopolitanism" provided the consistent core that saw the group through their radical days and into an anti-Stalinist, later anti-Marxist stance that has become identified as "neoconservatism." There was no dramatic change, no sudden transition from radicalism to conservatism. They had always been "cosmopolitan" and antitotalitarian. But nearly everybody else who has studied this group of New York Jewish intellectuals believes that there was a dramatic shift from their young, radical days, to an older, postwar conservatism. Alexander Bloom, as we shall see, argues that their belated return to a Jewish identity was the occasion of a turn toward a conservative, even anti-Communist political stance.[3] Russell Jacoby compares the Jewish radicals of the 1930s with their non-Jewish colleagues, and finds that in contrast to their Jewish comrades, the non-Jews invariably clung to their radicalism well into the 1960s.[4]

> Estrangement from a Christian civilization, runs the usual argument, edged Jews into reformism or revolution. Yet this argument can be reversed, or at least recast: personal alien-

ation does not engender a hardy radicalism. The angst that
expresses the pain of separation also craves union—or its substitute, recognition and acceptance. The social critique
founded solely on alienation also founders on it. (Jacoby 89)

Alexander Bloom presents a compatible, although slightly different argument. Bloom contends that the New York Intellectuals did indeed change their political stance during the 1940s, from their previously Marxist-Trotskyite radicalism, to a more conservative support of American politics. The earlier radicalism, the wartime patriotism, and the postwar conservatism, all derived from struggles over alienation and assimilation, and ambivalence toward Jewish identity. This was the New Yorkers' tender spot that Arendt touched with her report on Eichmann.

Both Bloom and Cooney present the New York Intellectuals as the doted-upon sons of immigrant Jewish families. "Parents measured success by educational achievement, and as the young boys proved precocious, they were singled out in the public schools and shone in adults' eyes. While this marked a boy for educational heights at an early age, it also brought with it personal pressure to succeed" (Bloom 13). This is confirmed by Irving Howe, who described immigrant Jewish culture in New York as "utterly devoted to its sons . . . the sons—*they* would achieve both collective Jewish fulfillment and individual Jewish success."[5] Cooney notes that the assumption of male privilege characterized their young manhood: "And it was the sons who took center stage. An air of masculine clubbiness hangs around the early years of the New York Intellectuals. Young women were sometimes present, sometimes mentioned, but seldom treated as equals" (Cooney 13). The preference for boys was community wide. The sons may have felt the pressure of expectations from their parents, but the entire New York Jewish community was prepared to applaud their achievements. In contrast, "Those women who made their mark intellectually in the early years succeeded through determination, talent, and sometimes a husband's or companion's connections, but not through equivalent encouragements or opportunities supported by a whole culture" (Cooney 11).

Both Bloom and Cooney discuss the youthful "swagger" allowed these bright boys, a theme we shall pursue in more detail in the following chapter. "They might be *pishers* or cocky, but being bright raised them above the level of potential 'cranks' or 'eccentrics.' Youthful swagger would be tolerated. With the support and tolerance of the community, it could be turned into attributes which would lead them out of the ghetto" (Bloom 15). Bloom goes on to discuss the special closeness between these Jewish boys and their mothers, but we shall save that for the next chapter, and focus here on the Jewish sons' relationship to their Jewishness.

The young men, who, like other sons of American immigrants, were being pushed to succeed as Americans, sought to leave behind their poverty and the parochialism of their parents. A secular education replaced the traditional Jewish education, although the emphasis on education remained central, to the point of being sacred. Bloom refers to it as "the new religion" (28). It was difficult to distinguish the specifics of Judaism from their general embarrassment about their parents' Old World mannerisms, and the simplest solution was to distance themselves from everything associated with their past. The inseparability of the Jewish and immigrant components of their identities made it extremely difficult for the young men to distinguish between the two sufficiently to retain the Jewish, while abandoning their parents' poverty or provincialism. It was easier to move away from it all.

For many, their immigrant parents had set the stage for the move away from Judaism by changing their Jewish-sounding names upon arrival in the United States. William Phillips (Litvinsky), Daniel Bell (Bolotsky), and Philip Rahv (Greenbaum) were three prominent members of the *Partisan Review* whose male predecessors had changed the family name. We will refrain from noting the anglicized first names: the surfeit of Philips, Lionels, Williams, and so forth.

Lionel Mordecai Trilling is actually an interesting study in ambivalence toward his Jewish background. He was raised in an orthodox household, and his Bar Mitzvah took place at the Jewish Theological Seminary of New York, where he led services and presented an original speech before family and friends. He was tutored for the Bar Mitzvah by Max Kadushin, the respected traditional Jewish scholar, who had been the disciple of Mordecai Kaplan. Lionel Trilling's father had also been a precocious scholar of Judaism in his native Bialystock, destined for the Rabbinate, by choice of his parents. However, he broke down when reading the Haftorah at his Bar Mitzvah, an event that so humiliated himself and his family that he was sent to the United States. His American life was dominated by business failure and mediocrity. Young Lionel's mother was determined that her son would distinguish himself, if not as a rabbi, then at least as a scholar.[6]

One needn't be a psychologist to imagine that a name like Lionel Mordecai, and the father's traumatic history with Jewish studies, would guarantee some severe tensions in the son with regard to Judaism. He became the first Jewish professor in the English department at Columbia University—a distinction, sure enough, but also one that could easily aggravate mixed feelings about one's Jewish identity. He wrote in 1944 in the *Contemporary Jewish Record:*

> As the Jewish community now exists, it can give no sustenance to the American artist or intellectual who is born a Jew. . . . I know of no writers who have used their Jewish experience as the subject of excellent work; I know of no writer in English who has added a micromillimeter to his stature by "realizing his Jewishness." (Wald 34)

A year before his death Trilling wrote that the word *shame* best characterized the way young middle-class Jews felt. He remarked: "Self-hatred was the word that later came into vogue but shame is simpler and better" (Wald 36).

Trilling made a distinction between the subjective experience of Judaism and the objective label imposed by the world, and believed the objective labeling was the more significant in his life; that is, if the world hadn't imposed it upon him, he would have been unaware of his Jewishness. He managed to prevail over the anti-Semitism at Columbia University to become the first Jewish assistant professor in the English department, all the while claiming,

I cannot discover anything in my professional intellectual life which I can significantly trace back to my Jewish birth and rearing. I do not think of myself as a "Jewish writer." I do not have it in mind to serve by my writing any Jewish purpose. (Bloom 24)

The complexity of the pull of Judaism meant that even though the young intellectuals sought escape from it, they were unable simply to appropriate a non-Jewish American past. The obvious way to deal with the lack of identity was "cosmopolitanism," or internationalism. During the Depression of the 1930s the internationalist pull of Marxism proved especially attractive. They assumed a "universalist" attitude toward their Jewishness, not quite denying that they were themselves Jewish, but rejecting the traditional religious and cultural customs, and insisting that their Jewishness had no influence whatsoever upon their intellectual work.

The group that founded *Partisan Review*, William Phillips, Phillip Rahv, and their friends, Lionel Abel, Harold Rosenberg, Alfred Kazin, Edmund Wilson, Dwight MacDonald, and others, were radicals: Marxists, Trotskyites, part of the "Old Left" that was characteristic of the American immigrant response to the depression. A split between Stalinists and Trotskyites resulted from the Moscow trials, and was reinforced by the Hitler-Stalin nonaggression pact of 1939. The entire group remained steadfastly antiwar as Hitler rose to power in Germany and began his assault on Europe. Even while the United States began to mobilize for war, this group held to the belief that all wars were symptomatic of capitalism, and would bring cultural repression and lead to fascism at home. They saw their mission as one of bringing a cosmopolitan, European-influenced culture to uncultured, agrarian, populist America. They were, without a doubt, cultural imperialists with little tolerance for "low-brow" or "mass" culture. It never occurred to them that they were frightened, as much as disdainful, of what they regarded as the parochialism of "American" culture, which was also profoundly Christian. Nor did it occur to them that while they were enlightening America in the name of an international, that is urban, culture, they were likely also influenced by a Jewish concern with Christian American agrarianism.

Once out of college, with the Depression in full force, Philip Rahv and William Phillips raised enough money to buy the *Partisan Review* some independence from its former Trotskyite sponsors. It was to be a cosmopolitan literary and political magazine, a vehicle for publishing their radical internationalist ideas, free of the coerciveness of Communist party influence over art and ideas. In a sense, it broke with the confining "political correctness" of the Old Left. As Trotskyites, they had broken with the Stalinists, and felt vindicated by the 1939 Hitler-Stalin nonaggression pact. They were against both Hitler's and Stalin's totalitarianism, but did not focus at all upon Nazi anti-Semitism. As stalwart internationalists, they maintained a stance of unwavering neutrality—against involvement in European politics, against both fascism and capitalism. They sought to maintain their intellectual purity by staying clear of contaminating mainstream politics: "Radical intellectuals had no business, Philip Rahv argued, taking sides in this contest of national imperialism. 'Who will annihilate the potential German revolution, if not the French and the British imperialists—once they have removed Hitler?'" (Bloom 125).

Even as war broke out in Europe, their stance held steady. They maintained that "once intellectuals became involved with the Bourgeois order, they could not escape it" (Bloom 128). The *Partisan Review* published a position statement of the League for Cultural Freedom and Socialism, which had been formed to defend artistic independence among radicals against the coerciveness of the Communist party. Its attitude toward the war reflected that of the New York Intellectuals at the time:

> Our entry into the war, under the slogan of "Stop Hitler!" would actually result in the immediate introduction of totalitarianism over here. Only the German people can free themselves of the fascist yoke. The American masses can best help them by fighting *at home* to keep their own liberties.... American intellectuals must now signalize their opposition not only to war in the abstract but specifically to American entry into this war. It would be a betrayal of the human spirit for them to keep silent at this time. (Bloom 126)

Only after the Japanese bombed Pearl Harbor—actually, not until 1942—did Rahv and Phillips move toward limited support of American involvement, which was already a *fait accompli*. They argued that Roosevelt and Churchill were more tolerable (the lesser of two evils) than Hitler, and shied away from opposing the war effort. They broke with Dwight MacDonald over this, leading MacDonald to accuse them of being timid, fearful of the unpopularity of opposing U.S. involvement in the war.

The first step they took toward support of the American war effort was a response in keeping with American outrage over the Japanese bombing of Pearl Harbor. This stance permitted them to avoid making themselves into pariahs, virtually alone in opposition to United States involvement in the war, while it allowed them to continue to avoid making a direct response to the Holocaust. Perhaps unconsciously, they were seeking refuge in America, feeling they could ill afford to affront so many Americans by their opposition to the war. Bloom identifies their support of the war effort as "their first commitment to American government policy and the maintenance of American society" (131). After the bombing of Pearl Harbor, *Partisan Review* published an editorial in which the five editors announced that because of their differences, the journal could have no editorial line on the war, and pledged to maintain "cultural values against all types of coercion and repression" (Wald 208). But in Wald's thirty-page chapter on the New York Intellectuals' attitude toward the war, ironically entitled "The Second Imperialist War," there is no mention at all of the editors' response to Hitler, the Holocaust, or the needs of the European Jews for rescue and support.[7]

Indeed, and somewhat outrageously, they buttressed their new-found, if cautious patriotism with optimism over America's cultural future: now that so many "European" (Jewish) refugees were arriving in New York, New York might soon replace Paris as the world's cultural and literary center! Still, they refused publicly to acknowledge that Nazi anti-Semitism was the source of this American windfall.

THE NEW YORK INTELLECTUALS AND THE HOLOCAUST

With regard to the extermination of the Jews, underway in Hitler's Europe, and obvious at least to the extent that it accounted for the migration of the European intellectual elite to New York, the editors of the *Partisan Review* maintained a remarkable silence. They now officially supported the American war effort, but still declined to mention the Holocaust as a justification for American involvement. Their commitment to universalism "left little room for the expression of Jewish themes or even for much comment on Nazi anti-Semitism before the war" (Bloom 138). But knowledge of Hitler's anti-Semitism abounded, even if the grisly extent of the horror was not common knowledge until after the war. As noted, the New Yorkers were already celebrating the arrival of prominent intellectuals and writers to their city, and must certainly have been aware that the flight of prominent Jews such as Freud and Einstein indicated some horror for Jews in Germany and Austria. Bloom observes: "It is remarkable how rarely the pages of *Partisan Review* and the various other writings of the New York Intellectuals contained references in the 1930s to the persecution of the Jews" (Bloom 138). "The lack of discussion on the topic of Jews and their persecution stands out starkly" (Bloom 139).

In November of 1938, Sidney Hook had published an article in the *New Leader* entitled "Tragedy of German Jewry," but it opened with a "cosmopolitan" disclaimer, in which he reminded the reader that the Jews were not the only people suffering: "Let us bear in mind that in protesting against Hitler's anti-Jewish brutalities we are also protesting against the hounding of other religions and political minorities" (Bloom 138). In spite of its title, the bulk of the article is devoted to an indictment not of Hitler, but of Stalinism: "Let us also remember that it was from Stalin that Hitler learned the art of wiping out whole groups and classes of innocent citizens. We cannot with good conscience protest against Hitler's treatment of the Jews and remain silent about the six million...who fill the concentration camps in Russia" (Bloom 138).

It is true that this was "only" 1938, hence the systematic extermination of the Jews had not been publicly discussed, much less implemented. But Hitler had been in power for five years, and his anti-Semitism was no secret. American Jews had begun to respond to it with the call for a boycott, and as David Ben Gurion had noted, "No one needed official announcements to know that Hitler had intended to exterminate the Jews—it was all in *Mein Kampf*" (Segev 79). Hook's article is remarkable testimony to the tenacity of his avoidance of Judaism: even when ostensibly talking about Nazi anti-Semitism, Hook saw fit to defer to what we may presume he viewed as the "equally pressing needs" of other victims. It is as though some misguided sense of honor prevented him from dwelling upon or identifying with the needs of his own people.

Not until 1944 did Alfred Kazin break the silence by mentioning both the Nazi genocide and the remarkable silence of his colleagues about it in an article published in the *New Republic.*

> Something has been done—and not by the Nazis—which can never be undone. The tragedy is in our minds, in the basic equality of our personal culture; and that is why it will be the tragedy of the peace.... Something has been set forth in Europe that is subtle, and suspended, and destructive.... That something is all our silent complicity in the massacre of the Jews.[8]

Kazin thus became the "first New York Intellectual to argue for an extended sense of guilt for the Nazi crimes" (Bloom 139). Others joined him in this attitude after the war, but during the war itself his statement evoked a vague embarrassment from the *New Republic* and his readers. Kazin claimed he was horrified by the response to his article. Other intellectuals still argued from the universalist position, still expressed more interest in world trends on general themes, or, like Sidney Hook, hid any concern they had for the plight of the Jews under an internationalist umbrella, where they could express equal horror for other atrocities, thus continuing to distance themselves from the European Jews.

In a more recent interview with Bloom, Kazin admitted that the problem was fear of seeming "too Jewish," of undoing those decades of assimilation by denying one's background. "Let's face it.... If these intellectuals had gone on a great deal for stuff about the Jews and the war, the way, for example, the Yiddish press did, they would have seemed a good deal less 'American,' less assimilated."[9]

When, after the war, the full story of the Nazi crimes began to unfold and it became evident that even Kazin had underestimated the extent of the slaughter by one-half, the New Yorkers admitted to what they termed a "low charged guilt . . . a quiet remorse" (Howe, in Bloom 140). Bloom notes, "Having neglected their own roots in the pursuit of intellectual prominence and political goals, they found themselves face to face with their origins and a reality larger than they could have envisioned" (140). I believe that their guilt was as highly charged as their response to Hannah Arendt's *New Yorker* articles.

It is edifying that Kazin was among the very few New York Jewish intellectuals who, far from adding his own brand to the public humiliation of Arendt, actually attempted to defend her against her inquisitors.

POSTWAR POLITICS AND THE NEW YORKERS

The shock and realization that they were, after all, Jews, forced the New York Intellectuals to make some adjustment in their stance toward American politics. Cooney argues for the consistency of their political position—antitotalitarianism—in the face of changing Soviet politics. The credibility of that perspective is derived from the fact that the Intellectuals had associated much earlier Hitler with Stalin, regarding both as totalitarian, while supporting Trotsky. They had also sought independence from Communist party influence over art and literature (see pp. 97, 134–5). After the war, their stance became overtly anti-Communist, beyond mere anti-Stalinism, although the group did not want to be associated with Senator Joseph McCarthy. They sought to oppose Stalin without being identified with McCarthy, who, with his "agrarian-populist-fascism" seemed anathema to their Cosmopolitanism.

Bloom argues that the real change between the early and later politics of the *Partisan Review* had less to do with opposition to totalitarianism than with the need of its contributors to feel assimilated into American life. After the war, Judaism and conservative Americanism may not have appeared so antithetical as they had in the thirties. The intellectuals' belated awareness of the Holocaust was the catalyst for their increasingly conservative political stance. They were, as the title of Bloom's book suggests, prodigal sons, welcomed home by a Jewish community who had been waiting tolerantly for their boychiks to return.

Daniel Bell acknowledged no conflict between their new conservatism and their former radicalism. "A radical is a prodigal son. . . . He may eventually return to the house of his elders, but the return is by choice. . . . A resilient society, like a wise parent, understands this ritual, and in meeting the challenge to tradition, grows" (170 Bloom). This admonition about the benefits bestowed upon American Jewish society by the sons who had spent several decades avoiding their Jewishness is self-indulgent, to say the least. It stems from an assumption of privilege, available to few. But their expectations of loving acceptance from the community were not unfounded. They were the pride of the Jewish community of their youth, "the bright *pishers* from Brownsville," and they found, in the postwar Jewish community, a receptive audience for their newly discovered interest in Judaism, people who were relieved to find justified their faith that the young men would turn out all right.

The Intellectuals had discovered that they were now experts on the condition that they claimed plagued postwar American society: Alienation. Their return home was thus not to traditional Judaism, but to what they, as intellectuals and social scientists, defined as the alienation of modern America as a whole. Their stance was now to put themselves forward as men who had special expertise to offer to the nation that had just discovered its own alienation. The irony is that to the extent they no longer felt so alienated from modern America, they no longer had a call to be specialists in marginality, and to the extent that their arguments won acceptance, they were no longer marginal men. Nonetheless, Bloom assures us, "Undaunted by the internal contradiction, they staked out their claim" (Bloom 151).

Bloom is skeptical about the proclaimed motivation of those who now defined themselves as uniquely positioned to contribute "insightful criticism and comment" about contemporary American life. He is more tempted to present it as self-serving opportunism. This is a far cry from Cooney's more compassionate argument that the Intellectuals were politically consistent throughout the decade, while society changed around them. Rather, Bloom concludes, "As radical intellectuals in the 1930s, alienated Jews in the 1940s, and ex-radicals in the 1950s, they frequently discovered their own position remarkably appropriate for the contemporary situation.... Beginning their reevaluations on personal grounds—shocked by the Holocaust into redefining their own identities—they later found a public application for the results of these investigations" (Bloom 155).

Their goal seems to have been finding the grounds upon which to present themselves as experts, sages, secular rabbis to American society, thereby fulfilling both their parents' dreams and their own. They now basked in the respect of the most highly educated members of American society, and one can almost see them reaching for approval from the doubters with an increasingly conservative stance. But they knew they had to reconcile their current conservatism with their previous radicalism. For this they found "liberal anticommunism" a convenient position, carving out, as it did, a place to stand between McCarthyism, with which they did not want to be associated, and socialist sympathies, from which they now also sought to distance themselves.

THE NEW YORK INTELLECTUALS AND HANNAH ARENDT

Ironically, Hannah Arendt's *Origins of Totalitarianism* helped them to find this middle ground and to justify it, by associating "radical evil" with both the Right (Hitler) and the Left (Stalin). With her first major work, she appeared to provide scholarly justification for their new conservatism, and this from a European Jew, a refugee from the Holocaust. They could identify with her criticism of Hitler (where they had missed the boat earlier), as well as with her anticommunism, necessary for their new-found Americanism.

Alan Wald explains that Arendt's book could be read as bolstering the anti-Communist hysteria of the 1950s, because its method was such a departure from the usual Marxist class analysis of the history of the Soviet Union. "Its conflation of Stalinism and Hitlerism was developed without a comparison of class structures and economic systems, and it was based on the metaphysical assumption that the most appropriate measure for believing that the two social orders were a single genus was the degree of 'radical evil' that they embodied" (Wald 269). It thus could be used to fan the belief that "the Soviet Union was to be expected to behave as Nazi Germany had in the 1930s" (Wald 269). Wald is quick to point out that this was undoubtedly not Hannah Arendt's intention, describing her as "a maverick thinker of considerable creativity who feared that the United States might itself move in a totalitarian direction under the impact of McCarthyism" (Wald 269). He also reminds us that she had at least partly assimilated the tradition of dissident communism through her husband, Heinrich Blucher.

The New York Intellectuals seized upon her book, lavishing upon its author extravagant praise, such as Kazin's description of Arendt's thinking as possessing "moral grandeur," and MacDonald's description of her as "the most original and profound... political theoretician of our times" (in Wald 269). The group of former left-wingers was delighted to take advantage of her argument to formulate an anti-Communist stance that did not sound like the same sort of stuff upon which Senator McCarthy was building his career. They called it "liberal anticommunism." Bloom suggests that it served the purpose of offering them

> a philosophy of their own, free of the disquieting notion that they might be McCarthyites, and, they hoped, free of lingering suspicions about their own past activities.... The liberals regarded their position as both personally fulfilling and politically correct—as satisfying intellectual requirements as well as international realities. (Bloom 228)

Arendt had coined the phrase "radical evil" to describe the unprecedented destructive capacity of totalitarian systems.

Her argument was that totalitarianism was a development of modernity that could be distinguished from earlier, historical examples of political evil, such as tyranny. In appearing to equate Nazis with Bolsheviks Arendt provided precisely the material for which anti-Communists had waited. "Arendt's arguments became the philosophical cement which firmly set this new view of political realities" (Bloom 220).

During the first decade after her arrival from Europe, and after the *Origins of Totalitarianism* was published, Arendt was a respected figure among the *Partisan Review* crowd. But she was never a part of the inner circle. While its members took advantage of her scholarship to explain and justify their current concerns, she was never herself an insider. She had received her initial attention in the United States from this group, and Alfred Kazin had been helpful in finding a publisher for an American edition of *The Origins*. Still, a number of factors distinguished Arendt from the *PR* group. She had grown up in Germany, not New York, and had received a classical German education at Marburg and Heidelberg, not CCNY. She had never "passed through a Leninist phase" (Wald 269), although she was married to a Marxist. Like many members of the *PR* crowd, she had little Jewish religious training—in fact, probably less than most of them, because she was female and the daughter of enlightened German Jews, not East European immigrants to America.

Two additional factors that obviously distinguish her from the group of New York Intellectuals are overlooked by these otherwise thorough accounts of Arendt's relationship with the *Partisan Review* "boys" (as she referred to them). First, the fact that she was a female and unattached to a male in their circle created distance.[10] Secondly, that she had actually had to flee the Nazis to save her life, as well as the lives of her mother and her husband was also a major difference in her life experience, and her relationship both to the Holocaust and Judaism. The price Arendt would have paid for ignoring Hitler and the Holocaust most certainly would have been death. She could hardly have afforded the "cosmopolitan neutrality" assumed by the *Partisan Review*.[11]

There were still other distinctions between Arendt and the New York Intellectuals. In the 1930s and 1940s Arendt had been a Jewish activist more than an employed scholar, because of both the condition of exile that she had endured for over a decade, and because the academic world in both Europe and the United States was not only anti-Semitic, as the *Partisan Review* crowd knew, but also excluded women. In fact, only after *The Origins* was published in 1951 did she become, in her words, a "cover girl"—appearing on the covers of *Time* and *Newsweek* the same week—who was invited to teach at the nation's most prestigious campuses. She maintained her independence from academic life, however, and never took a fulltime position at a university.

In this context, then, the emotional response to *Eichmann in Jerusalem*, which Bloom describes as "a hailstorm of criticism and enormous debate, well beyond political discussion" (Bloom 329), becomes more comprehensible. On the simplest level, in *Eichmann in Jerusalem* Hannah Arendt changed her mind about the existence of "radical evil." That is why the subtitle of the book, "The Banality of Evil," which Arendt claimed was incredibly overinterpreted, and with which she had meant to imply no theory, was so upsetting. Arendt meant that great evil exists in the world, but does not have otherworldly, demonic sources: people can cause great evil, often with an entirely banal mind set. Thus Eichmann may have been "banal," but the destruction he caused was not. Nonetheless, without the concept of "radical evil" to link Stalinism with Nazism, the New York Intellectuals had a harder time believing in the credibility of their "liberal anti-Communist" stance. If communism wasn't as radically evil as Hitler's fascism, or if the concept of evil itself was more subtle and complicated than had been presented in *The Origins*, they must come to terms with their own political reversal, from leftist to anti-Communist politics. Without the concept of radical evil to enable them to be outraged by both communism and fascism, the New York Intellectuals would have to face the complexities of the Holocaust, as well as their abandonment of radical politics. They might, after all, be no different from the McCarthyites, whom they knew were a threat to free speech, democracy, and everything they had stood for throughout their early years.

Arendt's changed ideas about the nature of evil were thus perceived as a betrayal—which explains both the excessive emotional loading of the criticism of her work, and, for example, Lionel Abel's preoccupation with the "contradictions" between *The Origins* and *Eichmann*. Abel was the one who had contradicted—indeed, reversed—himself politically, as he moved from socialism in the thirties to anticommunism in the fifties. In *The Origins* Arendt had appeared to be saying that Nazism and Stalinism were not all that different. In opposing Communism in the 1950s, Abel could believe that he was really defending the Jews, as well as other Americans, from another menace as dangerous as Hitler. If Arendt, whose authority rested upon actual encounters with the Nazis, had changed her mind about the "radical evil" of Nazism and Communism, how was Abel to explain his politics to himself? He was left standing at the altar, like a jilted lover. How could *she* contradict herself like that? But Arendt was not a bride: she was a scholar whose ideas had evolved over a decade, and her more recent ideas were subtler and more complex than her earlier work, hence politically harder to deal with.

There is an additional dimension that accounts for the excessive emotion in the response to *Eichmann in Jerusalem*, and it has, not surprisingly, to do with Jewish identity. Bloom astutely couples publication of *Eichmann* with the simultaneous publication of another book seldom associated with Arendt's volume: Nathan Glazer and Daniel Patrick Moynihan's *Beyond the Melting Pot*, also published in 1963. Bloom suggests that both books "signaled a return to questions about Jewishness and ethnic identity" (329). Not only her relinquishment of the concept of radical evil but her unwillingness to polarize Jews and Germans into innocent victims and radically evil predators caused anxiety among the New Yorkers. Irving Howe himself later suggested that repressed feelings—the tonguetiedness of the late 1940s which had left the question of six million Jewish deaths unanswered—gave way as "the long-suppressed grief evoked by the Holocaust burst out. It was as if her views, which roused many of us to fury, enabled us to finally speak about the unspeakable."[12] One can hardly imagine a more self-revelatory admission that guilt over one's own behavior with regard to the Holocaust had now been converted into fury at Arendt. Bloom adds, "The emotions which the debate tapped, whether because of an outpouring of suppressed grief as Howe suggests or because of other considerations about Jewish identity, demonstrated the degree to which Jewishness remained a sensitive issue" (Bloom 331).

Eichmann in Jerusalem pulled the rug out from under the New York Intellectuals in at least two important ways: it robbed them of an easy position for justifying or rationalizing the contradictions in their political odyssey from the Trotskyite days of their youth to the quasi-McCarthyite days of their middle age. It also robbed them of easy access to a simplified, purified Jewish goodness: it made them think about the complexities and tragic choices faced by Jews during the Holocaust, rather than allowing them to reappropriate a less troublesome, more romantic version of Jewish identity. Jews were human beings and, as such, flawed as well as admirable. In a word, Arendt made the Holocaust real, rather than mythical or ideological. The New York Intellectuals turned on Hannah Arendt for writing *Eichmann in Jerusalem*, because the book made them think about their relationship to their Jewishness, and their conservatism. She had a credibility they could not have with regard to the Holocaust, and now she was not permitting easy access to the oversimplified moral and political categories which would have enabled them, and others, to characterize their earlier behavior as moral. Not all the Jews had behaved admirably, she suggested, and many of the Nazis may have been "ordinary," mindless bureaucrats, rather than crazed, anti-Semitic killers.[13] The complexity of her categories proved too stressful for these intellectuals, who were, in effect, "born-again Jews," and who craved simplicity for the categories of good and evil.

This sounds like enough to explain the excessively vitriolic reaction to *Eichmann in Jerusalem*. Can there be more?

CHAPTER 5

Race, Gender and Judaism: The *Eichmann* Controversy as Case Study

Israeli guilt and embarrassment over lack of action and powerlessness against the Nazis, as well as over their contempt for the Holocaust victims; New York Jewish Intellectual guilt over their avoidance of the Holocaust: these would seem to be sufficient to account for the excessive response to Arendt's *Eichmann in Jerusalem*. What can additional probing possibly add to an understanding of the *Eichmann* controversy?

I mentioned previously that the New York and Israeli complaints about Arendt's "betrayal" differed somewhat. That the rage had different sources is evidenced in the different treatment of Hilberg's and Arendt's books. The New Yorkers were primarily angry at Arendt, while they remained for the most part respectful of Raul Hilberg's monumental *The Destruction of the European Jews*, which was published a year before Arendt's report, and made many similar arguments about the Judenrate.[1] The Israelis were more evenly incensed at both works, squelching translation of both into Hebrew.[2] This implies that the Israelis were equally upset by Hilberg's and Arendt's indiscretion at airing controversial Jewish issues outside the "safe" confines of Israel as the Jewish homeland. While neither scholar was raising issues that were new to the Israelis, they were, for the first time, raising them outside Israel. The Israelis were sensitive to the fact that their attitude and response to the Holocaust may not have been adequate; both Hilberg and Arendt aggravated that tender issue. The New York Intellectuals were sensitive about their Jewish identity as well as their belated and inadequate response to the Holocaust. They had a stake in Arendt's earlier position about "radical evil," as we saw, but were relatively untouched by Hilberg's criticism of the European Jewish leadership. Thus their initial response to Arendt was more volatile than to Hilberg.

There is an additional dimension that is obvious, but also easy to avoid or deny. Arendt was a *woman* raising sensitive issues about the effectiveness of Israeli and New York Jewish *men*. She was unaware of writing "as a woman," but I believe that is how her opinions were received. To claim that gender cannot possibly have had anything to do with the response to her report on Eichmann is a denial of the first order. Male offense taken at an outspoken, "uppity," or "sassy" woman is legendary, the stuff of high and popular culture, from Greek and Shakespearian drama to stand-up comedy and television sitcoms. Stereotypically, men will tolerate criticism from other men and regard the same talk from a woman as "shrewishness" or "back talk." Women who are publicly (or privately) critical of men, especially prominent well-respected men, risk a range of criticism from "nagging wives" to "castrating bitches." An American first lady with a mind and opinion of her own is either a dangerous conniver, or wearing the pants in the family. That such a woman herself might actually aspire to high office and political power is rarely even considered. A woman in private life who values her own ideas as much as her husband's may "drive him to drink," or to other women.

But it is not adequate to generalize from stereotypes to the particular case of Hannah Arendt's trouble with Jewish men in New York and Israel. The fact that she was a woman, and so far as I know, the only woman, who spoke out critically and publicly on this emotionally laden issue, where the parties responsible for decisions were primarily men, is an obvious fact. The implications of this situation are less obvious, and gender as a factor in the *Eichmann* controversy needs to be carefully established. To avoid suspense, let me state at the outset that it is my hunch that Arendt's most strident critics, the *Partisan Review* crowd in New York, and Ben Gurion and the Mapai in Israel, felt not only guilty and powerless about their responses to the Holocaust, but "unmanned" by the power of the Nazis and what appeared to be the collusion of most of the Western world in the face of the slaughter of the European Jews. When Hannah Arendt, a woman, and a tough-talking (or tough-writing) refugee from the hell that had been Europe, seemed to be questioning the behavior of the (male) leadership in Europe and postwar Jerusalem, it was as though she were exposing the men in all their weakness, a weakness that was experienced by them as impotence, as specifically male sexual powerlessness. While the men may have quarreled among themselves about how to respond during and after the war, and had often been unsparing in their criticisms of each other, both across international boundaries and within the New York Intellectual and the Zionist communities, hearing the same criticism from a woman was intolerable, tantamount to forcing them to reexperience their impotence in front of a "mixed" audience.

On their own merit, Arendt's arguments undoubtedly would have drawn criticism, even if a man had written them. But the same controversy initiated by a man would not have been so one-sided. Arendt's Jewish critics attacked her like an infuriated mob, while a few gallant gents tried to rescue her, or at least argue that she should be spared. Had a man written *Eichmann in Jerusalem*, there would have been two volatile sides to the issue, just as there had been to the major Jewish issues of the previous two decades: negotiate with the Nazis or not? Armed resistance or survival tactics? Those battles were fierce and hard fought, but there was a "critical mass" of opinion on both sides. That Arendt was the *only* woman to criticize the entirely male leadership of both European and Israeli Judaism, and that she drew so much universally severe criticism from men who had disagreed with each other on other important issues, points to a role for gender in catalyzing their rage.

But why should the Jewish men in Israel and America have been so vulnerable as to experience public criticism on a political issue as a sexually charged threat? To answer this we must explore the scholarship on Judaism and sexuality.

NAZIS AND SEXUALITY

There have been several excellent studies of Judaism and sexuality, from a variety of perspectives, ranging from studies of Biblical and European history to contemporary gender politics and film studies. All presuppose on some level the significance of the phallus as symbol, and thus are more or less psychoanalytic in approach. We shall consider various approaches to the "problem" of Jewish masculinity in this section; then look at recent work on Jewish womanhood; and finally return to both New York and Israel for a gendered interpretation of the *Eichmann* controversy.

George Mosse, in his highly respected *Nationalism and Sexuality* identifies the origins of modern gender stereotyping, and particularly the need for a male-dominated gender hierarchy, with the rise of the modern nation state.[3] He describes his project as "Analyzing the relationship between nationalism and respectability . . . tracing the development of some of the most important norms that have informed our society: ideals of manliness, which will loom so large in these pages; and their effect on the place of women; and insiders who have accepted the norms, as compared to the outsiders, those considered abnormal or diseased" (Mosse 1). The nation-state was the ordering principle of the (post eighteenth-century) modern world, and "respectability," which involved sexual norms and definitions of "normal" and "abnormal" behavior, the ordering principle of society within the nation-state. Mosse focuses most of his attention upon the Germans, paying some attention also to the English and considerably less to the French and Italians. Jewish men came to represent "abnormality" in terms of the emerging German definition of maleness, as did homosexuals, and women who did not conform to their prescribed roles.

German manliness at the turn of the century was a revival of an idealized projection about classical Greek masculinity. "The present-day Germans and the ancient Greeks were considered the twin pillars of the Aryan race" (Mosse 171). But in German hands, the Greek ideal of nude male youth and beauty became de-eroticized, de-sexualized, abstracted and universalized. The passionate Eros described in, for example, Plato's *Symposium* had no place in the German concept of manhood. While women were excluded utterly from the German ideal, the exclusively male company was not allowed to indulge in even a hint of homo-erotic pleasure. Manliness was, as an ideal, at least, about the *absence* of sexual passion.[4]

In contrast to the lithe, athletic, dynamic Greek male, European national womanhood was represented by mediaeval images: seated women, draped rather than naked, both virginal and maternal, pious and sedate, and not sexual. Women "stood for immutability rather than progress, providing the backdrop against which men determined the fate of nations."[5] As the modern era dawned and the world became newly ordered, "nationalism and respectability assigned everyone his place in life, man and woman, normal and abnormal, native and foreigner; any confusion between these categories threatened chaos and loss of control" (Mosse 16).

The association of racism and oppression with sexuality is not unfamiliar: literature on white Christian genocide against native Americans, and on anti-black racism in the United States, is suffused with theories about the inseparability of racism and sexual oppression. But Mosse argues that the association is not so much universal as historical: as nationalism arose so did a particular form of gender stereotyping, and a prescription for sexuality that would permit the ordering of society into respectable and unrespectable categories of human beings. Mosse views racism as an intensified form of nationalism, with "normal" sexuality an important component of the racist stance.

> The stereotyped depiction of sexual "degenerates" was transferred almost intact to the "inferior races" who inspired the same fears. These races, too, were said to display a lack of morality and a general absence of self-discipline. Blacks, and then Jews, were endowed with excessive sexuality, with a so-called female sensuousness that transformed love into lust. They lacked all manliness. Jews as a group were said to exhibit

female traits, just as homosexuals were generally considered effeminate. (Mosse 36)

The German youth movement spawned in 1901, started by a group of Berlin schoolboys, quickly gained popularity as a training ground for *mannerstaat*, the state as an expression of manliness. Boys were encouraged to develop close-knit groups, to roam the countryside without adult supervision, and to create their own mode of life, *Wandervogelin*. Encouraging teenage boys to find their own forms of unsupervised amusements may strike the contemporary adult as a foolhardy, perhaps even perverse way to build a nation. And indeed, German nationalism in the twentieth century may unwittingly provide a case study of what may happen when adolescent boys being pushed to be "manly" create a world after their own image. Mosse tells us that "The older comrades and adult leaders presented it as a quest for the 'genuine' in nature and the nation—as an elite of males that would give a fresh impulse to German national consciousness" (Mosse 45).

Idealizing the nude Greek body, and encouraging German teenage boys to roam the countryside searching for manhood in the purity of nature was an invitation to trouble, if the German ideal of manliness also precluded sexuality. Worshiping the nude male body in nature seemed precariously close to what "abnormal" homosexuals and the urban "decadents," artistic young men and women in European cities around the turn of the century, might be doing.

The line maintained in order to idealize the exclusive community of German male youths without promoting eroticism or homosexuality was, to say the least, a fine one. It required not only the availability of "nature" as a setting, but a strident and constant distinction between normal men and women, on the one hand, and "abnormals," on the other. German youths were to enjoy their nudity only in a natural context, whereas the decadents of the "unnatural" cities were defined as abnormal. "What counted in the end was the 'framing' of the nude body by nature. . . . Nudity as distinct from mere lack of clothes must be represented as part of the pure, reverential contemplation of nature" (Mosse 57).

Mosse describes the attempt to ease German anxiety about sexual boundaries by stressing exaggerated differences between the sexes and their intended contributions to the well-being of the nation. Predictably, the men were presented as dynamic, warriors, nation builders, while "German womanhood was praised [as] . . . the priestess of the battlefield, the maiden with the shield, the spirit that awaits a masculine leader—no relation to the soldier girl fighting with gun and cannon in a modern army" (Mosse 101). But with so much at stake, and boundaries so essentially shaky, simply defining women as other was insufficient, giving rise to an even more strident hatred of "active" women. "Those who did not live up to the ideal were perceived as a menace to society and the nation, threatening the established order they were intended to uphold. Hence the deep hatred for women as revolutionary figures, almost surpassing the disdain which established society reserved for male revolutionaries" (Mosse 90). What was threatening was the crossing of boundaries, and the threatened destruction of order. "Men were always uneasy about women who crossed over into the world of masculinity. These were thought to be 'modern women' of an independent cast of mind" (Mosse 102).

But what does this description of Christian European sexual pathology have to do with our understanding of the Jewish male reaction to Hannah Arendt and *Eichmann in Jerusalem*? In the mind of a paranoid, a perceived threat—in this case, the threat of losing one's masculinity—cannot be contained by controlling only one portion of the world—in this case, women. The male community that was to symbolize the nation felt vulnerable not only to assaults from active women, but from other sexual deviants. German manhood felt threatened by homosexuals, certainly, but also by effeminate men: Jews. Racism, which in this context can certainly be regarded as an exaggerated form of nationalism, needs visible targets against which to define one's own sense of privilege.

One might be tempted, naively, to wonder why Jewish men who found themselves identified with women and homosexuals by racist, sexist Nazis, shouldn't have developed a sense of solidarity, of shared victimhood with Jewish women at least. But our century of racism, sexism, and homophobia has taught us that such an outcome is unlikely. The victims are never entirely free of the temptation to identify with or admire their oppressors, as a way of escaping the unattractiveness of their victimhood. For example, many contemporary black feminists argue that African American men learned about patriarchy and sexism from their white patriarchal slave masters: learning to oppress women was a way of identifying with some of the power of the master, at the same time it maintainined the ordered hierarchy of the race-gender system.[6] Likewise, although the Nazis did not encourage Jews to collude in the oppression of Jewish women—indeed, they attempted to emasculate Jewish men in a way that white men have been accused of attempting to do to black men—for Jewish men, identifying with the German nationalistic model of masculinity was one avenue of escape from their sense of victimhood.

> German Jews, for example, were proud to be both German and Jewish, and until the victory of National Socialism, many Germans accepted that claim. Yet even here, there was a price of admission. As rabbis preached the virtues of self-control, chastity, and manly bearing, Jews were to become "respectable" and abandon any signs of their ghetto past. . . . Assimilation always included a flight from a former identity. (Mosse 187)

Internal contradictions in their ideology were not a problem for the racists. While Jewish men were regarded by the Germans as effeminate, like women or homosexuals, they were not usually accused of being homosexuals. Instead, they were regarded as a sexual threat, preying upon gentile women. This may have been consistent with the definition of femininity as lacking control over one's passions, but reconciling the accusations of sexual proclivities toward Christian women with the accusations of effeminacy and homosexuality took some stretching. It was also in conflict with what even the Germans had to admit: Jews had a strong family life, and were actually "respectable" in the middle-class way so valued by German society.

The means by which to reconcile so many contradictions was, perhaps not surprisingly, a conspiracy theory. The Jews' "uncontrolled sexual drive directed against gentile women" was aimed at "corrupt(ing) the nation's mothers, thus preventing the birth of healthy children. Moreover Jews were accused of inventing birth control—another means of destroying the Aryan race" (Mosse 140).[7] Jews were, simultaneously, accused of *spreading* homosexuality throughout Aryan society, as yet another way of attaining cultural dominance in Germany by decimating the Aryan race.

Some of the fuel for this theory was provided by a Jew, Otto Weininger, whose *Sex and Character* (1903), one of the most influential racial tracts of the twentieth century, "profoundly affect(ed) the views of Adolf Hitler and many other racists" (Mosse 145). Weininger was a self-hating racist, and a raging misogynist. He argued that women "were totally preoccupied with their sexuality, whereas men knew how to be social, how to fight, how to debate—understood science, commerce, religion, and art. Women never grew to maturity" (Mosse 145). Jews, in Weininger's opinion, were like women, possessing no moral sense, knowing only sexual passion. Weininger committed suicide shortly after his book was published.

Weininger was not a German nationalist. But Hitler was, and so was Heinrich Himmler. Weininger's views of the sexual dangers posed by effeminate, lustful Jewish men, as well as a deep fear of homosexuals, played a dynamic role in Nazi ideology. Himmler was the driving force behind the persecution of homosexuals during the Third Reich, which included the death penalty for any man who kissed another man. In November 1937, Himmler delivered a speech on sexuality, in which he advocated expelling members of the SS who behaved rudely or drank too much, commanded his men to marry to produce Aryan children, and advocated prostitution as a corrective to the absence of feminine contact in the military, as well as another way of producing German children. The recommendation to visit prostitutes was actually in conflict with Hitler's views, which tended toward a more thorough repression of any sexual activity outside of marriage. Himmler concluded his 1937 speech with a furious denouncement of homosexuals, reminding his audience that "Germany is a masculine state.... There have been matriarchies and Amazon states, but 'for centuries, yea, millennia, the Germans ... have been ruled as a *Mannerstaat*'" (Mosse 167). He reminded his audience that "The conspiracy of homosexuals must be viewed side by side with the world Jewish conspiracy.... Both are bent on destroying the German state and race as the implacable enemies of German virtue and purpose of will" (Mosse 168).[8]

It is easy enough to see that a nation capable of committing racist genocide would likely have other "problem" areas including sexuality. It is more difficult to acknowledge that the problems afflicting Nazi Germany might also characterize saner cultures, such as our own. As Mosse puts it in the conclusion to his book, "What began as bourgeois morality in the eighteenth century, in the end became everyone's morality" (Mosse 191). While the specific German danger appears to be over, nationalism certainly is not. And so the question of the links between racism, sexism, and nationalism remain. Sexism is an essential component of racism. The accusations that the men of a certain culture are either "not masculine enough" or have excessive sexual urges, are indispensable components of the mechanism of racism. The cycle of oppression is completed, both racially and sexually, only when the men and women of an oppressed group are pitted against one another because the men believe they should be masculine in the same way they regard their oppressors to be. The victims thus themselves become oppressors, in a hierarchy of sexual and racial domination as inclusive as the food chain. Remove either sexism or racism from the world and the other will also wither and die.

The *Eichmann* controversy can teach us about the tragic consequences of the internalization of racism as it converts feelings of guilt and inadequacy into rage, which erupts in the form of sexism. So we must turn now to a discussion that will be much more disturbing than discussing the Nazis' sexual obsessions. We consider the extent to which Jewish men may have internalized ideas about masculinity that come from a Christian nationalist culture, and to consider whether the treatment Hannah Arendt received may be an example of how racist definitions of sexuality are internalized, found discomfiting, and finally externalized in the form of aggression against "masculine" women.

RACISM, SEXISM, AND JEWISH MASCULINITY

Some scholars treating the theme of Judaism and masculinity locate the sources of the problem deeper in the psyche, and further back in Jewish history. The psychoanalytic approach to the study of Jewish men and cultural masculinity regards Jewish circumcision as a symbolic castration, which has "always" created difficulty for Jewish men in relation to non-Jewish men. This may seem an esoteric and essentialist approach, perhaps not as relevant to our concerns as a more straightforward historical discussion of, for example, political powerlessness as an undermining influence for Jewish men (and women). But if we want to understand the relationship between anti-Semitic racism and the public disempowerment of Jewish women as well as men, an investigation into the hagiography of sexual symbolism is appropriate.

The phallus itself is not a universal or essentialist image, but rather something with its own history. Yet mystification of the phallus is so pervasive, and so symptomatic of the problem of a phallus-worshiping culture, that we forget, as Marx said in reference to the mystification of capital and fetishism of commodities, that we ourselves created it.[9] In nature, there is no such thing as a "phallus."

Daniel Boyarin argues that throughout Jewish history, Jewish men have had to respond to the "problem" of the "Jew as castrated": "It is circumcision that most fully inscribes Jews as nonmale."[10] The sense of differentness, the specialness of the Jewish male relationship to God embodied in circumcision may require the existence of goyim as "other," but that "other" has also historically had more power. How that power may have become associated with the penis, thereby creating the phallus, is a question that goes to the heart of psychoanalytic feminism. How did male privilege and power become associated with the phallus? There is abundant feminist literature on the subject.[11] For the purposes of our discussion here, it will have to suffice that the startling insight that no man actually possesses a "phallus," reveals our unintentional participation in perpetuating the myth of its power.

Boyarin's argument is that Jewish men participate in the (gentile) myth of a phallus, and the resulting feeling of inadequacy that they don't possess it. They suffer from "phallus envy," much as Freud argued that women suffer from "penis envy." Indeed, Boyarin would have us understand that Freud created the myth of female penis envy as a diversion from the more central problem he himself experienced: envy of the gentile phallus, or in the pre-Freudian terminology of his day, envy of the power of the goyim. "Phallus envy" pushes Jewish men in two directions. First, at least unconsciously, Jewish men desire to be more like the goyim. Modern Zionism may be viewed as the culmination of this wish, which has manifested itself throughout the ages as instances of Jewish militancy and violent resistance. Advocacy of Jewish violence is an imitation of non-Jewish behavior, contrary to the teachings of Jewish tradition. Secondly, as with any men who doubt their masculinity, there is a desire for ever clearer distinctions between themselves and their women. In the Jewish tradition, this need receives its ultimate expression in the culture of Talmudic study, and the complete gender segregation of orthodox Jewish worship. Thus from the very beginning of Jewish history—long enough ago to make it appear almost essentialist—Jews envied the power of their oppressors, perceived in explicitly male terms, and sought to compensate by appropriating their violent behavior, and segregating themselves as fully as possible from Jewish women.

The circumcised penis thus evokes unconscious fears of castration in Jewish men, demands compensatory male activities, and may account for the exclusion of women from the most sacred aspects of Jewish life. Jewish men in a gentile world need ways of reassuring themselves of their intact maleness, and the study of Torah "is the quintessential performance of Jewish maleness." Talmudic study is characterized by homosocial bonding and the "inscription of sex through gender differentiating practice."

> The House of Study was thus the Jewish equivalent of the locker-room, barracks, or the warship—and compare the historically similar taboos on the presence of women in those environments.... The performance of maleness through study became particularly fraught, I suggest, precisely because this performance was read as female in the cultural environment within which European Jews lived from the Roman period onward. (Boyarin 78)

Sigmund Freud, far from naming Jewish male castration anxiety, provides further evidence of it with his psychoanalytic theory. Freud did not expose for the world a *gentile* preoccupation with masculinity that needed an emasculated Jewish "Other." Rather, he described the *universality* of phallus worship and "Oedipal" conflict, thus associating Jewish problems with gentile masculinity. From Freud's perspective, Jews and gentiles share the same gender problems! Boyarin regards the Oedipus complex as "an act of repression/overcoming."[12] At the center of his theory Freud placed "an active, phallic, mother-desiring, father-killing 'normal' (that is, gentile) man" (Boyarin 311). Freud's (unconscious) wish to be like the goyim is expressed in placing a violent gentile inside the "normal" unconscious of every Jewish man.

Zionism is another aspect of the Jewish response to envy of the gentile phallus. Freud, Mosse, Boyarin, and as we shall soon see, Paul Breines, regard Zionism as a psychosexual as much as a political movement: an effort on the part of Jews to regain lost masculinity on an explicitly European gentile model. As George Mosse observes "Zionists and assimilationists shared the same idea of manliness."[13] Boyarin concurs that Zionism "is truly the most profound sort of assimilationism, one in which Jews become like all the nations" (Boyarin 368). "The project of these Zionists was precisely to transform Jewish men into the type of male that they admired, namely, the 'Aryan' male. If the political project of Zionism was to be a nation like all other nations, on the level of reform of the Jewish psyche it was to be men like all other men" (369).

The paradox is that Zionists explicitly justified the need for a Jewish state in terms of Jewish Otherness: Zionism insists that Jews are unlike gentiles, and will never be accepted in gentile society. But in needing their own land to dominate, Zionists fell victim to the dominating influence of masculinist European behavior. The nationalist stance toward territory was, in effect, an imitation of Aryan domination. In Freudian terms, the Zionist response to anti-Semitism was "the erection of a state" as an antidote to the emasculating wound of circumcision. The extension of this attempt to masculinize Jews ultimately manifested itself in the contemptuous Israeli attitude toward the victims of the Holocaust which, if we remember the insights of Israeli paratrooper Joel Palgi and use of "sabon," or "soap" to refer to the victims, came close to identification with the oppressor in its affirmation of Jewish weakness. It demanded heroic death rather than "mere" survival.[14]

European Christianity thus may claim credit for the invention of the phallus. In Boyarin's terms, the phallus is the very symbol of the mythical powers of the Goyim—not part of Jewish culture—and Jewish male phallus envy is really a wish to be a Christian, a wish for assimilation, a self-destructive impulse. In his view, both Zionism and the attempt to "masculinize" Jews by building muscles are misguided attempts to ape oppressive behavior. Judaism offers a tradition of gentle, civilized men who should not compensate by insisting upon an exaggerated contrast between themselves and women, or apologize for their gentleness or passivity. Boyarin values the Jewish talent for survival developed over the millennia; he regards all resistance and militancy in Jewish history as undesirable, attempts to imitate Jewish oppressors. His argument is intriguing, although it runs the risk of essentialism: are Jews, in "essence" (four millennia of history renders moot the distinction between nature and history) different, more passive and peaceful, than other men?

Paul Breines offers a different perspective on the subject of Jewish masculinity, focusing on American popular culture in the twentieth century, and Zionist politics in Israel.[15] Breines avoids Boyarin's tendency toward essentialism with his insistence that Jewish men are not so different from other men. Jews have responded to situations throughout history both passively and actively, and in their history have utilized both militancy and passivity as means of survival. "Jews will do, so to speak, what a man has got to do when faced with the opportunity for toughness; they will be as tough as the proverbial next guy" (Breines 49). Thus for Breines, it is puzzling that the nonviolent image of Jewish men is the one that has prevailed, and that in the popular imagination, Jewish men are gentle and frail, less "masculine" than other men. "There have also always been tough, fighting Jews," hardly an aberration from "authentic" Jewish behavior (Breines 49).

Breines does not answer the question why, with two traditions of Jewish male behavior, including militancy, Jewish men have a "masculinity" problem: they are perceived, and also perceive themselves to be less "manly" than the goyim. But he does propose a theory for the gendering of recent Zionist history. The Six-Day War of 1967, and to a lesser extent, the Yom Kippur War of 1973, dramatically changed Jewish self-perception for the first time in recent history, and marked a dramatic reversal from the self-loathing caused by the image of the Holocaust victims in Jewish consciousness.[16] These two wars have led to a renewed "revisionist" interest in Jewish history and literature, as Jewish history is reinterpreted with an emphasis on "tough" Jewish images.

Both Breines and Boyarin regard Freud as an important guide to unconscious attitudes about Jewish masculinity, although not his celebrated psychoanalytic theory as such, but Freud's own involvement with Jewish male feelings of inadequacy and desire to be relieved of them. They focus upon Freud's relationship to his own Judaism and masculinity, and utilize the now famous "hat-in-the-mud" story recounted by Freud in his *Interpretation of Dreams*. When Freud's father was a boy, an anti-Semitic bully knocked his new hat into the mud and shouted, "Jew, get off the sidewalk!" Jakob Freud told this story to his young son Sigmund, who demanded to know how his father had responded. The father recounted that he had picked up his hat and walked on, without defending himself or confronting the anti-Semite. In *The Interpretation of Dreams*, Freud relates his profound disappointment in his father's response. He would have preferred that his father had stood up for himself in a more manly fashion.

Boyarin uses the story as a demonstration of Freud's "phallus envy": his unequivocal discomfort with his father's "feminine" passivity in the face of the anti-Semitic bully. In contrast, Breines, following close analysis of the language of Freud's account of the incident in *The Interpretation of Dreams*, believes that Freud's response was essentially ambivalent, revealing the tension between the two traditions, aggression *and* passivity, that characterizes Jewish masculine experience throughout history. Freud *both* wished that his father had responded more aggressively (the assimilationist stance) *and* knew that Jewish teaching frowns upon violence, even in response to rude, but not overtly dangerous, anti-Semitic behavior (the "Jewish" stance). The assimilationist would have fought back; the more "Jewish" stance was to do what Jakob Freud actually did, pick up his hat and walk on, not allowing the brutishness of the anti-Semite to determine his own behavior.

Breines sees in Sigmund Freud's ambivalence, the availability of both stances: The emphasis on nonviolence as the most moral, profoundly Jewish stance, as well as at times the most prudent way of promoting survival in a hostile world; and the more militant fighting stance that Jews have had to assume from time to time throughout their beleaguered history. He believes there is no "essential" Jewish nature—neither tough nor gentle—but that both images of Jewish men have existed since the beginning of Jewish history, and that *ambivalence* is the most characteristic Jewish stance toward the conflict between toughness and gentleness. Breines describes his own ambivalence: a desire to avoid appearing "feminine," existing alongside a reverence for the Talmudic teachings of nonviolence, an awareness that nonviolence is "more moral." Referring to Freud, and other Jews who have been influential in his life (I. B. Singer, Philip Roth, and his father are cited) Breines notes, "We are all (Jewish) men who do not want to appear to be women" (Breines 36). "At that very moment—when ambivalence, basic to his Jewishness, was most poignantly on display—Freud was at *his most* Jewish. As I may well be in making the point" (Breines 41).

In Breines's view, Freud's attitude toward Zionism, and also toward his friend Theodor Herzl, is further evidence of Freud's uncertainty about the aggressive masculine stance. Freud regarded Herzl as both admirable and dangerous. He distanced his own work from Herzl's, as revealed in a letter to Herzl's son: "Your father is one of those people who have turned dreams into reality. This is a very rare and dangerous breed. It includes the Garibaldi's ... the Herzl's.... I would simply call them the sharpest opponents of my scientific work" (Breines 31). The scientific work he referred to was the interpretation of dreams. As a physician and analyst, Freud studied dreams, where men like Herzl attempted to make them come true. "I deal in psychoanalysis, they deal in psychosynthesis" (Breines 32).

Breines reminds us that the Jewish male dilemma about masculinity bears consequences for Jewish women. In the preoccupation with defining maleness, Jewish women disappear, as do non-Jewish men who are not anti-Semitic aggressors. The assumption that "real" men are big, strong, and combative, and not Jewish, reduces the world to only "weak" Jews and "strong" gentiles, overlooking the possibility of strong Jewish women and non-Jewish men who are not anti-Semites.[17] What would have happened had a non-Jewish passerby witnessed the insult to Freud's father, picked up and returned Jakob Freud's hat, with apologies for the appalling conduct of the anti-Semite, perhaps even berating the aggressor for his ignorance and boorishness? What if a Jewish girl had come along, berated the bully for his ignorance and boorishness, sent him on his way, and returned the hat to young Jakob Freud? The dichotomy between Jew and "he man" or tough guy instantly disappears.

Boyarin argues that Theodor Herzl was driven to become "The Father of Modern Zionism" out of a desire to be like the European goyim, and regards the argument for the "necessity" of the state of Israel as a response to German anti-Semitism: an opportunity for Jews to have a state of their own where they could be just as aggressive and imperialistic as the Europeans. Breines too has grave reservations about the masculine, aggressive form Zionism has taken. Both Nationalism and Socialism, the two components of the word *Nazi,* are powerful forces in Israel, giving some credence to Boyarin's more extreme insistence that Zionism is an imitation of the worst the Western European tradition has to offer: racial chauvinism and imperialism. The socialist aspect of the Israeli settlement, manifested in labor Zionism, may seem benign in comparison to nationalism and imperialism, but Breines is effective in identifying it with masculinist politics, as we shall see when we return to a discussion of the New York Intellectuals' socialist politics.

Breines also regards the "need" for a state as a masculinist stance. "Zionism has been straightforward in its contention that a Jewish state is the key to the normalization of the Jewish situation and that the abnormality of the Jews was a political problem caused by statelessness. And statelessness, according to Zionism, is the cause of meekness, frailty, passivity, humiliation" (Breines 47). Indeed, in the terms being developed here, to the extent that Hannah Arendt argues for the necessity of the political state as a vehicle for endowing the individual with identity, she, too, is "masculinist" in her thinking. Breines suggests that Arendt's *Eichmann in Jerusalem* fed into the hysteria over whether Jews had behaved in a sufficiently masculine fashion during the Holocaust. Arendt and Bruno Bettelheim "raised similar questions of Jewish passivity and weakness in the face of Nazi brutality" (Breines 70). We have seen that neither Arendt nor Bettelheim *raised* the questions, rather they were already preoccupations of the Israelis. Breines also suggests that some of the later rebuttals to Arendt (he cites post-1967 studies by Isaiah Trunk and Lucy Davidowicz) were "shaped by a shift toward a tough Jewish consciousness that had been set in motion by the Israeli victory in June, 1967" (Breines 81). From Breines's perspective, both Arendt's and Bettelheim's questions about Jewish response to the Holocaust *and* the furious response of Jews throughout the world, were influenced by a preoccupation with whether the Jewish people had behaved in a sufficiently active, masculine fashion.

That Arendt had a penchant for the active "masculine" stance in history and politics is no secret. Whether that was what was operative in her analysis of the Eichmann trial is another matter. It is true that she advocated formation of a Jewish army to take its place among the forces allied against Hitler. In his intriguing portrait of Arendt entitled, "I Somehow Don't Fit" Anthony Heilbrut describes her as "admittedly radical, but in no way Marxist, militantly agitating for a Jewish army but wary of a Jewish state, she was a European Zionist rapidly disabused of her Zionism through her experience of American life."[18]

The Israeli state, Brcines argues, actually embodies the double-edged Jewish relationship toward militancy. Justification for the existence of the state comes from the persecution suffered by the Jews. Zionism, in order to justify an armed, militant state capable of defending Jews, *needs* the image of Jewish victimization throughout history, and most dramatically during the Holocaust. "Zionism is at once a decisive break with the traditions of Jewish weakness and gentleness and also not so decisive a break: it rejects meekness and gentleness in favor of the normalcy of toughness, while preserving the older tradition of the Jews as a special or chosen people, which *depends* on imagery of Jews as frail victims" (Breines 50).

Thus there is scholarly precedent for regarding the centrality of gender as an issue for Jewish men. "Masculinity" on a gentile model in the terms of this discussion, is of supreme value in Western culture: it defines what is admirable. Mosse, Breines, and Boyarin all regard the Zionist stance as self-consciously masculinist, and unconsciously assimilationist. For all their insistence on separation from the gentile world, Zionists are defined by that world, and seek, in desiring for Jews to be a nation "like all other nations," to be "just like the goyim": aggressive, self-contained, obsessed with defense and militarism, in a word, masculine. Masculinity is associated with Christianity, or at any event, with non-Judaism, and we can begin to see similarities in the problems faced by both the Zionists and the New York Intellectuals: both were struggling with assimilation, both sought to escape the stigma of femininity associated with Jewish maleness. Assimilation was the avenue to maleness on a gentile model.

Assimilation, in these terms, is gendered: its achievement is maleness. The masculinity of assimilation is what unites the positions of the Israelis and the New York Jews and enables us to understand the gendered dimension to the attack on Hannah Arendt for *Eichmann in Jerusalem*.

One other source should be mentioned on the subject of masculinity and Judaism before returning to the manifestation of these themes in the behavior of the *Partisan Review* editors. David Biale's discussion in *Eros and the Jews* of "cultural constructions"—stereotypes—in Israel and America from the mid-twentieth century onward will enable us to focus on masculinity and Zionism as well as on American Jews.[19] Biale's chapter on American popular culture and Jewish sexuality follows his discussion of "Zionism as Erotic Revolution," so once again the contrast between Israeli and Diaspora Jewish masculinity is made.

It is no secret that Zionism intended to build new Jewish bodies, and a healthier attitude toward sexuality. "Physical strength, youth, nature and secularism were the constellation of Zionist symbols set against the degeneracy, old age, and urban and religious signs of the exile. To build a Judaism with muscles meant to create a sexually healthy Judaism" (Biale 179). Postcards published by early Zionist congresses "typically featured virile young farmers in Palestine contrasted with old frail Orthodox Jews in the Diaspora" (Biale 179). One popular song in Palestine in the early part of this century claimed "We came to the land to build it and be built by it," and Biale explains that being built by it involved using agricultural labor to reconstruct both body and psyche.

If the reconstruction of mind and body through physical labor sounds somewhat Germanic, even in a Hegelian-Marxian sense, the association is not far off: the Zionist youth movement was influenced by the ideas of the German *Wandervogel*, the neoromantic German youth movement, even though the *Wandervogel* was frequently anti-Semitic, and a precursor to the Nazi youth movement (Biale 185). It is thus also not surprising that the prototype of the new body to be built by the land was virile and masculine. The Zionist revolution also proposed to create a stronger, healthier Zionist woman, and a different concept of marriage. But by all accounts, the image of strength was explicitly masculine, and misogyny continued in its most conventional and pervasive forms. "Erotic Zionism was based on a cascade of masculine images, contrasted with the 'feminine' weakness of the Disapora" (Biale 186).

For all the disdain of the "weakness" and "femininity" of Diaspora Jews, the Zionist settlers had themselves arrived recently from Europe, and as we might expect, many of the sexual attitudes of the European Jews remained. Indeed, to the extent that the settlers, or at least the male settlers, sought to distance themselves from the powerlessness of their past, they would seek to exaggerate the distinctions between Jews of the Yishuv and those of the Diaspora. More virile sexuality among Zionist Jews was at the top of the list of distinguishing characteristics.

Zionist women were not thoroughly convinced that the new sexual ideology had their best interests at heart. Biale comments, "Even within the ideology itself, which was articulated overwhelmingly by men, there was a contradiction between the principle of equality and the homoerotic imagery of the youth movement. As long as Zionism was seen as the creation of a virile New Man against the allegedly feminine impotence of exile, women would have difficulty finding a truly equal place" (Biale 187).

One woman who had immigrated to Israel during the Third Aliyah observed, "In relations between men and women there were many inhibitions. In effect, the mentality of the shtetl continued" (Biale 197). Biale notes that while the men believed they had broken thoroughly from the past, the women, "who were largely excluded from formulating Zionist ideology," were less convinced that sexual mores had changed (Biale 197). The Zionist ideology was created by men, and reflected their wishes for a new image of their sexuality. It was stridently affirmed that the New Man with his new strong body and new eroticism was to be distinguished from the sickly, effeminate Jew of exile. Biale also confirms what has been noted by Mosse, Boyarin, and Breines: "Zionism, it seems, has not only liberated the Jew from sexual neurosis, but it has turned him into a quasi *goy*" (Biale 204).

In his discussion of American popular culture, Biale cites the works of Philip Roth, Woody Allen, and Jackie Mason (and we would certainly add Henny Youngman), heirs of the "Borsht Belt" Jewish humor, to demonstrate how the feelings of Jewish male inadequacy manifest themselves in the form of self-deprecation and a strident misogyny directed at Jewish women.[20] Beyond reflecting spontaneous projected self-hatred, or "barely repressed aggression" among modern Jewish men, this misogyny was actually encouraged by the rabbis of the time. "Echoing earlier German Zionist critiques of Jewish women, a Conservative Canadian rabbi, David Kirshenbaum, writing in 1958, specifically blamed the materialism of Jewish women for the increasing rate of intermarriage. 'No wonder' Kirshenbaum wrote, 'Jewish men prefer gentiles!'" (Biale 208).

In his discussion of Jewish sexuality in popular culture, from "The Jazz Singer" to "The Heartbreak Kid," "Norma Rae," "The Way We Were," and "Crossing Delancey," from Philip Roth and Saul Bellow to Adrienne Rich and Irena Klepfisz, Biale touches on the symbolism of circumcision, sex with the goyim, assimilation, Jewish lesbians ("You know of course that there are no Jewish lesbians because to begin with Jews are not supposed to be sexual. Especially not Jewish women."—Adrienne Rich, quoted in Biale 225), and the sexuality of radical politics. He notes that "the wedding of Jewish political radicalism to sexual liberation is not simply the creation of nostalgic fiction. Emma Goldman . . . personified the combination" (Biale 220).

But in spite of the fact that Biale includes women, and well-developed feminist sensibilities, in his discussion, he acknowledges "Like the historical tradition as a whole, most of the images of both male and female Jewish sexuality in

America that we have discussed so far were produced by men" (Biale 224).

ASSIMILATION AS GENDERED: THE *PARTISAN REVIEW* CROWD REVISITED

Reference to first-generation American Jews always assumes the male gender: the community was focused on its sons. The New York Intellectuals are referred to with a specifically male terminology: "pischers" and "boychiks," who were welcomed back to the community as "prodigal sons" even after they had turned away from Judaism for decades. On the one hand, their retreat from Judaism was similar to the experiences of the children of many immigrants to America: embarrassment at their parents who spoke English with an accent, ate "un-American" food, were too emotional, or traditional, or religious, compared to the Anglicized version of the cool, rational American. The paths away from the old world and into assimilated Americanism have traditionally been education, the active life, and the adaptation to "American" customs and cultural experiences. What is not usually recognized is the extent to which these "traditional" pathways to assimilation assume that the child with ambitions to be "Americanized" is male. The traits defined as American are invariably traits to which a *boy* would aspire: active, resourceful, athletic, rational—in sum, a "man of action." Quiet, bookish, sentimental, unathletic boys are not quite American, and it goes without saying that they are unmasculine as well: "sissies."

Recall that "swagger" was allowed these bright young Jewish boys because it was regarded as a ticket out of the ghetto. Imagine a Jewish girl allowed by her parents and community to swagger, encouraged to be bright and outspoken, in the hope that such behavior could lead her away from the Jewish community! A Jewish girl's ticket to success in America was marriage to a bright, ambitious Jewish boy.

But if the assumption was that the males of any given immigrant community would lead the next generation to Americanism, how was the Jewish community explicitly affected? If Christian (or American) culture was regarded as masculine, compared to Judaism's "feminine," we can see that before the Jewish boys could, like other immigrant sons, become fully Americanized, they would need to become masculinized in their own eyes, and in the eyes of American society. Other European ethnic groups had an equally gender-biased but somewhat simpler task in order to become assimilated. They were already regarded as masculine: now all they needed was to become American. They were masculine, in this scenario, because they were European Christians. Asian American and African American men had their own gender troubles in the United States.[21] But Italians, Irish, Polish, and other European immigrants were never regarded as feminine, even if their Catholicism made them the targets of Protestant bigotry. Jews had to become gendered males in order to become assimilated into American life.

They might accomplish this task by becoming athletes: baseball, football, and boxing were available to boys as facilitators in the Americanization process. If they succeeded in physically battling the anti-Semitism of their teammates with fists, athletic prowess, or both, they might succeed in winning the (somewhat qualified) respect of the Americans, and be welcomed into the brotherhood of American sports. The less athletic might become experts of the games: sportswriters and sportscasters, readers of the sports page, and regular spectators at games. This was, of course, less satisfactory, and less efficient as an avenue of assimilation than actually establishing one's athletic prowess. But there is an entire literature—mostly first person—on the centrality of sports as a pathway from the immigrant family into American life. It goes without saying that this pathway excluded girls and women.

In the families that nurtured the New York Intellectuals, the athletic path was not encouraged. An exaggerated closeness between the sons and their mothers made it unlikely that they would be permitted to risk the dangers of playing ball and roughhousing in the streets. While the ambitions of the immigrant fathers might rest on the performance of their sons, the fathers remained distant from the everyday workings of family life.

> The relation of the mother to her child grew especially close in this atmosphere. "From infancy on," Irving Howe later observed, "the child is petted by his mother. She keeps him in the feminine pattern as long as possible.... She doesn't want to cut his curls... or to have him enter athletic activities, for fear he might be hurt.... She constantly hovers over him, developing in him—as if with unconscious skill—the sense of dependence on her which he is later to find so difficult to overcome."... During adolescent rebellion the sons found clearer targets in the overattentive and restrictive pattern established by their mothers. (Bloom 18–19)

One needn't be a psychoanalyst to anticipate the boys' perceived need to exclude women from their "American" adult lives. Their mothers, and by extension all women, were associated with the dependency and the parochialism of both childhood and the ghetto. Perhaps Jewishness itself carried this association with femininity, as the fathers seemed to exclude their sons from their lives completely. Jewish immigrant fathers spent their time working, at the synagogue, and perhaps also at political meetings. The fathers often felt like failures, wanted their sons to be different from them, and expressed this inarticulately, by maintaining distance rather than closeness. "Disappointment, [Robert] Warshow... observed, 'was often the only thing [fathers] could clearly communicate'" (Bloom 19).

This was a tragic situation for both fathers and sons, with implications that were also harmful to the women. Contemporary psychoanalytic feminists have written about the reproduction throughout the generations of polarized gender roles likely to result from distant fathers and overinvolved mothers. The result is likely to be men who have difficulty making any emotional connections, and women who have difficulty with separation and autonomy. The psychodynamics of generations brought up entirely by mothers has been studied in detail elsewhere, by feminist psychoanalysts, and, from an entirely different perspective, by the New York Intellectuals themselves, who were hardly reticent about writing about themselves and their fathers.[22]

So the calling of the sons was scholarly, not athletic. This was traditional enough for a Jewish boy, and satisfied parental ambitions, although it hampered the assimilation process because it was at odds with the American image of masculinity. But a solution was achieved that satisfied the need to "succeed" in terms different from that of the fathers, and which would also avoid the stigma of Jewish male "sissies." Instead of turning to Talmudic study, they become "cosmopolitan" intellectuals: rational, universalist, not tribally Jewish. This served its purpose as a vehicle for escaping Judaism, while being rational, "universal" (non-Jewish) scholars fulfilled enough of the requirements of gentile American manhood. Rationality, or universalist scholarship, was still quite manly, in American terms. The boys were also drawn to radicalism—Marxism, Communism, Trotskyism—and as we shall see, this served the purpose of engendering the intellectuals as male.

In his discussion of twentieth-century "tough Jews" of America, Breines cites gangsters, cowboys, and radicals as well as soldiers and athletes, as masculine images with appeal to Jews. "The gangster as well as the cowboy and leftist emerged in the era of Jewish emancipation and thus, like the Jewish soldier, arose from the experience of Jews engaged in extensive intercourse with the non-Jewish world" (102).[23] Breines goes so far as to hint that with a little stretching of categories, Karl Marx himself might qualify as a tough Jew. In any event, Trotsky most certainly makes the list.

> The notion of tough Jews would surely be too loose were Karl Marx squeezed into it. On the other hand, I do think that his concept of class struggle can be understood as a theoretico-philosophical form of Jewish toughness, especially when seen against the backdrop of the many rabbis in Marx's family tree. And consider the figures from the later Marxist and the broader socialist-anarchist traditions who can more readily be seen as tough Jews. Leon Trotsky is the prototype. Author of countless books (including a defense of revolutionary violence) and organizer of the Red Army in the Russian Revolution and Civil War, he is a Jewish intellectual on horseback. (Breines 103)

The *Partisan Review* crowd were unabashed admirers of Trotsky. They invited him to contribute to their publication, although they resisted adhering to the party line he demanded and the control he wanted to assume over editorial policies. Trotsky believed the *Partisan Review* editors were insufficiently committed to revolution, and the liaison never succeeded.²⁴ But Trotsky's appeal was enormous, and he was lionized by many of the intellectuals. "Many *Partisan* writers fastened onto Trotsky in an uncritical way, idolizing his skills, overvaluing his contributions, and finding reflections of their own calling in his actions" (Bloom 112). Irving Howe observed, "Trotsky . . . was a man of heroic mold, entirely committed to the life of action, but he was also an intellectual who believed in the power and purity of the word" (in Bloom 112). Most telling was Trotsky's psychological appeal to the Partisans, as a *Jew* who appeared to be cast in an heroic (masculine) mold:

> A final attribute of Trotsky's helped cement the emotional relationship between him and many of the young radical critics and writers. He was a Jew. Trotsky, like the young men from the immigrant ghettos, was not devout—this was an age of radical cosmpolitanism. Still, childhood in the Jewish communities created invisible ties which would continually direct the young radicals' lives. So, too, did the unstated awareness of Trotsky's Jewishness provide a final psychological link. He was all they were or wished to be—a young Jew who coupled his radical commitment with his intellectual abilities. (Bloom 112)²⁵

If the New Yorkers' commitment to "cosmopolitanism" was a way to move away from the parochialism and the associated femininity of their Jewish parents, their radical commitment was a way of achieving masculinity, activism, and effectiveness rather than passivity, and victimhood. It was an efficient vehicle for distancing themselves from their fears about the "feminine" associations of Jewish maleness. If Israeli Zionism was, paradoxically, assimilationist in its mimicry of European virility, American radicalism also had a hidden assimilationist agenda. Ironically, the young Marxists utilized its virile associations as a way of proving their virile Americanism.

Now, one may be inclined to respond, "Perhaps their radical commitment had nothing to do with their fears of effeminacy. Perhaps it reflects only heartfelt political convictions." I do not imply that, at least at that stage of their lives, the New Yorkers were not genuinely committed to Bolshevik politics, or that they assumed a disingenuous radical stance for the sole purpose of establishing their masculinity. However, I believe that their radical political commitment also served a psychological purpose: soothing unconscious "Jewish" fears that they were insufficiently masculine. And while they left behind the exclusively male House of Study, they sought to duplicate the exclusive masculinity both at *Partisan Review* and as radicals.

For a variety of reasons, ranging from a preoccupation with masculinity as a symbol of one's distance from immigrant Jewishness, to the family structure and parenting practices of Jewish immigrant families, which will be discussed in due course, the New York Intellectuals created an environment where women were, at best, peripheral. We have seen that Arendt, after her arrival in New York, was admired from a distance. Mary McCarthy and a very few other talented literary women were included in the circle, but only as extensions of their *Partisan Review* boyfriends.[26]

For example, in 1937, Philip Rahv met Mary McCarthy at a party at James T. Farrell's. She was not yet the well-known literary figure she was to become, but she was clearly a bright, educated young woman. After a trial summer of living together in a friend's borrowed apartment, Rahv and McCarthy rented their own place. Although she was unknown, Rahv brought McCarthy to *Partisan Review* as an editor in charge of theater criticism. McCarthy claimed she received the assignment because she had once been married to an actor and was "supposed to know something about the theater." Bloom notes: "Although she was clearly a woman of intellectual skills, it is also clear that her position on the *PR* editorial board derived essentially from her relationship with Rahv. When she left him, she left the magazine" (Bloom 73).

McCarthy left Rahv for Edmund Wilson after little over a year. Wilson had been an intellectual model for the younger men at *Partisan Review*, and the fact that he had "taken Rahv's girl" caused tensions, gossip, and rejections of both Wilson's and McCarthy's work. Wilson scolded the editors on her behalf: "I've thought there was something wrong in your shop ever since you passed up that short story of Mary's. You people owed her a chance to develop, since she was one of your original group" (Bloom 124). Meanwhile, back at the editorial offices, one long-employed secretary remarked to William Barrett that "it was too bad William [Phillips] and Philip [Rahv] were not of opposite sex, for then they could have gotten married and had babies instead of *Partisan Review*" (Bloom 74).

While the editorial offices of the *Partisan Review* thus became a bastion of male exclusivity, the remarkably explicit association between masculine sexuality, radical politics, and Judaism completed the gender therapy.

> The idea of brotherhood appealed on many levels, combining the highest idealism with the most practical of needs. If young intellectuals longed to merge with the international proletariat, they also wanted to get together with each other and have some fun. In classmates who had gone "proletarian," Alfred Kazin saw youths who "*looked* as if they had found the right answer. And they were ... easy with girls, passing them around at dances with comradely contempt, as if being militant about everything brought advantages." (Cooney 46)

Cooney muses about what appeal such contempt could possibly have had for the "girls" involved, while it offered the young men a sense of social acceptance in the same way as any gang membership would, even in the absence of the New York Intellectuals' lofty self-importance. William Phillips and Philip Rahv, founders of *Partisan Review*, referred to their fundraising dances as the "best dance floor in the city."[27]

While they were busy using *PR*'s radical commitment as a vehicle for giving them group access to local girls, their commitment to Marxist politics itself was expressed in terms of virility. Swaggering Mike Gold, Communist and editor of *The New Masses* since 1928, challenged the *Partisan Review* intellectuals to meet his standards of masculinity. "For [Mike] Gold, the worker seemed always virile, masculine, and heroic, while intellectuals remained somehow effete" (Cooney 33). Phillips and Rahv joined Gold's ranks for awhile, but when, several years later, they split with the Stalinists, Gold berated them for ingratitude. He implied that only his brand of communism had saved them from effeminacy.

> Gold remembered "the same people only a decade ago" as "eunuchs" seeking potency, needing sex, and desperately making the "ivory tower . . . into a bedroom." To affirm his own working-class virility, Gold declared loudly, "I want to spit whenever I think of it." (Cooney 116)

But let us assume that Mike Gold had some unusually intense conflicts about his masculinity, not emblematic of the *Partisan Review* crowd who were, after all, his rivals. We can still gasp with incredulity at Lionel Abel's association of Marxism with both Judaism and masculinity. Abel described Harold Rosenberg's view that

> Marxism was two things: it was Talmud, to be sure. But it was also Cabala. And he thought that the role of the literary men should be to develop the arcane, cabalistic side of Marxist doctrine. . . . I shall never forget the evening when he proved that Helen of Troy—his argument involved both word magic and economic determinism—was really a loaf of bread![28]

One could dismiss this as high-spirited boyishness, a version of fraternity house mirth. Cooney observes: "When life broke through ideology, the young intellectuals kicked up their heels and reveled in using and abusing Marxism for a bit of intellectual strutting and chicanery" (Cooney 45). But the good fun was not without its misogynist side: it involved associating the manly Marxism with Judaism, and then using both, somehow, to turn a legendary beautiful woman into a loaf of bread: good enough to eat! Sounds like a frat house gang bang at Helen of Troy's expense. It also combined the traditional male exclusiveness of Talmudic study with the more contemporary virility associated with radical militancy, thereby retaining the best of both worlds: the male worlds of Jewish Study and radical activism.

One might think that the security of being lovingly supported by one's culture—even in assuming a rebellious stance against one's own cultural traditions—would foster enough self-confidence to forestall compensatory denigration of one's sisters. But there is evidence that these young men, striving with the help of their own Jewish community to leave Judaism behind, found it necessary to associate their mission with manliness, and to treat women with a swaggering disrespect. According to the scholars of Jewish sexuality we have considered, *to the extent* that this particular generation of Jews sought to deny their Jewishness, they would embrace what they perceived as the dominant culture's definition of masculinity.[29]

JEWISH WOMEN

Thus far we have considered primarily male sources on the "problem" of Jewish masculinity. Although a full-blown discussion of Jewish feminist scholarship is beyond the scope of this study, a sense of its parameters is important for perspective. It is also important to consider more explicitly what the relationship between Jewish men and women has been, both culturally and in terms of Jewish law and tradition. There is a vast and growing literature on the subject, too, but here we will only review conditions during the modern era, which has been our focus.[30]

In our discussion thus far of Jewish masculinity, we have enlisted the help of male scholars who appear to be extraordinarily aware of and sensitive to the general issues of feminism as well as specifically Jewish feminism. Mosse, Boyarin, Breines, and Biale all regard as problematic the association of masculinity with aggression, militancy, and domination. They express a sense that there is something wrong with the cultural expectation that men, whether Jewish or not, need to behave in a bellicose fashion, that muscles and strength are associated with manhood, and that gentleness and passivity are regarded, disdainfully, as "feminine." They all seek to validate on some level the Jewish male history of passivity. Paradoxically, then, while these serious scholars raise questions that are compatible with a feminist perspective, about the dangers inherent in associating masculinity with violence and physical aggression, they obscure Jewish feminist issues by presenting Jewish men as "already liberated" by the Jewish tradition itself: gentle, passive, family oriented. The problem is perceived to be the dominance of gentile society, which makes Jewish men ashamed of their own cultural traits. This stance perpetuates the myth that Jewish women are somehow better treated by their men than non-Jewish women, and less likely to suffer the worst that patriarchy has to offer. It perpetuates the stereotype that Jewish men actually are gentler, kinder, more thoughtful, studious, reliable, "good husbands." How could such men be "oppressors," as "angry feminists" are perceived to accuse all men of being?[31]

This stance is a preemptive strike. It is a defense against the fear of "race betrayal": that in criticizing Jewish men, Jewish women undermine the need for unity, solidarity, in the face of a much greater oppression. As Cynthia Ozick confesses about her own Jewish feminist concerns: "Sometimes I feel ashamed. The problem—the status of Jewish women—shames me with its seeming triviality, its capacity to distract, its insistent sociological preoccupation, its self-centeredness, its callous swerve away from all those hammer blows dealt to the Jewish people as a whole."[32] The problem is not unique to Jewish women. It has been faced recently and publicly by African American women who object to the public creation of a Black Patriarchy, marked most recently with the institution of men-only marches; who object to excusing domestic violence perpetrated by African American men with the rationalization that the black men are oppressed (more so than African American women?), which somehow makes the abuse of women more acceptable. These feminists have been accused of undermining the racial solidarity of African Americans with "trivial," "selfish," or "divisive" problems. The accusations of racial or community betrayal leveled at women who challenge male behavior is used to undermine feminist concerns. It takes a particularly tricky turn when the men of a community themselves appear to be making feminist arguments their own. When Jewish men object to Jewish male violence, and we appear to have evidence of the "kinder, gentler" Jewish man, it is even more difficult for a Jewish feminist to get a foothold. "What more do Jewish women want?"

For starters, Jewish feminists seek acknowledgment of an inherent and pervasive male bias in Jewish culture and Jewish religion. As Susannah Heschel puts it in the introduction to her volume:

> The problem, as today's writers see it, runs throughout the course of Jewish history, penetrating the basic theological suppositions of Judaism: its imagery of women and men, its liturgy, its conceptions of the Jewish people and community, its understanding of God as Father and King. Woman as Other is expressed, for instance, by Judaism's "purity" laws, in which women convey impurity not to themselves or to other women, but only to the men with whom they come into contact.... Women are placed behind a curtain in some synagogues, or denied aliyot and positions of leadership, not for any reasons concerning them but because their visible presence might affect the concentration of men at prayer. (Heschel xxii)

Heschel goes on to suggest that if woman is regarded as Other "in the synagogue, *halachah*, liturgy and theology," then "she is bound to be treated as Other in the home, the family and the community." From this perspective, Jewish feminist cultural and religious issues are inseparable.

Critics of the feminist stance respond that Jewish women are not regarded as "Other," implying inferiority, but are "different," a difference that is natural, intended by the Creator, inscribed in the Torah, and interpreted in the Talmud which is as sacred as the Torah. The acknowledgment of difference represents a mark of respect for women. Moshe Meiselman states, "Men and women are equally judged and given equal rewards, but for different tasks—men for the creation of a link in the chain of Torah scholars, women for the creating of a Jewish home."[33] Far from being oppressed, women's separate excellence is valorized by the Jewish tradition. Jewish women are particularly well taken care of: exempted from many of the rigors of communal religious worship and thus saved for their own equally important duties of raising observant Jewish children and keeping the home kosher; protected by the *ketubah* (marriage contract) from the vulnerability that a single woman suffers in a male-dominated world; given a respite from sexual pressures by the laws of *niddah* and *mikveh*, which also ensure that sexual passion is preserved in marriage. The fact that it is extremely difficult for a Jewish woman to divorce her husband is also for her own good, since a woman needs the protection of marriage. The problems of *agunah*—women abandoned but not divorced by their husbands and thus legally incapable of remarrying—are overlooked in this argument. The laws of inheritance that seem to favor sons are actually a "great blessing" to daughters. Meiselman remarks, "The fact that daughters do not inherit if there are sons seems prima facie to be a gross inequity, but on a deeper investigation it will be seen to be a great blessing" (Meiselman 88). It protects a wife and daughters from being creditors in the event that the patriarch dies insolvent. "The choice represents a realistic approach to the needs of women. The law recognizes that it is easier and preferable for men to go out and earn a living than for women" (Meiselman 91). Meiselman neglects the "protection racket" logic of this arrangement: "We have an obligation to protect you from the fact that we won't allow you to earn an independent income."

Furthermore, women are spared the obligation to study Torah, because their household and family duties would keep them from being able to focus with sufficient energy and concentration on the sacred text. Maimonides wrote, "The sages commanded a man not to teach his daugher Torah. This is because women are not disposed to dedicate themselves to study and will turn the words of Torah into foolish words according to their limited understanding [due to their lack of interest]. Our sages said that anyone who teaches his daugher Torah is to be considered as if he had taught her trivial and unimportant things."[34] Meiselman rephrases this, as part of his explanation that Judaism has women's best interests at heart: "One does not *impose* Torah knowledge upon women, as one does upon men, for they are not required to study" (38). However, a father *may* teach his daughter, if she shows the proper motivation. But because girls and women are not *required* to study, the *mitzvah* of studying is not as valuable as it is for a boy who is *commanded* to study Torah. Since women's domestic duties are commanded, they constitute a more valued *mitzvah* for women, and Torah study becomes, as it were, a less "cost-effective" way of being a good Jew, for women and girls.

The sequestering of women in a balcony or curtained section of the Orthodox synagogue is, to this way of thinking, also not a sign of women's inferior status in Jewish worship, but reflects deference to the weakness of men. Men are so incapable of resisting the sexual allures of women that the mere sight of females in shul would cause them to lose concentration in their prayers. The explantion for keeping women out of the sight of men (also covering the hair of orthodox women at all times with either a scarf or a wig) is intended to protect men from their own inability to resist temptation. One feminist has suggested that this argument has all the logic of a proposal to hospitalize healthy people to keep them from being contaminated by the sick. If women are more capable of maintaining spirituality, even in mixed company, why are they not given the most sacred duties and commanded to worship communally? The men should be kept at home and out of the mischief they seem bound to get into whenever they see a woman.

There is also the puzzle of why Jewish orthodoxy, which requires so much restraint and dedication in every aspect of life, from dietary laws, to the times of prayers, to a monthly prescribed schedule of sexual intercourse, fails in demanding of men that they keep their minds and hearts on their prayers, even in the presence of women. Just how libidinous does the Creator suppose observant Jewish men are? Cynthia Ozick wonders, "Is the pious Jewish male more subject than other males to sexual arousal under inappropriate conditions? In fact, observant Jewish men are without doubt better prepared than others for sexual self-restraint, and it is not pious Jewish males who are weak in the face of women—only their arguments" (Heschel 141). The assumption of Jewish male susceptibility to sexual temptation seems perversely to confirm the deadly racial stereotypes we have discussed of the irrepressible sexual urges of Jewish men.

The prayer Orthodox Jewish men recite each morning includes the verse, "Blessed art Thou . . . who has not created me a woman . . . for women are not commanded in all of the Mitzvot," and in spite of Meiselman's insistence that this only thanks God for the extra *duties* of being a man, the prayer's gratitude for male privilege reverberates throughout Jewish culture. The woman's equivalent prayer, blessing God for creating her "in accordance with His will," seems to be an acknowledgment of a consolation prize. Imagine a situation where white people daily thank God for not making them black, while black people thank God for making them "in accordance with the white man's [the equivalent of "His" in the orthodox Jewish woman's prayer] will"! It is impossible to regard such a prayer as anything other than brainwashing, an apology for racism.

Tempting as this line of inquiry may be, further investigation would take us too far afield from the specific question we are considering: whether Arendt's treatment by Jewish men in Israel and New York was influenced by Jewish attitudes toward women, whether as a woman, she was regarded as particularly "out of line" with her public criticism of Jewish male leadership. I offer here only an outline of the major questions of Jewish feminism and a brief review of gender relations in modern Jewish practice, in order to prepare the stage for addressing that question.

The central dilemma for Jewish feminists is to recast the role of women in Jewish religious practices without losing the sacredness of traditional Jewish teachings, or relegating women to a marginal status in the most revered aspects of Jewish life. The challenge is to change Judaism to include women in its most sacred aspects, without losing the weight of tradition that is the essence of Judaism. Orthodox Jews believe this to be an impossible, indeed, heretical undertaking:

> Orthodoxy . . . responds to modernity by insulating itself from modernity's challenges. Historical method is accepted only warily, and in any case, never applied to the key texts, the Bible and the Talmud, which are held to be the literally revealed word of God from Sinai. Any challenge to that revelation is not recognized.To Orthodoxy, the historical method suggests that the Talmudic rabbis were not transmitting the revealed word of God, but were actually creating something new. (Heschel xxv)

On the other hand, Conservative and Reform Jews regard the history of Judaism as a history of response and adaptation to changing circumstances. The tradition of flexibility, of retaining the center while responding to the environment, is the secret of Jewish survival over the milennia. But Heschel argues that "Conservative Judaism remains theologically confused." "Ultimately, since the Jewish history we know is the history of Jewish men, it is precisely that historical consciousness that is invoked by Conservative leaders when they want to oppose any changes in the status of women" (Heschel xxix).

Cynthia Ozick regards the silence of the Torah on the universal denigration of women as a scandal. The abuses of women by society in general are "so wide flung on our planet that they seem, by their undeviating pervasiveness, very nearly to have the sanction of nature" (Heschel 146). The majesty of Torah is precisely that it stands in opposition to many "natural" injustices of the world.

> In creating the Sabbath, Torah came face to face with a nature that says, "I make no difference among the days." And Torah made a difference among the days. In giving the Commandment against idolatry, Torah came face to face with a society in competition with the Creator. And Torah taught the Unity of the Creator. In making the Commandment against dishonor of parents, Torah came face to face with merciless usage of the old. And Torah ordained devotion to parents. In every instance Torah strives to teach *No* to unrestraint, *No* to victimization, *No* to dehumanization

The exception, Ozick writes, is with regard to women. "Here alone Torah confirms the world, denying the meaning of its own Covenant. . . . The Covenant is silent about women; the Covenant consorts with the world at large" (149–50). So exceptional is the omission of the Torah with regard to women, that it begs for the study of Oral Law: "The Oral Law, with its rabbinic piecemeal repairs, is the first to inform us that such a precept is implicit though absent—otherwise whence would the Oral Law derive its repairs?" (150). Ozick concludes, "With regard to women, the Commandment separating Torah from the world is the single missing Commandment. Torah—one's

heart stops in one's mouth as one dares to say these words—
Torah is in this respect frayed" (150). The missing commandment is "Thou shalt not lessen the humanity of women!"

Critics of Jewish feminism would likely respond that respect of women is taken for granted in Jewish teachings: a commandment is unnecessary. But if feminist complaints about *halakha* and a male bias in Jewish worship were truly unfounded, Jewish practice would reflect the unspoken commandment to respect women. Is there such a legacy of equality in Jewish culture? A brief survey of the separate spheres traditionally occupied by Jewish men and women in Europe and America leaves some doubt about the matter.

In her introduction to *Found Treasures: Stories by Yiddish Women Writers*,[35] Irena Klepfisz discusses Yiddish as a spoken language associated with women in Eastern Europe and Germany, during the past few centuries. Although men as well as women spoke Yiddish, because the language was used in matters of daily life, home business, and social relations, it was called *mame-loshn*, the mother tongue, and contrasted with the written language, Hebrew, the language of rabbis and scholars, of tanakh and halakha. Hebrew was the "male" language, called *loshn-kaydesh*, the holy tongue. Hebrew was used primarily in prayer and study in order to preserve the sacredness of the Torah. The language was as sacred as the text. Only men read Torah, but both men and women spoke Yiddish. Yiddish-speaking men were primarily working class, and there was thus an artificial gender segregation associated with the two languages that also reflected class and value hierarchies.

During the eighteenth century, Yiddish was "discovered" and legitimized by Hasidic men as a medium for writing in a more accessible, democratic language. Klepfisz notes, "Early (male) Hasidic attitudes to Yiddish demonstrates what feminists have found in other Western cultures: women's perspectives and contributions are deemed inferior or insignificant until men decide otherwise, legitimize them through defeminization and claim them as their own" (30). Zionists used Yiddish in newspapers and journals to reach Diaspora Jews, but

Hebrew was to be the official (masculine) language in the future Jewish state.

As a more popularly accessible language than Hebrew, Yiddish became the language of political debate, and the means of expression of the more progressive Zionists. Women's Yiddish writings were ostensibly welcomed into the more progressive branch of the European Zionist movement, but Klepfisz suggests that "male Yiddishists were probably more conflicted over women's presence in their circles than they wanted to admit," and soon sought greater legitimacy for Yiddish as a medium of secular artistic, moral, and intellectual expression. "To do so, they needed to defeminize it, to dissociate it from its recent 'degenerate' history and its older demeaning connection with women and illiterates" (34).

Sholem Aleichem and two earlier Yiddish writers, Mendele Mokher Sforim and I. L.Peretz, wrote in Yiddish as a "self-conscious and inherently progressive act: an identification with the masses through their spoken language" (36). But these intellectuals were somewhat ambivalent about being entirely identified with the language of the masses, indeed, with a language associated with women. They sought more: legitimacy for Yiddish that had been reserved for the Hebrew language, as holy (or at least, rational) and masculine. Sholem Aleichem claimed Mendele as his "grandfather" (there was an approximately twenty-year age difference between them, but who's counting when you're founding a tradition?) and "instantly created a male Yiddish literary dynasty which mirrored the rabbinical scholarly dynasty. Just when Yiddish was being championed as an authentic national *mame-loshn*, Sholem Aleichem declared— and everyone agreed—its literature now belonged to the fathers" (Klepfisz 37). Yiddish had been parochial, and now that the men had appropriated it for progressive political purposes, they wanted to claim "universality." Universality has been associated with the male perspective since the beginning of history, and we have seen that the New York Intellectuals claimed a version of it—"cosmpolitanism"—as a way of avoiding their Judaism.[36] Klepfisz regards the move as utterly false: sheer appropriation by men of a medium women had been using. The result, she indicates, was all too similar to what usually happens when men "discover" and desire to claim something that women have previously had access to: the women disappear, as though they had never been a part of the action. Not surprisingly, Yiddish women writers have dissappeared from public awareness to be reclaimed by feminists in volumes such as *Found Treasures*. We now associate the written Yiddish "tradition" with men: Sholem Aleichem, I. B. Singer, et al. The complex political, and fairly recent history of Yiddish writing has been forgotten as thoroughly as the women who first wrote in the language.

The history of the popularization of Yiddish is an example of the deeply rooted association of the masculine with the scholarly and legitimate, the male aversion to anything identified with femininity in the Jewish tradition, and the resistance to associating anything feminine with either the scholarly or the sacred.

In a sense, our consideration of the Jewish male "problem" with a "feminine" image gives the game away. It is traumatic for a man to be considered unmasculine. The reverse is not the case. Accusing a woman of being "masculine" may not be what she wishes for herself, and may be intended as an insult, but it also carries a certain respect: she is a woman to be contended with, not easily dismissed. A "feminine" man need not be taken seriously. Boyarin believes that in nineteenth-century European culture, the association of Jewish men with femininity has carried the correlating association of Jewish women with aggressiveness and masculinity. Boyarin surmises that this may be because some Jewish women were provided with a better education and better training for the world than their non-Jewish European sisters. This more worldly training for Jewish women in a Victorian world may have been the result of a number of influences: the German-Jewish desire to be a part of the German enlightenment, *bildung*, which also gave rise to the Reform Jewish movement; the fact that the Jewish regard for Torah study as a man's highest calling necessitated equipping Jewish woman with greater skills for operating in the marketplace; the fact that traditional Judaism forbade the study of Torah and Talmud to women, meant that the education they received was more secular and "enlightened" than that of their brothers.

Ironically then, some Jewish girls, while denied access to Torah by Jewish law and tradition, were assigned more active roles than those set aside for non-Jewish girls. They were expected to be competent enough in the world to support their husbands, who if possible, should be allowed to be religious scholars. Thus they were encouraged to have a secular education, and perhaps some business training, as well as the traditional domestic training reserved for Jewish girls.[37] While the Jewish girls were thus denied access to the exclusively male House of Study, and to what Judaism valued most highly, they acquired worldly skills and a secular education that rendered them more adept at functioning in the gentile world than their menfolk. They appeared, in stereotypical comparison to Victorian gentile girls, "masculine."

There may be some truth to this description of the exceptional educational opportunities afforded Jewish middle-class girls. However, there is little in Marion Kaplan's *The Making of the Jewish Middle Class* to confirm the sense that Jewish women experienced their opportunities in such optimistic terms. Kaplan argues that Jewish women were indeed powerful influences within their families, hence within the German-Jewish community, for keeping an identification with Judaism alive—although increasingly in the privacy of home and synagogue, and "despite their relegation to insignificance in religious and political matters."[38]

Contrary to the contention that Jewish women were more adept at moving in the secular world than their men, Kaplan observes, "With few exceptions, Jewish women had less opportunity than men to leave the home, family and immediate community, to meet and merge with the majority. Conversely, they had more occasion to cultivate family, friendship, and communal ties, the few arenas in which Jewishness could still be expressed without interference. Socially prescribed roles thus reinforced their allegiances" (Kaplan 15). During the years of the rise of the Jewish bourgeoisie in Germany, "more than ever before, women were defined through the family. A value system which described women as domestic, weak, modest, dependent, self-denying, emotional, religious, and virtuous gained currency.... At the same time, men under pressure to succeed in the outside world viewed these traits as encumbrances" (Kaplan 16). In sum, "perched rather precariously on a pedestal, married women remained respected, protected, and powerless" (17). Kaplan assures us that this had as much to do with traditional Judaism itself, as with the desire to become more like the Germans: "Jewish tradition defined women by their primary work, childbearing. Excluded from metaphysical covenant between God and man as well as from the earthly synagogue community, women's only access to God and to the holy community was in their function as mothers" (Kaplan 41).

In her chapter describing Jewish women's efforts to attain a higher education in Germany, she outlines the resistance of *both* German academia *and* Jewish parents. Among the Jewish upper bourgeoisie, when a girl finished her schooling at age sixteen, she faced "six to ten years of uselessness before [she] would be ready to marry," and some Jewish parents, even Orthodox, were prevailed upon to provide their daughters with a higher education, at least to avoid the disgrace of her earning money during those years. Still, daughters faced parental resistance, which often made a lasting impression, and the predictable prejudice against both Jews and women from the German professoriate.[39] Whatever the particular familial decision, "Girls' education stood in a clearly secondary position to that of their brothers. In fact, in many families it seems to have been absolutely acceptable for a daughter to replace one of the servants, so that money could be saved for the son's education" (Kaplan 141).

Jewish manhood was identified with femininity by gentile society, while scholarship was identified with masculinity by the Jewish tradition. In the wings stood trouble waiting to happen in the form of a Jewish woman scholar named Hannah Arendt.

THE *EICHMANN* CONTROVERSY, GENDER, AND JUDAISM

Arendt was not the only Jewish woman scholar in the world when she wrote. But she was one of the most prominent intellectuals of her day when she published *Eichmann in Jerusalem*, having already earned a respected reputation with *The Origins of Totalitarianism*, *The Human Condition*, and scores of scholarly essays. Still, to reiterate the haunting phrase quoted in Heilbut, she "somehow didn't fit."[40] By that phrase she meant that she could not identify herself by political category, but it also applied to her scholarship. She was not accepted by the academic establishment as a recognized scholar until near the end of her life. She was regarded neither as a philosopher nor a political scientist. She was often accused of being a "journalist," or a "commentator." But *The Origins* had earned her front-page notoriety, and she had a large reputation. People knew who she was, in contrast to, for example, Raul Hilberg, who was a respected but bookish academic. Unlike other "Jewish women scholars," such as Marie Syrkin, Lucy Davidowicz, Rosa Luxemburg, or even Emma Goldman, she did not "fit" with any group that could be named: not Zionist, Socialist, or Anarchist. These women, for all their erudition and provocativeness, were less threatening than Arendt because they belonged to, and did not challenge the leadership of, male-led groups. The latter two, who were indeed big-time troublemakers, did not identify themselves as Jews, and to the extent that they ran afoul of male-dominated leadership, were shot or exiled.

Hannah Arendt was the only woman with a public reputation who challenged the Jewish male leadership on both sides of the Atlantic, for their ineffectiveness during the worst crisis in Jewish history. In that stance she was utterly alone. Still, what would Hannah Arendt have thought of the idea that part of the source of the fury directed at her over *Eichmann in Jerusalem* was the result of the fact that she reminded Jewish men of their sense of inadequacy, in a specifically gendered way, in the face of Nazi power?

After the initial attack in the *Partisan Review*, Arendt wrote to her friend Mary McCarthy, "My reason for breaking with the P.R. people has nothing to do with the content of Abel's review, but with the choice of the reviewer. What is involved is (a) that they knew that Abel had written a piece against me before [a negative review of *Between Past and Future*], hence was hostile to begin with and (b) that they showed an extraordinary lack of the most elementary respect for myself and my work in choosing somebody like Abel as a reviewer."[41]

In the same letter she offers commiseration to Mary McCarthy, whose novel *The Group* had received similarly hostile treatment on a somewhat smaller scale. She refers to the group of negative reviewers as "the boys": "That the 'boys' have tried to turn against you seems to me only natural and I think it has more to do with 'The Group' being a best seller than with political matters" (Brightman 147). Editor Carol Brightman notes that the reference to "the boys" in this letter, "alludes to a larger circle of New York intellectuals than the *Partisan Review* editors, to whom the term *boys* commonly referred" (Brightman 148n.2).

The disparaging reference to "the boys" hints at some awareness on Arendt's part that gender was playing a role in the treatment she and McCarthy were accorded. It is also likely that referring to the intellectuals as "the boys" both confirms the thesis that gender was central to their identity and reveals that it went unrecognized in the sense that "boys" seems a natural reference. Nobody would associate "the girls" with a group of intellectuals. Arendt suggested to McCarthy that jealousy of her success and notoriety may have played a role in the hostile reception her book received. Norman Mailer's haughty dismissal of McCarthy's book as a "lady book" in the *New York Review* supports the male jealousy theory.[42] McCarthy's suspicion that Elizabeth Hardwick was responsible for the review assignment does nothing to diminish the likelihood—even if a woman competitor had relinquished the podium to a resentful man. Besides, Hardwick was the wife of the editor of *The New York Review*.

But still, we seem to have adequate explanations for the attack on Hannah Arendt, without the added gender factor: embarrassment at the inadequacy of their response to the Holocaust of the New York Intellectuals, and embarrassment over the Israeli sense of helplessness as Jews were slaughtered. In addition, there are the complexities of party politics in Israel, and the New Yorkers' political migration from radicalism to conservatism, with *Eichmann in Jerusalem* appearing to undemine the more confirming *Origins of Totalitarianism.* Surely *anybody*, male or female, who aggravated these tender feelings or provoked hidden guilt and ambivalence would evoke a rageful response.

The New York Jews and the Israelis had very little in common prior to their excoriation of Hannah Arendt's report on the Eichmann trial. The New Yorkers had been denying Judaism all their lives, while the Israelis had settled a land precisely because their Jewish identity was central. But we have seen that there is an issue that they faced in common: the judgment of the non-Jewish world, both European and American, that they were insufficiently masculine. The surprising singularity of the agreement of the New York and Israeli Jews over Arendt's report is not so paradoxical once gender is factored in. Both the official spokesmen for nonassimilation, the Zionists, and the radical intellectuals of the 1930s, who wanted nothing more than to leave Judaism behind, can be understood as defending their maligned manhood in their fury at Hannah Arendt. Both the Israelis and the New Yorkers were responding to gentile racism that associated Judaism with femininity, accepting the challenge to be "real" men, and in that sense, desiring to assimilate to the non-Jewish standards of masculine deportment. Hannah Arendt touched *that* nerve.

Arendt was the "big strong woman" who, in Breines's scenario (Breines 39) happened on the scene of anti-Semitic aggression, recovered Jakob Freud's hat, and destroyed the oversimplified categories of tough gentile man and passive, feminine Jew. She was a Holocaust refugee who refused to be a victim. Remember that Israeli Zionists had been struggling with their image of Holocaust Jews: did the victims die inglorious deaths because they were not "tough" enough to resist the Nazis? Or, during the time of the Kastner affair and its aftermath in the Eichmann trial, were the truly despicable victims the ones who negotiated with the Nazis, while the "innocent" Jews who died were more heroic? Either interpretation represented a false dichotomy, tainted with gender. "Good" and "bad" were polarized, good associated with masculine, bad with feminine. The Zionists, so many of whom had recently been diaspora Jews themselves, were desperate to distinguish themselves from the weak, feminine Jews: the task was to identify which group of Europeans should be labeled that way.

From this perspective, whether or not Arendt was a woman may have been of secondary significance to the Israelis in comparison to the fact that she was supposed to be a European survivor, but refused to be a victim. Instead, she was reading them the riot act, sufficient threat in itself to the dearly held gendered stereotypes. It also might account for the fact that their responses to Hilberg and Arendt were similar. In terms of prevailing gender stereotypes, both scholars were "women" challenging the potency of the Israelis.

The New York Intellectuals' gender problem took a different but related form. They themselves stood "accused" of being emasculated, both by Israelis, because they were assimilationists, and by Americans, because they were Jews. As a European Jew (female) and a refugee of the Holocaust, Arendt reminded them of the falseness of their attempts at assimilation. They were Jews who had denied their Jewishness and sought to establish their muscularity by means of radical politics. They had moved away from radicalism, at least in part, out of belated recognition of their Jewishness. But they too saw the world in terms of polarities, and their latest one was centered on an exaggerated association of Hitler, Stalin, and Evil, which appeared to be validated by Arendt's earlier work. Her complicated message about the Holocaust now forced them to face the complexity of being Jewish, and reminded them of their less than heroic stance during the war. Since their avoidance of Judaism all their lives had, I suspect, something to do with a desire to be "masculine" on a non-Jewish model, accepting the reality of Jewishness rather than an idealized vision of Jewish goodness, was bound to be troubling. It was even worse because Arendt was a Holocaust refugee herself, a European-educated scholar, and a "big strong woman." I will decline here to speculate about the "special" relationship between Jewish sons and their mothers, and what this "big strong Jewish woman" must have evoked in them unconsciously.

Gender also played a part in the specific accusation against her, of being insufficiently identified with the Jewish people, of "blaming the victims," of being too shrill and angry in her tone, of, in a phrase, being disloyal to the Jews. On its most general level, Arendt was caught in a web of double standards. She was expected by the Jewish community to put her loyalty to her own people before her "objective" scholarship in a way that appears utterly disingenuous coming from a group of men who had built their careers distancing themselves from loyalty to "their own people"—right up through the Holocaust. But as a woman, she was denied access by Jewish tradition and law to the basis of Jewish scholarship, the Torah and Talmud. If she were to be a scholar, in an important sense she *had* to be a "non Jewish" scholar, a classical or a universal scholar. But, to the extent that she was a classical or universal scholar, she was usurping the Intellectuals' access to assimilation, which was associated with masculinity.

In other words, Arendt was dismantling categories for the New Yorkers as well as the Israelis: for the Israelis she was the "strong Jewish woman" from the Diaspora, a combination they had not believed possible. For the New Yorkers, she was a Jewish woman who presented herself as a universal scholar: also tantamount to cross dressing, if we take seriously the argument that their cosmpolitanism, which was related to their radicalism, was an effort at assimilation associated with masculinity.

Why, then, weren't the New York Intellectuals enraged by *The Origins of Totalitarianism*, which appeared a decade earlier, and was written by the same universalist woman scholar? The answer to that question is that the *Origins* confirmed the Intellectuals in their turn away from radicalism to an Americanism that was not perceived to be incompatible with their newly acknowledged Jewishness. In contrast, *Eichmann in Jerusalem* reminded them, without the comfort of confirming their political stances on anything, that *they* had betrayed themselves during the Holocaust by adhering to a "cosmopolitan" stance that was indeed insufficiently identified with the Jews suffering in Europe. They accused Arendt of what they feared about themselves. Hilberg was spared the bulk of their rage because he was like them: an American Jewish man, rather than a woman from Europe who had a more legitimate claim to Jewish heroism by virtue of her classical German training and her real scrape with danger in Nazi Germany. In the gender-distorted currency of the day, she was "more of a man" than any of them.

CHAPTER 6

Transition

THINKING ABOUT *EICHMANN*

Perhaps we understand something more of the world and ourselves through the discussion, actually an unmasking, of the hidden dimensions of gender and Judaism in the treatment of Hannah Arendt over *Eichmann in Jerusalem*. But do we learn anything about Hannah Arendt?

The tendency among contemporary scholars is to split Arendt's work into an "early" part, concerned with politics and action, and a "later" part, concerned with thinking and "the life of the mind," including her efforts to construct a theory of political ethics. I suggested earlier that to divide her work in this way is to distort it by inviting an equally skewed division into a "Jewish" Arendt—concerned with specifically Jewish politics, totalitarianism, the Holocaust—and a "universal" or "classical" Arendt—concerned with philosophy and European scholarship. Arendt herself made no such distinction between her early and later years. But she probably would agree with much of the contemporary scholarship that confirms the insularity of her scholarly work from the influences of her Jewishness. Contemporary feminists are less sanguine about her ability to escape the influences of gender in her scholarly work, but she undoubtedly would have been equally strident in affirming her immunity from that charge as well.[1]

Paradoxically, while Arendt is supposed to have escaped "contamination" from her Jewishness and her femaleness in her scholarship, recent assessments have attempted to demonstrate that she was unable to escape the influence of Heidegger. Her relationship with Heidegger is employed as a means of undermining her loyalty to the Jewish people: apparently her affair with the German philosopher nurtured an anti-Semitic streak in herself. The need to dissociate Arendt from her attachment to Judaism is extraordinary, and makes one wonder what is at stake for the scholars engaged in this effort.[2] That she had been attached to Heidegger in her student days, and managed to reach a reconciliation with him after the war's end is taken as evidence that she was "under his spell," that his teachings had a definitive influence upon her work, and that she somehow adapted to his anti-Semitism in her scholarly and/or public life. Such an approach is disrespectful of Arendt, reducing her to a woman so dependent upon her relationship with a teacher, lover, boyfriend—whatever the male influence is called—that she was unable to think for herself, or separate even a troubling romantic attachment from her scholarly and political convictions. The attempt to reduce Hannah Arendt to Heidegger's influence and then to use that to attack her loyalty to the Jewish people resembles the accusations of the New York Intellectuals that she was a "self-hating Jew," a projection perhaps of their own ambivalence toward Judaism.

While Arendt never denied that she was either Jewish or female, it is nonetheless troubling to acknowledge that Arendt herself would likely have denied the impact of both her Jewish and her female identity upon her scholarship. I have argued for the impact of gender upon the way her highest profile work dealing with a major Jewish issue was received. But we have yet to consider whether her Jewish identity or her female identity actually shaped the content of her scholarship itself. I shall leave other feminist scholars of Arendt to deal with the issue of what impact her gender may have had upon her scholarship,[3] and confine myself to the neglected issue of whether evidence of her Jewishness affected the scholarship that she, as well as the rest of the scholarly world, regarded as immune to the influences of ethnic or cultural identity.

I do not regard Hannah Arendt either as an unproblematic example of "Jewish consciousness" or, on the other hand, as suffering from an inadequate identification with the Jewish people. I see no evidence that she ever denied or insufficiently identified with the Jewish people as such; indeed, she identified herself specifically as a Jew before anything else, to both Jaspers and Gershom Scholem.[4] She was not a "self-hating Jew" who lusted after or identified with Martin Heidegger *because* he was an anti-Semite. I surmise that she suffered from conflicts about her own legitimacy as a scholar, for the reasons suggested at the close of the previous chapter: Jewish women did not have a history of being nurtured and supported as scholars by their own community, and Jewish scholars did not have a history of being nurtured and supported by non-Jewish academics or intellectuals throughout history. Hannah Arendt thus was the victim of "double jeopardy," similar to what black feminists describe as the problems of being both African American and female. In Arendt's case, she would have stood a better chance of being taken seriously as a scholar by the Jewish community had she been a man, but even a Jewish man who sought recognition from European scholars and academics would have had to prove that he was not "merely" a Jewish scholar. "Cosmopolitanism" was the response of the New York Jewish Intellectuals to the challenge to rise above their Jewish parochialism. Arendt was one step ahead of the American men in that she had actually received a classical European education under the tutelage of Heidegger and Jaspers. But both her Jewish and female identities hampered the world's acceptance of her legitimacy as a "universal" scholar, a neglect for which her unconventional career path provides evidence. Academia was another arena in which she "somehow didn't fit."

If Arendt was somewhat defensive about her legitimacy as a scholar, I suggest that avoidance of her Jewishness and femaleness, at least when it came to her scholarship, was largely a manifestation of that defensiveness. In the preceding chapters on race, gender, and their impact on the controversy over *Eichmann*, an important substantive issue of cultural pluralism today remained unexplored: What impact, if any, does cultural identity or gender have upon scholarship and upon one's ability to raise "universal" questions from a nontribal perspective? Arendt's professed separation of her scholarship from her Jewish identity reveals her conviction that being a Jew (or a woman) had a negligible impact on her scholarship. But if we look closely at her work, especially after *Eichmann in Jerusalem*, we find an approach to social and ethical questions more Jewish than has been acknowledged. Especially with regard to *The Life of the Mind*, the questions Arendt raises are profoundly "Jewish" in style and content. Her avoidance of Jewish scholarship as a potential avenue to addressing the issues she raised contributed to her less than satisfactory treatment of them in *Thinking*. Nonetheless, despite the fact that she sought answers to her questions in Greek, German, and Christian sources, completely overlooking Jewish scholarship, the solutions she proposes are more "Jewish" than she or anybody else has allowed—even though they are presented in the words of Socrates.

It goes against the grain of scholarly deference to Greek and European Christian influences to look for the Jewish influences in Arendt's most philosophical work. *Thinking*, the first volume of *The Life of the Mind*, is focused solely upon classical thought: Greek, Roman, Christian, German, and even, briefly, Chinese, but not Jewish sources on ethics or the nature of thought itself. Arendt wrote *Thinking* because she had been so profoundly misunderstood when she argued in *Eichmann* that the evil of the Holocaust was the likely result of a massive failure to think. *The Life of the Mind*, from this perspective, was a philosophical explanation and justification for Arendt's argument in Eichmann, as well as a response to the controversy. *Eichmann in Jerusalem* may be understood as an "act of thinking." Arendt had risked revealing herself in the process of thinking in that controversial book, and *The Life of the Mind* is a fullblown theoretical explanation of what she was thinking about, having been so profoundly misunderstood in *Eichmann*.

Unfortunately, the world was no more ready for Arendt than it had been for Socrates. In the response to *Eichmann*, Arendt was all but invited to drink the hemlock. Jaspers himself made the comparison between Socrates and Arendt in a letter of 25 July 1963 (L.332, p. 511), when he attempted to comfort Arendt as the furor over her Eichmann book battered her severely, and the lethal dimensions of what she yet faced became apparent: "Because you have touched an extremely sore spot for many people, shown their lives to be informed by a lie, they hate you. . . . What you have communicated was, though hidden in books, in large part already known. Your power as a writer—like Lessing's—has made it widely known now. Truth is beaten to death, as Kierkegaard said of Socrates and Jesus. Things haven't come to that and won't come to that" (512).[5]

What did Arendt mean when she wrote that a failure to think might be sufficient to cause political catastrophes? Arendt was not trying to establish a predictive link between thinking and the avoidance of evil. She was not so naive as to believe that all people would ever think (although she held it to be a theoretical possibility), or that evil could actually be eliminated from the world. Nonetheless, contemporary commentary on *Eichmann in Jerusalem* projects an instrumental mentality onto Arendt, presenting her concern as confined to criticism and judgment of Eichmann himself: "If only Eichmann had thought hard, he would not have committed his monstrous crimes."[6]

But I read *Eichmann in Jerusalem* as *itself* an example of Arendt thinking: it is an *act* of thinking, oriented toward the future, rather than an excoriation of the failures of the past. Arendt took upon herself the role of the Socratic gadfly, the electric ray, and shocked her readers by dismantling the pre-fabricated categories people believed permitted them to understand Eichmann. She dismantled the conventional judgment of Eichmann. She thought about and examined the unexamined assumption that evil deeds must be done by evil people. "Now that the devil himself was in the dock he turned out to be an 'idealist,' and though it may be hard to believe, it is quite possible that the one who sold his soul had also been an 'idealist'" (*Eichmann* 42). This sounds shocking, but in fact it is completely compatible with her general mistrust of doctrinaire thinkers. The *content* of one's ideas may or may not be dangerous, but more importantly, when one submerges oneself in an ideal one invariably stops thinking, or at best thinks primarily in terms of abstractions and generalities that isolate us from the plurality of the world. It would have been much easier to continue to think of Eichmann as exceptionally bad, hate filled, a racist, perhaps insane, perhaps very stupid. But Arendt found none of those traits in the man she saw on trial.

Rather than bringing an established perspective to the trial in Jerusalem, Arendt looked and listened, and allowed herself to be surprised by the unexpected. In her report she quoted people verbatim, seeming to assume that any thinking person would recognize the use of language she pointed to as instances of the inability to think and to question. Anyone who could refer to killing as "a medical matter" could not be thinking. On page 77 of the book, she simply quotes the language used by the Nazis to describe the murder of the Jews: "the final solution," "the final aim," a "stage," "physical extermination," "evacuate," and the forced emigration of Jews as a "solution" that was "obsolete." The language lures us into the false belief that rational thought processes are going on. She demands that we think about our own uncritical use of language. The technique she used in *Eichmann* is similar to her approach in "Lying in Politics," where she was deeply worried about President Johnson's and his advisers' departure from reality with regard to the Viet Nam War.[7]

Her method is an undoing, a deconstruction: using Eichmann and Zionism in the same sentence is profoundly unsettling, to say the least. Associating Leo Baeck with the Fuhrer was truly a boorish move, but probably the result of overzealousness rather than cold heartedness.[8] Barnouw uses the term to which Arendt made reference in her letter to Scholem, to describe her method of displaying verbatim quotations and allowing the reader to supply the analysis: *oratio obliqua*. "By using the narrative strategy of *oratio obliqua*, Arendt was able to let Eichmann's voice be heard *and* judged through the perspective provided by the context. It was an indirect way of judging, but a very effective one."[9] It may have been effective, but it also was misunderstood, as we have seen, at least by Scholem, Syrkin, and Abel, who failed to perceive any irony at all.

Arendt's exhortation to reject conventional wisdom and reified ideas, and to think critically about our use of language was directed more toward the "experts" of the present and future than toward Eichmann, for whom it was too late anyway. It is not that Arendt refused to say "Thou shalt not kill," but rather that she refused to say "Evil deeds are committed by evil people." If worldly evil is made possible by "nothing more" than the unwillingness or inability to think, then everybody who did not actually resist the Nazis is in some way guilty of contributing to the Holocaust. This places a harsh demand upon most of us, who prefer not to see the connection between passivity and responsibility. Arendt remarked in her reply to Scholem, "I understand that there was no possibility of resistance, but there existed the possibility of *doing nothing*. And in order to do nothing, one did not need to be a saint, one needed only to say: 'I am just a simple Jew, and I have no desire to play any other role.'"[10] This, she implied, would have been a more effective and responsible stance for Leo Baeck to have assumed.

Eichmann in Jerusalem was intended to arouse people who smugly believed they knew exactly how to understand Eichmann and his kind. It was intended to unfreeze those frozen interpretations about the nature of evil without offering a comfortable category into which Eichmann and other perpetrators of political evil would fit. This met with a response that was not so different from the one that Socrates received at the hands of the respectable Athenians.

Thinking and "Thinking and Moral Considerations," the essay that preceded and in a sense encapsulated it, may from this perspective be understood as elaborations of what Arendt had intended in *Eichmann*. Thinking must be available to everybody, and not the privilege (or burden) of a select few; it must avoid offering a doctrine, must "unfreeze" existing categories and dogmas. "It is in its nature to undo, unfreeze as it were, what language, the medium of thinking, has frozen into thought—words (concepts, sentences, definitions, doctrines)"

("Thinking and Moral Considerations" 434). "The consequence of this peculiarity is that thinking inevitably has a destructive, undermining effect on all established criteria, values, measurements for good and evil" (434). Arendt utilizes the life of Socrates, and his own explanation of what he thought he was doing in the *Apology* when he was on trial for his life, to help her describe the task of thinking.[11] *The Life of the Mind* is Arendt's *Apology*.[12]

THE POLITICAL CONSEQUENCES OF THINKING

Plato's *Apology* is, of course, no apology at all. Rather, it is a magnificent portrayal of Socrates in a controlled rage at the uncomprehending respectable citizens who are about to send him to his death for the crime of thinking. Socrates claims to have "not the slightest skill as a speaker—unless, of course, by a skillful speaker they mean one who speaks the truth."[13] The fact that he claims to have spent his life speaking the truth without the skills of a rhetorician has offended some people so profoundly that he is on trial for his life. Socrates guesses that his difficult questions upset people by undermining their confidence in what they believe. His demand that they think makes them nervous and ultimately angry at him. His assault on their complacency is itself a description of thinking and its dangers when others respond to the challenge to think. It is also a description of Arendt's "crime" in writing *Eichmann in Jerusalem*.

Socrates was told that the Oracle of Delphi had declared him the wisest man in the world. Since he did not experience himself as wise he sought to confirm the truth of the Oracle's proclamation by interviewing men with reputations for wisdom: politicians, poets, skilled craftsmen. His discovery: "When I began to try to show him [the politician] that he only thought he was wise and was not really so, my efforts were resented both by him and by many of the other people present. However, I reflected as I walked away: 'Well I am certainly wiser than this man. It is only too likely that neither of us has any knowledge to boast of; but he thinks he knows something which he does not know, whereas I am quite conscious of my ignorance. At any rate, it seems that I am wiser than he is to this small extent, that I do not think that I know what I do not know'" (p. 50, 21b–d).

As he interviewed the local sages Socrates discovered that ordinary folk are probably more perceptive than the experts. "People with the greatest reputations were almost entirely deficient, while others who were supposed to be their inferiors were much better qualified in practical intelligence" (51). Of the poets: "It is hardly an exaggeration to say that any of the bystanders could have explained those poems better than their actual authors" (51). Even the craftsmen he interviewed, although understanding the technical aspects of their respective trades, were actually blinded by their limited expertise. "On the strength of their technical proficiency they claimed a perfect understanding of every other subject, however important; and I felt that this error more than outweighed their positive wisdom" (52).

The first step in achieving wisdom, then, is the acknowledgment that one has something left to learn. Those who live with the conceit that they know something—anything—fully, are the biggest fools. But of course they are also likely to be the most influential men in politics, and so they are the most dangerous to attempt to instruct. Nevertheless, Socrates claims that his life would be barren unless he continued to play this dangerous game of thinking and demanding the same of others. He proclaims that he will teach *anybody* to raise the hard questions—without fee—but that he has nothing of substance to teach. He teaches *how* to think—he teaches "method"—but there is no gratifying product as reward for the risk taking. As a result of this conventionally unrewarding endeavor, Socrates notes, "I have incurred a great deal of bitter hostility; and this is what will bring about my destruction, if anything does; not Meletus nor Antyus, but the slander and jealousy of a very large section of the people" (59).

When the jury decides for the death penalty, Socrates retorts, "It is not a lack of arguments that has caused my condemnation, but a lack of effrontery and impudence, and the fact that I have refused to address you in the way which would give you most pleasure" (74), in the posture of a supplicant before them. Socrates is condemned to death for challenging people to think, and for addressing them in terms that they are not prepared to hear. Both the tone and the content of his message make people uncomfortable. Thinking unfreezes frozen concepts, unsettles complacent truths, wakens the mind from lazy slumber. Many would prefer to be left sleeping. Still others sleep under the illusion that they are awake. Jaspers describes Socrates' "crime" in terms which may be applied to that of Arendt.

> The people confused the man who had transcended Sophism with Sophism itself. For the new method by which he refuted it was intolerable. Socrates questioned unremittingly; he drove his listeners to the basic problems of man, but did not solve them. Confusion, a consciousness of inferiority, and the demands he raised created anger and hatred.[14]

ARENDT AS JEWISH GADFLY

I have likened Hannah Arendt to a Socratic gadfly in *Eichmann in Jerusalem* and to Socrates once again with my statement that *The Life of the Mind* is Hannah Arendt's *Apology*. What has happened to the Jewish woman I promised to present? Has she disappeared again? The Socratic analogy is one way of interpreting what happened to Arendt in the Eichmann controversy. Karl Jaspers lovingly offered her that image. I believe there are some good reasons why Arendt could avail herself of the Socratic analogy. Her report on Eichmann was provocative and disturbing. It *was* a challenge to think, and portions of her audience were quite willing to slaughter her for it. But *Eichmann in Jerusalem* was *also* a work of astonishing political naivete. Far from intending that statement to be an incrimination of Arendt, I believe that in general her naivete empowered her work, gave her the freedom to say what she believed without being shackled to conventional ideas. But in *Eichmann,* she rared back and let loose with a powerful intellectual and ethical challenge, apparently oblivious to the fact that her scholarly Jewish audience did not regard her as a Greek, or even a German male, and therefore was loathe to accept her challenge. She was received as a *Jewish Woman* writing about things that were inappropriate for her to address, especially in public. She did not perceive these facets of her identity as problematic to the way her writing was received, and therein lay her naivete.

Arendt's critics did not accuse her of being a Socratic gadfly. That would have been a remarkable compliment coming from Jewish and non-Jewish detractors alike. Indeed, Jaspers offered her that as solace in a letter intended to soothe her as the attacks over *Eichmann* multiplied. Instead, she was accused of talking out of turn, of indiscretion. The explicit rationale about "betrayal of the Jewish people" was linked to the charge that she had been tasteless, had embarrassed the Jews by exposing "private" Jewish matters before a "public" (gentile) audience. For example, Irving Howe's lament in *Commentary* that *The New Yorker* does not publish rebuttals, and that Arendt's report would thus be "elevated" in the minds of the "lowbrows" who read the magazine to the stature of "literature," can be viewed as an expression of fear that what she wrote would be read as authoritative by non-Jews and nonintellectuals.

> Hundreds of thousands of good middle-class Americans will have learned from those articles that the Jewish leadership in Europe was cowardly, inept, and even collaborationist; that the Jewish community helped the Nazis achieve their goal of racial genocide; and that if the Jews had not "cooperated" with the Nazis, fewer than five to six million Jews would have been killed. No small matter: and you will forgive some of us if we react strongly to this charge.... A terrific piece, a great story: you don't argue with literature.[15]

This charge of indiscretion from members of the Jewish community resounds with the ambivalence of cultured, educated, "assimilated" Jews when one of their number behaves before non-Jews in a manner deemed "too Jewish." Even Scholem, a Zionist emigre to Israel who did not believe assimilation was possible, feared not only that Arendt had betrayed the Jewish community, but that she had acted in a way unfit for a Christian audience. "Shah! Not in front of the Goyim!" underlies his message to Arendt.

Assimilated Jews were themselves aware of the importance of keeping their Jewish lives apart. "A man in the street and a Jew at home" was the catch phrase that captured the demands upon the Jewish European bourgeois. Arendt was well aware of "the rule," and made reference to it in her discussion of anti-Semitism in *The Origins of Totalitarianism*. Once again, what usually goes unrecognized is how gendered is the prescription. Of course, it says explicitly "a *man* in the street," suggesting that Jewish women were not expected to make public appearances. But beyond that, as Marion Kaplan explains, Jewish women were assigned the role of maintaining the Jewishness of the home as a refuge for the men in the street.

John Murray Cuddihy discusses this cultural (but not the gendered) division in *The Ordeal of Civility*.[16] He argues that assimilation of the Jews to gentile society called for "the bifurcation of private affect from public demeanor."[17] This demanded a difficult transition from the lack of differentiation between private and public in the ghettos of Eastern Europe and the immigrant-settled slums of Lower East Side Manhattan, to the civility and manners, and the differentiation between manners and morals, of European and American Christianity. "Jewish Emancipation involved Jews in collision with the differentiations of Western society. The differentiations most foreign to the shtetl subculture of *Yiddishkeit* were those of public from private behavior and of manners from morals. Jews were being asked, in effect, to become bourgeois, and to become bourgeois quickly." The clash between shtetl Jews and the Protestant bourgeoisie can be characterized by the familiarity and passion of Jewish ghetto life (perceived as plain crudeness by Christians) versus the refinement of manners of the dominant Christian culture. "'Niceness' is as good a name as any for the informally yet pervasively institutionalized civility expected. . . . Intensity, fanaticism, inwardness—too much of *anything*, in fact—is unseemly and bids fair to destroy the fragile solidarity of the surface we call civility" (Cuddihy 14).

Cuddihy's description of the repression of passion and intensity needed to assimilate to Christian culture echoes Mosse's description of Germanic (and English) masculinity at the turn of the century. Cuddihy overlooks gender in his description of the pathway to assimilation of European and American Jews, but we can supply the missing dimension in a manner compatible with Marion Kaplan's reading of the rise of the Jewish middle class if we remember that Jewish women were expected to remain out of public life. Acquiring "gentility" was a male project in the sense that it was the men who attempted to unlearn their Jewish passion and "crudeness" publicly. According to Kaplan, while Jewish middle-class women also sought to run a "respectable" (if Kosher) bourgeois household, their passion and affectionate demonstrativeness, at least for their children, was a well-known trait, sometimes displayed publicly to the embarrassment or envy of gentile witnesses.

By all accounts of their penchant for inhouse rivalries and talent for vociferous political disputes, however, both the New York Intellectuals and the Israelis failed in the task of leaving their passion behind. This may have been the result of their ascent from the working classes, and their unfamiliarity with assimilated Jewish bourgeois mores. For them, as we have seen, masculine assimilation was associated not so much with repression of emotion as such, as with scholarly objectivity in the case of the Americans, and militancy and physical prowess on the part of the Israelis. Nonetheless, elements of Cuddihy's description of the need for circumspection and indirectness seem to explain the accusation that Arendt had defied the standards of good taste as well as community loyalty with her outspoken criticism of European and Israeli Jewish men during the Holocaust.

Arendt defended herself by claiming that far from being guilty of an unseemly display of passion in public, *she* was adhering to a dignified scholarly objectivity. That is, she accepted the assimilationist bifurcation of public from private life, insisting that she had been impartial, rather than emotional in her assessment of the Eichmann trial. She refused, she insisted, to reveal any engaged partiality in her work, because she was fully aware of "what happens when emotions are displayed in public and become a factor in political affairs."[18] Ironically, then, both Arendt and Scholem accused each other of acting "too Jewish" in public: he told her she should have been more circumspect in criticizing Jews, and she in turn claimed that she would not sacrifice her scholarly perspective to tribal loyalty. She had also advocated a Jewish army be formed to join the fight against Hitler, thereby attaching herself to both the American and the Israeli masculine assimilationist postures. In "usurping" the masculine assimilationist stands of both the New Yorkers and the Zionists, Arendt provided fuel for the unlikely convergence of their opinions of her work.

But the fury over her report on Eichmann was also fueled by an unacknowledged gender factor: as a woman who was making a "cosmopolitan" or universalist argument about the Nazis, Arendt usurped the New York Jews' masculine stance. As a woman discussing the less than "heroic" behavior of the Israeli Zionists, she undermined the Israeli's claim to masculinity as well. Arendt was assuming the assimilated stance of the Jewish men: scholarly and "cosmopolitan." She might as well have been cross dressing. Jewish assimilation is so profoundly a male project that when Arendt was accused of not writing from a Jewish perspective, or of betraying the Jewish people, the hidden message was really, "Stop acting like a Jewish *man* publicly: act more like a Jewish woman!" which was tantamount to bellowing at her, "Be silent!"

There was thus no way for Hannah Arendt publicly to identify with the Jewish people, as was being demanded of her, without relinquishing either her independent scholarly stance—that is, her ability to simply "think what we are doing"—or relinquishing her Jewish womanhood. Her very presence embodied the deconstruction of accepted categories: a Jewish woman scholar acting publicly, and claiming to speak from a universalist standpoint. No wonder her subsequent work, her response to the *Eichmann* controversy in *The Life of the Mind* , was concerned with dismantling frozen categories. In her work on thinking, she took the stance that thinking has no final product, is an activity that prevents ideas from becoming reified into a static body of rules or ethics, that thinking will always be a challenge to society because it questions all conventional wisdom. Socrates was a natural spokesman for that position. Who would listen to such thought coming directly from the mouth (or typewriter) of a Jewish woman? With Socrates as front man, Arendt might get people to stop and think, which was also the substantive message of her life's final project.

Even less acknowledged than Arendt's undoubtedly unconscious tactic of putting her ideas into the mouth of Socrates himself, was another dimension that also went unrecognized by both Arendt and other contemporary scholars: how very Jewish it was to make the dismantling of accepted doctrine and conventional wisdom the core of her theory about the relationship between thinking and preventing worldly evil. Nothing could be more Jewish than a philosophy based upon the smashing of idols, even idols that take the form of reified, rigid ideas. In the chapters that follow I shall present Arendt's philosophy as an example of Jewish thinking, unacknowledged as Jewish either by herself or her critics and admirers. The first step is to define, to the extent that it is possible, the nature of Jewish thinking.

CHAPTER 7

Biblical and Rabbinic Approaches to Thinking

THINKING LIKE A JEW

That Hannah Arendt was a Jewish woman is significant, both politically and intellectually. While descriptions of group membership, labels of religion, ethnicity, gender, and race can be used for racist purposes, to reduce people to stereotypes and dismiss them, the influence of identity upon one's work and its reception cannot be ignored. Searching for the role played by Arendt's religion and gender does not reflect the impulse to "reduce" her to a Jewish woman, with the implicit assumption that if we know that much, we know all we need to about her. Rather, the impulse is the reverse: can we know enough about her work and its meaning if we insist that her Judaism had nothing significant to contribute to what she wrote?

The controversy generated over *Eichmann* was influenced by Judaism and gender, however unacknowledged by all concerned. The controversy prompted Arendt to investigate the relationship between thinking and political action, a project which was both a continuation of her argument in *Eichmann in Jerusalem*, and an emphatic statement that she would continue both to *think* and to insist that thinking and its absence bore worldly consequences, as the response to her thinking on Eichmann had demonstrated.

Paradoxically, although her detractors accused her of "not thinking like a Jew," even while she herself insisted that "thinking" could not be specifically "Jewish," she *did* "think like a Jew" more than she or anybody else would admit. In this and the chapter that follows, we shall consider what "thinking like a Jew" might mean.

What can it mean to "think like a Jew"?[1] In our age of multicultural awareness, it may seem emotionally liberating to acknowledge the influence of history and identity upon creative work. However, labeling a type of thinking "Jewish" also has a recent history of anti-Semitism, enough to make many Jews wary of the enterprise. Hitler, of course, used the label "Jewish" as a modifier signifying "debased": rationale for genocide. Arendt and Jews of her generation knew all too well that being labeled a "Jewish" anything, thinker included, was potentially lethal. How can I, more than half a century after the Holocaust, and lacking direct experience of the most extensive display of anti-Semitism in history, now use the term *Jewish thinking* as a way of understanding, rather than circumscribing or demeaning, the significance of Arendt's scholarship?

Beyond the political danger of typologizing racial, ethnic, religious, or gendered characteristics, the attempt to render in worldly terms approaches to truth and knowledge that stem from a religious outlook may be inherently problematic. Contemporary writers who describe a Hebrew style of thinking often emphasize our inherent deference to the Greek claims to philosophy and epistemology: as secularly educated Westerners, our unconscious approach to understanding Hebrew thought may be "Greek." We are tempted, almost unconsciously, to *translate* a Hebrew approach to truth, and to an ethic understood by Jews as process, into the "Western" or "classical" tradition. This may be an epistemologically impossible undertaking, which can succeed only by misrepresenting the religious character of "Jewish" thinking.

Further aggravating the difficulties of comparing religious thought to philosophy, literature, or history in an effort to compare "styles" of thinking, is the variety of styles that have characterized Jewish religious thought itself. This should come as no surprise, given the extraordinary length of Jewish history. Even deprived of the continuous physical availability of a homeland, the history of the Jewish people spans over four thousand continuous years, grounded on one central text, which has, in turn, spawned additional literature and commentary. Any tradition spanning four millennia would of necessity have had to sustain changes in response to historical developments, and to exhibit flexibility in order to survive.

We can anticipate a problem in defining not only "Jewish thinking" but also in defining who is a Jew, at least in the postenlightenment age when there are three, probably four major religious interpretations of Judaism (Orthodox, Conservative, Reform, and Reconstructionist), and where many Jews do not practice their religion at all, and yet still consider themselves Jewish. A number of scholars, including Hannah Arendt, have noted the modern phenomenon of the secular Jew, and it describes many of the labor Zionists, who are stridently Jewish, but not religious in an orthodox fashion.[2] Indeed, difficulties in Israel from its inception to the present-day conflict over a peace treaty with the Palestinian Arabs, involve severe tensions between secular Zionists and orthodox Jews in Israel.

Yosef Hayim Yerushalmi offers a description of the secular Jew in his study of *Freud's Moses*:

> The Psychological [i.e. Secular] Jew seems, at least to the outsider, devoid of all but the most vestigial content; it has become almost pure subjectivity. Content is replaced by character. Alienated from classical Jewish texts, Psychological Jews tend to insist on inalienable Jewish traits. Intellectuality and independence of mind, the highest ethical and moral standards, concern for social justice, tenacity in the face of persecution—these are among the qualities they will claim, if called upon, as quintessentially Jewish.[3]

In his introduction to Yerushalmi's monograph, *Zakhor*, on the relationship between historiography and Jewish memory, Harold Bloom grapples with the question of who is a "Jewish" writer. He suggests that there may be a reciprocal relationship between who is defined as a "Jewish writer" and how "Jewish writing" is defined: "Kafka and Freud are so strong and so Jewish that we redefine the Jewish on their basis, but what is it about them that is Jewish?"[4] "You cannot decide whether modern Jewish writing possesses common elements without defining the undecidable issue of who is or is not Jewish. Is Proust somehow a Jewish writer? If he was, then what about Montaigne? Clearly Jewish ancestry is hardly in itself a sufficient cause of Jewish writing, nor can we associate Jewish imagination with normative Judaism" (*Zakhor* xxii).

Bloom defers to "common consent" as a means of defining a Jew and asserts that Kafka and Freud are probably regarded as "the" Jewish writers of the modern age. These are hardly the most obvious choices, and the definition of "common consent" remains remarkably undefined. Bloom ultimately imposes his own definition that the essence of being a Jewish writer involves an obsession with interpretation. Taking his cue from the omnipresent New York bus and subway billboards for Levy's Rye Bread, Bloom cheerfully observes, "You don't have to be Jewish to be a compulsive interpreter, but, of course, it helps" (*Zakhor* xxiii). With regard to Kafka and Freud,

> I think that finally their Jewishness consists in their intense obsession with interpretation, as such. All Jewish writing tends to be outrageously interpretive, so that the Nietzschean question applies poorly to them—'Who is the interpreter, and what power does he seek to gain over the text?'" (*Zakhor* xxiii)

According to Bloom's perspective, Jewish writing is characterized by a dialogical stance, based upon this will to interpret, to engage in dialogue with a text. But the basic text for Jewish writers, argues Bloom, is always the Bible. The suggestion is that the centrality of the Bible in Jewish life, or in the Jewish unconscious, fuels the passion for writing and interpretation, even for "secular," nonreligious Jews. The Bible is a template for every other text. Biblical scholars argue that the Jewish Text possesses certain features that make it distinct among religious texts.

THE BIBLE

The literature on Biblical Narrative, as well as on the legal and poetic aspects of the Bible, is enormous, too extensive to address in any detail here. Still, there are stylistic traits that may be identified as characteristic. When we refer to "Jewish thinking," chances are that Talmudic and Midrashic thought is what we have in mind as the foundation and model. But the Talmud and Midrash are intimately connected to, inseparable and indeed sometimes indistinguishable from, the Bible.[5]

A unique characteristic of the Jewish Bible is its extremely spare style, referred to by one scholar as its "spare and almost calligraphic description of events."[6] Barry Holtz remarks, "The Bible is loathe to tell us the motivations, feelings or thoughts of characters. Rarely giving us descriptive details either of people or places, it is composed in a stark, uncompromising style" (Holtz 180). Action is conveyed with an absolute minimum of embellishment, necessitating many inferences through the dialogue that comprises much of the text. Yet it is extremely rare that more than two people converse at one time, and there is no identified narrator, attributed author, redactor, or patron. The Bible is historically organized, in a basically linear fashion, although there are interludes interjected into many stories that are out of chronological sequence. And, remarkably, the Jewish Bible does not sermonize: "It allows its messages to arise from silences in the narrative. In a sense it is *weighing* messages, in that discordant voices in the tradition are allowed silently to clash, even as the narrative plunges inexorably forward" (Holtz 63). It is almost as though the Bible were written in order to be interpreted. Its richness is the result of its spareness, of its lack of explanation or excuse for contradictions and plural accounts of the same event. It is both straightforward and enigmatic: an invitation to thought, dialogue, and interpretation. The Hebrew Bible was the first major book among ancient peoples to be written in prose. "It is peculiar, and culturally significant, that among ancient peoples only Israel should have chosen to cast its sacred national traditions in prose."[7] Robert Alter suggests that there must be significance to this. The two innovations that result from this style are the predominance of dialogue as the primary means of conveying the story, and the "deliberate avoidance of epic." Epic poetry was associated with paganism and polytheism, and the spurning of the epic form was regarded as necessary for conveying the monotheism of Jewish history.

Narrative prose, the new format or genre, was compatible with the monotheism of Jewish religion. It was appropriate to the invisibility of the Jewish God, as well as the indeterminacy, or ineffability of both the shape of that God and God's messages, meaning, and morality.

> Meaning, perhaps for the first time in narrative literature, was conceived as a *process*, requiring continual revision—both in the ordinary sense and in the etymological sense of seeing—again—continual suspension of judgment, weighing of multiple possibilities, brooding over gaps in information provided. (Alter 12)

I have written elsewhere that there exists a Biblical Dialectic, contradictions in the text, remaining intact, to be struggled with by the reader.[8] Some of the more obvious moments are discussed at the end of chapter 8 (pp. 208 ff.). Biblical scholars have noted tension or conflict in the text in the form of, for example, conflicting renderings of the covenant with Israel: is it "unconditional," or "conditional"? Both aspects seem to be in evidence in the story of Abraham in Genesis 15 and 17. Is Israel's tenure in the promised land contingent upon good behavior, as it were, upon the Jews successfully fulfilling God's commandments to the letter? or is it unconditional, bequeathed "for an everlasting possession"? Why two apparently contradictory versions of God's covenant with Abraham, especially in such close proximity in the text as to be virtually impossible to overlook? Joel Rosenberg suggests, "Obviously they represent a polarity that lies at the heart of ancient Israelite history. . . . both ideologies are skillfully interwoven and alternate almost in the fashion of a Sonata. . . . If one believes moral struggle to be everlasting, then the two covenants are not in contradiction" (Holtz 67).

The existence of dual and often apparently contradictory versions of accounts of events in the Bible, as well as the double conception of covenant, is so prevalent that the serious reader comes to expect it. It is undoubtedly the result of the extreme age of the Bible and the fact that it was written (or compiled, since the orthodox believe that the entire Bible was actually dictated by God) by multiple authors, at different times. Differing versions of stories were included side by side, with no effort made to "clean up" discrepancies or edit out inconsistencies. The conflicts themselves were assumed to have significance, and the Rabbis set about the task of deriving meaning from the ambiguities and inconsistencies. What a modern reader would regard as historical and literary contradictions became the raw material for Talmudic study.

TALMUD

The Torah, sacred core of Jewish worship, is the five books of Moses, which are traditionally assumed to have been dictated by God to Moses on Mount Sinai. The Torah itself has the power of revelation, coming directly from God. Torah scrolls are inscribed by hand according to ancient methods. The scrolls are clothed in velvet and silver in Western synagogues (different cultures have different specific customs, but the scrolls are always protected in some decorous and loving manner) and kept in a special "arc" in the synagogue, taken out each Sabbath according to ritual. A portion of the Torah is read aloud before the congregation each week, and in some congregations the service also includes a short interpretative talk, or *drash*, given by the rabbi or an adult member of the congregation. Congregants read the Torah portion silently in their Bibles as it is read aloud from the scroll to all. The form of the Jewish Sabbath service reenacts the emergence of the "oral tradition" some 2500 years ago.

The early rabbinic interpretations, which are now referred to as the "Oral Tradition," emerged after the destruction of the first temple in Jerusalem in 586 B.C.E., although its compilation in the Talmud wasn't "closed" until the fifth century, nearly one thousand years later. A scholar named Ezra returned from exile in Babylon, called a convocation of the Jewish people in 444 b.c.e., and read the Torah aloud. As he read, others, his followers, the *soferim* ("bookmen," "students," "scribes") offered interpretation, which is referred to as "giving the sense" of the Torah. The exegesis of Scripture is referred to as *drash* in Hebrew, and means "interpretation" or "translation." It is the basis for the word *Midrash*, and had as its purpose originally the application of Torah to everyday life. That early moment of public discussion and interpretation marks the moment when the Torah was officially accepted as the center of Jewish life. The sanctification of Torah was thus inseparably linked to a moment of interpretation, and also reflected the political necessity of keeping the Jewish people together when their physical center had been destroyed.[9] For several centuries there was only this oral tradition, of discussion, debate, and interpretation of God's Torah carried on among educated rabbis.

The impulse to record the teachings was born of political necessity, for the sake of the survival of the Jewish people after the second destruction of the Jerusalem temple in 70 A.D. But codifying the teachings of the rabbis gave rise to questions about whether what was being written down carried the same weight as the Torah, was equally the work of God, with the same power of revelation. Perhaps the inscribed teachings of the early rabbis was "only" the work of men, even if those men were revered. The men engaged in actually recording the oral tradition, insisted that they were inscribing God's words, not adding their own. God on Sinai had actually spoken everything that would become part of the oral tradition, knowing that it would take millennia for all of God's teachings to be articulated and put to use in the world. That is, the rabbinic interpretation of God's word was also part of God's word.[10]

Whether inspired by God or men, what emerged was the "written Torah," which was really the Torah itself (which had always been "written"), plus the Rabbinic commentary, newly committed to text. Rabbi Akiba, an early Jewish martyr, was one of the first to compile fragments of the Oral Torah into a written code during the second century. This code marks the initiation of the Talmudic tradition and is referred to as the Mishnah ("Recitation," or "Recapitulation") of the Oral Torah. The Mishnah is the core document of the Talmudic tradition. It is in part a code of Jewish law, rules for daily life extracted from the text of the Bible. But legal disputes are unresolved and liberally sprinkled with nonlegal materials, including stories and interpretations of Scripture. It has been referred to as "the earliest teaching text, the oldest curriculum of Jewish learning in the world today" (Holtz 131).

The Mishnah became the basis for further study, which continued to elaborate, expand, apply its teachings to specific situations, and even contradict the earlier teachings, while still retaining a sense of the sacredness of the earliest Mishnah commentary. Study sessions in which the commentary was commented upon took place in the homes of the rabbis engaged in the study. The Rabbis who inscribed the Mishnah claimed that the laws of the Mishnah, like the Torah itself, were revealed by God to Moses on Sinai. A contemporary political interpretation of what appears to be the willful muddling of the distinction between the word of God and the words of the Rabbis, might lead us to see that in a time of acute political crisis, with the Temple destroyed and the diaspora upon them, the Rabbis, perhaps desperately, "borrowed" the authority of God and Moses, to enhance their own authority, in an effort to forge a bond capable of keeping the Jewish people faithful when it seemed they would be scattered before the wind. From a certain perspective, it worked.

Not only is the boundary between Torah and Talmud indistinct, but also in a sense that is difficult for a modern reader to understand, the boundary between the written Torah and the world itself is indistinct. Susan Handelman remarks, "Far from being a physical book, the Torah, in the Rabbinic view, is a blueprint of creation and, therefore, there is a direct correlation between the world and Torah. The Torah is not seen as speculation *about* the world, but part of its very essence. Where ought one look to fathom the secrets of creation, to comprehend the laws of nature? To the Text.... While Torah is considered to be a blueprint of the universe, it is also a guide to the most minute and mundane details of daily life."[11]

The sense that to the Talmudic Rabbis, Torah is not really a "physical" book, is vividly conveyed in Rabbi Hanina ben

Tradyon's vision as he was being burned alive by Roman soldiers who had wrapped him in a Torah before lighting the flame.

> Rabbi Hanina ben Tradyon also chose to teach Torah in public in spite of the decree, holding a Sefer Torah in his arms. After his capture they wrapped him in a Sefer Torah and piled branches about him, lit them, and placed wet wool over his heart so that he would not die quickly. He told his disciples what he saw: The parchment is burning, but the letters are flying free![12]

The cumulative and dialogical structure of Talmudic thought, which is what makes its study so daunting, is clearly in evidence in the very composition of a page of text, as well as the method of study. The oldest moments of the Mishnah, the earliest stages of the conversation, are set in the *middle* of the page, in large type. Talmudic discussion, or *Gemara*, continues in type set around the Mishnah, with many digressions until the next Mishnah is printed, and is in turn responded to. Medieval Talmudists, most notably Rashi, were later added to the dialogue.

A sort of pluralist reading of the Talmud was in this way encouraged—indeed demanded, if one were to proceed through the text. Each page calls for a dialogical reading.

From this perspective, it is clear that the Talmud both is and is not a "lawbook." Many aspects of Jewish "law" are virtually unenforceable: Who really knows which kitchens in a given community are kosher, or which members of that community secretly violate the Sabbath? Furthermore, while the Talmud provides the basis for discussion and decision about the law, "rulings are always part of an ongoing process, which needs to be determined according to individual instances."[13]

What may, to contemporary Western readers, appear to be an invitation to chaos rather than order, is in fact a remarkably open system, based upon interpretations organized horizontally, through history, rather than vertically. Even historical time is given no automatic deference: earlier and later interpretations are potentially equally valid. What appears to be disorganization, then, really resembles more the "disorganization" of democracy: a plurality of responsible voices, each qualified by virtue of practice, experience, and assumed responsibility to render judgment worthy of serious consideration. Placing value on a plurality of voices may not be the most efficient way to organize a community, but it is certainly by definition less authoritarian than other possible systems. "In the Jewish view, every particular had equal status with every other: the literal had as much importance as the spiritual; there was no hierarchy of interpretation. Interpretation was a horizontal process, where many meanings simultaneously existed together, and there could be no end to the law."[14]

The technique for studying Talmud is itself open-ended and dialogical. The Talmud is rarely "read" in a solitary manner, as other texts are. Rather, it is studied as active dialogue with a partner. Goldenberg offers a description of the typical Yeshiva.

> There, students study in pairs, reading every word of the text out loud, never going on to the next phrase until they have exhausted the meaning of the one under discussion. The Talmud itself, after all, originated as oral discussion, and still has the form of an elaborate conversation carried on over centuries. Its standard way of citing an opinion is "Rabbi X says ..."; later generations of rabbinic disciples listened to Rabbis and answered back. This mode of study, called in Aramaic havrata ("fellowship"), turns text study into dialogue and makes books into tools for overcoming, not strengthening, isolation. It makes the tradition of rabbinic learning a powerful source of community cohesion, a source of speech rather than silence. This activity was usually called not "study" but "learning" and in every Jewish community an invitation to fellowship could take the form of the proposal "let's learn together." The life of the mind and the life of society were thus made one. (Holtz 169)

This ability to fuse the life of the mind with the life of the community resembles what Hannah Arendt was searching for in *The Life of the Mind*, as we shall see later on. Still, let us not be overcome by this rather romantic vision of community life and learning. Perhaps what is described is no more than a cooperative effort at self-indoctrination? Then the "life of the mind" would hardly be as vital as it seemed at first glance.

One important aspect of Jewish tradition militates against uncritical dogma at the heart of Jewish religious thought and practice: there is tension built into the very act of codifying the Bible. The Talmud itself reflects a spirit of tension and self-criticism. Although codifying the Oral Torah after the destruction of the second temple in Jerusalem was necessary if the Jewish people were to survive, there were, nonetheless, profound objections to setting the teachings of the rabbis to text, precisely because the indeterminacy of dialogue was valued, while the possibility of dogma in written text was worrisome.

> The same centuries that saw the composition of these great codes also saw unending *opposition* to the activity they reflect. There has always been a fear among rabbis that codifying presented a double threat to the authentic tradition: it could distract people from studying the *really* important texts (principally the Talmud), and a truly authoritative code might well freeze the law in a way even the most tradition-minded leaders did not wish to see. (Holtz 163)

Such fears about the consequences of codifying ethical dialogue, and worry over providing too easily accessible a set of rules, should dispel initial concerns about a doctrinaire approach to ethics in early Judaism. Conflict, dialogue, and interpretation are built into the structure and substance of Jewish ethical thought. This describes a central concern of Hannah Arendt's search for a worldly philosophy. She was profoundly apprehensive about the consequences of ethical or philosophical codes and their penchant for closing down challenge and discussion.

In spite of its centrality, both spiritually and intellectually, and in spite of its sacred status, the Talmud as a text is "unfinished." It demands dialogue, interpretation, and application to contemporary situations if it is to be fully engaged. It is both a practical guide for living and a way of establishing contact and continuity with the holiest, most spiritual aspects of Judaism. The Talmudic debates and dialogues over interpreting the Torah are seldom resolved with any finality, and one can imagine that such indecisiveness can be extremely frustrating when its job seemed to be the application of Biblical law to everyday life. But the primary purpose of the Talmud was not to determine the law. "The Talmud is a scholastic text. Its chief purpose is to preserve the record of earlier generations studying their own traditions and provide materials for later generations wishing to do the same. It is a book produced by and for people whose highest value was the life of study" (Holtz 156). The ultimate uncertainty of the Talmud is captured in the following description: "It is rich with stories that may—or may not—reflect the way certain events happened, and it is full of legal discussions that may—or may not—report the actual content of early rabbinic scholarly certainty. Everything is fascinating, everything is potentially an open window on the past, but nothing can be trusted" (Holtz 157).

MIDRASH

From a certain perspective, the Talmud, with all its uncertainty, inconclusiveness, and intensity, *is* the core of Jewish thinking. Its approach to the truth of the Biblical text, however, is neither straightforward reverence nor obedience. The Talmud utilizes a dialogical, dialectical method, challenging and interpreting every mark in the Torah, *even while* regarding it as perfect, sacred, and coming directly from God. The completeness and perfection are simply unabsorbable by human beings as such and so we have to work toward an always incomplete and imperfect understanding of God's perfection *through* engaging in dialogue, questioning, challenging, and interpreting the Bible.

Still, in the more than 1500 years since its compilation, there have been other key moments and important texts to represent Jewish thought. After the Talmud came Midrash: later interpretations of Torah and Talmud in the forms of sermons and stories, which may be regarded as elaborations of the sparseness of the Biblical text itself. "Midrash comes to fill in the gaps, to tell us the details that the Bible teasingly leaves out.... Midrash attempts to elucidate confusions and harmonize seeming contradictions" (Holtz 180).

The Midrashim are not regarded as any more conclusive than the Talmudic commentary, and serve equally as invitations to further dialogue. In fact, Midrash, of all the rabbinic commentary, is probably the most recognizable style to a contemporary reader. It most resembles a literary interpretation of the Bible as text. However, the interpretations themselves are then regarded as Biblical literature, read as such, and further commented upon. The two major styles of Midrashim are *halakhic*, and *aggadic*: legal commentary, and narrative sermonizing, respectively. Once again the border is not finite, and Holtz reminds us, "It should be obvious that these are rather artificial distinctions and terms. In fact, there is very little in Jewish literature which is either pure *halakha* or pure *aggadah*: the driest legal texts are often dotted with aggadic asides; the aggadic stories are often brought to teach a story about the law" (Holtz 179). This is consistent with our observation that the Talmud is not really a law book: neither is Midrash.

THE MIDDLE AGES

Thus far, we have listed the sources of Jewish thought in Torah, comprised of Biblical narrative, law, poetry, and in Mishnah, Gemara, Talmud, and Midrash—a mere two thousand years of Jewish thought, dialogue, and text. This barely brings us to the Middle Ages. But there is also a body of Medieval Biblical commentary, whose most important figure is Rashi (Rabbi Schlomo Yitzhaki, or Schlomo ben Isaac, 1040–1105). So important was Rashi's interpretation that Medieval editions of the Bible were printed with the commentary of the most revered Rashi always printed in the column next to the bound edge of each page, right at the "heart" of the Bible. Surrounding the Biblical text and Rashi's commentary were the writings of other, later commentators. A page of the Bible or the Talmud provides vivid testimony to the role of interpretation and dialogue in Judaism. Each page is a network of text and commentaries written at different moments of Jewish history. "The arrangement in *Midra'ot Gedolot* encourages dialectic among the distinguished voices on the page, confirming the well-known witticism that where there are two Jews, there are three opinions" (Holtz 215).

The medieval commentaries themselves take two different forms: *Derash* and *Peshat*. *Derash* refers to the style of Biblical exegesis that extracts hidden or latent meaning in the text, and *peshat* refers to a more contextual, literalist approach to the Bible.[15] The Middle Ages also saw the effort, for the first time, especially by Spanish and French Jews, to engage in dialogue with thinkers of other cultures—particularly scholars from Arab lands. Efforts were also made, most notably by Maimonides, to "translate" the Bible into Aristotelian categories. "Rational modes of thought lent the Jewish commentators historical perspective, an appreciation of rhetoric, and a conviction that the Bible must make sense. Some, like Maimonides, felt such a strong need to harmonize the Torah and Aristotle that they reverted to the methods of *derash* to force the Bible into the Procrustean bed of Aristotelian logic" (Holtz 221).

MYSTICISM

The final aspect of traditional Jewish thought to be mentioned here is the mystical movement. Perhaps in response to the extreme rationalization of Jewish thought during the Medieval fascination with Aristotle, there arose an effort to return Jewish thinking to its spiritual roots. This took the milder form of a return to *derash* as the central Midrashic approach, and the disappearance of *peshat* until the nineteenth-century enlightenment once again attempted some sort of assimilation with non-Jewish Western rationalism. The return to spirituality in the middle ages also took the more radical form of Jewish mysticicism. There arose the Kabbalists, with their principle text *Zohar* (Moses ben Shem tov de Leon) and the more modern, eighteenth-century Hassidism, still a powerful force in Judaism today (Ba'al Shem Tov, Levi Yizhak, Isaac Luria). Kabbalism was a complicated system of mystical symbols that also brought erotic imagery to the Jewish male relationship to God, while Hassidism was an Eastern European movement that sought to bring the average Jew into the movement by applying a more directly accessible emotionalism.

Let us pause to summarize before shifting perspective somewhat to consider Jewish consciousness of history. We have noted the Bible's innovative prose style, spare and dialogical, accompanied by an invitation to engage in dialogue and interpretation. Without attempting to diminish the richness and complexity of "Jewish thinking," it may be possible to define as a common thread "tolerance for ambiguity," or even "tolerance for contradictions." Biblical and Talmudic scholars seem to have a remarkable capacity to absorb, internalize, utilize contradictions—both across time and internally—on any given issue or question. One could never describe this sort of Jewish thinking as one dimensional, linear, or rigid.

The ability to absorb and maintain contradiction and indeterminateness growing out of constant interpretation suggests that Talmudic thinking is eternally dialectical—both internally, in the form of endless debate and interpretation, and externally, in terms of the emergence of the major moments in the history of Jewish thought. The major moments in Jewish thought have been defined here as (1) Bible and commentary on the Bible in the form of Talmud and Midrash, continuing for at least two millennia until the time of the medieval Biblical commentaries; (2) increasing rationalization of the Talmud in an effort to assimilate Biblical thought with Greek, Arabic, and Islamic philosophy; and (3) a mystical or emotive response to the extreme rationalism of medieval Jewish philosophy.

JEWISH HISTORICAL CONSCIOUSNESS

Finally, let us consider a Jewish stance toward time with a comparison of Yosef Hayim Yerushalmi's perspective on the role history has played in Jewish thought with that of Amos Funkenstein.[16] The title of Yerushalmi's book, *Zakhor* is the Hebrew command, "Remember!" Yerushalmi argues that memory and history have been both central and at odds with one another in Jewish consciousness. While memory—the retention of past and identity and, by implication history—is essential, historiography—the writing of that history–has held little appeal to Jews. This renders the Jewish concept of history fairly idiosyncratic. From early on Jews were preoccupied with the interpretation and meaning of their own history. This preoccupation stood in marked contrast with the Greek focus on nature, regarded as essentialist and archetypal. In the Jewish Bible, history is told for the purpose of teaching the Jewish people Judaism, keeping them together as a community, and providing the basis for their continued faith in God. The purpose of Jewish Biblical history is thus spiritual and political. The accounts in the Torah are selective, recorded with a purpose beyond the mere recounting of facts. Thus while the Bible exhorts Jews to remember, to maintain a living contact with the past, the definition of the past is not "historical" in the modern philosophical or scientific sense.

Only since the late nineteenth century was there a more systematic Jewish attempt to write history. But the new interest in history was part of the effort to assimilate—intellectually as well as socially. The willingness to write history was the result neither of a newfound interest on the part of modern European Jews, nor even an assimilationist effort to mimic the intellectual style of the Christians. Rather the Jews were writing history *for* the Christians to read: "For the first time it is not history that must prove its validity to Judaism, but Judaism that must prove its validity to history, by revealing and justifying itself historically" (*Zakhor* 84).

Nowadays we witness a Jewish preoccupation with history, and the reverse of the Jewish tendency of the middle ages: a lack of interest in developing discourse between Jewish, Christian, and Muslim philosophy. History has become more important as Jews have become assimilated, almost as a compensation for lost faith and knowledge about Judaism itself. "In this sense, if for no other, history becomes what it had never been before—the faith of fallen Jews. For the first time history, not a sacred text, becomes the arbiter of Judaism" (*Zakhor* 86).

Amos Funkenstein presents a different perspective on the Jewish attitude toward history. He believes Yerushalmi overstates the distinction in Jewish culture between memory and history, claims that Jews have always been aware of and interested in their history as such (i.e., not only as reflected indirectly in ritual, prayer, and tradition), and that they are not so different from Christians or Greeks in this regard. "It is my contention that, with or without history proper, creative thinking about history—past and present—never ceased. Jewish culture was and remained formed by an acute historical *consciousness*, albeit different at different periods. Put differently, Jewish culture never took itself for granted" (Funkenstein 11).

Early Jewish and Greek historical consciousness resembled each other in their awareness of themselves as young cultures. "Both saw their origins in historical rather than mythical ties; both preserved a memory of relatively recent origins, preceded by a nomadic prehistory.... Awareness of the unity of history as a whole also has its dual origin in Israel and in Greece" (Funkenstein 11–12). Likewise, early Christian historical writings borrowed, indeed, "appropriated the history of Israel until the coming of Christ in that they viewed it as a gradual 'preparation'" (Funkenstein 13). Funkenstein also argues that the Jewish sense of time does not differ dramatically from the Christian or the Greek. "Contrasting the Jewish (or Christian) and the Greek perception of history, some scholars characterize the one as 'linear' the other as 'cyclical.' Neither is the case. Where and when do we find, for the first time, an explicit insistence on the uniqueness of historical events—or on the uniqueness of history as a whole? Perhaps not before Augustine" (Funkenstein 13).

Funkenstein's mission is to "contribute to the demystification of collective entities." He seeks to avoid an essentialist view of the Jews as unique in history, as well as the assimilationist dilemma described by Yerushalmi, that the Jewish sense of "chosenness" renders the study of Jewish history incompatible with Jewish spiritualism. Funkenstein acknowledges the uniqueness of Jewish history but refuses to make an essentialist argument about Jewish uniqueness. He is both a Zionist and a political egalitarian, a potentially paradoxical position that provides insight about the possibility of maintaining cultural identity and continuity without either dominating other groups or assimilating and disappearing as a group. While Funkenstein professes the inappropriateness of Jewish essentialism, he stresses *history* as the basis for understanding what *is* unique about the Jews. "I have . . . indicated what I believe is the main theme of historical reflection among Jews: the grounding of their uniqueness *in* an understanding of history" (Funkenstein 21). With this perspective Funkenstein overcomes the (Greek-inspired) penchant for polarizing essentialist nature with the contingency of history. With a perspective more compatible to that of Karl Marx, Funkenstein assumes a dialectic between nature and history; Jews *are* unique, because of their specific history, which continues to affect who they are as people. This dynamic describes the formation of all ethnic, racial, and religious groups.

Thus Funkenstein avoids mystification of Jewishness or any other culture. He believes that overstating the uniqueness of Jewish history has contributed to Israeli political injustices in Palestine. "Depersonalization of the Palestinian, denial of their personal and political self-identity, has become an oppressive political reality. As a Zionist and as a historian, I fear these developments and abhor their consequences. By destroying the identity of the other we, too, will destroy our own" (Funkenstein 49). Now these are sentiments with which Hannah Arendt would agree, and with which, in fact, she did agree.[17] The concluding thoughts of this celebrated scholar echo Arendt's fears that the German executioners of the Holocaust were not a race of devils, but ominously human.[18]

> Theologians seem to emphasize the "incomprehensibility" of the Holocaust and the "madness" of those who caused it because they cannot find any theological meaning in it. . . . If, however, we turn from God to humankind, the Holocaust is neither incomprehensible nor meaningless. It was neither bestial nor indeed pagan. It was, instead, an eminently human event in that it demonstrated those extremes which only man and his society are capable of doing or suffering. It pointed at a possibility, perhaps unknown before, of human existence, a possibility as human as the most sublime instances of creativity and compassion. (Funkenstein 337)

In contrast, then, with Yerushalmi's reading of the uniqueness of Jewish history, and the millennia-old Jewish aversion to writing or rewriting their own history, Funkenstein offers a dialectic between Jewish memory and Jewish history, developing throughout the ages. Drawing parallels between the structure of historical thought in Hegel and Maimonides, Funkenstein notes, "Just as Hegel's *objective Geist* uses the subjective, egoistic freedom of man to further the objective goals of history . . . so also Maimonides' God fights polytheism with its own weapons. . . . Maimonides spoke of the 'cunning of God'" (Funkenstein 144). The analogy is to Hegel's reference to the "cunning of reason," his way of describing the "objective meaning" that emerges even as history is characterized by subjective needs, acts, and perceptions. The dialectic between tradition and change is the ability of Jewish law to develop in opposition to its own insistence on immutability. The laws are sacred and absolute, and yet constantly being reinterpreted and adapted to changing historical circumstances. "Should laws be changed? Maimonides, we have seen, insists on the validity of every iota of the law even in the messianic age" (147). Maimonides was no democrat, did not believe in "the capability of the masses to rise to the level of the philosopher," and insisted that the laws must be presented to the masses as absolute. But he held a "doctrine of contingency" based upon the Aristotelian doctrine of equity, which allowed a certain amount of flexibility in the law. In sum, while "The absolute immutability of the law may be a necessary fiction for the masses . . . the legal experts of every generation have the right and duty to adjust the law *in causu necessitatis*" (Funkenstein 146–47).

Funkenstein argues for the persistence of a Jewish historical consciousness, a dialectic between history and memory, stability and adaptability. This does not describe Jewish uniqueness, as though Jewish culture survived in isolation from other cultures with whom the Jews were in contact. Cultures influence one another. Shaped as they were by history and mutual interaction, rather than "determined" by essentialist concepts of "race," cultures *can* be distinguished from one another.

Funkenstein thus also notes a certain Jewish reticence about history: a sense of detachment, or reluctance to touch it. "The traditional Jewish attitude toward time and history was neither affirmative nor negative, but indifferent" (Funkenstein 254).

Both awareness of history and ability to change are very much a part of Jewish law and culture, although inexplicitly. It is as though the "trick" in adapting to the demands of history is not to talk about what is changing. This would take the form in Jewish law of enacting a change without explicit blessings of rabbis who may understand the need for change, but who have the wisdom to resist the temptation, in the vernacular of the present day, to "make too big a deal out of it."[19] The rabbinic term for the ability to embrace change without being explicit about it, thus easing the pain of change, and preserving the sense that *halakha* is sacred, is "a fence around the Torah," or "fences to the law."

> Now it is true that Jewish law—the *halakha*—developed of old, mechanisms of change and adjustment to new circumstances. The famous word-pun of Rabbi Moses of Pressburg—"everything new is forbidden by law"—was itself "new," characteristic of the reaction against the reform movement. The very term "novelty" carried . . . a highly positive connotation within legal scholarship. But changes and adjustments, even radical ones, had to appear under the guise of conservation, of being merely "fences to the law." (Funkenstein 253)

In sum, a Jewish perspective on history according to both Yerushalmi and Funkenstein, who otherwise have significant disagreements on the subject, involves a self-consciousness of the importance of knowing about history; belief that history involves discrete events, some of which are (subjectively) more important than others and must be actively remembered; deference to the Bible as the main "source book" of Jewish history, and a simultaneous deference to the interpretations of the scholars, the rabbis, who have indicated little interest in writing, but much in interpreting, Jewish history. Both Funkenstein and Yerushalmi note a Jewish "indifference" toward post-Biblical history, a sense that what Jews need to know about themselves *is* indeed historical, but is contained within the Bible to be interpreted by and for later generations.

In what follows, we shall attempt to bridge the millennia and derive a modern definition of "Jewish thinking."

CHAPTER 8

Greek and Hebrew: The Structure of Thinking

Thorlief Boman's *Hebrew Thought Compared with Greek* is a classical exegesis on the difference between Greek ideas as presented in Plato's dialogues and Hebrew ideas set forth in the Torah. Boman relies heavily on a comparison of the structure of the Greek and Hebrew languages.[1] His approach thus has the advantage of being grounded in specific texts, and is historically contained. Some scholars have suggested that Boman treats the differences between Hebrew and Greek thought from an unconsciously "Greek" perspective: statically, and too abstractly, as though Hebrew thought at least wasn't characterized by a living and dynamic historical reality.[2] Nonetheless, his treatise is considered a classic, and for good reason. Arendt herself used it as a reference when she sought to understand the differences between Greek and Hebrew thought,[3] and if we accept it on its own terms, as a non-Jewish effort to understand Jewish thought, and use Max Kadushin's distinctly Jewish treatment of the same issues for contrast, we should be in a position to understand some of the aspects that distinguish Jewish thinking from Greek and Christian approaches to knowledge.[4]

THE STRUCTURE OF HEBREW THOUGHT COMPARED TO GREEK

In his short, elegant monograph, Boman analyzes differences in language to demonstrate structural differences in the Greek and Hebrew approaches to truth: Greek truth is static, while the Hebrew is dynamic. To demonstrate, Boman compares the Greek and Hebrew visual worlds, differences in Greek and Hebrew conceptions of time and space, and the Greek logical versus Hebrew psychological approach to "reality."

Boman focuses on the use of verbs, and particularly the Hebrew verb *hayah*, to be, in comparison to the Greek εἰμί as evidence that the Hebrews conceived of a world in flux, while the Greeks regarded the world in more static terms. As reflected in the Hebrew language, existence is constantly changing, linked inextricably to the material world. In contrast, Greek reality resides in eternal essences, beyond appearance, regarded as transient, an unreliable indicator of truth. To use modern philosophical vernacular, Hebrew thinkers believe truth is found in *existence*, while Greek thinkers regard truth as *essential* rather than existential.

For example, the Hebrew verb *hayah*, compared to the verb *to be* in English is a "true verb with full verbal force," as in "Javeh hurled a great wind, and a mighty tempest *was* (Jonah: 1.4)" (Boman 38). This reflects the Hebrew belief in the givenness of God, in contrast to which everything in the universe is transient. Truth *is* the power to create, destroy, change. From the Hebrew perspective, stasis, the "essential" being of the universe, is illusory. In stark contrast stands the Greek *concept*, represented for Boman by Platonic thought. What Plato seeks, of course, is the eternal essence, the unchangeable universal beneath fleeting, changing empirical surfaces. Heraclitus alone, of all Greek thinkers, was intrigued by the dynamic, changing quality of the world, an interest to which Boman refers as "un-Greek" (Boman 52).

Static (Greek) versus dynamic (Hebrew) thinking can be further comprehended by comparing the words *davar* and *logos*, both of which mean "word." But each word also has an additional meaning, and the difference permits us to understand yet another distinction between Greek and Hebrew thought. In Hebrew, *davar* means not only "word," but also "thing," while in Greek *logos* or "word" means also "speech" and "reason." The Hebrew is grounded in the material world, while the Greek term has a more abstract job description. This might seem at odds with Boman's contention that Hebrew thinking is dynamic, while Greek is static, but the conclusion he draws is just the reverse. "Things" in the world are related to action and change, since the world itself is perennially changing. "Word" and "deed" mean the same thing for Hebrew thinkers, whereas for the Greeks "word" was associated with thought and reason, regarded as approaches to the eternal.

Comparing the Greek and Hebrew for "word" reveals further differences in perspective. *Logos*, the Greek word derived from λέγω or speak, really has more to do with gathering and arranging than with speaking. "The basic meaning of the root *leg-* is, without doubt, 'to gather,' and indeed not to gather pell-mell, but to put together in order, to *arrange*" (Boman 67). In contrast is the Hebrew *davar:*

> Dynamic both objectively and linguistically . . . the basic meaning is "to be behind and drive forward," hence "to let words follow one another" . . . *davar* means not only "word" but also "deed": Abraham's servant recounted to Isaac all the "words" that he had done (Gen. 24.66). . . . the *word* is the highest and noblest function of man and is, for that reason, identical with his action. (Boman 65)

Thus two basic words teach us about differences in what was regarded as primary descriptions of mental life: for the Hebrew, dynamic, masterful, energetic; for the Greek, ordered, moderated, thought out, calculated, meaningful, rational.

Comparison of the verb *know* and its association with sight in the Greek and sound in the Hebrew gives us access to still another distinction. Truth to the Greeks was largely visual and pictorial. The words *know* and *see* are derived from the same verb, εἴδω. Even Plato's quest for hidden, eternal essences was conceived as "seeing," only with an inner, deeper sight, "the mind's eye." When we contrast the Hebrew preference for the invisible "revelation" of the word in sound to the Greek association of knowledge with light and sight, we begin to understand why Greek thought was more compatible with the Christian rather than Jewish perspective. Jewish suspicion of pictorial representation is derived from the belief that God cannot be seen or even envisaged, hence any attempt to render God in images is idolatrous, blasphemous. Jewish disinterest in the visible stems from the prohibition against iconic representations of God.

> Israelite faith permitted no bodily representation of God either in sculpture or in painting; the Decalogue's ban on images corresponds to Jewish character and Jewish thinking.... Where the pagan paints his god or forms him out of stone, the Jew paints the symbol of God's word: the Torah shrine and lamp or else the *action* of his God and so the sacred history. He does not employ God's image, face and form, but at most employs a hand of God to indicate his *action*.... Thus this art is truly Jewish in kind; the invisible being of his God is made visible in his *acts* through which he also *speaks*. (Boman 113)

In contrast, of course, is the Christian belief that Jesus is the visible manifestation of God. Not only the association of knowledge with light and specifically with the sun in Plato's *Republic* for example, but the very word for both theory and God in Greek is derived from the verb, θεωρέω, or behold. The Greek word for God is θεός, also derived from the verb θεωρέω, and specifically, Boman tells us, from the word for spectator.

The Greeks, for all their emphasis on the relationship between seeing and knowing, distinguished spiritual from physical beauty, elevating the spiritual and even arguing that inner, "invisible," spiritual beauty could determine its outward appearance. (See Plato's *Symposium* and *Phaedrus* for examples.) But there is no question that the Greeks esteemed what could be seen, in a dramatic departure from the Hebrew notion of truth.

Thus the Jewish incapacity to see or visualize God translates into a tendency to mistrust visible representations of truth, or the pursuit of truth perceived in visible terms. The word of God, or truth is *heard*, rather than seen. Surprisingly, Boman does not make reference to the most important call to Jewish prayer, "Shema Israel..." ("Hear O Israel the Lord our God, the Lord is One"), during which pious Jews cover their eyes to enhance the sense of hearing. Instead, he leads us indirectly to the Hebrew association of hearing with Truth, through a discussion of Time and Space. Greeks think spatially, while Hebrews think temporally. "We *see* the spatial and *hear* the temporal" (Boman 142).[5]

So thoroughgoing was the Greek disdain for time that time itself was rendered *spatially*. If this should seem familiar, it is because the Christian European tradition also adopted this way of conceptualizing time. Time is associated with geometrical shapes—usually circular or linear—and with words that indicate a spatial consciousness: what is future lies "before" us, what is past lies "behind." This is just the opposite of the Hebrew concept, which is focused on human action rather than geometrical space. The past came "before" (*quedem*) because our ancestors lived before us, where the future is "after" (*ahar*).

Rather than conceiving of time visually, the Hebrew experience of time is rhythmical: moments or pulses. "The Hebrews . . . orient themselves temporally not toward the circular movement of the sun, but toward the regular change of the moon's phases, toward the rhythm. . . . Lines and forms . . . play no role for them" (Boman 134). "The shortest time in Hebrew is not a point nor a distance, nor a duration, but a beat" (Boman 136). The difference translates into an emphasis in Jewish thinking on subjective experience, rather than what is objectively observable. Lacking an interest in geometric shapes, the Jews regarded numbers as repetitions of human activity rather than as abstract entities conceptualized visually as quantities.

Plato believed that geometry was the science that permitted one to approach essential reality, while the Jews regarded form, shape, and outline as unreal, something that does not exist in the world. "The Hebrew language formed no specific expressions for designating the outline or contour of objects and did not even need them" (Boman 156). This perspective is reflected in the indefinite and sometimes movable boundaries between past, present, and future found in Biblical narrative and Talmudic discourse, and in the distinct Jewish sense of history, discussed in the previous chapter. Even the Torah, which seems to be the defined, time-bound starting point for Jewish thought and ethics, is itself the still incomplete core of interpretive process. For the Greeks, however, form was superior, closer to truth than content.

The Jews were not abstract thinkers—at least not in the Greek sense. But paradoxically, their concept of God, although not abstract, is certainly intangible compared to the gods of Greek religion, while the Hebrew concept of truth, and reality, is much more worldly, tangible, and human than that of the Greeks. However, in spite of its dependence upon worldly behavior and thought for its vitality, the Torah does not lead away from itself for confirmation, as the Greek texts do. Understanding the Torah calls for ever more careful reading, "listening" to the text more intently; Greek texts point outward for their ultimate meaning, toward vision and abstraction.

Boman concludes his monograph with a wonderfully concise summary, leaving us with an abstract, as well as an an impressionistic description of the differences between Hebrew and Greek thinking. He suggests that the distinction between the two modes may be conceptualized by asking the question, What do they mean by truth? His answer is that the Greeks regarded truth as an unveiling, "that which is revealed, clear, evident, or that which is to be seen clearly" (202). This is evident in the Greek word for truth, ἀλήθεια, which translated literally means "not hidden." Truth in Hebrew is expressed by means of derivatives of the verb *aman*, "to be steady, faithful." Jewish tradition asks for certainty in the sense of reliability, steadiness, constancy, trustworthiness, while the Greeks ask for visible signs and revelations.

The impressionistic images Boman leaves us with are of Socrates, standing stock still in the agora, seized by a problem, deep in thought, immovable; and the Jew in prayer, rocking back and forth, lost in spiritual devotion. "The Greek most acutely experiences the word and existence while he stands and reflects, but the Israelite reaches his zenith in ceaseless movement. Rest, harmony, composure, and self-control—this is the Greek way; movement, life, deep emotion, and power—this is the Hebrew way" (Boman 203).

RABBINIC THOUGHT

Boman thus offers a clear and well-respected "translation" of elements of the structure of Jewish Biblical thought into terms that are comprehensible within a framework of "Western" Greek and Christian thought. We must acknowledge the cultural limitations of such an enterprise. Does it distort rabbinic or Talmudic thinking when we distill abstract structure from its religious content?

Three problems come quickly to mind as we attempt to compare religious and philosophical thought. The first, of course, is that the Bible is the word of God, and too literal an association of God with philosophical truth may be inappropriate. Belief in God is spiritual, grounded in faith rather than rationality. Belief that "truth" exists in any sort of philosophical sense is usually grounded in a more formal rational stance. Although the argument can be made that the search for philosophical truth begins in a "leap of faith" that truth exists, and that some philosophical stances may be likened to religion, such a comparison cannot be assumed.

The second problem involves the context for religious Judaism, indeed for all religions which assume a following: a group, a community of the faithful, in contrast to the solitary pursuit of philosophic truth, each philosopher on his own.

Finally, as is the case with most religions, Jewish thought is centered on a sacred Text, the Torah, which is accepted as Truth absolutely, although open to infinite interpretation. What is compatible with philosophy, perhaps, is the Jewish rejection of dogma, implicit in Judaism's penchant for plural interpretation and its embrace of the infinite. We also face a problem in trying to compare secular philosophical and epistemological ideas about truth, with truth as the Jewish religion conceives it.

Three elements, then, are problematic in attempting to extricate a "Jewish style of thinking" in order to place it in the world of secular thought: (1) the initial faith in God; (2) the existence of a community of believers; and (3) the centrality of the Torah as sacred text. In addition, there is the problem, discussed previously, of distinguishing between Torah and Talmud.

How does "Jewish Thinking" fare when defined by a religious Jewish scholar, rather than a secular scholar such as Boman?

Max Kadushin, the eminent traditional Jewish scholar, comes close to making the argument that Talmudic thinking cannot be compared to any sort of philosophical thought. The difficulty in describing a rabbinical approach to concepts, ideas, definitions, values as such, he argues, lies in the fact that those terms have no abstract or independent significance in the Hebrew tradition. The lack of a distinction between form and content in Jewish thinking is central to his discussion. But where Boman treated this from the Greek perspective, assuming boundaries as definitive, and then "removing" them from the Greek picture as a way of explaining the Hebrew stance, Kadushin, grounded in the Jewish stance, attempts to explain the lack of boundaries without the aid of conventional (Greek-Christian) definitions. The result is somewhat amorphous to those of us educated in the formal Western tradition. He refers to the collapse of form and content in Jewish thought by the term *value concept*, a term so vague as to defy customary definition and very nearly, comprehension.

> Any attempt to formulate rabbinic values does violence to them. The only authentic way to express abstractly a rabbinic value is by means of the term for it found in rabbinic literature. Even to define the term is to distort the value. A definition would have to present the value as a complete idea, a proposition; it would thereby change the character of the value. We may say, therefore, that the rabbinic value terms stand for ideas, but not for complete, fully formulated ideas. The rabbinic value terms can thus be characterized as undefined concepts. (Kadushin 2)

"Value concept," as Kadushin uses the term, implies the inseparability of abstract ideas from their concrete manifestation in an unspoken, almost nonarticulable awareness of the concept by members of "the group," defined as members of the Jewish faith. A "value concept" is an inexplicit but somewhat prescriptive affirmation of the group's perspective on the world: something between a definition, or the name of a concept, and a behavioral rule. It is ineffable but worldly, a concept at work in the world which cannot be wrested from its context. This sounds like an effort to define that intangible "something" that distinguishes a community from a mere crowd of people. It is abstract, somewhat inarticulate, and yet visible in terms of its effects: perhaps something like a Socratic wind. Kadushin endeavors to conceptualize, with the use of one awkward, inelegant term, the convergence between the abstract and the concrete. He appears not at all fazed or influenced by the struggles of Karl Marx and his German predecessors to unite theory and practice with elaborate philosophical systems.

"Value concept," as Kadushin uses the term, indicates a fluidity and dynamism in rabbinic thinking, a lack of boundaries—at least between theory and practice—and across generations. The fact that "the concepts are not only communicable, but they are common ideas, folk ideas" (Kadushin 4) implies an accessibility to "all" the members of the group. The concepts are not rarified philosophical terms, but generalized perspectives that come to life in the form of worldly actions, and are transmitted from generation to generation by their unspoken tangibility. They "are the means of rendering the experience of God a normal element in the life of every man" (Kadushin 7).

Kadushin refers to the "worldliness" of the value concepts, and believes that their rootedness in daily life prevents them from being comprehensible in terms of a logical system. He refers to the worldliness of Jewish thought as its "organic" quality.[6] Rather charmingly, he insists that philosophy calls for too much head-breaking exertion to be of much use to ordinary people: "Such systems, requiring tremendous mental effort and concentration, never were, and could be, guides in daily conduct for most men, not even for philosophers in their off moments" (Kadushin 32). While the rabbinic value concepts may be complex and disorganized compared to philosophy, they are more available to ordinary folk, in contrast with philosophy that is "stiff, brittle and artificial" (Kadushin 32). Although generated and articulated by Judaism's most educated rabbinical scholars, Jewish thinking does not present itself as a system or a totality of thought: it is responsive to the plurality of daily needs and is accessible, because of its everyday applicability, to ordinary observant Jews. Whether or not such a description of rabbinic thought is an idealization or a reality, we get a sense of what one respected traditional scholar believes Jewish thinking should be.

In spite of the fact that *value concept* is a term almost too awkward and vague to be useful to us, Kadushin's perspective conveys certain aspects of rabbinic thinking that are compatible with Boman's portrayal of Hebrew thought, and actually adds a certain dimension: a wariness of dogma.

> The value concepts are dynamic. They cannot be organized into a static system, one neat proposition following another, because the concepts are single words or terms, not propositions.... All this would be impossible were the value concepts congealed in a static, hierarchical system of thought. Were that the case, instead of leaving room for the *differentia* of personalities, the value concepts would impose a uniform set of ideas upon everybody, a rigid structure of dogmas. (Kadushin 5)

Such an aim is, of course, not only compatible with Greek thought, at least as exemplified by Plato, but is the very purpose, or hope of the philosopher. Moreover, while Kadushin reiterates the intangibility, and also the dynamism of Jewish thought as described by Boman, he inadvertently confirms, in more traditional religious terms, what the secular scholars of the previous chapter discussed as the ongoing interpretation, the dialectic, that forms the basis of Jewish thought: inherently plural, involving a collection of voices from the generations across the world.

I must admit that I, for one, am not comfortable with Kadushin's insistence that the term *value concepts* adequately captures the availability of Talmudic wisdom to members of "the" Jewish community. Kadushin is attempting to render the religious and ethical dimensions of the Talmud in terms that are comprehensible to secular scholars, without losing sight of what he takes to be the incompatibility of religion and philosophy. Jewish thought is prescriptive without being codified or rigid; it is derived from a specific text for a specific community. It sounds like nothing could be further from a description of philosophy, which is abstract, essentialist and universal, and regarded as the exclusive domain of *specialists*. Kadushin may be trying to have it both ways, with his argument that the sort of thinking he is describing is "rabbinic," that is, the work of specialists, full time Jewish scholars, and yet available to all members of the Jewish community.

SCAFFOLDING

A summation, or codification of the complexity of Jewish thinking would, from a Jewish perspective, be a violation of the spirit of Jewish thinking itself. However, out of deference to Western standards of scholarship—whether modeled on the Greek or not—a "working definition" of Jewish thinking is in order if we are to return to the question of the extent to which Jewish thinking either influenced or should have influenced Hannah Arendt's search for a worldly philosophy in *The Life of the Mind*. To that end, let me attempt to draw together some threads, with the full understanding that the result is an artifice, a scaffolding with which to continue work, rather than a vain effort to reduce four thousand years of history to a few succinct themes, or intellectual values, or epistemological rules.

The basic features that characterize a "Hebrew" or Jewish style of thinking are: (1) groundedness in a basic text, the Torah, which in spite of its centrality to Jewish thinking is regarded as incomplete, and dependent upon reading and interpretation for its vitality; (2) an unwillingness to codify, or "complete" the Torah, and by extension, an unwillingness to regard truth as ever complete or definable in the way that Greek thought regards definitions, categories, metaphors as "real"; (3) lack of boundedness—between text and life, idea and thing, word and world, past and future, that stems directly from the combination of centrality and indeterminateness of the Torah; (4) a lack of emphasis on visual images as a means of access to truth or meaning; and finally, (5) a worldliness, growing from the lack of boundary between the word and the world, and a consequent democratic potential growing from the dependence on particularity, people and the world, which stems directly from the belief that abstraction and essence are neither privileged nor ultimately distinguishable from particular and material as approaches to "truth."

With the understanding that they are not readily separable, these characteristics will now be elaborated, however briefly. It will be obvious that they tend to flow into and circle back upon one another.[7]

Centrality of the Torah. There is no getting around the fact that the Torah is at the center of Judaism. The specificity of this circumstance may seem to make it impossible to compare Judaism to anything besides other organized religions. However, the Torah is unusual among religious texts, precisely because of a peculiar feature of Jewish thinking, the refusal to regard the Torah as either complete, contained within the physical text itself, or codifiable. It is not "applicable" to the world, not a handbook for orthodoxy, but rather a part of worldly life itself. It is thus also the source of the existence of the Jewish community in the world. In an important sense, then, the centrality of the Torah, while defining the Jewish community, and creating its exclusivity, is also a model for flexibility between any text, or source of thinking, and worldly life. This is in part due to the indeterminacy that characterizes the Jewish approach to text and life more generally, and more specifically, to the explicit unwillingness of the earliest Talmudic rabbis to "codify" the Torah, to create an artifact out of it, which might run the risk of making it into an idol. This reticence with respect to Torah initiated the age-old tradition of interpretation that keeps the boundary between Torah and world dymanic and vital.

Reluctance to codify. In Jewish thinking, both Torah and Talmud are always incomplete, always in process of being understood and made real by human beings. One "reads" the world as one reads a text—or in the case of the Jews, "The" text. This creates a certain difficulty in distinguishing method from substance in Jewish thought.

Somewhat paradoxically, the indeterminateness of the rabbinic teachings also reflects their inherent worldiness. "While Torah is considered to be a blueprint of the universe, it is also a guide to the most minute and mundane details of daily life" (Handelman 38). Boman attributes this to the materiality and dynamism of Hebrew thought: truth is reflected in the changing world, as compared to the Greek belief that truth *is* essential, transcending any mundane embodiment. The rabbinic teachings are never "complete" because that would separate them from the world and the community which puts them to use: the indeterminateness ensures involvement in everyday life and with everyday people. Each generation must think, discuss, interpret, and implement the teachings for itself. There is no closed system that may simply be applied to the world.

Lack of boundedness. Jewish thinking is characterized by a rejection of closure, which involves many dimensions. The lack of boundedness probably stems from the invisibility and incorporeality of the Hebrew God, and the prohibition against even attempting to render an image of God. We have seen that the boundary between the Torah and Talmud is questionable; the boundary between the text and the world, or word and world (*davar* = both word and thing in Hebrew) is questionable; the boundary between past and present is willfully tampered with, as memory is maintained by the reenactment of history in rituals and prayers, performed by each new generation of Jews.

Related to the lack of boundaries is the lack of interest in historical writing observed by Yerushalmi and Funkenstein. Although refraining from historical commentary is a phenomenon responsive to social and historical developments themselves, there is certainly a long tradition among the Jews of regarding interest in any history except that presented in the Bible as sacreligious. From this perspective, causality, time, materiality, all are indefinite. This may seem chaotic, nonsensical, "irrational": but only if one insists that the ultimate "rational" perspective is Greek. Most scholars comparing Jewish and Greek thinking do so from a Greek perspective, translating the "illogic" of Hebrew thought into Greek logical categories. A Greek perspective would grant primacy to the abstract laws of nature or the universe, with a book, even the Bible, regarded as subordinate to that essential reality: at best a book, if accurate, only reflects the primacy of nature. The

Jewish perspective regards the boundary between text and world as utterly permeable.

Lack of interest in visual imagery. Jewish thinking, reflecting its disinterest in visual imagery, does not make the customary distinction, following Greek thought, between form and content. Form is inseparable from content, and yet the meaning of the content is not self-evidently empirical. Like the invisible, incorporeal Jewish God, Truth is indefinite, incapable of being articulated in the form of a doctrine. Truth and thought, ideas, are always incomplete, and their life is rooted in the world and in people thinking.

Perhaps the insignificance of visual imagery and its relation to the unacceptability of written codification of even the most sacred Jewish teachings is symbolized most strikingly in Moses's smashing of the tablets upon his descent from Sinai. He found his people prostrated before a golden calf they themselves had fashioned, and furious, he smashed the tablets upon which the Ten Commandments had been inscribed by God. God's very words, at least in their concretized form, were the victim of Moses's rage at his people, who had reified a symbol of a god into gold. Moses reversed the sins of his community by smashing the tablets, the physical form containing the teachings of the One Hebrew God: smashed stone was truer to the teachings of that God than a gold statue to be worshipped. And as evidence of the eternal *and* intangible nature of God's teachings, Moses received a second set of tablets. Tablets can be replaced and duplicated: only the teachings are real and they can never be captured in stone.

This does not mean that all Jewish thinkers have succeeded in thinking without images. The most obvious example of the difficulty of succeeding in this mandate is the use of the male generic for God. If God has no body, why the insistence on God's maleness? Why is it unthinkable to entertain use of the female generic as a way of forcing the observant Jew to cease thinking of God as a man?[8] Likewise, how could Moses have spoken to God on Mount Sinai? How could Jacob have claimed to have seen God's face when he wrestled with the "angel," and named the spot *peniel*, or "the face of God"? "And Jacob called the name of the place Peniel: 'for I have seen God face to face, and my life is preserved'" (Gen. 32:31). How can this be reconciled with the fact that at Exodus 33:20, where Moses asks God to "Show me, I pray Thee, Thy glory," God responds, "Thou canst not see My face, for man shall not see Me and live." God then told Moses of a place between some rocks where he could hide his face for his own protection while God passed by, presumably in the form of fire. "And the Lord said: 'Behold, there is a place by Me, and thou shalt stand upon a rock. And it shall come to pass, while My glory passeth by, that I will put thee in a cleft of the rock, and will cover thee with My hand until I have passed by. And I will take away My hand, and thou shalt see My back; but My face shall not be seen" (Exod. 33: 21–23).

In spite of apparent contradictions, or enigmas, or perhaps, intentional puzzles to be interpreted by the generations, in spite also of the failure on the part of even the most revered Jewish thinkers to adhere to the letter of Jewish teachings, we press on with the effort to discover the underlying spirit characterizing Jewish thought.

Inherent worldliness and democratic potential. There is an assumption that the Torah is open to interpretation not only by experts, the rabbis, but by any Jew who gives it serious thought, even the simplest person.[9] The indeterminateness or the inconclusiveness of the boundaries of the Torah implies a dialectical relationship between the divine authority of the Torah and its interpreters. Theoretically, the authority of interpretation is available to all Jews. However, I suspect more problems than Kadushin acknowledges in legitimating Talmudic interpretation. It would seem to involve a question of the politics of the authority of Judaism: who belongs to the priesthood? Nonetheless, at least in theory, the text of the Torah is brought to life in practice, by even the simplest people, hence the dialectic of intepretation is an opportunity extended to all members of the community. At minimum, it is an ethical approach to life that involves thinking without codified rules. Susan

Handelman captures the difference in this respect from Greek thought: "The infinity of meaning and plurality of interpretation are as much the cardinal virtues, even divine imperatives, for Rabbinic thought as they are the cardinal sins for Greek thought" (Handelman 21).

It might be romantic to expect each generation to perform the function of prophets, to think about, interpret and reapply the traditional teachings to its own worldly activities; and it may be naive to hold the view that average people have the will, the intelligence, and the time to engage in such an undertaking. But I am going to argue that that is precisely what Hannah Arendt sought in her idealistic quest for a way of thinking accessible to "all." The "all" in Jewish thinking is clearly restricted to the Jewish community, and at that, primarily to its male members who are commanded to study Torah, as compared to women who are advised against it. So the apparent absence of boundaries between text and world, and past and present, is, in a manner of speaking, assumed because the text is after all one Torah and the community is one people. Nonetheless, there is room for remarkable diversity, plurality, and contradiction within that community and in relation to that text. And perhaps, in Hegelian fashion, if we immerse ourselves entirely in essential aspects of our own particular community and tradition, we will be able to emerge with recognition about how something similar but not identical might work for other communities, with other texts. But that is for future speculation. In terms of what we need here, it is sufficient to note that for all its vitality and incompleteness, the Jewish text presupposes a Jewish community, with both positive and negative aspects: a chance for real discourse, as well as the possibility of parochialism.

The democratic potential is, of course, an ideal. In terms of complexity and inapproachability, Talmudic learning certainly rivals the most difficult philosophical systems in the history of the world as an intimidating undertaking. Still, it is significant that one studies the Talmud with other people: pairs of scholars, and under the close supervision of a rabbi. (And of course the word *rabbi* means simply "my teacher," connoting not an expert with a doctrine, but a personal guide to a method and practice.) While all boys were exposed to some training in Torah and Talmud, only a tiny minority went on to become Talmudic scholars. Still, one could make the argument that Jewish teachings are democratic in spirit, are intended to be available to the entire community, even if in practice the everyday work of poor people reduced their time with the teachings to a few memorable quotations from the rabbis, folk tales, and daily prayer.

All of this may be reflected in Boman's rather abstract rendering of Hebrew thought as "dynamic," in motion, as reflected in the Hebrew language and through the attitude toward the teachings and prayers. Can we move, with this self-contained description of the perspectives of a "closed" community into the larger world that Arendt wishes to empower with similar traits of "thinking"? That is the task at hand.

CHAPTER 9

Toward Understanding Arendt as a Jewish Thinker

A JEWISH SOUL IN A GERMAN SCHOLAR

Arendt's intellectual and political agenda was "Jewish" in a way that has been insufficiently recognized, and which was neither acknowledged nor understood by Arendt herself. I propose a double-edged argument: (1) Hannah Arendt was more of a "Jewish thinker" than she realized, and (2) if she had been able to embrace more explicitly some of the tenets of a Jewish approach to morality and acting in the world, she might have been more successful in elaborating upon "the Eichmann problem," her contention that failure to think can result in historical catastrophes.

In order to argue that Arendt was more of a Jewish intellectual than she thought, and at the same time, not quite enough of a Jewish intellectual, it will be necessary to establish links between the description of "Jewish thinking" in the previous two chapters, and Arendt's efforts to discuss thinking and its relationship to political action in *The Life of the Mind*, *The Human Condition*, and related writings. Nazi totalitarianism, and specifically the Holocaust, had forged in Arendt her central identity as a Jew. After publication of *Eichmann* she was spurned by Jews in America, Europe, and Israel. Arendt responded by developing her thinking toward *The Life of the Mind*. Her project was to expand upon the argument which had been so profoundly misunderstood in *Eichmann*, that the absence of thinking may be sufficient to allow political catastrophes to take place. She sought to explain the role of thinking in political life, and to articulate a conception of thinking grounded in the world and available to everybody—not just to "professional thinkers." But in this last great work of her life, she overlooked the impact of her identity as a Jew upon her thinking, or believed that as important as that identity might be, it need not affect the life of *her* mind.

Arendt demonstrated remarkable, perhaps psychologically suspicious oversights in neglecting to include Jewish thought in any of her discussions of philosophy or ethics. Apparently in her opinion, one could be a political Jew, or a religious Jew, while remaining immune to Jewish intellectual influences. From her perspective, intellectuals are free of ethnic, racial, or political influences. This "universalist perspective" on intellectual life may partially account for the difficulty Arendt had in arriving at a philosophy that would "work" in the world. This may seem counterintuitive: an articulation of thinking that would be available to all, and not just specialists, would seem to demand the avoidance of any specific cultural perspective. Arendt did not seek a description of thinking specific to Judaism or specific to anything else—although the Euro-Centric assumptions dominating her work are undeniable. But while she needed a universally accessible perspective, and while I believe such a quest reflects her genuinely democratic instincts, avoiding the specificity of different cultural perspectives hampered her effort to bring thinking into the world. Her discussion of thinking in *The Life of the Mind* is not culturally specific enough to be worldly.

This is strangely discordant with her otherwise particularist, materialist tendencies.[1] Philosophy in her view is at risk of being irrelevant when it becomes rarified and untouchable—available only to specialists and not ordinary people. Here I do not question why she held what for her was an uncharacteristically idealist view of intellectual life. I do not question why there were gaps in Arendt's claim to Jewish identity, nor do I judge the fragmentation of her Judaism. I am not trying to argue (along with her *Eichmann* critics) that if she had been a "good" or "loyal" Jew, we should have been able to see her claiming her identity in various predetermined places. She *was* a "good and loyal" Jew, if not a religious one, at least in terms of claiming that identity publicly, consistently, and with what often appears to be a combination of pride and stubbornness. I intend in this chapter and the two that follow, only to fill in the missing pieces in Arendt's quest for a worldly way of thinking. If she had been willing and able to claim her Jewish identity as a thinker as well as a political actor, would her final intellectual quest have been more successful than it was? Perhaps this question will shed light on more general problems of integrating one's cultural or racial identity with one's creative work or public identity in our multicultural age.

The contradictions in Arendt's final project may have reflected a conflict within Arendt, between the political Jew and the intellectual German. Perhaps Hannah Arendt's Jewish soul was raising questions for which the German scholar Arendt could not find answers. But all these musings are grounded in the understanding that *The Life of the Mind*, apart from being unfinished, is a flawed work: that there are contradictions, specifically in *Thinking*, that are serious enough to undermine the power of the book. Like all of Arendt's work, there is plenty in *Thinking* to teach and enlighten, and to provoke thought and debate. However, Arendt did not succeed in articulating a worldly philosophy free of universals or absolutes, yet more reliable than "opinion," and available to anybody with the inclination to think. One might argue that "failing" at that task still leaves her in rather august company: it is no disgrace. Still, she might have gotten closer to succeeding at her self-appointed task had she considered the work of Jewish thinkers, along with her Greeks and Germans.

I do not refer to Judaism in the abstract, as an ephemeral or essential quality residing in all Jews whether religious or not, determining their thoughts, actions, and heroes. I propose neither a theory of essentialist, transhistorical characteristics of the Jewish people conceived as a race nor a reductionist or determinist theory about group membership. Rather, my argument is that cultural tendencies, shaped by history, exist and inform an outlook on the world. Cultural membership may influence, but need not define or determine a person's creative work, political convictions, or stance toward the world, either consciously or unconsciously.

Preliminary to a fully developed discussion of *Thinking* in the next chapter, we consider here, with the help of Margaret Canovan's excellent book, the tensions that undermine *Thinking* and contribute to its lack of resolution.[2] In her penetrating and thorough analysis of Hannah Arendt's political thought, Canovan argues that the advent of totalitarianism and its continued threat shaped all of Arendt's political theory. Understanding her preoccupation with the problem of totalitarianism enables us to understand the coherence of Arendt's work. Canovan presents a convincing case, characterized by a meticulous analysis of unpublished papers and manuscripts from the Arendt archives. On the whole, her reading of Arendt is compatible with my own. Still, I believe there is a missing dimension in Canovan's study.

Canovan traces Arendt's lifelong attempt to understand the phenomenon of totalitarianism. She addresses the intellectual and moral influences of Greek, Christian, and German scholars: Socrates, Jesus, Augustine, Machiavelli, Kant, Heidegger, Jaspers, Weber, and even Marx, upon Arendt. The chapter on "Morals and Politics in a Post-Totalitarian Age" is a lengthy and subtle analysis of the disturbing separation in Arendt's work of politics from morality. In this chapter Canovan distinguishes two sorts of morality in Arendt's work, personal morality and the morality required of the citizen. The public, more political morality has a chance of preventing political evil in the world. Precisely this concern for the world is what Eichmann lacked. Indeed, Eichmann thought he was doing the right thing in carrying out his job of organizing the murder of Jews. "It was not that Eichmann lacked a sense of moral obligation—he was quite concerned to do the right thing—

just that, in the circles in which he moved, he met no one who seemed to think that the Final Solution was wrong, and plenty of people for whom killing Jews had become a duty; unpleasant, like so many duties, but something that had to be done" (Canovan 160). Thus the private mores or customs of a society sometimes prove insufficient to prevent the occurrence of political evil and historical catastrophes. "The question 'What barriers should have been able to prevent this monstrous evil?' at the same time gave back the frightening answer, 'Not ordinary morality, for ordinary decent moral people adapted to Nazism with ease as soon as it became the established order' " (Canovan 160).

Canovan writes that Arendt found the sources of private morality—the internal dialogue of the philosopher represented by Socrates and Christian morality represented by Jesus—to be of limited use in the world. Socrates' "pure" philosophy, characterized by an internal dialogue with the self, entails a withdrawal from the world. This can only prevent evil in a circuitous and unreliable manner. Socrates' injunction that it is better to suffer than to do wrong, represented a personal, but not a politically moral stance.[3]

Arendt proposed a public morality required of the citizen, involving concern for the world, distinguishable from the private morality that had proven so inadequate in the face of the Holocaust. "Politically, on the contrary, what counts is that a wrong has been done; to the law it is irrelevant who is better off as a result—the doer or the sufferer."[4] "The political answer to the Socratic proposition would be: What is important in the world is that there be no wrong.... Never mind who suffers it; your duty is to prevent it" (Canovan 178, citing Arendt, "Collective Responsibility" [1968]). Canovan suggests that Arendt became committed to republican principles in the hope that they would enable politics to embrace a public morality. "Arendt emerged from her encounter with Nazism, then, as a radical republican in the tradition of Clemenceau, the French Revolution and the Enlightenment, convinced that republican institutions and public-spirited citizens provided the strongest possible defenses against totalitarianism" (Canovan 163).

If totalitarianism was the problem, and "radical republicanism" Arendt's solution as perceived by Canovan, the term *plurality* in Arendt's work is also central. The importance of plurality in Arendt's theory is well known, but focusing upon it as her central contribution, an encapsulation of her contribution to political thought, is one of Canovan's original contributions. By the word *plurality*, Arendt meant both individualism and something more than that. She meant to signify the underlying equality of condition that characterizes human life—we all have the same basic biological needs, and the same human dignity or worth at the core of our existence. But each person is also an individual, distinct from others. Plurality in Arendt's terminology refers to this public acknowledgment of both the equality and distinctiveness of all people.

While Canovan may be correct in her appraisal of where Arendt headed politically with the experience of the Holocaust (although that judgment seems questionable in light of a reading of Arendt's *On Revolution*, where she mounts a concerted attack upon the ideas of the French Revolution), I believe it is not the most important aspect of her work, and will not carry us very far toward an understanding of Arendt's final effort, *The Life of the Mind*.[5] To my way of thinking, Canovan was hot on the trail of the "essential Arendt" until she followed her down the path of radical republicanism. Canovan lost the trail there, and I propose picking my way back to Arendt's awareness that "when the chips were down," as she was fond of saying, politically she was a Jew. She wrote to Jaspers in 1946 (L.50, 12/17/46). "Politically, I will always speak only in the name of the Jews whenever circumstances force me to give my nationality."[6] In her address accepting the Lessing Prize of the Free City of Hamburg in 1959, "On Humanity in Dark Times: Thoughts on Lessing," she remarked:

> I so explicitly stress my membership in the group of Jews expelled from Germany at a relatively early age because I wish to anticipate certain misunderstandings which can arise only too easily when one speaks of humanity. In this connection I cannot gloss over the fact that for many years I considered the only adequate reply to the question, "Who are you?" to be: A Jew. That answer alone took into account the reality of

persecution. . . . I was only acknowledging a political fact, through which my being a member of this group outweighed all other questions of personal identity or rather had decided them in favor of anonymity or namelessness. Nowadays such an attitude would seem like a pose.[7]

A list of Arendt's political heroes, cited by Canovan, consists, with the single exception of Clemenceau, not of radical republicans, but of Jewish rebels.

> Her own heroes and heroines were fighters for principles of this kind: the heroes of the Dreyfus case, Bernard Lazare, "a partisan of the impartiality of the law," and Clemenceau, defender of "such 'abstract' ideas as justice, liberty and civic virtue"; Judah Magnes, who strove for justice for Jews *and* Arabs in Palestine; Rosa Luxemburg, who fought for justice and political freedom. (Canovan 194–95)

The list of political heroes is remarkable for the striking discord it establishes with the *intellectual* heroes associated with Arendt, and regarded by Canovan and other scholars as the central influences on the development of her philosophical thought. The *political* heroes, with the exception of Clemenceau, are all Jews, and Clemenceau's commitment to justice, liberty, and civic virtue was admirable to Arendt because it involved the unpopular idea of fairness to the Jew, Dreyfus, during an anti-Semitic rampage in France. The major *intellectual* influences on Arendt include Socrates, Aristotle, Kant, Heidegger, Jaspers, and occasionally Marx. In contrast to the political heroes, not one of Arendt's intellectual heroes is a Jew, except Marx, who alone among the stellar group cannot really be regarded as one of her "heroes": Arendt's disagreements with Marx's theory were so profound, that he is better understood as a well-respected "foil" for her own theory.

Considering the uniformly Jewish identities of her political heroes, Arendt's avoidance of Jewish intellectuals notwithstanding, Judaism is the dimension I would add to Canovan's identification of totalitarianism as the centerpiece of Arendt's moral and political concerns. The specific horror of totalitarianism that shocked the world was the assault on the Jews during the Holocaust. If Canovan is correct (and I believe on the whole that she is) in identifying totalitarianism as Arendt's main political and moral preoccupation, the specific dimension overlooked in her analysis is the attempted genocide of the Jewish people. This is the gritty core, the catalyst that turned Arendt's attention toward totalitarianism.

THE POLITICAL TROUBLE WITH PHILOSOPHY

But what was the problem with Arendt's work on thinking? What tension so undermined her final effort, *The Life of the Mind*? Canovan suggests that Arendt's concern to unite thinking with politics, or to articulate a worldly way of thinking, led her in two incompatible directions. The tension is signified by her adherence to the influence of Heidegger, on the one hand, and Jaspers, on the other, echoed in her divided loyalty to Plato and Socrates. Heidegger and Plato represent the "purer" philosophical thinkers, while to Arendt, Jaspers and Socrates embodied the effort to bring philosophy into the world. As philosophers, Heidegger and Plato represent a quest for "pure" or absolute truth, not compatible with the world or with politics. The search for this rarified sort of truth calls for solitude: the philosopher is alone, not a worldly character, and so the relationship between his truth and the world remains problematic. In addition to the isolation required by the activity of philosophy, the substantive truth sought by the philosopher is antithetical to the democratic life. It is unified and absolute, incompatible with dialogue and plurality. The danger is that this sort of "truth" is compatible only with political coercion: it courts totalitarianism with its singular and coercive worldview. On two counts then, philosophy appears to be incompatible with the pluralist political world: its absolutism of content and the solitude and withdrawal required by its activity.

However, Socrates, whom Arendt considered the most "political" thinker of the four, was also in her terms the "purest" philosopher, because he thought for the love of thinking, rather than for any result in the world. Besides, as mentioned above, his dialogues were often internal, with himself, and thus removed from the everyday world. In contrast to Socrates' style of thinking, the "great philosophical systems," Arendt believed, "can hardly be called the results of pure thinking," because the authors of these systems had to stop thinking to write the stuff down.[8] "The activity of thinking is as relentless and repetitive as life itself, and the question whether thought has any meaning at all constitutes the same unanswerable riddle as the question of the meaning of life; its processes permeate the whole of human existence so intimately that its beginning and end coincide with the beginning and end of human life itself."[9] This view of thinking is compatible with the productless activity symbolized by Penelope's web, an image Arendt offers in *Thinking*. "The business of thinking is like Penelope's web: it undoes every morning what it has finished the night before" (*Thinking* 88).

Arendt never resolved these tensions in the nature of thinking. They dogged her from her earliest writings, right up to her work on *The Life of the Mind*. Canovan captures Arendt's dilemma this way:

> We can find in these early reflections from the 1950s two alternative views of the political implications of philosophy, associated with two pairs of opposed philosophers, Plato versus Socrates and Heidegger versus Jaspers. When Arendt is focusing on Plato or Heidegger she is inclined to fear that philosophy is intrinsically solitary, antipolitical and sympathetic to coercion; whereas, when she concentrates on Socrates or Jaspers she is tempted to believe that true philosophy may be communicative and in harmony with free politics. No sooner does she formulate either side of the dilemma, however, than she qualifies it and tries to find some way of mediating between the two sides that will allow her to avoid having to choose between them. (Canovan 264)

If "truth" were not conceived as absolute, would it be more compatible with the political world? In her efforts to connect thinking with worldly concerns, Arendt also entertained a conceptualization of "thinking" not involved in pursuit of absolute truth and not tied to philosophy. This looser definition of thinking resembles a dialogue that does not end: a productless quest, a process of questioning more compatible with a worldly way of thinking that removes Plato from consideration. At times Arendt argued that Heidegger's philosophy was compatible with this conception of dialogical thought, thereby associating him more closely with Socratic than Platonic thought.

Arendt's inability to renounce her attachment to Martin Heidegger was a big problem for her intellectually, politically, and personally, and we might as well address it now. It is probably still the single most tenacious grievance cited by Jews who believe Arendt had trouble with her own Jewish identity. She never publicly denounced Heidegger the Nazi. Even if her contorted efforts to present him as a "worldly thinker" had reflected an accurate reading of his work, it still leaves an enormous problem in reconciling how a "philosopher of the world" could have been such a political fool. In other words, Heidegger stands as a powerful symbol of the irrelevence, perhaps even the danger of philosophy when it comes to worldly ethics. Heidegger the philosophical genius of the twentieth century never renounced his involvement with the Nazi party, and Arendt never publicly renounced Heidegger.

Privately, in letters to Jaspers in the early years after the war, she was clear and unsparing in her disdain for Heidegger and his politics. She referred to him as a "potential murderer" and a liar.[10] Unfortunately for Arendt, this clear-headedness never made it into any of her public statements about her former mentor and lover.[11]

In 1946 Arendt wrote "What is Existenz Philosophy" in which she critically associated Heidegger with system building and a philosophy of egoism. Twenty-five years later, in "Heidegger at Eighty," she had him, approvingly, in Kant's camp, as one of the great destroyers of coercive metaphysical systems. Reading the two essays back to back is a dizzying experience: they appear to contradict each other so profoundly that one wonders whether Arendt was writing about the same man. In the 1946 essay she depicts Heidegger as a thinker who sought to reconstruct systematic philosophy, to rebuild a metaphysics that had been brought crashing to earth by Kant. This is in keeping with the totalitarian tendencies that she associated with Heidegger right after the war. In that early essay, written soon after she was reunited with Jaspers after a hiatus of twelve years, during which each feared the other had been killed, Jaspers is presented as the true heir to Kant, Heidegger as someone who sought to restore the old order:

> As opposed to Jaspers, Heidegger seeks with the new content to revive Systematic Philosophy in the completely traditional sense.... Heidegger's attempt despite and against Kant to reestablish an ontology led to a far-reaching alteration of the traditional philosophical terminology. For this reason, Heidegger always appears on first glace more revolutionary than Jaspers and this terminological appearance has very much interfered with the correct estimate of his philosophy. He says explicitly that he wishes to found an ontology and he can have nothing else in mind than to undo the destruction, begun with Kant, of the ancient conception of Being.[19]

In startling contrast, in "Martin Heidegger at Eighty," written over two decades after Arendt had visited and "reconciled" with Heidegger in 1949, she presents Heidegger as eclipsing even Kant as the greatest destroyer of the old metaphysical systems: "As to Heidegger's share in the collapse of metaphysics, which was immanent anyway, what we owe him and only him, is that the collapse took place in a manner worthy of what had preceded it: that metaphysics was *thought* through to its end." ("Heidegger at Eighty" 297)

In the earlier essay, Arendt presents Heidegger's philosophy as focused on an abstract, egoistic "self" to the detriment of involvement in the particularities of the world: "The 'self' has entered in place of man.... In this absolute isolation, the Self emerges as the concept really contrary to Man.... The Self as conscience has put itself in place of humanity, and the Being of the Self in place of the Being of Man." Even more damning: "Heidegger has therefore attempted in later lectures to bring in, by way of afterthought, such mythologizing confusions as Folk and Earth as a social foundation for his isolated Selves. It is evident that such conceptions can lead only out of philosophy into some naturalistic superstition" ("Existenz" 51)

Again, in contrast to her criticism of egoism in the 1946 essay, Arendt wrote in 1971: "The thinking 'I' which 'stands within' the raging storm, as Heidegger says, and for which time literally stands still, is not just ageless; it is also, although always specifically other, without qualities. . . . The thinking 'I' is everything but the self of consciousness" ("Heidegger at Eighty" 298). In a final, rather weak effort to save Heidegger from responsibility for his murderous political stupidity, Arendt notes that he was young enough not to have known what he was doing (he was in his forties). "Every thinker if only he grows old enough, must strive to unravel what have actually emerged as the results of his thought, and he does this simply by rethinking them" ("Heidegger at Eighty" 298).[13]

Arendt's inability publicly to disavow Heidegger may reflect an idiosyncratic weakness on her part: she "just couldn't get over him," in the worst romantic way. But that failing is of little interest to us intellectually, and probably better material for a psychoanalyst—or data for the author of a mass-market book on "Women Who Love the Wrong Men," or something of that sort.[14]

What is more significant for the argument I am making here is that Arendt's inability to "get over" Heidegger *intellectually* may reflect a weakness on her part for the legitimacy of German philosophy. It may reveal to us the Jewish pariah within herself at war with what she perceived to be the greater legitimacy of the German scholar she aspired to be. She tried to twist Heidegger into a thinker who would contribute to her own scholarly agenda, perhaps borrowing his name in an effort to lend legitimacy to her own project of bringing philosophy closer to the political world. We shall see these efforts dramatically in evidence in her discussion of the Jewish philosopher Philo of Alexandria in *Thinking*. Canovan also provides us with an example, as she notes incredulously that in Arendt's 1954 manuscript, "Concern with Politics in Recent European Philosophical Thought" (presented at the 1954 APSA meetings), written almost twenty years before she wrote "Heidegger at Eighty," Arendt had appropriated Heidegger in an eccentric manner. "The most remarkable feature of this 1954 manuscript is the surprising (not to say bizarre) suggestion that the philosopher who may be able to show us the way out of this difficulty [the dichotomy between philosophy and politics] is, of all people, Martin Heidegger. The Nazi fellow traveller whom we have seen Arendt dismissing in her essay on 'Existenz Philosophy' as the philosopher of 'egoism,' now appears as a guide to thinking about pluralistic politics" (Canovan 263). Canovan bluntly accuses Arendt of twisting Heidegger to serve her own purposes. "It seems likely that she was reading her own political philosophy into his writings, revealing what may seem a pathetic eagerness to rescue him from the political company he himself had chosen" (Canovan 263).[15]

In Canovan's reading, Socrates and Jaspers were more reliable figures than Heidegger to represent Arendt's hope that philosophy and politics were after all compatible. However, this stance is also not without problems. As we have seen, even Socrates, who in my reading emerges in Arendt's work as the ultimate philosopher of the public realm, was actually more engaged in a dialogue with himself than with others. Although Socrates did not seek an end product with his thinking, one might still argue that he was not, after all, so much engaged with as forced into the public realm. Besides, Arendt worried that even the pluralism of never-ending dialogues with others may lead to the predominance of opinion, rather than truth, or even thinking, in the world. So again she was left with the dilemma that dialogue is not after all compatible with philosophy: either the person engaged in a thinking dialogue with self is as withdrawn from the world as the philosopher seeking absolute truth; or the engaged dialogian can come up with nothing more satisfying than opinion as a guiding principle for political action.

WARM-UP EXERCISE: AN IMPRESSIONISTIC READING OF "TRUTH AND POLITICS"

Arendt's most explicit treatment of the relationship between Truth, truths, and opinion written before "Thinking" (and its exploratory essay, "Thinking and Moral Considerations") may be found in her essay "Truth and Politics"[16] In that essay, Arendt distinguishes among three different sorts of truths, philosophical, rational, and factual, and avers that none of the three has ever been welcomed into the political realm. Of the three, factual truth is most compatible with politics: absolutely necessary for political freedom, and also for the form of discourse that *is* compatible with politics: opinion. Philosophical as well as religious truths are no longer taken seriously enough to pose a threat to a political man. "Neither the truth of revealed religion, which the political thinkers of the seventeenth century still treated as a major nuisance, or the truth of the philosopher, disclosed to man in solitude, interferes any longer with the affairs of the world" (T. and P. 235).

Factual truth is another story. In principle, facts are necessary for the very formulation of opinions. How can one form an opinion without facts? However, in an age where the worldless fabrication of totalitarianism is possible, facts have come under a new form of political attack. They, like philosophical truth, are in danger of becoming transformed into opinion once they enter the political realm: "What seems even more disturbing is that to the extent to which unwelcome factual truths are tolerated in free countries they are often consciously or unconsciously transformed into opinions—as though the fact of Germany's support of Hitler or of France's collapse before the German armies in 1940 or of Vatican policies during the Second World War were not a matter of historical record but a matter of opinion" (T. and P. 236). Contributing to our sense of instability in the world, wholesale systematic lying in totalitarian regimes is accompanied by the conversion of fact into opinion in the "free world."

At a certain point in this difficult essay, Arendt turns to a discussion of what can be done to safeguard facts in the free world, since they are absolutely indispensable to the formation of opinion and to free political discourse. She considers universities to be one place where facts can be safeguarded (although that strikes one as a rather lame hope, and indeed, she herself acknowledges the vulnerability of the academy to political regimes). In the end, she suggests safeguarding facts in the form of stories, and there her language becomes poignant and revealing, reaching a crescendo with a proclamation of faith in the power of factual truth to survive. While reading the concluding paragraphs of "Truth and Politics," I found my mind slipping into a metaphorical state, with facts and factual truth playing the role of Jews endangered by a totalitarian politics. Ultimately, facts (or in my fantasy drama about this essay, Jews) persevere because they must, with the preservation of their story providing the ultimate guarantee of survival. "And the surest sign of the factuality of facts [read: Jews] and events is precisely this stubborn thereness whose inherent contingency ultimately defies all attempts at conclusive explanation" (T. and P. 257). "Truth [read: Jews], though powerless and always defeated in a head-on clash with the powers that be, possesses a strength of its own: whatever those in power may contrive, they are unable to discover or invent a viable substitute for it. Persuasion and violence can destroy truth, but they cannot replace it" (T. and P. 259). Truth is preserved by narrative when it enters the political realm. "Reality is different from, and more than, the totality of facts and events which, anyhow, is unascertainable. Who says what is—*legei ta eonta*—always tells a story, and in this story the particular facts lose their contingency and acquire some humanly comprehensible meaning" (T. and P. 262).

What is preserved by the storyteller no longer resembles anything we might recognize as philosophical, rational, or factual. But it is the last resort for truth under fire: a hiding place in a time of dire need. Truth can be destroyed by being turned into opinion but, disguised as story, it may very well survive to serve the world. Arendt concludes "Truth and Politics" with a proclamation of faith in truth's ability to survive the effort to reduce it to opinion in the political realm, lending a rather spiritual feel to the end of the essay: "The political function of the storyteller—historian or novelist—is to teach acceptance of things as they are. Out of this acceptance, which can also be called truthfulness, arises the faculty of judgment" (T. and P. 262). Ultimately truth must remain opposed to politics, but thank God, the political sphere is limited:

> What I meant to show here is that this whole sphere, its greatness notwithstanding, is limited—that it does not encompass the whole of man's and the world's existence. It is limited by those things which men cannot change at will. And it is only by

> respecting its own borders that this realm, where we are free to act and to change, can remain intact, preserving its integrity and keeping its promises. Conceptually, we may call truth what we cannot change; metaphorically, it is the ground on which we stand and the sky that stretches above us. (T. and P. 263–64)

This proclamation of faith reads like a prayer for the survival of truth [read: Jews], and the belief that if all else fails, it can be preserved in the form of a great story. If one squints to shift focus slightly, as when viewing a hologram, one can see a parable about Arendt's faith in the survival of the Jews, and all pariah peoples, by continuing to tell their story. The existence of a central story, either text or oral tradition, thus has something to do with the survival of truth. Without such a text or tradition, the prospects for truth surviving in the political realm are rather dismal.

Arendt struggled in vain to overcome the dilemma posed by the solitary nature of the philosophic pursuit and the public nature of politics. Even while attempting to dampen the dangers of absolutism in philosophy with the image of a never-ending productless dialogue, she was left with its solitude and worldlessness. As far as Arendt was concerned, philosophy and politics, truth and public life, remained incompatible. Arendt spent decades maneuvering the terms *philosophy*, *truth*, and *thinking*, in an effort to find a place in the world for the life of the mind. I shall argue that the tension she experienced can best be understood as a struggle between her training as a German Christian scholar and the Jewish aspects of her soul. That Jewish soul was forged by a heritage and culture that is extremely difficult to erase, and by Arendt's own life experiences as a refugee from anti-Semitic genocide, which she tried and failed to keep corraled in her political ideas.

In the previous two chapters a concept of "Jewish thinking" was proposed, with deference to its variety and complexity. The effort was made to avoid reducing Jewish thinking to a formula. Now, to freshen awareness of what is involved in "Jewish thinking" so that a discussion of the Jewish aspects of *Thinking* may become clearer, recall that Jewish thinking involves: (1) a central text, even though that text's boundaries are indefinite;

(2) lack of codification, an emphasis on continual reinterpretation through dialogue; (3) lack of boundedness, and the assumption that the bond between past, present, and future is subjective, forged by human actions; (4) lack of interest in visual imagery as an approach to truth or meaning; (5) and assumption of a community and potential for democracy in that all the members of the community are expected to participate to the extent possible. In Thorlief Boman's terms, Jewish thinking is dynamic compared to the more static quality of Greek thought.

There are five dimensions to Arendt's approach to thinking that appear throughout her writings and which can be identified as exhibiting a certain Jewish style, in terms of the characteristics set forth previously. I shall describe in encapsulated form the five dimensions here, although such a formulaic approach is obviously an oversimplification. Regard them as handles, useful for orientation as we step into this labyrinthian terrain. The Jewish characteristics of Arendt's quest for a worldly philosophy are: (1) her refusal to codify, to present formulae for thinking, her aversion to dogma and closure, and her belief that absolutes and universals are antithetical to the plurality needed in a free public sphere; (2) her emphasis on the "ineffability" of thought, her belief that making complex thoughts too tangible and explicit may result in them becoming reified, or "frozen" dogma; (3) her emphasis on plurality, described in *The Human Condition* as the need for a community of equal individuals in order to ensure freedom, also evident in her insistence upon a plural approach to truth, rather than a quest for universals; (4) her emphasis on "worldliness" or the importance of keeping thought grounded in the world, rather than hoping for a systematic, absolutist, or universalist philosophy; and (5) her ideas about the role of history, which are remarkably compatible with the Jewish approach to history.

It is time to turn to a detailed reading of the *Thinking* volume of *The Life of the Mind*. The tensions described by Canovan are certainly in evidence, but their genesis is not a divided loyalty in Arendt's heart between Socrates and Heidegger. It is broader than that, a divided loyalty between Arendt's Jewish soul and her German education.

CHAPTER 10

The Pariah and Parvenu in *Thinking*

SEEING AND HEARING

In the introduction to *The Life of the Mind* Arendt states that the impetus to begin the project was her experience at the trial of Adolf Eichmann in Jerusalem. "Factually, my preoccupation with mental activities has two rather different origins. The immediate impulse came from my attending the Eichmann trial in Jerusalem."[1] She continues, "In my report of it I spoke of the 'banality of evil.' Behind that phrase, I held no thesis or doctrine, although I was dimly aware of the fact that it went counter to our tradition of thought—literary, theological, or philosophic—about the phenomenon of evil" (*Thinking* 3). This is an obvious reference to the response to her report, her book *Eichmann in Jerusalem,* and the furor over her phrase "the banality of evil," which was misinterpreted to mean that she did not regard the Nazi crimes as exceptionally evil. What she meant was that exceptional evil can present itself in the guise of ordinariness—banality—making it even more insidious and dangerous. Her reference to the controversial phrase and her insistence that she intended nothing doctrinaire in its use, along with her statement that she was "dimly aware of the fact that it went counter to our tradition of thought..." indicate to me that the controversy itself, as well as her experience in

231

Jerusalem, were in the forefront of her mind when she began work on *Thinking*.

The second dimension that Arendt identifies as influencing her "preoccupation with mental activities," also prompted by her experience in Jerusalem, was the renewal of her interest in "the problem of Action, the oldest concern of political theory." She was concerned with the traditional dichotomy in political theory between thought and action, theory and practice, and as Canovan and other Arendt scholars have noted, she sought to reconcile the gap with her work on *The Life of the Mind*. The project is expressed by the question that Arendt claims "imposed" itself upon her: "Could the activity of Thinking as such, the habit of examining whatever happens to come to pass or to attract attention, regardless of results and specific content, could this activity be among the conditions that make men abstain from evil doing or even actually 'condition' them against it?" (*Thinking* 5).

She begins the volume with an affirmation of faith. Acknowledging the modern "deaths" of God, metaphysics, and philosophy, noting that the consequences of these losses are widespread and concern everybody, she insists that people (men) are and always have been thinking beings, who ought to be able to think their way out of the threat of meaninglessness in modern life. "Our *ability* to think is not at stake; we are what men [sic] always have been—thinking beings" (*Thinking* 11).

The need to think is associated with the quest for meaning, though not necessarily with truth, for "truth and meaning are not the same" (15). The quest for meaning is universal. All human beings can think, and all people crave meaning in their lives. "If, as I suggested before, the ability to tell right from wrong should turn out to have anything to do with the ability to think, then we must be able to 'demand' its exercise from every sane person, no matter how erudite or ignorant, intelligent or stupid, he may happen to be" (13). The absence of thought is not stupidity; many intelligent people fail to think, or lose the "habit of examining."

From the very start of the volume, then, Arendt seeks access to "meaning" in contemporary life, insists that all people must be capable of seeking it, and hopes that it will affect action in the world. The agenda is clear, and she launches upon the journey. She begins with an exploration of "Appearance," discussing what the world is that Thinking might affect it. The world is phenomenal: we *see* it. All existence presupposes a *spectator*, which in turn presupposes plurality. "Everything that is, is meant to be perceived by somebody. Not Man but men inhabit this planet. Plurality is the law of the earth" (19). "Our mental apparatus, though it can withdraw from *present* appearances, remains geared to Appearance" (24). This emphasis on appearance, at least in Boman's terms, reflects a thoroughly Greek perspective.

However, when we look closely at Arendt's discussion of seeing and hearing, we discover evidence of a troubled tension between the explicit Greek and unconscious Hebrew influences that plagues the entire volume. In her discussion of "Metaphor and the Ineffable" she contrasts the Greek association of thinking and seeing with the Hebrew association of hearing and truth. The Greek sense has dominated "from the outset in formal philosophy." Still there have been notable exceptions: theorists of the Will use metaphors taken either from the appetites and passions, or, she suggests, "from hearing, in line with the Jewish tradition of a God who is heard but not seen" (111).

The passages that follow are remarkable. Arendt notes that hearing is hardly ever associated with philosophy, except "in the late writings of Heidegger, where the thinking ego 'hears' the call of Being" (111). She then suggests that the medieval Jewish efforts to reconcile Biblical teachings with Greek philosophy resulted in the capitulation of Hebrew standards of Thinking to the Greek.

> Medieval Jewish writings testify to a complete victory of intuition or contemplation over every form of audition, and this victory was, as it were, foreshadowed by the early attempt of Philo of Alexandria to attune his Jewish creed to his Platonizing philosophy. He was still aware of the distinction between a Hebrew truth, which was heard, and the Greek *vision* of the true, and transformed the former into a mere preparation for the latter, to be achieved by divine intervention that had made man's ears into eyes to permit greater perfection of human cognition. (*Thinking* 111)

The full extent of the tension between Arendt's German philosophical training and the tug of her Jewish heritage can be gleaned from these passages. Heidegger is presented as thinking more like a Jew than Philo of Alexandria. Arendt's reference to Philo's religion is condescending: it is a "creed" compared to the more respectful reference to Greek *philosophy*. Being aware of the distinction between the Greek and Hebrew stances toward truth, Philo reduced the Hebrew perspective to a mere preparation for the Greek, effectuated by the Hebrew God, who transformed man's ears into eyes, "to permit greater perfection of human cognition."

If Arendt's reading of Philo is accurate, one can hardly imagine a more dramatic description of an assimilationist attempt to fit Judaism with the dominant culture. As we saw in chapter 7, Philo, along with other Medieval Jewish scholars, attempted to reconcile, in some way, Hebrew thought with Greek philosophy. In Arendt's reading, Philo uses the Hebrew God against the traditional Hebrew perspective itself, thereby subordinating hearing to sight as a way of gaining entree into Greek philosophy. One wonders why Arendt doesn't regard this as precisely the sort of assimilation to dominant society that she would have detested, had it occurred in the social realm. Instead, she seems rather patronizing, presenting Philo as a primitive, using a conception of God to turn ears into eyes. In the discussion that follows, she makes it clear that she regards the privileging of sight as appropriate. "There is first of all the indisputable fact that no other sense establishes such a safe distance between subject and object; distance is the most basic condition for the functioning of vision" (*Thinking* 111). Hearing creates dependency: "In hearing, the percipient is at the mercy of something or somebody else" (*Thinking* 112). Sight is associated with freedom, while hearing implies obedience:

> The Hebrew God can be heard but not seen, and truth therefore becomes invisible: 'Thou shalt not make unto thee my graven image or any likeness of any thing that is in heaven above or that is on the earth beneath.' The *invisibility* of truth in the Hebrew religion is as axiomatic as its ineffability in Greek philosophy from which all later philosophy derived its

axiomatic assumptions. And while truth, if understood in terms of hearing, demands obedience, truth understood in terms of vision relies on the same powerful self-evidence that forces us to admit the identity of an object the moment it is before our eyes. (*Thinking* 120)

She goes so far as to refer to sight as "noble," quoting approvingly from the work of her (Jewish) friend Hans Jonas. She presents philosophy as compatible with science, basking in the reflected glory of science as the only reliable means of achieving worldly knowledge. We know that Arendt herself entertained doubts about the prestige accorded science, and we shall see the trouble the centrality of science creates for her efforts to bring Thinking into the world. But it is important to note her temptation to respect philosophy for its reliance upon sight, and to regard it as compatible with modern secular knowledge for that very reason. "What recommended sight to be the guiding metaphor in philosophy—and along with sight, intuition as the ideal of truth—was not just the 'nobility' of this most cognitive of our senses, but the very early notion that the philosopher's quest for meaning was identical with the scientist's quest for knowledge" (*Thinking* 121).[2]

Arendt's admiration for sight as a path to knowledge is a significant inconvenience when she attempts in this same work to separate worldly thinking, the quest for meaning, from traditional "truth-seeking" philosophy, which she herself has associated with science, rendering it inaccessible to most people. If her intellectual convictions weren't so thoroughly predisposed in favor of the Greek, "hearing" as a sense might have been more available to her, and she might have been able to utilize it to *close* the distance from the world created by sight. If indeed hearing promotes proximity, rather than distance, it might be of use in bringing the life of the mind closer to life in the world, as well as people closer to each other as they attempt to discuss the meaning of things. If she had been less predisposed to "sight" rather than hearing (except when Heidegger presumably embraced hearing), she might have considered the possibility that hearing promotes *listening*, rather than obedience, which may be more compatible with both community and plurality. In fact, she does come close, when she notes that thinking, as distinct from philosophy, "needs speech not only to sound out and become manifest; it needs it to be activated at all" (*Thinking* 121).

Ironically, from a certain perspective "Hebrew" thinking, more than Greek, *trusts* worldly appearances. For all its emphasis on the visible, the Greek tradition in philosophy also regards phenomenal appearances as deceptive. Reality is something hidden and essential. As I have argued elsewhere, Arendt has little patience for inwardness.[3] She associates free will with the capacity to present oneself as one wishes to appear in the world. "In addition to the urge toward self-display by which living things fit themselves into a world of appearances, men also *present* themselves in deed and word and this indicates how they *wish* to appear, what in their opinion is fit to be seen and what is not" (*Thinking* 34). Such a statement is oblivious of the realities of race and gender, where certain appearances (white, male) are privileged, and associated with, e.g. respectability, authority, rationality; while others, unable to make themselves appear as they wish, suffer the consequences society associates with appearance.

In her denigration of the invisible, Arendt dismisses psychology and psychoanalysis as discovering "no more than the ever-changing moods, the ups and downs of our psychic life.... The monotonous sameness and pervasive ugliness so highly characteristic of the findings of modern psychology, and contrasting so obviously with the enormous variety and richness of overt human conduct, witness to the radical difference between the inside and outside of the human body" (*Thinking* 35). Anyone familiar with psychology—although perhaps not the orthodoxy of Freudian psychoanalysis—could testify to the fact that the variety reflected in psychological approaches to the world is remarkably rich, every bit as infinite as the variety of outward responses presented in public.

But Arendt's mistrust of inwardness and emotion, at least as a determinant of worldly actions, is not the issue here. Her project is to link thinking and worldly activity, without establishing a hierarchy, or a causal chain. The primacy of appearance is a given, she insists, because there is nothing outside of the world that "causes" appearances (42). She concludes irreverently, and hilariously, "If the divine is what causes appearances and does not appear itself, then man's inner organs would turn out to be his true divinities" (*Thinking* 42). So much for any compatibility between religion and philosophy!

Arendt's conflicted views about the nature of thinking are responsible for her desire, on the one hand, to bring it into the world and, on the other, for her avoidance of some opportunities for achieving that goal. She will not embrace essential truths, nor will she abandon the "superiority" of the Greek concept of thinking. She goes to some lengths to dissociate thinking from pursuit of absolute, universal, or essentialist truths. But the alternative, "opinion," seems a flimsy basis for building a worldly ethic, destined to lead to the impasse of "cultural relativism." Is murder, racism, or sexism acceptable if it is firmly rooted in certain cultures, and in the opinion of some, acceptable? It hardly seems likely that Arendt would support such a position. She must take her stand somewhere between relativism and absolutism. And yet, to paraphrase Canovan, no sooner does a non-Greek, or non-Christian possibility present itself than she reasserts the primacy of sight, or makes some sort of claim for universality of the life of the mind: "The Thinking ego is sheer activity and therefore ageless, sexless, without qualities, and without a life story" (*Thinking* 43). She dissociates Thinking from God with the wisecrack that if we don't rely on sight, but on some "hidden, internal causes," we will be left with our heart, lungs, and large intestine as "true divinities," a position even more "sight oriented" than the Greeks themselves; and she presents Philo as either an assimilationist or a primitive—it is not clear which.

I do not intend this to be disrespectful of Arendt, implying that she was "untrue to herself" and presuming my own superior capacity to come to terms with "who I am," culturally speaking. I mean to take a compassionate look at a conflicted Jewish intellectual, perhaps seeking "parvenu legitimacy" in ways in which she was unaware. The tragedy is that the most powerful engine of her scholarly legacy was, in my opinion, her real pariahdom: She "just didn't fit," and she knew it—both politically *and* intellectually. In contexts not so public as her published scholarly work, Arendt claimed to believe in God, and we may be certain that she was not referring to her liver and pancreas.[4] But, as Canovan notes, "Her religion, whatever it was, remained strictly a private matter, showing itself only in an occasional telling aside in her writings" (Canovan 104). Thus she "knew" who she was privately, but insisted that publicly both acting and Thinking were unaffected by that private identity.

CLASSICAL AND JEWISH ORTHODOXY

Throughout *Thinking*, we see Arendt struggling with the two tendencies identified by Canovan as a struggle between allegiance to Heidegger, the "pure" philosopher, and to Socrates, the "philosopher of the agora." I recast this as a struggle between Arendt the German intellectual and Arendt the Jewish pariah. The ambiguity about Socrates, who sometimes seems more like a "pure thinker" than a "philosopher of the agora," as well as Arendt's changing portrayal of Heidegger, from more systematic than Kant to more "deconstructionist" than Socrates, is some indication that they are not the best symbols of her conflict. In my reading, Arendt's problem in *Thinking* reflects the tension within herself between Jew and German.

If we may allow ourselves to speculate for a moment on why she was so averse to Judaism intellectually, two things come readily to mind. First, of course, is that her formal education was German and Christian: she simply did not have much Jewish scholarly background. This was not unusual for an educated, assimilationist twentieth-century German Jew. The absence of Jewish education may have been exaggerated because of the absence of a Jewish tradition of educating daughters as scholars. But another reason for Arendt's intellectual aversion to Judaism could easily be the association of Judaism with orthodoxy. Arendt's association of hearing with obedience seems to indicate that this may have been on her mind. It is not an idle concern: if Arendt was committed to opening dialogue, to "unfreezing frozen thoughts," then orthodoxy of any sort would be incompatible with the worldly Thinking she sought.

The irony is that in her work, the "orthodoxy" of philosophy is Greek—and perhaps also German—and every bit as coercive as religious orthodoxy may be. Orthodoxy is "right" or "straight" opinion, or belief in its literal translation from the Greek. In her efforts to put thinking to work in the world, Arendt continually stumbles over the classical Greek and German belief that philosophy and politics do not mix; that thinking is not something everyone can do because it is associated more with the pursuit of truth than the articulation of meaning through opinion; that detachment rather than engagement, the distance of visual perspective, rather than the proximity needed for hearing, is the appropriate stance of the thinker; that Thinking is solitary rather than community oriented or generated.

I do not advocate Jewish or any other sort of thinking as by definition the most effective way of engaging the world in a dialogue about tolerance for diversity, how to avoid totalitarianism, and so forth. I do suggest that the Talmudic or Biblical approach to the world may embody qualities Arendt sought for keeping thinking dynamic, and that her avoidance of it was symptomatic of the cultural hegemony, the orthodoxy of "classical" philosophy. The tensions and conflicts in her final work may in fact reflect the limitations of the Greek and German approaches to philosophy, and Arendt's efforts to find a way out of them. But on the other hand, her attraction to the "legitimacy" of German and Greek philosophy prevented her from truly breaking with philosophical orthodoxy and from achieving her goals as the brilliant, original, maverick thinker she actually was. When Arendt strove against the limitations of classical philosophical orthodoxy, she was a pariah scholar, and a Jewish one by her own definition: by birth and political identity. When she retreated to the attractions of German and Greek scholarship, she limited herself by assuming the stance, again in her own terms, of the "parvenu," or assimilationist, at least intellectually.

Let us look more closely at the tension between the Jew and the German in *Thinking*. At times, Arendt describes Thinking in terms that seem wholly foreign to any "Jewish" conception of the life of the mind. Thinking has no worldly characteristics, and it must be performed alone: "For while, for whatever reason, a man indulges in sheer thinking, and no matter on what subject, he lives completely in the singular, that is, in complete solitude, as though not men but Man inhabited the earth" (*Thinking* 47). Additionally, thinking subjects everything in the world to doubt: "It is precisely the Thinking activity—the experiences of the thinking ego—that gives rise to doubt of the world's reality and of my own" (49). Thinking involves a withdrawal from the world: not even into a "self" because the "Thinking ego" is ageless, sexless, without even cultural dispositions. "Thinking . . . subjects everything it gets hold of to doubt . . . [and] has no such matter-of-fact relation to reality" (52). She contrasts thinking with common sense, which she describes as "The feeling of realness belonging to our biological apparatus" (52).

After following Arendt for a while down the path of the isolation and worldlessness of the thinker, we find her returning to a more worldly version of thinking. Now it has the capacity to change things, since according to the definition presented, it is a radically "deconstructionist" activity. Her discussion of the relationship between thinking and science is a good encapsulation of the Greek and the Jew embattled in *Thinking*. Science is associated with sight and knowledge, rather than "meaning." It also has the capacity to change the world in a way that resembles the deconstructive powers of Thinking, rather than the linear accumulation of facts. Science "constantly destroys authentic semblances." "It was Thinking that enabled men to penetrate the appearances and unmask them as semblances, albeit authentic ones; commonsense reasoning would never have dared upset so rapidly all the plausibilities of our sensory apparatus" (53).

Arendt contrasts "pure" Thinking with science, precisely because science is world oriented and results in a "product." Science and the search for knowledge never leave the "realm of appearances." Science seeks knowledge and both factual and rational truth, while Thinking seeks meaning. As such, Thinking is productless: it is not oriented toward an end product.

"Thinking withdraws radically and for its own sake from the world and its evidential nature, whereas science profits from a possible withdrawal for the sake of specific results" (56). Ultimately, Arendt identifies science with common sense. It is "refinement of common sense" anchored in the world, while pure Thinking is a self-contained activity in pursuit of meaning, which is never final or tangible.

In what is by now becoming a predictable pattern, the distinction between "worldless" Thinking and "worldly" science does not hold for long. Before we know it, Arendt is back trying to identify thinking with a search for meaning bearing worldly and human implications. The human "need" to think is probably what permits us to raise the more commonsensical and scientific questions. "It is more than likely that men, if they were ever to lose the appetite for meaning we call thinking, and cease to ask unanswerable questions, would lose not only the ability to produce those thought-things that we call works of art, but also the capacity to ask all the answerable questions upon which every civilization is founded" (62). Arendt evidences a faith that a link between thinking and the world exists but cannot be pointed to. It is invisible, ineffable: the point is not to ask for results or guarantees, but to keep thinking, out of "reason's own need"—or perhaps out of faith. Thinking has its results, but no one has sufficient control or prescience to determine what they must be.

But commiting herself to the potential worldliness of Thinking once again eludes Arendt's grasp. She calls again upon her classical authorities, Heidegger and then Plato, who describe Thinking as unworldly, almost antithetical to life. All Thinking—"every reflection that does not serve knowledge and is not guided by practical needs and aims"—is "out of order" (Heidegger). It involves a "stop and think." Thinking interrupts living. Arendt discusses the age-old battle between Thinking and common sense, early exemplified by the Thracian peasant girl who laughed at the sight of Thales falling into a well while he was intent upon the motions of the heavenly bodies above him, and more contemporarily caricatured by the absent-minded professor. Plato, with his simile of the Cave, reminds us that to ordinary people the preoccupations of philosophers seem otherworldly, more like death than life, while for philosophers it is the meaninglessness of unexplored daily activities that seem deathlike. "Seen from the perspective of Thinking, life in its sheer thereness is meaningless; seen from the perspective of the immediacy of life and the world given to the senses, Thinking is, as Plato indicated, a living death" (*Thinking* 87).

As Canovan points out, when Arendt isn't associating Heidegger with worldly Thinking, she rescues Thinking from its otherworldly, Heideggerian incarnation with the help of Socrates. But remarkably, the Socrates who emerges as the worldly thinker in Arendt's volume bears a striking resemblance to the pariah in her Jewish political writings. Thus the conflict between the classical and Jewish perspectives in Arendt's work is played out as a battle between Heidegger and Socrates, with Plato as a sort of mediator.

SOCRATES AS PARIAH

In her discussion of Socrates in the chapter "What Makes Us Think?" the Jewish aspects of Arendt's quest to conceptualize thinking as worldly surface most visibly. From a certain perspective, Arendt's model thinker, Socrates, is a Jew. This is not to say that she misrepresents Socrates. Indeed, if there are cultural or ethnic "traits" that emerge as a perspective on the world, which are not regarded as essentialist or biologically determined, we would expect for them *not* to be unique to the ethnic group in question. We do not seek to identify racial exclusivity, but cultural tendencies. Arendt may recognize tendencies in Socrates that we can identify with intellectual "Jewishness" as presented here. If Socrates remains recognizable, he may indeed have possessed characteristics that resemble Jewish characteristics. That doesn't mean that he needs to have been a Jew to possess them. But it can make us wonder why Arendt needed to go to Socrates to find them, and that inquiry may teach us something.

Arendt surveys "historically representative answers" to the question "What makes us think?" In early Greece, philosophy replaced religion (135): Thinking was an approach to the immortal. Plato associated the origin of Philosophy with the sense of Wonder. "The wonder that is the starting point of Thinking is neither puzzlement nor surprise nor perplexity; it is an *admiring* wonder" (*Thinking* 143). The Roman answer to why we think was nearly the opposite of the Greek: Thinking arises out of unhappiness. "Thinking then arises out of the disintegration of reality and the resulting *dis*unity of man and world, from which springs the need for another world, more harmonious and more meaningful" (153). There is no way to choose between these approaches to the question. Arendt finds a common thread in the various explanations, in the word *need*. We simply *need* to think.

The best way to understand what makes us think is to "look for a model, an example of a thinker who was not a professional" (167). She chooses Socrates, whom we would undoubtedly know even less about, were it not for Plato. Indeed, Socrates might not have made such an impression upon Plato, "if he had not decided to lay down his life, not for any specific belief or doctrine—he had none—but simply for the right to go about examining the opinions of other people" (168). Socrates had no doctrine, and left no text. Plato provided the text, and the vision that has come down to us bears an eerie resemblance to a Talmudic Rabbi with a following of devoted students. The text is not the Bible, but the method of study is similar—at least according to Arendt's description.

> The first thing that strikes us in Plato's Socratic dialogues is that they are all aporetic. The argument either leads nowhere or goes around in circles. In order to know what justice is, you must know what knowledge is, and in order to know that, you must have a previous, unexamined notion of knowledge.... None of the *logoi*, the arguments, ever stays put; they move around. And because Socrates, asking questions to which he does *not* know the answers, sets them in motion, once the statements have come full circle, it is usually Socrates who cheerfully proposes to start all over again and imagine what justice or piety or knowledge or happiness are. (*Thinking* 170)

This surely sounds more like Boman's description of dynamic *Hebrew* thought, rather than the peaceful stasis of his Greek. It is a description of Thinking as ceaseless activity with no anticipated end product. It represents a deconstructive approach to dogma, to codes, to any accepted doctrine. Even Socrates' focus on words themselves involves a critical reexamination of commonly accepted definitions. Words have a vital, dynamic quality: not closed entities, but something that must be brought to life in the world. "The word *house* is something like a frozen thought that Thinking must unfreeze whenever it wants to find out the original meaning" (171).

Although Socrates claimed to have no doctrine, nothing to teach, and indeed could be counted on to undermine any smugly assumed doctrine, he did say that he could teach virtue. But virtue was not to be confused with rules of behavior. He taught a method of questioning assumptions, and the activity, the process of questioning was itself virtuous. The method involved interactive dialogue with others, in the pursuit of meaning void of doctrine. He taught the method of questioning assumptions. "It seems that he, unlike the professional philosophers, felt the urge to check with his fellow men to learn whether his perplexities were shared by them—and this is quite different from the inclination to find solutions for riddles and then demonstrate them to others" (172).

Three images Socrates used to describe his task as thinker are the gadfly, midwife, and electric ray. He goaded people out of the complacent world of unquestioned assumptions; he "shocked" them into stopping and thinking, with unconventional questions and viewpoints; and he brought forth the thoughts and vital questions of others, nurturing the important ones once they were distinguished from shallow "wind eggs." Still, while he claimed that Thinking was the greatest good that ever befell Athens, and while he seems to have believed he could distinguish "healthy" thoughts from "windeggs," he did not have an answer to the question of what thinking was good *for*. Arendt hypothesizes, "We may be sure that a dialogue dealing with the question 'What is Thinking good for?' would have ended up in the same perplexities as all the others" (173). He was dealing with invisibles. The metaphor for Thinking is the wind: its effects can be felt and seen, while it itself remains invisible (174).

In fact, two of Socrates' more illustrious students, Alcibiades and Critias, got Socrates' lesson "wrong" by misinterpreting his call for no-doctrine to mean that all was permitted: "If we cannot define what piety is, let us be impious—which is pretty much the opposite of what Socrates had hoped to teach by talking about piety" (176). Obviously we would have difficulty defining Alcibiades and Critias as "Jewish thinkers."

The reason for the willful avoidance of doctrine, of the stance toward "unfreezing" words and concepts, rather than congealing thoughts into rules, is that the existence of rules causes people to cease Thinking. "What people then get used to is less the content of the rules, a close examination of which would always lead them into perplexity, than the *possession* of rules under which to subsume particulars" (177). Then people are dependent upon the existence of rules and have no capacity to distinguish good ones from bad. "The more firmly men hold to the old code, the more eager will they be to assimilate themselves to the new one, which in practice means that the readiest to obey will be those who were the most respectable pillars of society, the least likely to indulge in thoughts, dangerous or otherwise" (177). And lest we mistake her intentions, she lets us know, "I am alluding, of course, to what happened in Nazi Germany" (177).

Socrates pursued this dangerous undertaking of infusing Thinking into respectable society neither from altruism nor to transform Athens into a different sort of city. "He does not say that he began his examining in order to become such a great benefactor. As far as he himself is concerned, there is nothing more to be said than that life deprived of thought would be meaningless" (178). Arendt suggests that Socrates continued to think out of sheer Eros—love of Thinking—because it was what made his life meaningful.

It is difficult to write about Socrates—as he persisted unto death in asking uncomfortable questions and deconstructing accepted doctrine—without thinking of the Jewish Pariah in Arendt's work. Arendt did not respect assimilationist parvenus; and she expected people to refuse to act like victims. She favored a Jewish army during World War II, to liberate the Jews from the camps and to establish a record of refusing to be victims. But as I have argued elsewhere, her authentic heroes were pariahs, who knew where they stood with "respectable" society and insisted on their identity as pariahs, as self-proclaimed outsiders.[5] They claimed for themselves what society tried to impose upon them, thereby preempting victimhood.

Throughout history, Jews have continued to practice their religion even though it meant their doom as individuals: the religion lived on. Jewish martyrs make the statement, in essence, that life would be meaningless without their Judaism, that ceasing to study Talmud and to pray to their own God is a necessary condition for their life. Socrates continued to think out of "reason's own need," because life would be meaningless without it.

> It looks as though Socrates had nothing more to say about the connection between evil and lack of thought than that people who are not in love with beauty, justice, and wisdom are incapable of thought, just as, conversely, those who are in love with examining, and thus "do philosophy" would be incapable of doing evil. (*Thinking* 179)

But surely this is too much. Arendt cannot have had in mind a nonassimilationist European Jew when she wrote about Socrates! And is one justified in blithely associating practicing a religion with practicing "Thinking"? Especially when Boman left us with the contrasting image of Socrates, standing stock still in the Agora, and the Jew, rocking back and forth while he prays? Besides, Socrates has no doctrine, no text, he does not belong to a group of believers. What are the possible connections with a religious Jew?

Now it might be that Socrates had more of a doctrine than he acknowledged. If not, it is difficult to imagine why he was dangerous enough to have been executed. Arendt herself reminds us that the usual stance toward the philosopher is laughter. Even the little peasant girl knew to laugh at Thales's incapacity to navigate on the earth. What made Socrates so much more dangerous than Thales? The same questions could be raised in relation to Jews: What has made them the target of lethal oppression throughout the millennia? Likewise, they both do and do not have a doctrine. They have a God, a text, and a set of commandments, but there is, as we have seen, a profound reluctance to codify the text, which is continually being reinterpreted, to the point of rendering the boundary between text and interpretation indefinable, just as the boundary between word and thing or word and world is indefinite in the Hebrew language.

In Arendt's discussion of the "Two-in-One" of Socrates' internal dialogue, we find that Socrates did after all have a few positive propositions. Two, to be exact: "It is better to be wronged than to do wrong"; and "It would be better for me that my lyre or a chorus I directed should be out of tune and loud with discord than that I, *being one*, should be out of harmony with myself and contradict me" (*Thinking* 181). These hardly sound dangerous enough doctrines to have brought about Socrates' trial and execution for teaching false gods and corrupting youth. Arendt suggests that the real threat to any established order is Thinking itself. The danger is that thinking both challenges accepted conventions and creeds, and does not seek to bring forth a new creed.

> There are no dangerous thoughts; Thinking itself is dangerous, but nihilism is not its product. Nihilism is but the other side of conventionalism; its creed consists of negations of the current so-called positive values, to which it remains bound. . . . Thinking is equally dangerous to all creeds and, by itself, does not bring forth any new creed. Its most dangerous aspect from the viewpoint of common sense is that what was meaningful while you were Thinking dissolves the moment you want to apply it to everyday living. (*Thinking* 176)

THE WORLDLY RESULTS OF THINKING

"Thinking" as it is emerging in *The Life of the Mind* has some influence on the world, but that influence is neither simple nor direct. There are, reflecting the tension we have noted, two versions of Thinking as it emerges in Arendt's discussion: one "pure" and removed from the dailiness of the world; the other more engaged, although still indirectly, and potentially dangerous in terms of perceived threats to the political regime.

From my perspective, the first version is Greek, the second, Jewish. The "pure" thinker's solitude should keep him out of trouble, "off the streets" as it were, and in this way the incapacity of the thinker to do evil is by default: he or she doesn't do much of *anything* in the world, except think. The more "worldly" Thinking on the Socratic model is not really pluralist but dialogical. This thinker thinks out of Eros, out of love of Thinking and has an indirect impact on the world. The theory, which Arendt attributes to Socrates, is that anybody capable of love, and of appreciating beauty would, or perhaps could, do no wrong. We know that this is not necessarily true: people kill for the sake of and in the name of love. This may bring us closer to understanding why a version of Thinking modeled on love may be considered politically dangerous enough to invite killing. But what, more specifically, is the link between Socrates' erotic Thinking and the world?

Consider Arendt's brief remark early in *Thinking* that while Thinking itself has no product, some of the more practical or scientific questions could not have arisen without it. This gives us a clue about the worldly uses of Thinking. We think for the sake of Thinking, and then let go, relinquish control—something like Arendt's description of political action. Thinking, like acting, introduces something into the world, but cannot control its outcomes. Lenin's description of making a revolution also comes to mind: the revolutionary begins, but does not then control the course of events. Leading a revolution feels like riding a runaway train. Introducing an important idea into the world involves the same relinquishment of control over its destiny.

Arendt refers to thinking as "the habit of examining": "Could the activity of Thinking as such, the habit of examining whatever happens to come to pass or to attract attention, regardless of results and specific content, could this activity be among the conditions that make men abstain from evil doing or even actually 'condition' them against it?" (*Thinking* 5). Thinking of this sort resembles conditioning, training. In sports, one practices, trains, exercises the body, and rehearses the movements required in actual competition. One anticipates situations likely to occur, and tries to prepare for them. Baseball players endlessly practice fielding grounders and making double plays; football players anticipate different defenses and practice getting through, over, or around them; martial artists anticipate various attacks likely to occur in sparring matches and rehearse evasions, blocks, and counterattacks. But when the game begins, one can only hope that the training will assert itself and that the body will respond appropriately. One can never predict exactly what will happen, nor does one "think" before moving, any more than a bicycle rider "thinks" about maintaining balance while she rides. Responses must be almost automatic. Athletes refer to "muscle memory" to describe this highly prepared state, in which muscles respond from training almost as from instinct.

In a similar vein, perhaps the "habit of examining" conditions the individual to respond with critical perspective, almost instinctively, but with conditioned instincts, to the advent of evil. When one's Jewish neighbors disappear in the night, and so do the Jewish neighbors of all one's acquaintances, one is prepared to respond appropriately, if one has all along been in the habit of examining. We have reference here to Thinking as moral training: political disaster-preparedness training, as it were. A morally prepared polity will not be passive putty in the hands of a totalitarian dictator, because its instincts are prepared to respond swiftly: it is in condition. One would no sooner expect a populace to be prepared to respond to totalitarian terror without having been conditioned to think, than one would expect a team of beer-swilling, potato-chip munching, Monday-night football viewers to prevail in a football match-up with a professional team. Thus we begin to sense the danger to the authorities of the person who trains the populace in this vital art. Visualize Socrates as a freelance football coach trying to get a team of volunteers in shape to challenge the current Super Bowl champions. If they defeat the professional heroes, they threaten to undermine the multimillion-dollar sports economy that is professional football. The amateurs represent a genuine economic threat.

We now have some sense of what makes Thinking "dangerous" to an existing political and social order. We also have a hint of how it may affect the world. Still, has Arendt brought us to an understanding of how *everybody* is capable of thought? And what has happened to my argument that her approach to Thinking is both more Jewish than she believed and somehow also "not Jewish enough"? Her remaining discussion in *Thinking*, of "The two-in-one," will enable us to address these issues. There are limitations with Socrates as a model of a thinker, and Arendt is at a loss as to how to move beyond them.

"The two-in-one" refers to the "soundless dialogue" between me and myself that describes Socratic Thinking. While Socrates is remembered as the thinker who would engage *anybody* in dialogue (for free! because he promised no doctrine and claimed he had nothing to teach), his real Thinking seems to have occurred in dialogue with himself. That is, in spite of Arendt's presentation of Socrates as the philosopher of the agora, in spite of her presentation of his dialogues as "aporetic" and dynamic, there is still Boman's vision of Socrates the Greek, stock still, lost in thought, standing in the agora to be sure, but not really "there." Arendt attempts in her discussion of Socrates to move Thinking out of the mind of the philosopher and into the streets, the agora, the polis. Socrates is her chosen man. And though he talks to everybody, there is still the sense that he listens mostly to himself—which may be wise, but it doesn't do with Thinking what Arendt needs to have done. From this standpoint, Socrates *was* after all a Greek, and Arendt needs something more to complete her vision of Thinking.

Arendt is aware that while Socrates may represent the most "complete" worldly thinker she can find, there are still elements missing that she regards as essential. Socrates is a dismantler of dogma, a radical and challenging thinker. But he is not "worldly" enough in the sense that his dialogues are more internal than collective, and he thus resembles that rarified, unapproachable philosopher that discourages ordinary people from joining in his challenge to think. He professes to respect the opinion of ordinary folks more than experts, but he clearly prefers his own company in the enterprise of Thinking. Consider Arendt's reading of Socrates' positive maxim "Being one . . .": it is better to be out of harmony with the world than with myself. She regards this as an *un*political stance, in that the emphasis, overlooked by most modern translators, is on the "being one." *As an individual*—not as a member of a community—it is more important to be in harmony with oneself than with the community. As a member of a community, in contrast, one may have to compromise, be flexible, for the good of the common world, rather than for one's own sense of internal coherence or righteousness.

Neither, contends Arendt, can Socrates' first maxim, "It is better to suffer wrong than to do it," be described as "political," because it concerns the individual soul of the thinker, rather than the state of the world. It means only that "It is better for *me*, as a thinker, to suffer than do wrong." Although she acknowledges that it was a revolutionary statement in the context of its time, she insists that the political response in our own time would be to affirm the responsibility of all to prevent wrong from happening in the world, never mind who commits or suffers it. Arendt would politicize Socrates' statement as: "It is better to prevent wrong from happening in the world, than to either suffer or do wrong." This restatement reflects an objective stance, oriented toward the world, rather than a subjective stance oriented toward one's own soul. That worldly orientation, the objective rather than subjective standpoint, is what Arendt believes is prerequisite to political thinking.

Arendt leaves us with a conflicted image of Socrates— which is not surprising, since we have entertained a conflicted image of Socrates all along. Socrates was the "purest" thinker, and also the most public thinker in history. He left no written record of his thinking, sought no products, no doctrines, thought for the love of it. His thinking was a dialogue within himself, where he sought nothing more dangerous than harmony, and to do no harm. Yet if his thinking had no worldly product, why was he executed as a political troublemaker? Did he seek "pure" meaning or public dialogue? Did he seek inner peace, or to change the world?

The conflicted image of Socrates reflects once again Arendt's conflict between Jew and "classical" German or Greek scholar. Socrates is a pariah, and also the model of the wisest man in the history of the world. His internal dialogue would not have been sufficient to get himself killed, although it never would have earned him a reputation for wisdom either: no data left behind. He would have been laughable to a few peasant girls, as he stood in the same place in the agora, day after day, thinking. That Socrates is Greek. The "Jewish" Socrates tried talking to others in his community, and when in fact a few people clustered around him to debate the meaning of things, their leader was put to death. He, like Akiba, chose death rather than betrayal of either himself or his followers, and as he was dying, delivered a message to keep the faith.[6]

Arendt was tempted to view Socrates as a model of the worldly philosopher she sought, but she froze at the thought of relinquishing the image of Socrates the solitary classical philosopher, the purest thinker of all time. The pariah activist who engages in dialogue for the sake of disrupting complacency, and the "pure" thinker who thinks out of love, for reason's own need, may in fact reflect two sides of Socrates. But they also accurately reflect Arendt's conflict between the classical model of philosophy that she had been educated to revere, and the pariah activist needed by the Jews, and all potential victims of totalitarianism. The result is the lack of resolution in *Thinking* and the double-exposed picture of Socrates that Arendt bequeathed us. Arendt couldn't quite follow Socrates into the agora and use him as an example, because she couldn't turn off the German philosophical demands for purity and isolation from the masses. Arendt the Pariah drew a stunning portrait of Socrates the Pariah. She was more a Jewish thinker than she admitted, and yet, she backed off at the critical moment, leaving a lack of resolution in her quest for a worldly philosophy.

Now is the time to evoke the image of the Talmudic students paired off with one another, noisily debating and contesting every word of the most revered scholars of their tradition, and to consider whether that image might not be more compatible with Arendt's search for a universally available, worldly way of thinking than the silent Socratic two-in-one. The Talmudic students may have been specialists—chosen for a particularly intense encounter with Jewish scholarly teachings—but according to the Jewish teachings themselves, any (male) Jew can become a Talmudic scholar. Indeed, even the humblest working men and peasants were enjoined to spend their Sabbaths not languishing in well-deserved idleness but studying and discussing the Torah with their friends and family. All Jewish men were supposed to think and study; some more than others. The study, as we saw, entailed questioning the words of the authorities, by taking each word seriously. Likewise, the assumption was that the words are "real": they exist in the world and bear worldly consequences.

The importance of the Torah is not rarified, private, worldless awareness. The teachings, so fiercely debated, are directed toward activity. As members of the Jewish community, how should we act? What should we do? In Arendtian terms, however, the border between private and public is blurred, which may be yet another reason why she avoided utilizing Jewish thought for her philosophy. Still, what did she fear? So long as their culture remains viable, the members of the Jewish communities hardly seem to be in danger of succumbing to the temptation of becoming "mass men," which is what Arendt associated with the rise of "the social."[7] Arendt regarded the blurring of the border between private and public as politically dangerous because individual action, which she associated with freedom, was foreclosed. The likely result was mass society, a requisite for totalitarianism.

The teachings of the Torah are intended to shape and provide structure to daily life. But they are not intended to be doctrinaire, and they are, as we saw, subject to ceaseless debate and reinterpretation. They concern "conventional" morality, such as the injunction not to kill. But plenty of killing takes place in the Bible, committed by the patriarchs themselves, and sometimes the matriarchs, too, giving rise to questions about *when* one may kill, since it is obviously not an absolute, even though it is a commandment. As noted earlier, even the Ten commandments were lost once and resurrected.

The teachings of the Torah also have to do with debates about what to eat, when to bathe, how to dress and groom, when to have sexual intercourse, and with whom, and when to rest and pray. So the fierce debates among pairs of Jewish scholars result not in directly political actions, but certainly in worldly ethics that affect all the members of a community. This is not to be confused with "behavior" of which Arendt is so disdainful in *The Human Condition*. There, behavior is associated with private life, physical necessity, and the instinctive behavior of animals keeping themselves alive. In contrast, the private and physical activities of observant Jews are *human* in Arendt's terms, precisely because they are mediated by thought: they are neither automatic nor instinctive. And while the rules of *Kashrut*, for example, may seem doctrinaire, even dogmatic, they too have been the subject of rabbinic debate. They are set forth in the Torah, but rarely implemented without rabbinic dialogue about what is intended. It takes an act of interpretation, indeed, a history of interpretation to get from "Thou shalt not seethe the lamb in its mother's milk"[8] to keeping separate meat and dairy kitchens, and to declaring Cheerios kosher, but Ritz crackers not.

We conclude our search for Jewish themes in Arendt's work by returning to her more worldly writings: on political action and history.

CHAPTER 11

Jewish Themes in Political Action and History

JUDAISM AND THE SPACE FOR POLITICAL ACTION

Arendt wrote *The Life of the Mind* as part of a lifelong project that presented itself initially as Jewish: how to prevent a recurrence of anti-Semitic genocide. While she insisted that the Holocaust was not a uniquely Jewish problem, the systematic destruction of the Jews in Europe provided the specific catalyst that launched her on the quest for a type of thinking designed to prevent political evil. But the "Jewishness" of Arendt's scholarship is not restricted to the *Life of the Mind*, nor did the *Eichmann* controversy "make" Arendt a Jewish thinker. Hannah Arendt was one woman, whose work, as her life, is of a whole. There are Jewish themes to be found even in the work that seems most profoundly beholden to ancient Greece and classical imagery for the coherence of its theory: *The Human Condition*.[1]

I have written elsewhere, and in greater detail than I need go into here, about Arendt's Pariah as Jewish, a shadow figure to parallel the Greek hero who has received so much attention as Arendt's political actor.[2] Here I wish to focus briefly on Arendt's discussion of political action in *The Human Condition*, and then to move on to her ideas about history, in order to demonstrate the same pattern observed in *The Life of the Mind*: while she focuses on the Greek, Roman, and Christian references, avoiding Jewish sources and explicit discussion of Jewish themes, the substance of her questions and concerns is Jewish, at least in terms of the themes we have been discussing.

This statement may appear extravagant given the fact that *The Human Condition* has been utilized by Arendt scholars as an example of her thorough preoccupation with the Greeks. Arendt's treatment of political action and public life in *The Human Condition* is focused exclusively on the Greeks. The Athenian *polis* provided public space for Greek competition with the gods, the effort to win immortal fame, to wrest immortality from the hands of the gods and to provide meaning for the Athenian men who competed on this public stage. Her treatment of the subject is suffused with admiration for the Greeks and for an agonistic concept of heroism that has been regarded as conventionally "male," incompatible both with feminism, and with a "softer" more participatory version of democratic politics.[3]

But a close look at one dimension of Arendt's discussion of political action in *The Human Condition* reveals a Jewish foundation hidden beneath the Greek facade, and if we make allowance for the stereotypical association of Jewishness with femininity, the "maleness" of Arendt's polis life also disappears. The focus of my analysis is Arendt's conception of the importance of physical space as an arena for political action, and as a prerequisite of freedom.

Throughout *The Human Condition*, Arendt laments the loss of political spaces in modern life, stresses the importance of objectivity, and argues for the necessity of an actual public arena for the creation and maintenance of political freedom, which she attributes to the Athenians. There seems to be no doubt that she refers to actual, *physical* spaces, which are designed to survive the generations, as the following quotations indicate: "To live together in the world means essentially that a world of things is between those who have it in common as a table is located between those who sit around it; the world, like every in-between, relates and separates men at the same time. The public realm, as the common world, gathers us together and yet prevents our falling over each other, so to speak" (HC 52). "If the world is to contain a public space, it cannot be erected for one generation and planned for the living only; it must transcend the life span of mortal men" (55). "The point, then, is not that there is a lack of public admiration for poetry and philosophy in the modern world, but that such admiration does not constitute a space in which things are saved from destruction by time" (57).

This line of argument is maintained consistently, right up to the discussion of Action, which comes fairly late in the book. Arendt opens that discussion by reiterating her belief that public space is physical and provides a place for securing the immortality of human deeds against the ravages of time and history. "The organization of the *polis*, physically secured by the wall around the city and physiognomically guaranteed by its laws—lest the succeeding generations change its identity beyond recognition—is a kind of organized remembrance" (HC 198).

Then, astonishingly, in the course of the next few paragraphs, we see the walls of the *polis* crumble, as Arendt abruptly claims priority for human interaction as the basis for "organized remembrance," even in the *absence* of a physical space. On one single page (198), Arendt moves from a paragraph rather Hegelian in spirit, in which she suggests a dialectic between the tangible physical space of the polis and the intangibility of the words and actions of the people who appear there, to a description of public space as interactive, rather than physical. The dialectial moment is reflected in her description of Homeric performances.

> According to this self-interpretation, the political realm rises directly out of acting together, the "sharing of words and deeds." . . . It is as though the wall of the *polis* and the boundaries of the law were drawn around an already existing public space which, however, without such stabilizing protection could not endure, could not survive the moment of action and speech itself. (HC 198)

This description of the interaction between physical space and human activity raises a question about the inviolability of the physical aspect of the polis, which now appears to be shaped by people *and* space. But by the end of the page, the physical *polis* has fully receded, no longer necessary for what Arendt is arguing about "organized remembrance." The human dynamics, the actual interaction of people has replaced in importance the physical location for action:

> The *polis* properly speaking is not the city-state in its physical location; it is the organization of people as it arises out of acting and speaking together, and its true space lies between people living together for this purpose, no matter where they happen to be. "Wherever you go, you will be a *polis*": these famous words became not merely the watchword of Greek colonization, they expressed the conviction that action and speech create a space between the participants which can find its proper location almost any time and anywhere. (HC 198)

The "space," which now refers to human interaction, does not always exist and, Arendt notes, "To be deprived of it means to be deprived of reality" (198), a clear reference to what she describes as the disappearance of reality in totalitarianism.[4] In the ensuing discussion of "Power and the Space of Appearance," the creation of power is presented as a direct result of collective human action, even deprived of a physical space. "The space of appearance comes into being wherever men are together in the manner of speech and action" (199).

What accounts for this sudden switch in her thinking? Why focus on the quotation ("Wherever you go..." from Xenophon's *Anabasis*) that referred to colonial expansion, as though it had equally to do with loss of place? What loss preoccupied Arendt enough to lead from the stability of the Greek *polis* to the sort of political action that "creates its own space" among participants?

In "The Pariah as Hero," I explained this strange and sudden shift of Arendt's discussion of space, from inanimate to human, as her effort to create a place for the quiet hero, the outsider, the pariah. It now also seems clear that Arendt is evoking an image even more deeply rooted than her concerns for the survival of the Jews and other pariah peoples in the face of extreme political persecution. The hidden *polis* survives in the underground and resistance movements, in the absence of "the light of publicity," sure enough. But what the imagery on page 198 evokes even more dramatically is the destruction of the Temple in Jerusalem and the Jewish diaspora. That loss is more distinct and vivid than the destruction of any Greek *polis* I am aware of. The physical space that held the ancient Jews together was destroyed in fact, but the people lived on by means of "organized remembrance." Reference to the destruction of the Jerusalem Temple was undoubtedly far from Arendt's conscious mind. But why should the Greek polis that had been so important to her discussion, suddenly cease to be necessary to the preservation of a people? More likely, we have here another indication of her Jewish soul at work, while the German scholar to which she aspired went on discussing contemporary political dilemmas with reference to the ancient Greek, Roman, and Christian worlds.

Lest this interpretation seem too farfetched, too much of a wish or a fantasy on my part, consider one more dramatically and self-consciously Jewish image in her writings on the theme of the pariah in politics. In the preface to her collection of essays, *Between Past and Future*, she describes the "treasure" of the French resistance, which may be taken as a model for her most idealistic vision of participatory political action: those moments in history when people spontaneously band together to accomplish a goal in the world, irrespective of institutional government and administrative apparatus.[5] The exceptional moment in history intrigues Arendt and provides the model for political freedom, even though it does not provide a basis for "politics as usual." For Hannah Arendt, freedom is found in extraordinary historical moments, such as the Montgomery Bus Boycott during the Civil Rights Movement in the United States; the early student protest movements of the 1960s, beginning with the 1964 Free Speech Movement in Berkeley; and the Hungarian resistance to the Soviet Union. These are moments that appear spontaneous, although of course they had been years in the making: moments of clarity with regard to goals, a spirit of unusual comradery among the participants and, until provoked by aggressors, moments of peaceful and articulate protest.

Her discussion of the poignant temporality of the French resistance is of a piece with her discussion of the "movable" public realm, forced underground, in *The Human Condition*. Of the French resistance Arendt notes, "Without premonition and probably against their conscious inclinations, they had come to constitute willy-nilly a public realm where—without the paraphernalia of officialdom and hidden from the eyes of friend and foe—all relevant business in the affairs of the country was transacted in deed and word" (BPF 3). She cites the French poet and resistance fighter Rene Char, who describes his dread of losing that essential moment, forced by political disaster and bound to evaporate, taking with it the heightened sense of urgency and reality with which the participants were imbued. Arendt quotes Char's description of the return to politics and business-as-usual as an "'epasseur triste,' the 'sad opaqueness' of a private life centered about nothing but itself," or alternatively a return to "the old empty strife of conflicting ideologies" (BPF 4). The final paragraph of Arendt's description of loss of the special humanness of life in the underground, a life of pariahdom, is particularly remarkable. I quote Arendt quoting Char:

> What was this treasure? As they themselves understood it, it seems to have consisted, as it were, of two interconnected parts: they had discovered that he who "joined the Resistance, *found* himself," that he ceased to be "in quest of [himself] without mastery, in naked unsatisfaction," that he no longer suspected himself of "insincerity," of being "a carping, suspicious actor of life," that he could afford "to go naked." In this nakedness, stripped of all masks—of those which society assigns to its members as well as those which the individual fabricates for himself in his psychological reactions against society—they had been visited for the first time in their lives by an apparition of freedom ... because they ... had taken the initiative upon themselves and therefore, without knowing or even noticing it, had begun to create that public space between themselves where freedom could appear. "*At every meal that we eat together, freedom is invited to sit down. The chair remains vacant, but the place is set.*" (BPF 2; emphasis mine)

Consider what this paragraph reveals. Arendt is ostensibly discussing underground resistance, a form of civil disobedience.

It seems, thus, to confirm Canovan's reading by demonstrating Arendt's unwavering commitment to participatory democracy.[6] A closer look reveals that the language echoes her description of the conflict faced by Jews in mid-twentieth-century Europe who falsified themselves by dividing their lives into private and public: "A man on the street and a Jew at home." In the anti-Semitism volume of *The Origins of Totalitarianism*, she notes, "The adage 'a man in the street and a Jew at home' was bitterly realized: political problems were distorted to the point of pure perversion when Jews tried to solve them by means of inhumanity—for example in the question of mixed marriages[7] when the heavy burden of unsolved problems of public significance was crammed into that private existence which is much better ruled by the unpredictable laws of passion than by considered policies."[8] That is, political problems were privatized, and the attempt of individuals to work them out at home was bound to create misery and destined to fail.

The intrusion of public problems into private spaces results in the same sort of falseness of self described by Char, and remedied by involvement in the political activism of the resistance. In terms of Jewish identity, one refuses to become a parvenu and becomes, instead, a "conscious pariah." In "We Refugees" Arendt notes, "The less we are free to decide who we are or to live as we like, the more we try to put up a front, to hide the facts, and to play roles."[9] Ultimately, "the recovering of a new personality is as difficult—and as hopeless—as a new creation of the world. Whatever we do, whatever we pretend to be, we reveal nothing but our insane desire to be changed, not to be Jews" (63). The parallels between the "falseness" Char associates with the loss of political activism and the falseness of Arendt's Jewish parvenu seem unmistakable.

In "We Refugees," she describes the emotional havoc created by this sort of divided-self inauthenticity:

> Once we could buy our food and ride in the subway without being told we were undesirable. We have become a little hysterical since newspapermen started detecting us and telling us publicly to stop being disagreeable when shopping for milk and bread. We wonder how it can be done; we already are so damnably careful in every moment of our daily lives to avoid

anybody guessing who we are, what kind of passport we have, where our birth certificates were filled out—and that Hitler didn't like us. We try the best we can to fit into a world where you have to be sort of politically minded when you buy your food. (60)

Return now to the preface to *Between Past and Future*, with its haunting reference to the place set for freedom at every meal eaten by members of the resistance: "At every meal that we eat together, freedom is invited to sit down. The chair remains vacant, but the place is set" (BPF 4). The image was offered by the Frenchman (and non-Jew) Char, to refer to the vitality and optimism of life in the underground—nothing "Jewish" about it at all. But the quotation is chosen by Arendt, who had quite a different stake than Char in the liberation of France from the Nazis. She was a refugee in France during the period of occupation, was captured by the Germans, separated from her husband, put on a train, and shipped to an internment camp at Gurs. There she took advantage of a moment of confusion between French and German commands to slip away unnoticed, which ultimately led to her being reunited with her husband, and to their hair-raising escape to the United States.[10]

For Arendt, what was at stake in the French resistance was not the recapturing of her own country, but the defeat of the Nazis, and the possibility of physical survival in a country in which she was in exile. The liberation of France from the Nazis, of course, did not happen quickly enough and Arendt had to flee once again, as she had from Germany. The point is that she was a Jew in exile, and the image she borrows from Char puts me in mind not of a meeting of the French underground, but of a Jewish Passover Seder.

The place set "for freedom" in Char's terms takes the actual form at every Seder, of the place set for the prophet Elijah, who represents the possibility of freedom for Jews. The Passover Seder is the ritual reenactment of the Jews' passage from Egyptian slavery into freedom in the promised land, and the place set for Elijah is a central image in the Jewish imagination: a cup of wine for Elijah is poured and set at the Seder table. At the beginning of the second part of the Seder, after the meal is eaten, a child is sent to open the door of the house for Elijah, should he desire to enter. He is always "invited but not expected" at the Seder. The service also includes the remonstrance for all Jews to remember the unfortunates of every land, for "once we were slaves in Egypt": "Still we remember: 'It was we who were slaves, . . . we who were strangers.' And therefore, we recall these words as well: You shall not oppress a stranger, for you know the feelings of the stranger, having yourselves been strangers in the land of Egypt" (from the New Union Haggadah prepared by the Central Conference of American Rabbis, p. 56; quoted from Exod. 23:9). With regard to the specific imagery surrounding the ritual place set and cup poured for Elijah, "The prophet Malachi promised that Elijah would come to turn the hearts of parents to children, and the hearts of children to parents, and to announce the coming of the Messiah when all mankind would celebrate freedom. Hence, he has a place in every Seder. We open the door that he may enter, and set a cup of wine to represent the final Messianic promise for us and for all peoples: 'I will bring you into the Land'" (New Union Haggadah 68).

The Passover service is itself an example of "organized remembrance," reenacted over and over to evoke the feeling in the participants of bondage and liberation, as though each new generation of Jews were actually present in Egypt with their ancestors. There is no temple and no actual physical space: no *polis* for the Jews. Arendt does not associate any of the images discussed in her work with Jewish history, or the development of Jewish thinking. But her use of the term *organized remembrance* is so evocative of the Jewish command *Zakhor!*—"Remember!"—that we must turn to what she does say about history, to see if we can continue to trace these unacknowledged but persistent Jewish themes in her political theory.

JUDAISM AND ARENDT'S CONCEPT OF HISTORY

Arendt's essays "The Concept of History" (1958) and "On Humanity in Dark Times" (1959) provide further evidence of the hidden Jewish themes in Arendt's scholarship, this time through her concepts of history and community.[11] Recall that a Jewish perspective on history according to both Yosef

Yerushalmi and Amos Funkenstein, who otherwise have significant disagreements on the subject, involves self-consciousness of the importance of knowing about history; belief that history involves discrete events, some of which are (subjectively) more important than others and must be actively remembered; deference to the Bible as the main "source book" of Jewish history, and a simultaneous deference to the interpretations of the scholars, the rabbis, who have indicated little interest in writing, but much in interpreting, Jewish history. Both Funkenstein and Yerushalmi note a Jewish "indifference" toward post-Biblical history, a sense that what Jews need to know about themselves *is* indeed historical, but is contained within the Bible to be interpreted by and for later generations.

Arendt's 1958 essay "The Concept of History" provides the most direct account of her ideas about history. The structure and substance of the essay reveals the same dynamics that we observed in *Thinking*: the piece is ostensibly about Greek, Roman, and Christian history, but it nonetheless reveals distinctly Jewish concerns. The essay opens with a reference to Herodotus, who was given the title *pater historiae* by Cicero, and "has remained the father of Western history" (BPF 41). The Greek historical project was to find a realm for human "immortality" in the face of an implacable, cyclical "nature." Human mortality is described as a linear projection that "cuts through the circular movements of biological life" (42).[12] But history, Arendt notes, is actually older than Herodotus, "older, even, than Homer." Lest we be too hopeful that Arendt may here actually acknowledge Judaism as a venerable and valuable part of history, she identifies history's beginning "in the moment when Ulysses, at the court of the King of the Phraescians, listened to the story of his own deeds and sufferings, to the story of his *life*, now a thing outside himself, an 'object' for all to see and to hear" (45). History for Arendt begins not with the Jews, but with the Greeks, and proceeds through the Romans and Christians.

Arendt thus appears to regard history from a thoroughly classical perspective—as is her wont—but what emerges, unconsciously, is thoroughly compatible with the "Jewish" perspectives discussed earlier. Arendt's essay is a critique of the modern reification of history as a "process" amenable to manipulation by human beings. She condemns process thinking as a hubristic attempt on the part of men to replace God as the "maker" or "fabricator" of history.

Apart from the spiritual inadvisability of such hubris, Arendt worries about (at least) two factors associated with viewing history as primarily a process, rather than as the record of discrete events. If history is a process, and human beings can create and shape its outcome, then (1) the belief that "anything is possible," which she associates with totalitarian thinking, is a likely outcome; and (2) if people "make" history on a "fabrication" model (she cites Marx as an important spokesman for this perspective), then history must have an "end," a manmade end at that. The danger of belief in an historical endpoint is that violence is presupposed, justified, and deemed necessary for its achievement. For as Arendt notes, fabrication of anything involves violence: you cannot build a house without killing trees, disrupting the natural surface of the earth, transforming ore into metal by fire, and so forth. "What distinguishes Marx's own theory from all others in which the notion of 'making history' has found a place is that he alone realized that if one takes history to be the object of a process of fabrication or making, there must come a moment when this 'object' is completed, and that if one imagines that one can 'make history' one cannot escape the consequence that there will be an end to history" (BPF 79).

The rise of history as "process" is associated with modernity and alienation by Arendt, who claims unequivocally that "the modern concept of process pervading history and nature alike separates the modern age from the past more profoundly than any other single idea" (63). The link with alienation is that individual events and individual people lose their significance, are "meaningful" only when the end is achieved or the whole is comprehended. People become dispensable means to an end, rather than inherently valuable in their own subjectivity. "What the concept of process implies is that the concrete, the general, the single thing or event and the universal meaning, have parted company" (64). Process has usurped and replaced meaning. History is viewed not as the story of discrete and memorable deeds, or the sufferings of discrete, individual people with names and birth dates, but rather as "a manmade process, the only all-comprehending process which owed its existence exclusively to the human race" (58). Men pridefully take responsibility for manipulating history much as scientists believe they can manipulate nature. History is presumed to follow laws, like the laws of nature, and men assume a capacity for omnipotence as never before. This is a frightful development and Arendt laments the loss of human actions viewed as discrete, unpredictable, and not manageable.

Regarding history as process toward a manmade end is tantamount to playing God. The human claim that process determines ends eclipses the belief that meaning is provided by something larger than individuals. She contrasts this modern hubris with ancient perspectives, the Greek, Christian, and Jewish. The Greeks were preoccupied with greatness, competing with their gods for immortality: they aspired to immortality through their deeds. Christianity reflects the opposite perspective: men can achieve immortality in the afterlife, while the world itself is perishable. "In Christianity . . . it is the world that will pass away; men will live forever" (52). The Christian "reversal" of the Greek, in turn, is derived from "the altogether different teachings of the Hebrews, who always held that life itself is sacred, more sacred than anything else in the world, and that man is the supreme being on earth" (52). What is truly remarkable is that Arendt fails to recognize that this belief is the one that most resembles her own. She insists, consistently throughout all of her works, that to dignify individual human life is the highest value, and the ultimate determinant of morality.

Arendt's argument in this very essay, her reading of the dangers of making history into a process, is thus most compatible with what she herself identifies as Jewish priorities. However, in "The Concept of History," as in *Thinking*, Jewish thinking is presented as no more than a stepping stone to the more respectable Christian teachings, which then form the "significant" point of comparison with the Greek. Here she acknowledges that Jewish thought regards life as sacred, prohibiting the sacrifice of human life for an historical "end." But when it comes to actually putting the Jewish teaching to use, working with it and developing it to further her argument, we find her quickly dropping the Jewish in favor of the Christian or Greek. She cautions against overvaluing the human capacity to determine historical ends: "Neither freedom nor any other meaning can ever be the product of a human activity in the sense in which the table is clearly the end product of the carpenter's activity" (78). To support this caveat about human omnipotence, Arendt refers to Augustine. However, Augustine himself, as presented by Arendt, sounds very much like one of Yerushalmi's early Jews. Arendt tells us,

> The point, as he saw it, was that no purely secular event could or should ever be of central import to man. His lack of interest in what we call history was so great that he devoted only one book of the *Civatas Dei* to secular events; and in commissioning his friend and pupil Orosius to write a "world history" he had no more in mind than a "true compilation of the evils of the world." (BPF 65–66)

For Augustine, "history remains a storehouse of examples, and the locations of events in time within the secular course of history remain without importance" (66). This is consistent with Funkenstein's observations about Augustine. Although Augustine is the spokesman she turns to, Arendt concedes that his sense of the limited importance of secular history was not particularly Christian. "The single fact that the problem of history arose in Christian thought only with Augustine should make us doubt its Christian origin" (66).

With "The Concept of History" Arendt delivers a cautionary tale, warning about the hubristic dangers of overvaluing human will as a determining factor in history. The human being should not aspire to shape or fashion, that is to "make" history; and should not be so arrogant as to assume the posture of a God, pretending to know the significance of all worldly events, reducing the individual to the abstract universal as the meaning of individual lives and deeds are sacrificed to the god of "Progress." Arendt's humility regarding the limits of the human capacity to understand is also reflected in her statement at the beginning of *The Human Condition*, that people should not presume to know what "human nature" is. "To avoid misunderstanding: the human condition is not the same as human nature. . . . If we have a nature or essence, then surely only a god could know and define it, and the first prerequisite would be that he be able to speak about a 'who' as though it were a 'what'" (HC 9–10).

What "feels" Jewish about this stance is its unwillingness to specify, articulate, or visualize knowledge better left to God. Even though Arendt is not a religious writer, though her beliefs about God remained private, rarely being allowed to surface in her writings, her unwillingness to broach certain subjects, her conviction that certain things simply should not be articulated, or made explicit, is compatible with a Jewish aversion to (1) visualizing God; (2) reifying dogma in the form of finalized doctrine; and (3) stating explicitly what the future will look like. This aversion to articulating the future is compatible with Jewish agnosticism about the coming of the messiah and also the unwillingness to articulate or to write down change in Jewish law or custom. "Everything new is forbidden by law," and yet the willingness to adapt to changing historical necessity has been a prerequisite to Jewish survival.

I perceive residues of the invisibility of the Jewish God in Arendt's respect for "the ineffable." Arendt's deference to what may be comprehended, accepted, but is best left inexplicit or unarticulated, is also compatible with the Jewish attitude toward reform of tradition. Many people have regarded her as an "arrogant" thinker; few have noted or appreciated her humility, even reverence, in contrast to the human arrogance that she regarded as a component of totalitarian regimes, posing a lethal threat to the political realm as well as to human life.

To return to "The Concept of History," Arendt contends that the modern conceptualization of history as process carries the dangerous misconception (with the exception of Marx, as noted above) that human history is infinite—lacking either beginning or end. "This twofold infinity of past and future eliminates all notions of beginning and end, establishing mankind in a potential earthly immortality." Arendt's fear of this is utterly compatible with traditional Jewish *and* Christian stances. History began when God created the world (or when Christ was born) and will end when the Messiah returns. Since Arendt nowhere gives evidence of actually believing in a Messiah, one may wonder how this view of history as having an endpoint, symbolized by the expectation of a Messiah, can possibly be associated with her.

We may be able to make sense of Arendt's position if we call upon Funkenstein once more, who contrasts the Jewish attitude toward the coming of the Messiah with the Protestant.

> The driving force of Protestantism—the yearning for a *reformation*, for return to the original shape—had no precise equivalent in the traditional Jewish imagery. The belief in the future coming of the Messiah, who, "even if he procrastinates, will surely come," and the belief in the restoration of the Davidic Kingship, were not necessarily tied to the hope of a *better* Judaism, a purer community. Traditional Judaism lacked the image of an innocent, pure *Urgemeinschaft* that shall once again be restored. (Funkenstein 253)

We are reminded that Jewish imagery is simply not as concrete and pictorial, as *visual* as Christian imagery. Jews would no more predict a date for the arrival of a Messiah than they would attempt to draw a picture of God.

The sense of an ultimate but ineffable meaning to history that Arendt believes is necessary to avoid the arrogant stance that people alone make their own history, is thus compatible with the Jewish conception of the coming of the Messiah in the sense that it is an indefinite, ineffable, unarticulable, not humanly conceivable end. This is radically different from the end to history that Arendt associates with Marx: in her view man can neither make nor conceptualize an end to history. But Arendt's conceptualization of an "end" stands as an ineffable symbol for humility about human "prowess" in the world. This, I would argue, is a thoroughly Jewish stance.

Compatible with Arendt's belief that human beings should not inflate a sense of their own efficacy in the world, should retain humility in the face of God, is her concern about the loss of particularity that results from "process thinking." This, too, resounds with the Jewish perspective that "life itself is sacred, more sacred than anything else in the world, and that man is the supreme being on earth" (BPF 53). No theoretical end, no concept of absolute truth, is worth the knowing sacrifice of even one life. Jewish folk wisdom has it that if you save the life of one person, you save the world. Life is God's creation and it is sacred. Jewish law prohibits "mixing" things—certain fabrics cannot be worn together, certain foods cannot be eaten in the same meal—precisely because human beings should not meddle with God's creations. The Biblical prohibition against mixing milk and meat is, from one perspective, a prohibition that keeps sacred the bond between mother and offspring of any species ("Thou shalt not seethe the kid in the milk of its mother"); another Talmudic perspective has it that blood and milk are the fluids of life, and therefore belong in God's care alone. What God does not mix, neither should human beings presume to.[13]

Obviously, the "progress" of human beings has depended upon their willingness to mix and meddle with the natural world. I believe the sanction against "mixing" can still be understood as a symbolic reminder of the power of life forces, and of origins: a call for humility which it would be wise to heed. The most brilliant and effective scientists might do well to maintain contact with reminders of the ethical complexities, the dangers as well as the benefits of too aggressively rearranging the natural world.

COMMUNITY IN DARK TIMES

Another feature of Arendt's perspective on history, one with its Jewish undercurrents as well, appears in the essay "On Humanity in Dark Times," her acceptance speech of the Lessing Prize bestowed by the Free City of Hamburg.[14] There is a moment toward the beginning of the essay, where Arendt defines history as public stories, dependent upon freedom for survival: "When men are deprived of the public space—which is constituted by acting together and then fills of its own accord with the events and stories that develop into history—they retreat into their freedom of thought" (MDT 9). She describes Lessing as a man committed to maintaining freedom in the world, a man so mistrustful of absolute truth that he relished his partiality and valued above all other things, friendship. Justice, he maintained, "has little to do with objectivity in the ordinary sense" (6). "Lessing . . . rejoiced in the very thing that has ever—or at least since Parmenides and Plato—distressed philosophers: that the truth, as soon as it is uttered, is immediately transformed into one opinion among many, is contested, reformulated, reduced to one subject of discourse among others" (MDT 27).

From Arendt's perspective, Lessing stands for the importance of friendship and community over doctrine and ideology, even when ideology is regarded as "Truth." "Would any doctrine . . . however convincingly proved, be worth the sacrifice of so much as a single friendship between two men?" (29). Lessing valued friendship over brotherhood because friendship involves choice, and a certain distance necessary for free discussion. "He wanted to be the friend of many men but no man's brother" (30). This encourages us to consider the nature of community, and the extent to which it is comprised of membership by choice or birth. Arendt insists that communities of birth are fragile, have the most strength during times of crisis. She has reference to the Jews during the Holocaust. She professes her central identification with the Jews during and after the Nazi persecution, but also claims, "The humanity of the insulted and injured has never yet survived the hour of liberation by so much as a minute. This does not mean that it is insignificant, for in fact it makes insult and injury endurable; but it does mean that in political terms it is absolutely irrelevant" (MDT 16–17).

Arendt's ideas about the relative merits of blood ties versus the emotional ties of friendship or other sorts of community are complex. She clearly believes that blood ties, and by extension the biological ties of membership in an ethnic, religious, or racial group, are unreliable, even artificial as a basis for a long-standing community. In times of crisis, imposed political categories based upon notions of "race" or biology may force a community together, but as soon as the danger is past, or the singularly defined enemy is no longer a threat, the community dissolves. Those times of crisis, however, have the power to render friendship politically irrelevant, if friends are tempted to use their enclosed relationship to insulate themselves from political reality, when what is called for is confronting the trouble in the political world.

> In the case of a friendship between a German and a Jew under the conditions of the Third Reich it would scarcely have been a sign of humanness for the friends to have said: Are we not both human beings? It would have been mere evasion of reality and of the world common to both at that time; they would not have been resisting the world as it was. A law that prohibited the intercourse of Jews and Germans could be evaded but could not be defied by people who denied the reality of the distinction. (MDT 23)

On the other hand, under "normal" political circumstances, friendship, relations of choice rather than birth, are the more reliable guide to forging political communities: "Humaneness should be sober and cool, rather than sentimental; . . . humanity is exemplified not in fraternity but in friendship; that friendship is not intimately personal but makes political demands and preserves reference to the world" (25).

Arendt is using Lessing to describe the importance of staying "in the world" even in time of historical catastrophe when the world seems unendurable. But how is it possible for a group that has been threatened with annihilation to stay in the world? And "to what extent do we remain obligated to the world, even when we have been expelled from it or have withdrawn from it?" (22). Arendt's response is: Survival is possible if we continue to tell our story. "In reification by the poet or the historian, the narration of history has achieved permanence and persistence. Thus the narrative has been given its place in the world, where it will survive us" (22). So long as the story is preserved in the world, people have a chance to continue to find meaning from it. The text is all important; its meaning is never fully understood and so the story is never "closed" or completed. An association with the

Jewish attitude toward the Bible as the source of continuity, as narrative, history, the guarantee of future never fully understood, does not seem farfetched.

Arendt ends her essay on a note thoroughly consistent with the themes delineated in her "Concept of History," which also strikes me as compatible with a Jewish conception of history. She concludes with a quotation from Lessing that once again professes ignorance in the face of absolutes, and humility before the ineffable. Human power is simply limited, and awareness of that limitation promotes some sort of human discourse: "Let each man say what he deems truth and let truth itself be commended unto God" (MDT 30).

The themes that emerge from Arendt's discussion of Lessing is consistent with themes throughout her work. Absolute truths, doctrines, and dogmas are politically dangerous: dialogue, discussion, and fluidity are more reliable elements of thinking. The preservation of history through stories is one important access to "truth" conceived as facts rather than doctrines. The stories must be public, and by extension, available to interpretation, part of a public dialogue. The company we keep, as well as loyalty to that company, is critical in determining behavior. This is consistent with the approving quotation of Cicero in her essay "The Crisis in Culture": "I prefer before heaven to go astray with Plato rather than hold true views with his opponents" (BPF 224). During the "ordinary," less eventful periods of history, it is more conducive to political freedom for a community to be composed of friends who have chosen each other's company. But in times of political crises, the imposed community of "brothers" must not be abandoned. What holds a community together—whether brought together by friendship or an oppressor—is its stories, the telling of its own history.

There are many complexities that remain unaddressed and questions left unanswered in Arendt's essay on Lessing. The most glaring question is whether loyalty to friends who comprise a gang of murderous thugs is one possible outcome of this stance. But what is more directly relevant for our purposes here is how, once again, Arendt stresses the importance of narrative history over philosophy as a path to freedom and community coherence. This stance is altogether compatible with the Jewish perspectives on history we have considered, and speaks once again to the Jewish dimensions in Hannah Arendt's political theory.

CHAPTER 12

Conclusion

The conclusion is the author's moment to state bluntly what she fears may not have come across forcefully enough in her more extended discussion. I have taken pains to do justice to the complexity of the political, cultural, and gendered issues central to my arguments in this volume. Now I restate the major points in brief, with emphasis upon what I fear may have become lost along the way. Let us return to the issues raised in the introduction, to see whether we are any closer, after our excursion through Hannah Arendt's work, to understanding what influence the facts of her Jewishness and gender may have had upon her intellectual life.

JUDAISM

The most difficult questions raised in the introduction had to do with the nature of Jewish thinking, and Jewish identity, that each may be said to influence intellectual work. One difficulty is that Judaism is a religion, although in our contemporary secular world, also a cultural or "ethnic" identity. A person can identify herself as a Jew, and yet not be an observant religious practitioner. Or she can insist that Judaism has no influence whatsoever upon her scholarship or literary work, as so many twentieth-century Jewish intellectuals have done, and still "find" her Jewish identity late in life—perhaps when she understands that most everyone considers her a Jew in spite of all disclaimers. Still, how can a religion be said to have influence upon a nonreligious thinker, especially in areas not related to religion?

Hannah Arendt claimed her Jewish identity publicly, but kept her religious convictions private, was not a religious person or observant Jew, so far as I know, and believed that her scholarship was free of Jewish influence: she regarded herself as educated in the German tradition. How, then, can I insist that her intellectual life revealed Jewish influences? This was the question I raised in the introduction.

In the chapters describing Jewish thinking, certain elements emerged as most characteristic, derived from Biblical and rabbinic thought, from the Hebrew language itself, manifesting themselves, from the standpoint of contemporary scholars, in Jewish literature, and a Jewish sense of history. With the caveat that any such list is itself antithetical to Jewish thinking because of the second item on the list, they are: (1) centrality of the Torah; (2) reluctance to codify; (3) lack of boundedness, which also affects a sense of history and time, the sense that the past is not really "closed"; (4) lack of interest in visual imagery; and (5) inherent worldliness, or democratic potential, implying a community of adherents.

Let us translate these qualities into contemporary secular terms. The centrality of Torah can be understood as a focus on a central text, with the exceptional quality being that to religious Jews the Torah is both sacred and perfect, and yet not "complete" in the sense of never fully comprehended, even by the wisest of scholars. But the requirement to continue to try to understand, to interpret in good faith, is a sacred duty. Thus, Harold Bloom's insistence that "interpretation" is a central characteristic of a Jewish approach to the world. In the Jewish tradition, words are as "real" as any other things in the world. Because people can never know ultimate truth, there can be no codification that is not a misrepresentation of the complexity of truth. Interpretation requires fluidity and dialogue. The contemporary vernacular for codification is reification, and what is dangerous about it is that it halts thinking, and becomes oppressively dogmatic: codification is antithetical to freedom. The sense of history, the belief that the past is not "closed," is a way of connecting contemporary generations with the past, even as that past is being interpreted anew. The loss of community and tradition is a problem for many cultures in the modern age; the Jewish community's ceremonial reenactments of the important moments in its history are a way of both keeping community together and keeping a sense of the past alive, which also reinforces the sense of community. Obviously, it is one culture's solution to maintaining historical continuity; all cultures have some equivalent.

The lack of Jewish interest in visual imagery is antithethical to our empirically biased modern age. Its importance in Jewish thinking can be associated with the same impulse as the reluctance to codify, the desire to keep dialogue open: a picture or visual image is a form of codification. It freezes the developing truth about the concept. Paradoxically, in spite of the Jewish predilection for aural rather than visual access to truth, Jewish thinking is oriented toward the world. In modern philosophical terminology, it is materialist rather than idealist. To make philosophy work in the world was how Karl Marx viewed his Promethian task. Arendt was no less desirous of a way of thinking that would be accessible to all people. In the Jewish sense, that path leads to the convergence of word and world, the belief that Torah and Talmud blend into one another and are not entirely separable from worldly enactment: the most sacred passages of the Torah and Talmud are intended to have worldy implications. Max Kadushin's "value concept" is an attempt to express the blurred boundary between the sacred and the practical. The Hebrew word *Mitzvah*, commandment, also carries this connotation: the most important worldly duties are also holy. The most sacred of Jewish prayers all begin with the acknowledgment that we are made holy by being given commandments, things to do in the world: "Blessed art Thou, ruler of the universe, who has sanctified us by commanding us to...."

But more specifically, where do these Jewish themes appear in Arendt's political theory, in a way that supports my thesis that, unbeknownst even to Arendt, her work, her questions, her scholarly priorities, were Jewish? Let me pinpoint a few themes that are particularly relevent for Arendt's effort to describe thinking as capable of worldly intervention against the threat of political evil, available to all people, more solid than opinion, yet not as coercive as a codified doctrine, dogma or ideology. My approach has been two pronged: on the one hand, a summation of where Jewish thinking is evident in Arendt's search for a worldy philosophy, and on the other, a review of areas where Arendt might have been assisted by a more directly Jewish approach in her effort to break through the Greek-inspired dichotomies between "pure" philosophy and worldly dialogue.

Where Arendt, with the help of Socrates, exhibits a perspective more compatible with Rabbinic than Greek thinking, is in her insistence that all codification halts thinking, and courts the danger of dogma and authoritarianism. The aporetic Socratic dialogue that she admires so much, the unwillingness ever to stop examining accepted doctrine, sounds remarkably Talmudic. It is not the end product of thinking that carries worldly consequences, but the process of endless challenge and reinterpretation that bears the promise of preparing the thinker to question rules and dogma. This is not to be confused with the sort of endless thinking that simply keeps philosophers off the streets and out of trouble, because they are always engaged in a dialogue with themselves. Talmudic dialogue differs from the Greek philosopher's lonely quest in a number of important ways. It actually *is* a dialogue with another person; it presupposes that the participants in the dialogue are members of a community; and it is "material" in the sense of being oriented toward worldly behavior, both private and public.

These factors at face value were important to Arendt. But when we remember her discussion of friendship rather than birth as the preferred basis of a political community (from the essay on Lessing, "On Humanity in Dark Times"), it doesn't seem likely that Arendt would have been an advocate of "identity politics" based on race, religion, or ethnicity. Indeed, given the violent tribalism that plagues much of the contemporary world—Eastern Europe, the Middle East, Ireland, Los Angeles—her caution was no doubt wise. And yet people seem incapable of relinquishing these longstanding traditional identities, as unneighborly as they appear to be. What are the chances that an acknowledgment of one's ethnic identity is both psychologically comforting and capable of promoting peaceful coexistence with other races and religions? Why is it good to acknowledge and accept one's Jewish identity if it threatens to endanger one at the hands of anti-Semites? Or, as an African American student once asked me, rhetorically, "Why shouldn't I 'pass' if I can?"

At the time, I couldn't believe she was serious. Surely denying one's race and culture was bound to be emotionally destructive. But the ensuing discussion in the seminar made me take her question very seriously. If, as an African American woman in white society, she was likely to suffer economically, socially, and professionally, then why shouldn't she try to "pass," be taken for a white woman by white society, accrue the benefits of being white and deal with the emotional costs of the deception, the inauthenticity, on her own terms? In effect, she was asking, Why should I choose psychological over economic and social well-being, especially if poverty and exclusion are likely to wreak psychological havoc of their own? Why shouldn't I choose the pain of inauthenticity over the pain of poverty and lack of choices in life?

There are no ready answers to the question of why it is inherently good to accept one's ethnic heritage. However, one response is fairly obvious: it is not necessary to regard acceptance of one's ethnic identity in idealist terms. No culture is perfect, each has its good aspects and its bad. Jewish thinking is no panacea, any more than the sort of thinking that may be said to characterize any other long-standing community on earth. It carries no guarantee against dangerous misuse, violent defensive exclusionism, tribalism, nationalism, racism—all the dangers the modern world has to offer.

There exist in the world exclusionist Jews who are not interested in participating in any network of racial, cultural, or religious communities beyond their own. There are also

Christian and Muslim fundamentalists, black nationalists, and racial and religious chauvinists throughout the world who share the same adherence to exclusionism, and are prepared to make war upon any perceived challenge to their hegemony. This phenomenon is a plague upon the earth.

On the other hand, I share Arendt's concern that a world without boundaries and divisions will likely become a mass society, susceptible to a totalitarian order for its direction. Loss of identifying boundaries leaves people bereft of community. Arendt believed (when she wasn't lamenting the loss of small participatory communities, such as the *polis* of ancient Athens, or the New England small town) that national identity was necessary to provide such boundaries: statelessness deprives a person of grounding in the world. This is a rationalist approach to forging a community out of the modern world; it shuns the "irrationality" and the apparent biological determinism of race, religion, and ethnicity as the basis of modern community.

Here I disagree with Arendt. While it might be nice to be able to overlook communities of birth or biology and to choose one's own community, nationality, or political identity, such a situation is not possible given the tenacity of ethnic heritage— nor is it necessarily desirable. Arendt understood the importance of both history and community. Part of the sustaining power of ethnicity is its longevity. Race, religion, and culture have simply been around much longer than most nation states. People feel lost without them. This does not mean that cultural identity is determinist: that one must become a racial or religious exclusionist when accepting one's cultural identity. There are choices once one comes to terms with who one is, racially or ethnically. But avoiding the reality of centuries or millenia of heritage seems to me to run the risk of all psychological denial: one is never fully open to dialogue because one is too busy defending oneself against reality.

The point of this book has not been to establish that Jewish or Talmudic thinking is inherently superior to any other. Rather it has been to affirm that, as Arendt wrote to Gershom Scholem, she was a Jew, "as a matter of course." In a way, I am suggesting that her thinking was influenced by that fact, also as a matter of course, although the mechanism by which culture is transmitted to individuals is not something to which I claim special insight. We should not be surprised to find elements compatible with Jewish thinking in the work of Hannah Arendt: rather we should be surprised to find them denied and suppressed. And we can hypothesize that they might have been helpful to her, had she paid more attention to them.

Let us return to the question of how a Jewish approach might have aided Arendt in her quest for a dialogical, community-based, worldly model of thinking. Without implying that all Jews think progressively and open-mindedly, I insist that there are elements of the Talmudic approach to the world and community that would have helped Arendt in her quest for a worldly philosophy. The reluctance to codify, as discussed above, and throughout the second part of the book is one example. I have suggested that Arendt adhered to that reluctance, although she did not identify its attractiveness for her with Judaism. Another example is the creation of community. The "wisdom" or teachings of the Talmud is not intended for rabbis only. A community of Jewish men is assumed. The presence of women is acknowledged, but not as participants in the dialogue. Instead, the women simply perform the *mitzvot*, commandments, assigned to them by the male scholars who do participate in the dialogue. (We'll let that go for now, and deal with the necessity for change in another book.) Nonetheless the presumption of community is reinforced daily for orthodox Jews, and at least weekly for the more moderately observant, in communal worship. Jews must come together in a *minyan*, a group of a minimum of ten (men only for the orthodox), in order to conduct a religious service. Jews do not primarily worship at home or in private. They must collect in community shuls (the yiddish term for "schools," colloquial for synagogues), in order to reaffirm their membership in the community and to pursue their own interpretation of the Torah. Their membership in the community is confirmed by reciting prayers aloud and silently together, and by reading and rereading, and discussing the central text.

There is a prayer Jews say each time they cross the threshold of the synagogue, which affirms that the private household has been left behind and the community place of worship entered. It is effectively each individual's prayer for sanctification of the place of communal worship. It begins, "How goodly are your tents, O Jacob!; How beautiful your sanctuaries, O Israel! / Through Your great goodness I enter Your house; With reverence I bow before Your holy ark." The first verse is actually taken from a verse in the Bible (Numbers XXIV:5), where the prophet Balaam is commanded by Moabite King Balak to curse the Jews, and miraculously, out of his mouth comes the blessing, "How goodly are your habitations, O Jacob."[1]

The communal energy created each time the congregation meets closely resembles Arendt's concept of action in *The Human Condition*, and freedom in her discussion of the French Resistance, from the standpoints of both the necessity of a public space, revered by the community, and of the sheer force of human power created whenever individuals collect publicly. The power is created and recreated collectively, whenever the community actually convenes itself. The energy created in this sort of community may actually be capable of enduring beyond those "exeptional" political moments described by Arendt because it "refuels" on its own history each time it reconvenes. This conception of the role of a community of birth is recognized by Arendt only in time of political disaster, when the community is embattled—as we saw in her discussion of Lessing. Perhaps she feared the potential violent tribalism were the "irrationality" of community membership to be reified. But I believe there are choices, so long as people are in the "habit of examining": and acceptance of one's membership in an historic community does not inevitably lead to a violent mistrust of other communities, or demand withdrawal from the world.

One other aspect of Arendt's thought strikes me as particularly Jewish, and related to her refusal to "codify."[2] It is her respect for what she calls "ineffability." I read this also as compatible with the Jewish belief that God cannot be seen. There is great stress throughout Arendt's work on what cannot be made explicit. This is similar to what the rabbis described as the "fence around the Torah," and what I identified as one of the secrets of survival for the Jews: changes in custom occur, and are not made explicit until long after they are in place. Then they are "added on" to the teachings, and future thinkers are given the task of interpreting the meaning of any apparent contradictions.

Arendt's deference to the ineffable appears throughout her work, as a subtheme that bubbles to the surface occasionally. We saw it in the discussion of her "Concept of History": her unwillingness to allow human beings to convert history into a product, with an end that can be determined by any person. There was a sense that she wrote from a standpoint which, while not explicitly religious, was nonetheless spiritual in its willingness to relinquish human knowledge of important aspects of life. She simply refused to entertain the possibility of humanly available knowledge of life's meaning, or the description of an endpoint to history.

I see that same respect for the ineffable in her concept of political action which, in *The Human Condition* she describes as "in its most general sense . . . to take an initiative, to begin, to set something into motion. . . . It is in the nature of beginning that something new is started which cannot be expected from whatever may have happened before. This character of startling unexpectedness is inherent in all begininngs and in all origins."[3] But the political actor does not retain control over his (sic) act. Its significance is something left to later generations, to history. "Whatever the character and content of the subsequent story may be, whether it is played in private or public life, whether it involves many or few actors, its full meaning can reveal itself only when it has ended. . . . Action reveals itself fully only to the storyteller, that is to the backward glance of the historian, who indeed always knows better what it was all about than the participants" (HC 192). Arendt's political actor initiates something in the world, but then must relinquish it to future generations. The consequences of his act are neither fully knowable or controllable. Its meaning is ineffable, retained in narrative, interpreted by later generations.

Now one could argue that this does not sound particularly Jewish; if anything, it sounds Hegelian, as in Hegel's *Philosophy of History*, and specifically in his description of the flight of the Owl of Minerva. What makes Arendt's version more Jewish than Hegelian is her acquiescence to the unknowability of the end of history, which is also compatible with her professed agnosticism about human nature: "If we have a nature or essence, then surely only a god could know and define it" (HC 10). Not only does Arendt abhor the hubris of believing that a philosopher or a revolutionary can presume to know where history is headed, and sacrifice even one human life for his own projected creation. She also abhors the arrogance of believing that human history is something that people "make." Her humility in the face of the ineffable, her concession to what is believed unknowable strikes me as in keeping with a rabbinic stance toward history and truth.[4] Jews are not the only people with values that resemble this. But Arendt was a Jew who was escaping her cultural heritage in her scholarship. Her escape made her less aware than she might have been of some of the sources of her own ideas.

GENDER

Gender is the second dimension I have considered in relation to Hannah Arendt's work. The perspective I have taken is not the more traditional feminist stance, studying what influence Arendt's gender may have had upon her scholarly interests and the content of her work. Another feminist perspective, really a critique, takes a tack similar to the one I have taken with Judaism, and considers Arendt's flight from femininity in her scholarly life. Some of the same points I make in my discussion of her avoidance of intellectual Judaism may be made with regard to her attitude toward intellectual femininity: the model of scholarly legitimacy for Arendt was male and Christian. Possessing neither of those identifying characteristics, and knowing anyway that she was a scholar, Arendt simply dissociated scholarship, her intellectual life, from her biological and cultural life. I have argued that there was a price to pay for her dissociation of her intellectual life from Judaism: denial of a major part of her identity, and some missed intellectual opportunities. There also may be a price to pay for denying one's gender intellectually: the same problems with a divided life, culturally speaking, are sure to apply on the gender level as well. The ultimate risk of any sort of denial is inauthenticity and fear of self.

But that aspect of the gender dimension has not been my principal interest in this book. Arendt never claimed to be a feminist—although she never denied being a woman—but she *did* claim to be a Jew, all the while keeping that identity apart from her intellectual life. My involvement with gender and Hannah Arendt has had to do more with the fact that she was *received* as a "woman scholar,"[5] and was caught by surprise at the ferocity of the criticism leveled against her when she crossed an invisible line and publicly criticized the men of her own community. If she had been aware of how her reading public perceived her, she might not have been so taken by surprise by the furious response to *Eichmann*. But that's neither here nor there. I have laid out my argument for the impact of gender on the response of the New York and Israeli communities to *Eichmann in Jerusalem*, and will add nothing to that extensive discussion here. My concern is what sense can we make of the furor.

I suggested in the first part of the book, on gender and Judaism, that Arendt's report on Eichmann was so threatening to Jewish men, as well as to the protectors of their honor, Jewish women, because they had been labeled effeminate by the Nazis. I considered arguments that Jewish male defensiveness about masculinity may in fact be traceable to the covenant of circumcision, which in relation to the uncircumcised goyim may be experienced as a symbolic castration. This, I suggested, was probably less an inevitable, psychoanalytic association than a result of a history of oppression. There is nothing to suggest that the Biblical patriarchs felt less masculine than the people of other nations because of circumcision. Indeed, circumcision was regarded as empowering, a symbol of a special relationship between Jewish men and their God. They were powerful men, capable of spilling blood in the most violent way when required (Abraham even capable of sacrificing his beloved son—although not of consulting Sarah about it), and many of them were married to powerful women. The association of masculinity and power is the result of the phallus having been symbollically associated with worldly power, of which Jewish men have had little.

The myth of Jewish male effeminacy may have begun in the rabbinic period. More pertinent for the discussion here is its prevalence, for whatever reasons, in the modern age, and its availability to Nazis. The sexual symbolism coupled with real impotence in the face of the Nazi menace created an intensely gendered situation for Jewish men during this century of virulent anti-Semitism.[6] This might explain a good part of the viciousness with which the Jewish community attacked Hannah Arendt.

But the real lessons we can learn from the *Eichmann* controversy are more complex than simply, "Girls, if you want to play safe, be careful how you present your criticisms of men!" or "Guys, will you grow up and stop letting your sexual fears get in the way of every little thing!" As I indicated in chapter 5, part of the problem was that Arendt herself was more "macho" than the men she criticized experienced themselves as being. *She* wanted a Jewish army. *She* wanted Jews to stand up and fight for themselves, in a way we would normally associate with masculinity. From the perspective of some feminists, if militancy, armed retaliation, was her response to the attack on the Jews, she suffered from false consciousness. Indeed, Jewish feminist Daniel Boyarin would undoubtedly argue that Arendt's response was not only wrong-headed, but antithetical to his reading of what Jewish manhood is really about: he adheres to the admirability of Jewish passivity throughout history, and laments that aggression and combativeness have come to be regarded as the definition of masculinity in the modern world. Aggression and combativeness characterize the goyim, in Boyarin's schema, and Jewish male efforts to be more "masculine" on such a model are an assimilationist sellout of what is finest in the Jewish tradition.

To my way of thinking, the answer is not so much either to glorify or to condemn aggression and combativeness per se, but to dismantle the association of such characteristics with masculinity. There may, on rare occasion, very well be a place for violence in the world, although not for aggressive or instrumental violence as a way of achieving one's goals. But in extreme circumstances, when exceptional wrong is being done, violence may be a last-ditch defensive measure in order to secure one's preservation. There is plenty of violence in nature (all one has to do to get close to it is sit on the back porch and watch a bird extracting a living worm from its home in the earth), and although people are not interchangeable with nature, although what may distinguish us from the animals is our ability to use our intelligence to free ourselves from the determinism of nature, neither are we at a complete remove from it. We are a *part* of nature, however special our relation to it.

People have always found reason to fight; as civilization advances, we try to find ways to work out disagreements without resorting to instinctive brutality. But we are also "hard wired" for survival, which sometimes calls for fight rather than either flight or acquiescence. Extreme threats, such as genocidal menace, may very well call for armed resistance. What concerns me is that in those extreme circumstances when defensive violence may be necessary for survival, violence is perceived in gendered terms. The only thing that makes men more violent than women is essentialist sexism. When violent behavior is symbollically associated with manhood, the world is in deep trouble. Men are in trouble because they have bought the bill of goods that they are only truly "men" if they behave violently. Women are in even deeper trouble, having bought an even more dangerous bill of goods: that they are incapable of violence, even when it is neccesary to defend themselves. Occasionally, it is considered "natural" for the females of the species to defend their young and their homes with violence. But this is more in keeping with stereotypical "maternal instincts"—"mama bear" behavior—than with mature, rational women capable of defensive violence.

The lesson to be learned here is that there is a time for peace, and—with luck, intelligence, and the end of gender stereotyping—a much less significant time for war. But neither war nor peace, aggression nor passivity is the sole domain of either men or women. Hannah Arendt seemed to know this hard lesson, having gained it from her life's most trying moments. When she wrote *Eichmann in Jerusalem*, the world was not yet ready to hear her message.

APPENDIX

Reviews of Raul Hilberg's
The Destruction of the European Jews

The following are exerpts from a representative sample of reviews of Raul Hilberg's *The Destruction of the European Jews*. They have been chosen to reflect the prestige of the journals providing the reviews, and to demonstrate the respectful tone reserved for Hilberg, even when the reviewer had reservations about his findings or argument. They are intended to illustrate the contrast between the tone of the reviews of Hilberg's book, and those of Arendt's *Eichmann in Jerusalem*, while recognizing that the content of the two books dealt with similar issues.

ETHICS 72, 2 (January 1962)
The Destruction of the European Jews. By Raul Hilberg (Chicago: Quandrangle Books, 1961), pp. x+788.

This book recounts, in almost overpowering detail, the process by which the Nazi regime carried out its "solution" of the "Jewish question." In over seven hundred double-columned pages ... Hilberg traces the process of persecution which began with the economic, social and political destruction of the Jews of Germany in the prewar years and culminated in the mass murders of Auschwitz and the other "killing centers" of the "final solution." Murdering three million people—the approximate number killed in the assembly-line procedures employed in the final stages—is not a simple matter, especially if it is to be accomplished in relative secrecy.... The problem put even "Teutonic" thoroughness and dedication to a severe test, and it seems uncontestable that it could not have been accomplished without the relative docility of a population which had come to believe over the centuries that resistance only increased the fury and delayed the termination of persecution. Lacking the satanic ingenuity and the elaborate network of communication with which they were credited in Nazi mythology, the Jewish communities were, in an astonishing degree, taken by surprise, only slowly grasped the truth of their situation, and, reacting in traditional fashion, in large part supplied the discipline and organization which delivered them to the gas chambers.

But Hilberg's narrative is not concerned primarily with the Jews. His interest is in "the perpetrators," or, as he puts it, "the storm that caused the wreckage" . . . and he has therefore produced a narrative which abounds in organization charts, accounts of bureaucratic intrigue, and the names of officials.

Throughout, in fact, the work displays a political (and consequent moral) naivete which puts intrinsic limitations upon its usefulness for the purposes which Hilberg professes to be serving. The movement of the Nazi bureaucracy from state to state of "the destruction process" is not intelligible in itself. Understanding it requires more than an analysis of administrative hierarchies.

The closing sections of Hilberg's book are devoted to a consideration of "consequences" and "implications" of the events he describes. It is here, in his consideration of the various efforts at rescue, salvage, punishment of the perpetrators . . . that his political insight becomes most clearly deficient. The tone of these sections is bitter, and consistently so: it seems almost that everyone failed to react effectively or to appreciate the enormity of the crime.

On such problems studies such as this shed little light.

C.W.

COMMENTARY 33, 4 (April 1962)
Nazi Bureaucrats and Jewish Leaders*
*A review of *The Destruction of the European Jews*. By Raul Hilberg (Quadrangle Books), 788 pp.
H. R. Trevor-Roper

This is a forbidding book. It is nearly 800 pages long. The pages are double columned. It has nearly a hundred statistical tables. It is written in an austere style, without literary grace or emotion. And it deals with a subject of which, this year, we have already heard a great deal. I hardly thought, on taking it up, that I should be unable to put it down: that having postponed the reading of it till a time of leisure, I should then have read it through, almost without interruption, and quite without skipping, to the end. For this is not merely a compilation or a recapitulation of the the now documented facts. It is not yet another chronicle of horrors. It is a careful, analytic, three-dimensional study of a social and political experience unique in history: an experience which no one could believe possible till it had happened and whose real significance still bewilders us.

The great interest of Mr. Hilberg's book is that he has faced this total problem. He is not content to chronicle or to exclaim. While keeping to a narrative form, he has studied the social problem analytically: his narrative carries along with it a profound social content. This is why I call it "three dimensional." It reveals, methodically, fully, and clearly, the development of both the technical and the psychological process; the machinery and the mentality whereby one whole society sought to isolate and destroy another which, for centuries, had lived in its midst.

In all this process undoubtedly it was the Nazi party which gave the signal but it was the German bureaucracy in the widest sense—that is, not only the civil servants but the army and the business world—which made it possible. Again and again Mr. Hilberg makes this clear.

Here indeed we come to the central problem. For one thing which emerges clearly from Mr. Hilberg's study is that the Germans persuaded themselves that the extermination of the Jews was a necessity. Those who positively organized the extermination saw themselves as idealists, and they were anxious that this idealism, which enabled them to carry out a hideous task, should not be sullied by sadism or corruption. They must show that their action was materially and psychologically disinterested.

But even if we accept this, it is not the end of the problem. For there are always two parties to destruction: the destroyers and the destroyed. During the Eichmann trial in Israel a question constantly asked by younger Israelis was: But why was there no resistance? ... At Auschwitz the ratio of prisoners to guards varied from 20 to 1 to 35 to 1. And yet they went like sheep to the slaughter. The Germans themselves, who have long staggered the world by their bovine docility, were amazed. The Jews meekly accepted every successive order which rendered them impotent, they queued up for the deportation trains, they dutifully dug their graves and knelt down to be shot and tumble into them, they filed into the gas chambers. Resistance was negligible, German casualties almost nil. The last-minute resistance of the Warsaw Ghetto was a heroic exception.

For when the Germans had done their worst, we cannot escape the fact that the Jews of Europe, obedient to their leaders and to their own habits of mind, collaborated in their own destruction. Again and again this fact emerges from Mr. Hilberg's narrative. It is his most surprising revelation, and it will probably be the least welcome to his readers. But it is inescapable. For two thouand years, as he says, the Jews had been unlearning the habit of resistance, and in the end they could not, without a revolution, recover it.

The pattern of Jewish "appeasement" was the same everywhere.... Nor was it only the German Jews who walked into the trap. We cannot ascribe it to German docility.

It is easy to blame the *Judenrate*, but the *Judenrate* were not unrepresentative. As Mr. Hilberg says, they "*were* the Jewish leaders." All his evidence shows that, in their compliance, they accurately represented their followers. Compliance was the mentality of the Dispersion.... Even at the end (as the Hungarian episode shows) they did not wait to be deceived. They deceived themselves. Like the Germans, who did not wish to admit that, as a nation, they were murdering, the Jews did not wish to admit that, as a nation, they were being murdered.

Not the least of the contributions which Mr. Hilberg has made to history and sociology in this impressive work is his illumination of this great gulf between those who continued and those who sought to reverse a long-successful but, in its later and perhaps unique encounter with the German bureaucracy, ultimately disastrous tradition.

˜ ˜

AMERICAN HISTORICAL REVIEW 67, 3 (April 1962)
The Destruction of the Euroepan Jews. By Raul Hilberg (Chicago: Quadrangle Books, 1961), pp. x+788.

This is an impressive and depressing work. Professor Hilberg traces the steps taken by the German state, party, economic, and military bureaucracies to destroy Europe's Jews.

The author's method is simple in form. He reviews each step, following a chronological and geographical sequence across Europe and explicating the organizations and individuals involved on the basis primarily of exhaustive research in the German documents. This approach is productive both of the book's great merits and its defects. With great care and ingenuity Hilberg has unraveled agencies and jurisdictions, organizational responsibilities, and financial transactions that often baffle the scholar. The approach also reveals—and this is one of the main themes of the book—the involvement of vast numbers in the mechanics of mass murder. A modern society with its complex bureaucracy is potentially a menace to any moral order. Crime loses its criminality through the institutionalization: those who give orders see no blood; those who assist at the deed are mere technicians; those who kill only obey orders. By placing this whole story before the reader Hilberg performs an important service not only by pointing to the general danger, but also by restoring balance to our perspective on the past. He shows that the individuals involved in the murder process were not a selected crew of sadists, but a sample of the population; that if the SS did the shooting in Russia, the army did it in Serbia; that if the party bureaucracy pushed hard, the Foreign Ministry officials were doing their best to compete.

Nothing would be gained by listing minor errors. More important are those shortcomings produced by the author's methodology. First, Hilberg is sometimes carried away by his passion for detail into tedious efforts at precision that only tire the reader and mar the effectiveness of the account. Second, in trying to do practically all the research himself on the basis of documents, the author has sometimes redone episodes, like the proposed Grynzpan trial, that have already been analyzed more thoroughly by others. Furthermore, rigid adherence to the wording rather than the meaning of documents has in places led to distortion.

These deficiencies do not materially reduce Hilberg's contribution. Not only the process of destruction but its manifold implications and repercussions are described and analyzed with diligence and perception. The satellites of the Axis, both the willing and the unwilling, the rescue organizations and the Allied powers, the obedient victims and the murderers brought to trial, the survivors and the restitution officials all move across the somber pages of this book. Here the destruction process is seen through the eyes of its practitioners on a scale no other scholar has yet attempted. A German translation is desirable.

Gerhard L. Weinberg

AMERICAN JOURNAL OF SOCIOLOGY 68, 1 (July 1962)
The Destruction of the European Jews. By Raul Hilberg (Chicago: Quadrangle Books, 1961), pp. xii+788.

Professor Hilberg's volume is enormously useful as an approach to the problem. Its double-columned pages are packed with meticulous detail. He has carefully examined a great number of sources and has brought his materials together skilfully. His careful, lucid unfolding of how the tragedy developed brings home its full horror as few other treatments have.

Successful as the book is in describing how the killings were carried through, it nevertheless fails to explain why they took place. The author cannot understand the motives, either of the Nazis, or of the Germans, or of their collaborators, or of the conquered populations, or even of the Jews. Perhaps because he has so deeply immersed himself in the world of the bureaucrats, he cannot comprehend the human beings who were their victims.

Again and again Hilberg returns, as if it were critical, to the question of why the Jews failed to resist. It is as if, knowing that the tragedy should not have occurred, he insists that someone should have stopped it—Germans, Allies, or, if no one else, the Jews. And he draws upon a far-fetched conception of historical Jewish attitudes to account for their unwillingness to resist. Out of this misconception spring serious errors in interpretation.

The unwelcome possibility, which the author does not confront, is that nothing could have prevented the Holocaust once the war had begun—not the German people, nor the Allies, and least of all the Jews. In fact, the magnitude of the killing operations had no relation to the degree of resistance, but only to the extent of the Nazi power in various parts of Europe.

As an example of the supreme test of the compliance reaction in front of the grave, Hilberg cites the following eyewitness report: "The father was holding the hand of a boy about ten years old and was speaking to him softly; the boy was fighting his tears. The father pointed to the sky, stroked his head, and seemed to explain something to him.... Then I heard a series of shots" (1669). Perhaps no other attitude was dignified and reasonable in a world completely and brutally mad.

Oscar Handlin
Harvard University

NOTES

CHAPTER 1. INTRODUCTION

1. See for example, Dagmar Barnouw's fascinating study, *Visible Spaces: Hannah Arendt and the German-Jewish Experience* (Baltimore: The Johns Hopkins University Press, 1990); also *Feminist Interpretations of Hannah Arendt*, ed. Bonnie Honig (University Park, Pa.: Penn State Press, 1995), particularly Dietz's, Honig's, Pitkin's, and Benhabib's essays in that volume. The basic collection of Arendt's Jewish writings themselves is *The Jew as Pariah*, ed. and with an introduction by Ron H. Feldman (New York: Grove Press, 1978).

2. The "Jewish Writings" refer primarily to the essays collected in Ron Feldman's volume, op. cit. note 1. The complete citation for *Rahel Varnhagen* is Hannah Arendt, *Rahel Varnhagen: The Life of a Jewish Woman*, rev. ed. (New York: Harcourt Brace Jovanovich, 1974 [1957]).

3. Jaspers to Hannah Arendt, 23 August 1952. *Correspondence, Hannah Arendt, Karl Jaspers*, ed. Lotte Kohler and Hans Saner (New York: Harcourt Brace Jovanovich, 1992, pp. 192, 193).

4. *Correspondence*, op. cit. p. 197 Arendt to Jaspers, 7 September 1952.

5. I cite just two recent examples of scholarship that tends, in my opinion, to pull Arendt into "early" and "late," in a way that resembles a theme in Marx scholarship. Leah Bradshaw, in *Acting and Thinking: The Political Thought of Hannah Arendt* (Toronto: University of Toronto Press, 1989) suggests that when she was writing *The Human Condition*, Hannah Arendt believed in the complete primacy of action and was content with a view that maintained the utter separability of action from thought. In Bradshaw's scenario, Arendt later came to realize the interconnectedness of thinking and acting and tried to resolve the tension between them, only to overemphasize the importance of thought, once again divorced too completely from action. The tension between thinking and acting persisted, Bradshaw argues,

until Arendt went to Jerusalem to report on the trial of Adolph Eichmann. At that time, she turned toward the primacy of mental life but never resolved the "tensions" between her later interest in thinking and her early preoccupation with action.

Likewise, Ronald Beiner, an astute and evocative student of Arendt's theory of judgment, becomes ensnared in mapping the progression of her ideas about judgment from her earlier writings on the *Vita Activa* to the later preoccupation with *The Life of the Mind*. He notes a sharp turning point in her ideas in 1971, with her essay "Thinking and Moral Considerations": "Surveying Arendt's work as a whole, we can see that she offers not one but two theories of judgment.... In her writings up until the 1971 essay 'Thinking and Moral Considerations,' judgment is considered from the point of view of the *Vita Activa*; in her writings from that essay onward, judgment is considered from the point of view of the life of the mind.... As I interpret Arendt, her writings on the theme of judgment fall into two more or less distinct phases: early and late, practical and contemplative" (*Lectures on Kant's Political Philosophy*, ed. and with an interpretive essay by Ronald Beiner [Chicago: University of Chicago Press, 1982, pp. 91, 92]). Beiner, like Bradshaw, concludes that Arendt's work is seriously strained by the inconsistencies between her early and later work: "Arendt achieves a final resolution by abolishing this tension, opting wholly for the latter conception of judgment. This resolution ultimately produces consistency, but it is a strained consistency, achieved at the price of excluding any reference to the *vita activa* within the revised concept of judgment" (Beiner 139).

Both Beiner and Bradshaw may be correct in their perception of tensions between an "early" Arendt concerned with action, and a "later" Arendt concerned with the life of the mind. Margaret Canovan also sees a division in Arendt's work between the Socratic and Heideggerian, which translates into categories compatible with Beiner and Bradshaw: community oriented, and solitary philosophical. We shall discuss her work in more detail in chapter nine. But I am convinced that the intellectual "contradictions" in Arendt's work were not as profound as these scholars suggest, that action and thinking were always concerns of Arendt's, and that the tensions, which certainly do characterize (although, in my opinion, do not dichotomize) her work, are best understood as a tension between the largely unacknowledged interests of the Jewish scholar and the somewhat incompatible demands of the German philosophical scholar, which is closer to how Arendt presented her public scholarly persona.

On a lighter note, with regard to the segregation of Arendt into woman and Jew as well as scholar, consider the following correspondence with Gertrud Jaspers. Right after the war, when Arendt and Jaspers had made contact after twelve years of mutually fearing the other dead, Arendt enclosed cooking instructions along with the package of supplies she had sent to the Jaspers. She instructed the (Jewish) Frau Jaspers in the art of cooking bacon: "Furthermore, dear Gertrud Jaspers, don't rely on my not very highly developed housewifely instincts but write me what you'd like to have. In the last packages, I put in a kosher wurst; you have to be very careful with pork here because of trichinosis. If I should send bacon (I've forgotten the German word for it, the hell with it), please always fry it just this way: Put the slices in a moderately hot pan and fry them over a low flame. Keep pouring the fat off until the slices are crisp. Then nothing can go wrong with either the fat or the bacon" (*Correspondence*, op.cit, p. 24, 18 November 1945). Although I facetiously offer this charming letter as an example of Arendt as hausfrau, perhaps some more traditional Jewishness shows here unconsciously. In spite of instructing a sister in the art of cooking *traif*, she forgets the German word for it!

6. In *The Jew as Pariah*, ed. and with an introduction by Ron H. Feldman (New York: Grove Press, 1978), pp. 241, 245–47.

7. Some work is finally being done on assimilation and gender. A new volume has been published by the University of Washington Press, *Gender and Assimilation in Modern Jewish History: The Roles and Representation of Women*, ed. Paula Hyman (Seattle: University of Washington Press, 1995). See also Marion A. Kaplan, *The Making of the Jewish Middle Class: Women, Family and Identity in Imperial Germany* (New York: Oxford University Press, 1991). Other sources on Jewish feminism, although not specifically on gender and assimilation are cited in chapter 5.

8. George L. Mosse, *Nationalism and Sexuality: Middle-Class Morality and Sexual Norms in Modern Europe* (Madison: University of Wisconsin Press, 1985).

9. See, for example, bell hooks, *Ain't I a Woman* (Boston: South End Press, 1981), e.g., "While black men were not forced to assume a role colonial American society regarded as 'feminine,' black women were forced to assume a 'masculine' role. Black women labored in the fields alongside black men, but few if any black men labored as domestics alongside black women in the white household (with the possible exception of butlers, whose status was still higher than that of a maid). Thus, it would be much more accurate for scholars to

examine the dynamics of sexist and racist oppression during slavery in light of the masculinization of the black female and not the demasculinization of the black male" (22); and "Moynihan suggested that the negative effects of racist oppression of black people could be eliminated if black females were more passive, subservient and supportive of patriarchy. Once again, woman's liberation was presented as inimical to black liberation. The extent to which black men absorbed this ideology was made evident in the 60s black liberation movement. Black male leaders of the movement made the liberation of black people from racist oppression synonymous with their gaining the right to assume the role of patriarch, of sexist oppressor. By allowing white men to dictate the terms by which they would define black liberation, black men chose to endorse sexist exploitation and oppression of black women. And in so doing they were compromised. They were not liberated from the system but liberated to serve the system. The movement ended and the system had not changed; it was no less racist or sexist" (181).

See also Angela Davis, *Women, Race and Class* (New York: Vintage Books, 1983); and Patricia Hill Collins, *Black Feminist Thought: Knowledge, Consciousness, and the Politics of Empowerment* (New York: Routledge, 1990). Both scholars address the myth of the "dangerous" black matriarch, who somehow receives the blame for the "emasculinization" of African American men, as well as for all the problems African American families may suffer. Collins observes, "Far too many Black men who praise their own mothers feel less accountable to the mothers of their own children.... In the case of Black motherhood, the problems have been a stifling of dialogue among African American women and the perpetuation of troublesome, controlling images, both negative and positive" (116, 117). And: "The mammy represents the clearest example of the split between sexuality and motherhood present in Eurocentric masculinist thought. In contrast, both the matriarch and the welfare mother are sexual beings. But their sexuality is linked to their fertility, and this link forms one fundamental reason they are negative images. The matriarch represents the sexually aggressive woman, one who emasculates Black men because she will not permit them to assume roles as Black patriarchs. She refuses to be passive and thus is stigmatized. Similarly, the welfare mother represents a woman of low morals and uncontrolled sexuality, factors identified as the cause of her impoverished state. In both cases Black female control over sexuality and fertility is conceptualized as antithetical to elite white male interests" (78).

Angela Davis argues that the image of the black matriarch was created by white male scholars of slavery, who observed more shared domestic responsibilities and cooperation between men and women in slave households with regard to tasks performed, and this semblance of *equality* between slave men and women was perceived, through their gender-distorted eyes as "matriarchy." That is, the absence of patriarchal hierarchy within the slave families was labeled "matriarchy" because the women were not subordinate to the men: "The salient theme emerging from domestic life in the slave quarters is one of sexual equality. The labor that slaves performed for their own sake and not for the aggrandizement of their masters was carried out in terms of equality" (Davis 18).

10. As the African American poet Amiri Baraka (formerly Leroi Jones) observed recently in *The New Yorker*, regarding Louis Farrakhan: "First of all, I wouldn't go to no war and leave half the army home. . . . Logistically, that doesn't make sense." Henry Louis Gates further reports of his interview with Baraka: "He notes that Martin Luther King's 1963 March on Washington was 'much more inclusive,' and sees Farrakhan's regression as 'an absolute duplication of what's happening in the country,' from Robert Bly on the sacrilization of masculinity," in Henry Louis Gates, Jr., "Annals of Race: Thirteen Ways of Looking at a Black Man," *The New Yorker* 71, 33 (23 October 1995): 60.

11. See Jennifer Ring, *Modern Political Theory and Contemporary Feminism: A Dialectical Analysis* (Albany, State University of New York Press, 1991), esp. pp. 1–58.

12. This may sound like the traditional psychoanalytic "Catch 22": The evidence that we are resistant to something is precisely that we are unaware of the resistance and, thus, resisting all the more stridently. However, for more extensive discussion of the psychogenesis of the fear of female anger, see for example, Dorothy Dinnerstein, *The Mermaid and the Minotaur* (New York: Colophon Books, 1977); and Nancy Chodorow, *The Reproduction of Mothering* (Berkeley, University of California Press, 1978).

13. bell hooks, *Talking Back: Thinking Feminist, Thinking Black* (Boston: South End Press, 1989), p. 7.

14. bell hooks, op. cit., pp. 7, 128.

15. Carol Gilligan, *In A Different Voice* (Cambridge: Harvard University Press, 1982).

16. Catharine MacKinnon, "Feminism, Marxism, Method and the State: Toward Feminist Jurisprudence," *Signs* 8, 6 (1983): 35–58; and

MacKinnon, "Feminism, Marxism, Method and the State: An Agenda For Theory." In *Feminist Theory: A Critique of Ideology*, ed. Nannerl O. Keohane, Michelle Z. Rosaldo, and Barbara C. Gelpi (Chicago: University of Chicago Press, 1982), p.24

17. Sandra Harding, *The Science Question in Feminism* (Ithaca, N.Y.: Cornell University Press, 1986), p. 47. See also Evelyn Fox Keller, *Reflections on Science and Gender* (New Haven, Conn.: Yale University Press, 1985); Sandra Harding and Merrill B. Hintikka, *Discovering Reality* (Dordrecht, Holland: D. Reidel, 1983), especially the essay by Naomi Scheman on objectivity; Anne Fausto-Sterling, *Myths of Gender* (New York: Basic Books, 1985).

18. Nancy Hartsock, "The Feminist Standpoint." In *Feminism and Methodology*, ed. Sandra Harding (Bloomington: Indiana University Press, 1987), pp. 157–80.

CHAPTER 2. THE POLITICS OF THE *EICHMANN* CONTROVERSY

1. Elisabeth Young-Bruehl, *Arendt: For Love of the World* (New Haven, Conn.: Yale University Press, 1982), pp. 339, 379. See Young-Bruehl's excellent and thorough discussion of the writing of *Eichmann in Jerusalem* and the controversy surrounding it, pp. 328–378.

2. In Hannah Arendt, 1954. *Between Past and Future: Eight Exercises in Political Thought* (New York: Viking, 1954), p. 227.

3. Arendt, Hannah, "Thinking and Moral Considerations: A Lecture," *Social Research* 38, 3 (Autumn 1971): 417–440.

4. Arendt, Hannah, *The Life of the Mind: One/Thinking, Two/Willing.* (New York: Harcourt Brace Jovanovich, 1978 [1971]), pp. 3–5. Hereafter referred to in the text as either *Thinking* or *Willing*, with page reference following. See also Dagmar Barnouw, *Visible Spaces* (Baltimore: Johns Hopkins University Press, 1990). Referring to her unfinished *The Life of the Mind* and the work that led up to it, Barnouw notes: "Yet, where she talked explicitly and exclusively about thinking—in the 1971 lecture "Thinking and Moral considerations," in *Thinking*, the first volume of *The Life of the Mind*—she felt the need to justify her 'presumptuousness,' and in both cases she referred her readers to the case of Eichmann" (1ff.).

5. Arendt noted to Jaspers: "What is serious about this is that all the non-Jews are on my side now and that not a single Jew dares to stand

up for me publicly, even if he is completely with me" (L.343 11/24/ 63, p. 535). Mary McCarthy in "The Hue and Cry" (*Partisan Review* 31, 1 [Winter 1964]) noted: "So far as I know, all Miss Arendt's hostile reviews have come from Jews and those favorable to her from gentiles, with four exceptions: A. Alvarez, George Lichtheim, Bruno Bettelheim, and Daniel Bell. . . . It is as if *Eichmann in Jerusalem* had required a special pair of Jewish spectacles to make its 'true purport' visible" (82). Barnouw notes: "This is, on the whole, a useful observation, even though, as Dwight Macdonald points out, the exceptions are too many for her claim to be entirely convincing, especially since they include such substantial writers. But Macdonald, too, thought McCarthy's 'broader aim' was accurate: 'The reactions *in general* divide along Jewish and non-Jewish lines'" (from *Partisan Review* 31, 2 [Spring 1964]): 265–66.

6. Hannah Arendt, *Eichmann in Jerusalem: A Report on the Banality of Evil* (New York: Penguin, 1980 [1963]), p. 118. Hereafter referred to in the text as *Eichmann*, followed by page reference.

7. Barnouw, op. cit. p. 234.

8. Arendt was also not the only one to have made these charges. An Israeli counsel confirmed as much to her privately (see Hannah Arendt and Karl Jaspers, *Correspondence, 1926–1969*, ed. and with an introduction by Lotte Kohler and Hans Saner. Trans. Robert Kimber and Rita Kimber (New York: Harcourt Brace Jovanovich, 1991). Hereafter referred to in the text with the initial "L." for "Letter," followed by a number, date, page number, and author, where needed for clarification (L.343, 11/24/63, p. 534).

9. Barnouw, op. cit., pp. 232–33.

10. See for example her discussion in *On Revolution* of the patronizing attitude of the leaders of the French Revolution, in what she regards as their betrayal of the masses of poor people. Especially pp. 88–98 and 109–114. "Since the days of the French Revolution, it has been the boundlessness of their sentiment that made the revolutionaries so curiously insensitive to reality in general and to the reality of persons in particular whom they felt no compunctions in sacrificing to their 'principle,' or the course of history, or the cause of the revolution as such" (90). "It was the war upon hypocrisy that transformed Robespierre's dictatorship into the Reign of Terror" (99), and "It is true that the masses of the suffering people had taken to the street unbidden and uninvited by those who then became their organizers and their spokesmen. But the suffering they exposed transformed the

malheureux into the *enrages* only when 'the compassionate zeal' of the revolutionaries—of Robespierre, probably, more than of anybody else—began to glorify this suffering, hailing the exposed misery as the best and even only guarantee of virtue" (111).

11. See Hannah Arendt and Karl Jaspers, *Correspondence, 1926–1969*, ed. and with an introduction by Lotte Kohler and Hans Saner. Trans. Robert Kimber and Rita Kimber (New York: Harcourt Brace Jovanovich, 1991). Hereafter referred to in the text with the initial "L." for "Letter," followed by a number, date, page number, and author, where needed for clarification (L.332, 7/25/63 [Jaspers], pp. 511–15, and Arendt's reply, L.333, 8/9/63, pp. 515–18). "What I mean is that everyone who had a political role—even if he was against the regime and even if he was secretly preparing an assassination attempt on Hitler—was infected by the plague in both word and deed. In this sense, the demoralization of the country was complete—the only people not affected by it were those who sat steadfastly in their hiding places. You set the number at about 100,000, and I think that's a fair estimate. If those hundred thousand had come to power after Germany's defeat, things would probably look very different now" (518). Leni Yahil, in *The Holocaust: The Fate of European Jewry* (New York: Oxford University Press, 1990), also chronicles in detail instances of resistance. See full discussion of the European resistance in chapter 3.

12. Elisabeth Young-Bruehl, *Hannah Arendt: For Love of the World* (New Haven, Conn.: Yale University Press, 1982), p. 349.

13. For thorough accounts, see Young-Bruehl, op. cit., and Barnouw, *Dagmar, Visible Spaces* (Baltimore: Johns Hopkins University Press, 1990).

14. "Hannah Arendt on Eichmann: A Study in the Perversity of Brilliance," *Commentary* 36, 3 (September 1963): 201–208.

15. Raul Hilberg, *The Destruction of the European Jews* (New York: Holmes and Meier, 1985).

16. "The Aesthetics of Evil: Hannah Arendt on Eichmann and the Jews," *Partisan Review* 30, 1 (Spring 1963): 211–30.

17. See Appendix, pp. 289–295 and Hilberg, *The Destruction of the European Jews*, chapter one, "Precedents", especially pp. 19–24.

18. Young-Bruehl, op. cit., p. 360.

19. Young-Bruehl, p. 360. Irving Howe claimed in *Partisan Review* 31, 2 (Spring 1964): "*At no point*—was anyone, not Bell or Hilberg or Kazin 'shouted down.' Everyone who rose to speak was allowed to finish" (260).

20. "The Aesthetics of Evil," *Partisan Review* 30, 2 (Spring 1963): 214.

21. "The Hue and Cry," *Partisan Review* 31, 1 (Winter 1964): 82–94.

22. "A historical disaster has been transformed, I am sorry to say, into a journalistic occasion." "More on Eichmann," *Partisan Review* 31, 2 (Spring 1964): 278.

23. See discussion in Chapter 3, pp. 71 ff.

24. Feldman, op. cit., p. 241.

25. Ibid, p. 242.

26. Feldman, *The Jew as Pariah* (New York: Grove, 1978), p. 250.

27. Feldman, op. cit., p. 247.

28. Feldman, op. cit., p. 245.

29. Ibid, 248–49. Dagmar Barnouw observes: "Scholem chose to misunderstand what she said about Eichmann's professed fascination with Herzl's *The Jewish State*. . . . This, of course, did not make Eichmann a Zionist, nor does it suggest that Arendt considered him one when she reported that *he* considered himself converted to Zionism; and of course it did not make a Zionist a Nazi, nor did it suggest Arendt's establishing such an equation." Barnouw goes so far as to express astonishment at the public mentality that could so profoundly misinterpret Arendt's intentions:

"In her report on the Eichmann trial, Arendt showed how one quite normal man's inability to think for himself was fed by the moral inversion of totalitarian rule and, in turn, contributed to it until it reached stunning proportions. Most of her critics understood her description of this process to be an attempt to excuse the executioners and accuse the victims. It is this misunderstanding which is amazing, not the anger or the rage. It was caused by her refusal to use anti-Semitism as the main focus in her analysis of the crime and its punishment, which was connected with her insistence on being allowed to tell the story of Eichmann using a storyteller's strategies in negotiating distances and perspectives."

30. "In her lengthy chronicle of the destruction of European Jewry Miss Arendt adds nothing new to the vast literature on the subject. Basing herself largely on Raul Hilberg's impressive study (*The Destruction of the European Jews*) she goes over familiar territory" (Syrkin 7).

31. This is the subject of chapter 3, "Israel and the Holocaust."

32. Headline in *Intermountain Jewish News*, April 12, 1963. Cited in Macdonald, *Partisan Review* 31, 2 (Spring 1964): 262.

33. Daniel Bell, "The Alphabet of Justice: Reflections on 'Eichmann in Jerusalem,'" *Partisan Review* 30, 3 (Fall 1963): 417–29.

34. The issue of the education of Jewish women in the Germany of Hannah Arendt's childhood is discussed in detail in the section entitled "Jewish Women," of chapter 5, this volume.

35. Raul Hilberg, *The Destruction of the European Jews* (New York: Holmes and Meier, 1985).

36. See the appendix of reviews of Hilberg's book at the end of this volume, pp. 289–295

37. My evidence for this is somewhat anecdotal: presentation of these ideas at several annual meetings of the American Political Science Association were met with virulent outrage that simply recapitulated the tone of the *Eichmann* controversy itself, and caused one sympathetic colleague who had witnessed the uproar to remark to me, "I guess the *Eichmann* controversy is still alive." Readers' objections to my efforts to publish articles based on research for this book have been similarly strident, including reports to journals as disparate as *Tikkun* and *Political Theory*.

38. Dagmar Barnouw (1990) is somewhat of an exception to this, especially in her chapter on Rahel Varnhagen, where she notes, for example, "But Arendt does all these things to Rahel because she is profoundly angry with her out of a concrete sympathy with her life as a woman and a Jew. Putting herself in Rahel's place, seeing her so clearly, understanding her so well, she wishes passionately that the other Jewish woman, living more than a century before her, could have had the courage and the encouragement to change. No male, no gentile, would have been so angry with Rahel, nor would they have seen so clearly the waste of her life and the flaws in her life story" (70).

39. "Now let us, by a flight of imagination, suppose that Rome is not a human habitation but a psychical entity with a similarly long and copious past—an entity, that is to say, in which nothing that has once come into existence will have passed away and all the earlier phases of development continue to exist alongside the latest one," and so forth (Freud, *Civilization and Its Discontents*, trans. James Strachey [New York: Norton, 1961], p. 18).

40. For examples of Arendt's ability to distance herself from identifying with the female, see Arendt-Jaspers, *Correspondence* (L.258, 3/25/60 p. 391): "But that truly awful story about the girl confirms me in

my prejudice against women as professors. I may not have been able to manage a performance like that because I lack the uninhibitedness of the hysterical, but I can understand how fear would drive someone to simply lie in bed. That takes a certain courage, too, that I don't have. You thought: early stages of mental illness. You are probably right, but I don't think single women need to be crazy to do crazy things." Also, in *The Human Condition*, pp. 72–73: "Women and slaves belonged to the same category and were hidden away not only because they were somebody else's property, but because their life was 'laborious,' devoted to bodily functions.... The fact that the modern age emancipated the working class and the women at nearly the same historical moment must certainly be counted among the characteristics of an age which no longer believes that bodily functions and material concerns should be hidden."

CHAPTER 3. ISRAEL AND THE HOLOCAUST

1. "Raul Hilberg's basic work on the Holocaust also remains untranslated into Hebrew. Like Arendt, Hilberg placed part of the guilt for the genocide on the Jews themselves, implicating the Judenrats in facilitating the extermination program. The role of the Judenrats has always been one of the most sensitive issues of the Holocaust; it took seven years for Yad Vashem to publish a Hebrew translation of Isaiah Trunk's *Judenrat*, which was first published in New York. Ruth Bondi's *Edelstein against Time*—a humane, balanced account of the moral dilemmas faced by the man whom Eichmann appointed as 'Jewish Elder' of the Theresienstadt ghetto—was published only in the early 1980s, when it was seen as shattering a taboo. The same was true of Yehoshua Sobol's play, *Ghetto*, produced a few years later" Tom Segev, *The Seventh Million: The Israelis and the Holocaust*, trans. Haim Watzman (New York: Hill and Wang, 1993), p. 465.

2. (New York: Hill and Wang, 1993), trans. Haim Watzman.

3. Tom Segev, *The Seventh Million: The Israelis and the Holocaust*, trans. Haim Watzman (New York: Hill and Wang, 1993), p. 465. Page references follow in the text in parentheses.

4. Alexander Bloom, *Prodigal Sons: The New York Intellectuals and Their World* (New York: Oxford University Press, 1986), p. 329. Page references follow in the text in parentheses.

5. The term *Palestinian Jews*, and even *Palestine*, is problematic. It is technically accurate, since there was no "state of Israel" before 1948, and the British protectorate of Palestine included both Jewish and Arab territories. But since the current politics of the region remain tense, and struggle over territory still bitter, with Israel now referring to Jewish territory and Palestine referring to Arab territory, use of the term *Palestinian* to refer to Jews before the founding of the state of Israel is somewhat disconsonant. In this chapter, therefore, I shall use the terms *Palestine* and *Palestinian*, with the modifier of either *Jewish* or *Zionist*, only when the reference involves the legal or political aspects of the British protectorate before 1948. Otherwise, in deference to contemporary political instincts, when the term implies more the Jewish people in Palestine, (as in *am Yisrael* or *eretz Yisrael*) rather than the legal entity, I shall use the term *Israel* or *Israeli*. The most accurate term, and the one preferred by the Jewish people in Palestine before statehood to describe themselves, and which I shall also make use of, is *Yishuv*, or "settlement".

6. A more benign reading than Porat's regards the British as either passive or so preoccupied with their involvement in the broader war against the Axis powers that they overlooked the specific fate of the Jews. Porat is less sypathetic, and insists bluntly that the British simply did not care about the fate of the Jews and were actively working against the effectiveness of Israel's efforts to rescue European Jews. In her discussion of the pleas to the British to bomb Auschwitz she notes: "The reasons given by the Allies for their refusal to bomb Auschwitz are greatly suspect" (219) and concludes, "There is no way to avoid the conclusion that the Allies did not bomb Auschwitz because they were simply indifferent to the fate of the Jews" (219). She believes that far from being passive about the Holocaust, the British actively intervened against some of the rescue efforts: "A few decades later, when the archives were opened, it became clear that the British, who had been accused of passivity in the face of tragedy, had not been passive at all. This is perhaps the most heart-rending aspect of all the unsuccessful attempts to rescue the children. While Eichmann, his staff, and German Foreign Ministry officials exerted themselves lest a single Jewish child escape them, the British, self-righteous and seemingly passive, blocked all escape routes. In the middle were a handful of emissaries in Istanbul and officials in Palestine, who tried to break through the walls with their bare fists, and the children, who never came" (Porat 163).

7. "At the next meeting of the ZAC, in mid-January 1943, Gruenbaum argued that money from the Foundation Fund should not be used for

rescue operations: 'No, and I say it again—no! This tendency to consider Zionist activities secondary must be resisted.' ... Funds for rescue operations had to come from other sources" (Porat 76). Porat wonders whether "Gruenbaum had moved from one extreme—of rejecting the news [of the Holocaust] and denying its veracity—to another—of accepting it and totally despairing" (78).

8. With regard to the accusations that the Zionists would accept only "the best human material," which meant healthy young adults who agreed with them politically or children who could be socialized to labor Zionism, Porat believes, "Most of the leaders supported the decision to save 'any Jew who could be found' as the right decision" (Porat 247). She notes that "In mid-1943 the Rescue Committee decided to extend help to any Jew who could be helped. Smugglers and couriers were instructed to 'take any Jew ... any Jewish child' who could still be found" (246). But she also acknowledges that there was a problem:

> On the other hand, immigration permits continued to be distributed along party lines in the satellite countries, with which communication was better.... Toward the end of 1943... it emerged that, of the 857 refugees who had made their way to Istanbul through the Balkans, the majority were members of Agudat Yisrael and wealthy Jews, few of whom had ever given a thought to Palestine. No one from the pioneering movements was among them.... Zionists activists in occupied Europe were bitter; "I feel as if I had been spat on," wrote one. (Porat 246–47)

9. Bauer provides statistics to demonstrate his conclusion that "the boycott never posed a threat to the Nazi regime" because "Nazi policies, not unlike those of the American New Deal, concentrated on public works and priming the pump; they were implemented beginning immediately upon the assumption of power in January 1933. The results were impressive.... The GNP grew by 43 percent, the national index by 46 percent, the industrial index by 88 percent, and the number of employed by 36 percent." "To sum up: given the relatively insignificant part that foreign trade played in the German economy in 1933, even a successful boycott by Jews could have affected the German economy marginally at most" (see Bauer 12–15). Nonetheless, Nazi anti-Semitism was such that Jewish financial power was feared irrationally—and even against the early economic successes of the Nazi regime.

10. The title of a chapter in Segev's book, quoting the finding of the Israeli Chief Justice Heshin in Rudolf Kastner's appeal, who

claimed that negotiating with Nazis for the release of Jews had precedent in Jewish history: "But there is also another point of view, different and opposite, and this view also has roots in the pages of our history. Jeremiah the prophet, for example, preached surrender to the enemy and an alliance with him, while Rabbi Yohanan Ben-Zakkai chose to save what could be saved in a time of trouble. Despite this, no one accused them of selling their souls to the devil" (Segev 307).

11. "Even in 1942, the Jews of the Yishuv used this self-righteous doctrine of death with honor to excoriate their brothers in Europe who had not taken up arms against the Nazis. 'The problem with the Jews in the Exile is that they prefer the life of a beaten dog to death with honor,' said Yitzhak Gruenbaum. He reasoned that there was no hope of saving anything of the Zionist undertaking in the face of a German invasion. Given that, he said, 'we must at the very least see to it that we leave a Masada legend behind us'" (Segev 71).

12. Three men were arrested and ultimately convicted and sentenced to life imprisonment for assassinating Kastner. It was believed that they worked for an extreme right-wing underground movement that the secret service had infiltrated because it was illegal. It turned out that one of them, Ze'ev Eckstein, had been assigned to infiltrate the underground movement by the secret service. The other two suspects were Dan Shemer and Yosef Menkes (Segev 308).

13. Ben Gurion wrote to a friend, "I know almost nothing about the Kastner matter.... I did not follow the trial and did not read the verdict, except for a few sentences that appeared in the headlines" (Segev 293).

CHAPTER 4. THE NEW YORK INTELLECTUALS AND *EICHMANN IN JERUSALEM*

1. George L. Mosse, *German Jews Beyond Judaism* (Bloomington: Indiana University Press and Cincinnati, Hebrew Union College Press, 1995).

2. Terry Cooney, *The Rise of the New York Intellectuals: Partisan Review and Its Circle* (Madison: University of Wisconsin Press, 1986), p. 6. Page references follow in parentheses in the text with "Cooney."

3. Alexander Bloom, *Prodigal Sons: The New York Intellectuals and Their World* (New York: Oxford University Press, 1986). Page references appear in the text in parentheses with "Bloom."

4. Russell Jacoby, *The Last Intellectuals: American Culture in the Age of Academe* (New York: Basic, 1987). Page references appear in the text in parentheses with "Jacoby."

5. Irving Howe, *World of Our Fathers* (New York: Harcourt Brace Jovanovich, 1976), pp. 251–52.

6. Alan Wald, *The New York Intellectuals: The Rise and Decline of the Anti-Stalinist Left from the 1930's to the 1980's* (Chapel Hill: University of North Carolina Press, 1987), pp. 33–35.

7. Alan Wald, *The New York Intellectuals: The Rise and Decline of the Anti-Stalinist Left from the 1930s to the 1980s* (Chapel Hill: University of North Carolina Press, 1987).

8. Alfred Kazin, "In Every Voice, in Every Ban," *New Republic* (10 January 1944): 45–46.

9. Bloom, p. 138. Bloom refers to an interview that he conducted with Alfred Kazin on 23 October 1976.

10. Bloom describes Mary McCarthy's relation to the *Partisan Review* in these terms, for example: "Although she was unknown, Rahv brought McCarthy to *Partisan Review* as an editor; her duties were to handle theater criticism. McCarthy claims she received the assignment because she had once been married to an actor and was 'supposed to know something about theater.' Although she was clearly a woman of intellectual skills, it is also clear that her position on the *PR* editorial board derived essentially from her relationship with Rahv. When she left him, she left the magazine" (73).

11. See Elisabeth Young-Bruehl, *Hannah Arendt: For Love of the World* (New Haven, Conn.: Yale University Press, 1982), Chapter 4, "Stateless Persons", especially pp. 150–163.

12. Irving Howe, "Mid-Century Turning Point: An Intellectual Memoir," *Midstream* (June–July 1975): 25.

13. The significance of Arendt's ability to see the humanity in "her" Nazi, the one who arrested her before her escape to Paris becomes particularly telling in this context. See Young-Bruehl, p. 106.

CHAPTER 5. RACE, GENDER AND JUDAISM: THE *EICHMANN* CONTROVERSY AS CASE STUDY

1. See appendix.

2. See Young-Bruehl, pp. 347–48, op. cit. "On behalf of the Council of Jews from Germany, Siegfried Moses, formerly the state comptroller of Israel and a friend of Blumenfeld's, sent Hannah Arendt a letter. Moses, a scholar and an old acquaintance of Arendt's from Berlin, to whose 1962 *festschrift* she had contributed, made what he

called a 'declaration of war' against Arendt and her book. Moses indicated that the council was also preparing for war on the historian Raul Hilberg's *The Destruction of the European Jews* and on the psychologist Bruno Bettelheim's "Freedom from Ghetto Thinking." Arendt warned Moses in reply that Hilberg's book would have a limited, scholarly audience and that Bettelheim's article would not lend itself to discussion on a high intellectual level; she then suggested that he attack her book alone and not confuse his war by fighting on too many fronts." Arendt was not entirely respectful of Hilberg, writing to Jaspars in April of 1964: "I haven't heard anything about Hilberg's coming out on my side. He's talking some nonsense now about the 'death wish' of the Jews. His book is really excellent, but only because he just reports facts in it. His introductory chapter that deals with general and historical matters wouldn't pass muster in a pigpen. (Excuse me—I momentarily forgot to whom I was writing. But now that I've said it I'll let it stand.)" *Arendt-Jaspars Corespondence*, op. cit. (L.351, H.A. to K.J., New York, 20 April 1964), p. 550.

3. George L. Mosse, *Nationalism and Sexuality: Middle-Class Morality and Sexual Norms in Modern Europe* (Madison: University of Wisconsin Press, 1985). Page references follow in parentheses with "Mosse."

4. "The manly Englishman or German showed the restraint and self-control so dear to the middle class. Manliness meant freedom from sexual passion, the sublimation of sensuality into leadership of society and the nation.... Manliness was not just a matter of courage, it was a pattern of manners and morals. Masculine comportment and a manly figure exemplified the transcendence of the so-called lower passions" (Mosse 13).

5. Mosse 23. But Mosse discusses the later, partial, acceptance of women who sought to be athletic on a male model. There emerged works of art, monuments to these athletic German women, in which their nude forms were practically indistinguishable from a male nude. See Mosse, p. 129 and the photograph on the cover of the book.

6. See bell hooks, *Ain't I a Woman?* (Boston: South End Press, 1981), pp. 22, 181. See also fn. 9 chapter 1.

7. Mosse adds, "The condemnation of contraception by racists was not confined to Germany. Sidney Webb warned that unless the decline of the birth rate was averted, the English nation would fall to the Irish and the Jews" (Mosse 140).

8. Mosse suggests that Himmler's plan to snuff out, to obliterate entirely, the two million homosexuals that he believed lived in Germany

provided a forecast of the fate that awaited the Jews. "The way in which Himmler described the death that should await the incurable homosexual pushed to new lengths the process of eliminating the outsider and played its role in the Jewish Holocaust to come. The death of the outsider WAS used to obliterate his very existence.... The outsider was not merely killed; he was supposed never to have existed at all" (Mosse 169).

9. Karl Marx, "The Fetishism of Commodities and the Secret Thereof," *Capital*, vol. 1: "Whenever, by an exchange, we equate as values our different products, by that very act, we also equate, as human labour, the different kinds of labour expended upon them. We are not aware of this, nevertheless we do it. Value, therefore, does not stalk about with a label describing what it is. It is value, rather, that converts every product into a social hieroglyphic. Later on, we try to decipher the hieroglyphic, to get behind the secret of our own social products; for to stamp an object of utility as a value, is just as much a social product as language." In *The Marx-Engels Reader*, 2d ed., ed. Robert C. Tucker (New York: Norton, 1978), p. 322.

10. See Daniel Boyarin, *Judaism and Gender: An Autobiography of the Jewish Man*, forthcoming, p. 219.

11. See particularly, Mary O'Brien, *The Politics of Reproduction* (Boston: Routledge and Kegan Paul, 1981); Mary O'Brien, "Feminist Theory and Dialectical Logic," in *Feminist Theory: A Critique of Ideology*, ed. N. O. Keohane, M. Z. Rosaldo, and B. C. Gelpi (Chicago: University of Chicago Press, 1982); Dorothy Dinnerstein, *The Mermaid and the Minotaur* (New York: Colophon, 1977); Nancy Chodorow, *The Reproduction of Mothering* (Berkeley: University of California Press, 1978); Juliet Mitchell, *Psychoanalysis and Feminism* (New York: Pantheon, 1974).

12. "The Oedipus model itself ought to be interpreted as a repression of homoerotic desire. The fundamental ideas of human sexual development in Freud are a sort of screen or supervalent thought for a deeper but very threatening psychic constituent that Freud had found in his own hysteria, but that then panicked him: the desire for 'femaleness,' for passivity, to be the object of another man's desire, even to bear the child of another man. The analysand that Freud came to disbelieve was thus himself" (Boyarin 301).

13. Mosse (49): "German Jews were fond of evoking participation in Germany's wars, not only to prove their citizenship but also to demonstrate heroism and manly comportment. Highlighting this quest, Max Nordau at the Second Zionist Congress of 1898 called for the

creation of 'muscle Jews' as against pale-faced and thin-chested 'coffeehouse Jews.' Later, he expressed the hope that 'our new muscle Jews' might regain the heroism of their forefathers.'"

14. "The contempt that Zionists in Palestine had for the Jews killed in the Nazi concentration camps is, I put forth, a direct descendent of this anti-Semitic representation, but those who died in the hopeless Warsaw Ghetto 'Rebellion' were glorified as 'New Jews', as the Polish branch of the 'palmach', the Zionist shock troops. They had 'learned to die.' Over and over again, Zionist writers of the '40s wrote in near-fascist terms of the 'beautiful death' of the Warsaw rebels and the 'ugly death' of the martyrs of the camps. This represents identification with the oppressor in one of its most naked and obvious forms and has its effect in imitation of that oppressor as well" (Boyarin 382).

15. Paul Breines, *Tough Jews: Political Fantasies and the Moral Dilemma of American Jewry* (New York: Basic, 1990). Citations follow in the text in parentheses.

16. "As decisive as the 1967 Arab-Israeli War was in generating the Jewish American cult of both Israel and tough Jewish imagery, it left a small but significant gap, a gap then filled by the 1973 Arab-Israeli or Yom Kippur War. The Six Day War had placed Jewish power on the stage of world history.... The 1973 war, in which Israel was nearly defeated, reasserted Jewish vulnerability. Jewish toughness appears to be all the more necessary and ethically grounded" (Breines 175).

17. "We must acknowledge that what is excluded by such an assumption is not only the prospect of 'big, strong' women in the same muscular and fighting sense, but also the prospect that big and strong might have radically different terms of reference.... In addition to excluding women, the tale of the 'cap in the mud' also *banishes the figure of the non-Jew* who is not anti-Semitic" (Breines 38, 42).

18. In Anthony Heilbrut, *Exiled in Paradise* (New York: Viking, 1983), p. 402. See also Arendt-Jaspers, *Correspondence*, pp. 90, 91ff.

19. David Biale, *Eros and the Jews* (New York: Basic, 1992). Citations appear in the text in parentheses.

20. "If the sexual persona of the American Jewish male appears relatively harmless, the image of the Jewish woman often takes a vicious turn in the form of jokes about the "Jewish American Princess," or JAP.... the JAP, like the male schlemiel, is erotically blocked, but he

at least is comic and perhaps lovable in his ineptitude, whereas she is typically loathsome. His inner conflicts and neuroses are revealed and thus sympathetic, but her sexual pathology remains purely objectified and superficial, like her overdone makeup. Women become the site for projections of all that seems most hateful about Jewish sexuality" (Biale 207).

21. For a feminist reading of the "emasculation" of African American men, see for example, bell hooks, *Ain't I a Woman: Black Women and Feminism* (Boston: South End, 1981); Patricia Hill Collins, *Black Feminist Thought: Knowledge, Consciousness and the Politics of Empowerment* (New York: Routledge, 1990); Jacqueline Jones, *Labor of Love, Labor of Sorrow: Black Women, Work and the Family, From Slavery to the Present* (New York: Basic, 1985); Angela Davis, *Women, Race and Class* (New York: Vintage, 1983); Toni Morrison, *Race-ing Justice, En-Gendering Power: Essays on Anita Hill, Clarence Thomas, and the Construction of Social Reality* (New York: Pantheon, 1992), as well as a vast number of additional sources. For Asian American men, see for example, Stuart Creighton Miller, *The Unwelcome Immigrant* (Berkeley: University of California Press, 1969); Evelyn Nakano Glenn, *Issei, Nisei, War Bride: Three Generations of Japanese American Women in Domestic Service* (Philadelphia: Temple University Press, 1986); Asian Women United of California, *Making Waves: An Anthology of Writings By and About Asian American Women* (Boston: Beacon, 1989); Randall Miller and Alan Woll, *Ethnic and Racial Images in American Film and Television* (New York: Garland, 1987).

22. See Nancy Chodorow and Dorothy Dinnerstein, op. cit. above, n.12. Also Irving Howe, *World of our Fathers*, and Norman Podhoretz, *Making It*.

23. It is interesting to note the current African American male "gangsta" mystique—perhaps a similar effort to claim "manhood" on a model geared to earn the respect, or at least attention, of white gentile America.

24. Cooney notes, "Rahv was prepared to admit insecurity and uncertainty in the early issues of the magazine. But he was also prepared to react vigorously to Trotsky's critique and to challenge the exile's behavior. Rahv's letter, reflecting the combination of insecurity and bold assurance that shaped the new *Partisan Review*, spoke more frankly than any program published in the magazine itself. . . . Although Trotsky was a strategist and a theoretician of major stature, Rahv did not shrink from calling his judgment and his perspective into question" (Cooney 131). See also Alan M. Wald, *The New York Intellectuals: The Rise and*

Decline of the Anti-Stalinist Left from the 1930s to the 1980s (Chapel Hill: University of North Carolina Press, 1987), pp. 164ff.

25. Trotsky also cut a dashing figure, appealing to women, which had won him a job as a movie actor, something of a minor matinee idol, during his sojourn in New York before the Revolution.

26. See Cooney, op. cit. pp. 11–13. Discussion in chapter 4 above, pp. 69–70.

27. William Phillips, "How Partisan Review Began," *Commentary* 62 (December 1976): 43.

28. Lionel Abel, "New York City: A Remembrance," *Dissent* 8, 3 (Summer 1961): 257.

29. See Boyarin.

30. As just a sampling of sources on Jewish feminism, see for example, Susannah Heschel, *On Being a Jewish Feminist: A Reader* (New York: Schoken, 1983); Judith Plaskow, *Standing Again at Sinai: Judaism from a Feminist Perspective* (New York: Harper Collins, 1990); Rachel Biale, *Women and Jewish Law: An Exploration of Women's Issue in Halakhic Sources* (New York: Schoken, 1984); Frieda Forman, Ethel Raicus, Sarah Silberstein Swartz, and Margie Wolfe, ed., *Found Treasures: Stories by Yiddish Women Writers* (Toronto: Second Story, 1994); Judith R. Baskin, ed., *Women of the Word: Jewish Women and Jewish Writing* (Detroit, Mich.: Wayne State University Press, 1994); Susan A. Glenn, *Daughters of the Shtetl: Life and Labor in the Immigrant Generation* (Ithaca, N.Y.: Cornell University Press, 1990); Savina J. Teubal, *Sarah The Priestess: The First Matriarch of Genesis* (Athens: Ohio University Press, 1984); Marion A. Kaplan, *The Making of the Jewish Middle Class: Women, Family and Identity, in Imperial Germany* (New York: Oxford University Press, 1991).

31. That Jewish men are capable of domestic violence is well documented and, in a way, even more difficult to acknowledge and respond to because of their reputation as passive, gentle men and "good husbands." See, for example, Mimi Scarf's study, "Marriages Made in Heaven? Battered Jewish Wives," in Heschel, op. cit., pp. 51–64 (excerpted from her Masters' Thesis at Hebrew Union College, Los Angeles). The denial on the part of the wives of their husbands' violence—which resembles run-of-the-mill domestic violence in some ways and in others possesses distinctive characteristics—is pervasive, but

even worse is the refusal on the part of parents and parents-in-law to believe what Jewish sons and husbands may be capable of. There exists the assumption that even when Jewish men are "bad," they're not *as bad*—drunk, violent, possessive—as the goyim. Moshe Meiselman, while not addressing (or even acknowledging) Jewish male mistreatment of women in the marriage contract, congratulates Jewish law on not being as bad as, for instance, English Common Law, in reducing wives to the property of their husbands; e.g., "This [the Jewish] view contrasts sharply with the historic position of women in English law, where a woman was literally her husband's possession. Thus, until 1882 a woman could not enter a contract or even own property. Furthermore, until 1891 a husband had complete dominion over his wife, including the right to beat her and limit her freedom of movement. None of this is true in Jewish law.... Not only was beating a wife frowned upon and forbidden, but it was a valid ground for divorce" (Meiselman 97) (*if the woman could get anybody to believe her husband was beating her*). See also "Reyzele's Wedding, by Dora Schulner in *Found Treasures*, Forman et al., op. cit.

32. Cynthia Ozick, "Notes toward Finding the Right Question," *On Being A Jewish Feminist: A Reader*, ed. and with introductions by Susannah Heschel (New York: Schoken Books, 1983), p. 142.

33. Moshe Meiselman, *Jewish Woman in Jewish Law* (New York: KTAV Publishing House, 1978), p. 27

34. Quoted in Meiselman, p. 37

35. *Found Treasures: Stories by Yiddish Women Writers*, ed. Frieda Forman, Ethel Raicus, Sara Silberstein Swartz, and Margie Wolfe (Toronto: Second Story Press, 1994). Citations appear in parentheses.

36. See for example, Catherine Mackinnon in "Feminism, Marxism, Method and the State: An Agenda for Theory" *Signs* 7, no. 3 (Spring 1982) "The male epistemological stance, which corresponds to the world it creates is objectivity: the ostensibly uninvolved stance ... does not comprehend its own perspectivity, does not recognize what it sees as subjective like itself...." (p. 24.) Also Klepfisz, "Undoubtedly this defeminizing and separating the new from the old, the male from the female, were meant to "universalize" a literature which, until then, had been seen as rooted in the women's sphere. But, as feminist criticism has shown, Western concepts of the "universal" assume the primacy of *men's* feelings, experiences and perceptions; they treat

women's experiences as trivial or fail to differentiate them from men's In either case, women's experiences are erased" (Forman, et al. 37).

37. "In Eastern Europe Jewish women were gaining more and more access to practical secular education of various types, precisely because the community had not adopted the value system of Western Europe, and the more valorized talmudic study was reserved for boys while girls were allowed (and even encouraged) to pursue nonreligious vocations. This was consistent with a well-established social norm within which Jewish women were ideally the breadwinners for their scholarly husbands" (Boyarin 256).

38. Marion A.Kaplan, *The Making of the Jewish Middle Class: Women, Family, and Identity in Imperial Germany* (New York: Oxford University Press, 1991), p. 12. See also Susan A. Glenn, *Daughters of the Shtetl: Life and Labor in the Immigrant Generation* (Ithaca, N.Y.: Cornell University Press, 1990).

39. See Kaplan, "Jewish Women Confront Academia," in *The Making of the Jewish Middle Class*, pp. 137–52.

40. Heilbut relates the actual story leading her to make the remark. At a scholarly conference in the late 1960s, after she had become something of a hero to student radicals in the United States, she pleaded with her young audience not to turn her into a guru. "She closed the conference with a final, implicit plea that she not be turned into some intellectual guru. 'I would like to say that everything I did and everything I wrote—all that is tentative.' A questioner asked her to locate herself in the political spectrum. She replied, 'So you ask me where I am. I am nowhere. I am really not in the mainstream of present or any other political thought. But not because I want to be so original—it so happens that I somehow don't fit'" (Heilbut 436).

41. *Between Friends: The Correspondence of Hannah Arendt and Mary McCarthy,1949–1975*, ed.and with an intro. by Carol Brightman (New York: Harcourt Brace Jovanovich, 1995), p. 147 (H.A. to M.M. 20 September 1963).

42. "In 'The Mary McCarthy Case', *The New York Review of Books*, October 17, 1963, Norman Mailer charged the author of *The Group* with having written a 'lady book,' which did no more than match 'the best novel the editors of the women's magazines ever conceived in *their* secret ambitions.' Elizabeth Hardwick's unsigned parody, 'The Gang,' had appeared three weeks earlier" (Brightman 155n.2).

CHAPTER 6. TRANSITION

1. See Mary Dietz, "Feminist Receptions of Hannah Arendt" and other essays in *Feminist Interpretations of Hannah Arendt*, ed. Bonnie Honig (University Park, Pa.: University of Pennsylvania Press, 1995).

2. For example, in the recent *cause celebre*, *Hannah Arendt, Martin Heidegger* (New Haven, Conn.: Yale University Press, 1995), author Elzbieta Ettinger claims, "For Arendt, brought up in a completely assimilated social democratic family in Koenigsberg, the 'Jewish question' was limited to the name calling of street urchins and school children or to the occasional anti-Semitic remark of a teacher. According to her mother's instructions, she had to defend herself only from the children; her mother dealt with the teachers.... In a 1964 interview Arendt said: 'As a child I did not know that I was Jewish.... The word "Jew" was never mentioned at home when I was a child'" (4). It is difficult to imagine what Arendt's mother told her to defend herself against, if the word *Jew* was not mentioned. This also directly conflicts with Elisabeth Young-Bruehl's account in her classic biography of Arendt, of the Arendt family's friendship with the reform rabbi of Konigsburg, Hermann Vogelstein, of the fact that her grandparents on both sides were reform Jews, but observant enough to attend services, accompanied by their granddaughter Hannah, and to provide her with private tutoring from the rabbi, upon whom little Hannah developed a crush, declaring that she intended to marry him. She was deterred only when reminded that she would have to give up eating pork, of which she was fond. She amended her ambition to "Well, then, I'll marry a Rabbi with pork" (Young-Bruehl 8–9). The only sense one can make out of Ettinger's inaccuracy is her desire to separate Hannah Arendt from her Jewish identity.

3. See Honig, op. cit. Honig's essay in *Feminist Interpretations of Arendt* also appears, in virtually identical form, in Judith Butler and Joan W. Scott, *Feminists Theorize the Political* (New York: Routledge, 1992).

4. Arendt wrote to Jaspers on 17 December 1946, "I just noticed your question again about whether I'm a German or a Jew. To be perfectly honest, it doesn't matter to me in the least on a personal and individual level.... I'd put it this way: Politically, I will always speak only in the name of the Jews whenever circumstances force me to give my nationality. That is easier for me than for your wife, because I'm at a further remove from this whole question and because

I never felt myself, either spontaneously or at my own insistence to 'be a German'" (*Correspondence* 70). In a letter to Jaspers dated 7 September 1952, she discusses her decision not to publish *Rahel Varnhagen*, which she had given to Jaspers to read, and which he had expressed some criticisms about, because he believed that Arendt had not let Rahel "speak for herself" and had overemphasized the role Judaism had played in her identity. Arendt replied: "It was written from the perspective of a Zionist critique of assimilation, which I had adopted as my own and which I still consider basically justified today. But that critique was as politically naive as what it was criticizing. Personally, the book is alien to me in many ways, and perhaps that's why I feel it as particularly alien to me now, especially in its tone, in its mode of reflection, but not in the Jewish experience, which I made my own with no little difficulty. By virtue of my background I was simply naive. I found the so-called Jewish question boring. The person who opened my eyes in this area was Kurt Blumenfeld.... He used to say, 'Zionism is Germany's gift to the Jews'" (*Correspondence* 197–98). She also wrote to Jaspers on Jan. 29, 1946 (*Correspondence*, l. 34, p. 28) that she would continue to use the name Arendt, although she was newly married, "because I wanted my name to identify me as a Jew."

Arendt's letter to Scholem has been analyzed at length in the discussion of the *Eichmann* controversy above. Here the important point is her insistence on her Jewish identity. Scholem, remember, accused her of having insufficient *ahavath yisrael*, "love of the Jewish people," and she responded, "I have never in my life 'loved' any people or collective—neither the German people, nor the French, nor the American, nor the working class or anything of that sort. I indeed love 'only' my friends and the only kind of love I know of and believe in is the love of persons. Secondly, this 'love of the Jews' would appear to me, since I am myself Jewish, as something rather suspect. I cannot love myself or anything which I know is part and parcel of my own person.... Well, in this sense I do not 'love' the Jews, nor do I 'believe' in them; I merely belong to them as a matter of course, beyond dispute or argument" (New York City, 24 July 1963), in *The Jew as Pariah*, ed Ron Feldman (New York: Grove, 1978), pp. 245–46.

See also Pitkin's subtle discussion of the influence Heidegger may have had on Arendt's ideas in Honig, et al.; e.g., "But the matter is still more complicated, for the lesson Arendt learned from her romance with Heidegger parallels more than the lesson she thought Varnhagen learned at the end of her life. Both of these lessons also resemble a philosophical doctrine of Heidegger's, developed in *Being and Time*, the book on which he was working during his affair with

Arendt, and which they often discussed: the doctrine of *das Man*" (Honig 71).

5. Also, see L.337 10/22/63 Jaspers: "You have reached a point where many people no longer understand you." "Now you have delivered the crucial word against 'radical evil,' against gnosis! You are with Kant, who said, 'Man cannot be a devil,' and I am with you. But it's a pity that the term *radical evil*, in a very different sense that was not understood even by Goethe and Schiller, comes from Kant." In the next to last paragraph of Arendt's letter to Scholem, she writes: " I am now in fact convinced that evil is always merely extreme but never radical; it has no depth and no demonic dimension. It is able to devastate the entire world precisely because it spreads over the surface like a fungus. But only goodness is deep and radical. In the first section of *Religion innerhalb der Granzen der blosen Vernunft*, Kant defines 'radical evil' as a turning upside down of the relationship between duty and inclination" (*Correspondence* 774).

6. In *Hannah Arendt: Critical Essays*, ed, Lewis P. and Sandra K. Hinchman (Albany: State University of New York Press, 1994) Berel Lang, in "Hannah Arendt and the Politics of Evil," writes, "Eichmann in her judgment, simply did not think, perhaps he did not even have the capacity to think, about what he was doing—and the implications of her stress on this is that if he *had* thought about it, he would have acted differently or at least whatever evil he did would not have been banal" (Lang 264–75). Likewise, in "Thinking and Moral Considerations: Socrates and Arendt's Eichmann," in the same volume Joseph Beatty notes, "She would like to call Eichmann's acts 'evil' and argue that thinking would have precluded such acts" (Beatty 272). "With this groundwork established Arendt offers three arguments to support her claim that thinking excludes evil doing" (Beatty 268). Beatty criticizes Arendt's argument as logically flawed, asserting that "Arendt is building 'moral reasoning' into 'reasoning' such that if someone doesn't have the requisite moral concerns for others, i.e., if he doesn't make an appropriate (moral) response to others he isn't really *thinking*" (Beatty 273). He asks, "Why does Arendt maintain that, for those who think evil must necessarily occasion conscience and psychic punishment?" (272).

7. Arendt, Hannah, *Crises of the Republic* (New York: Harcourt Brace Jovanovich, 1972).

8. Young-Bruehl believes that the reference probably came from Hilberg. "This passage is quoted as it appeared in the revised edition

of *Eichmann in Jerusalem,* from which Arendt had eliminated the phrase that infuriated so many of her readers: she had referred to Baeck as the man 'who in the eyes of both Jews and gentiles was the Jewish Fuhrer.' Raul Hilberg, probably Arendt's source, had noted that Eichmann's assistant, Dieter Wisliceny, had called Baeck the 'Jewish Fuhrer,' but he did not imply that the phrase was used by others, Jewish or German" (Young-Bruehl 363). See also Young-Bruehl's discussion of Arendt's and Blumenfeld's somewhat critical but nonetheless admiring opinion of Leo Baeck (364ff.).

9. Barnouw, op. cit., p. 238.

10. Arendt, Hannah, *The Jew as Pariah: Jewish Identity and Politics in the Modern Age,* ed. Ron Feldman (New York: Grove, 1978), p. 248.

11. In *Thinking* (New York: Harcourt Brace Jovanovich, 1978), p. 173. "Hence, Socrates, gadfly, midwife, electric ray, is not a philosopher (he teaches nothing and has nothing to teach) and he is not a sophist, for he does not claim to make men wise. He only points out to them that they are not wise, that nobody is—a 'pursuit' keeping him so busy that he has not time for either public or private affairs. And while he defends himself vigorously against the charge of corrupting the young, he nowhere pretends that he is improving them. Nevertheless, he claims that the appearance in Athens of thinking and examining was the greatest good that ever befell the City. Thus he was concerned with what thinking is good for, although, in this, as in all other respects, he did not give a clear-cut answer. We may be sure that a dialogue dealing with the question 'what is thinking good for?' would have ended in the same perplexities as all the others" (173. See her more complete discussion of Socrates, 166–93).

12. I was gratified to find Carol Brightman coming to the same conclusion: "Arendt, [Jerome] Kohn suggests, 'actually believed that thinking conditions people to resist evil doing.' This novel view sets her apart from contemporary moral theorists, as well as from her beloved Kant. It suggests why the philosopher J. Glenn Gray, speaking of *The Life of the Mind* shortly before his death in 1972, told Kohn that 'this book is at least a hundred years ahead of its time.' It suggests, too, why someone might find in Arendt's meditations on Thinking, willing, and judging a spirit of inquiry more contemporaneous with Plato's *Apology*." Brightman does not pursue the analogy, but I shall (*Between Friends: The Correspondence of Hannah Arendt and Mary McCarthy, 1949–1975,* ed. Carol Brightman [New York: Harcourt Brace, 1995], p. xxviii).

13. Plato, *The Apology*, in *The Last Days of Socrates*, trans. and with an introduction by Hugh Tredennick (New York: Penguin, 1969), p. 45. Page references follow in parentheses in the text.

14. Jaspers, Karl, *Socrates, Buddha, Confucius, Jesus*, in *The Great Philosophers*, vol. 1 (New York: Harcourt Brace Jovanovich, 1985 [1957]), p. 11.

15. Irving Howe, "'The New Yorker' and Hannah Arendt," *Commentary* 36, 4 (October 1963): pp. 318–19. In his arrogance and condescension, Howe may have underestimated *The New Yorker*'s readership: it is hardly a mass-market publication such as *Life* magazine, *Sports Illustrated*, *Playboy*, or *Mechanics Illustrated*, mistaken for literature by "good middle-class Americans."

16. John Murray Cuddihy, *The Ordeal of Civility* (New York: Delta, 1974).

17. Cuddihy, p. 6. Cuddihy is not impressed by the capacity of Jewish or any other sort of intellectuals to be detached and scientific about their subject, especially when that subject is the explanation of the behavior of their own people: "I have never found particularly convincing the patently self-serving theory that intellectuals construct about themselves—that they are 'classless,' or constitute an 'interstitial' stratum (in Karl Mannheim's version), or are 'unattached' (in Lewis Coser's version). Intellectuals I have known are 'attached.' To *their* productions, as to those of the truck driver, we must address the nervy little sociology-of-knowledge question, 'Says who?'" (9).

18. Feldman, op. cit. p. 247.

CHAPTER 7. BIBLICAL AND RABBINIC APPROACHES TO THINKING

1. The more traditional way of approaching this question is to look to the Jewish philosophers for models of what "Jewish thinking" might be. If I argue that Arendt, in raising the questions she does in *The Life of the Mind*, was "more" of a Jewish thinker than she believed she was and yet was not quite "enough" of a Jewish thinker to answer her own questions, then I must have in mind some Jewish thinkers whom she should have either emulated or made use of. But I do not take that approach. The Jewish philosophers themselves, Maimonides, Spinoza, Mendelssohn, could be subjected to the sort of analysis I propose: to what extent were they, too, "assimilationist," in attempting to fit traditional Jewish teachings to a Greek or Christian model? For example, Maimonides sought the compatibilities between Aristo-

telian thought and the Talmud; Spinoza converted to Catholicism, and is often not regarded as a "Jewish philosopher" at all. Here I am more concerned with whether there exists, and how to describe, a certain style of thinking that might be called "Jewish." My effort is more compatible with contemporary multicultural analysis than with the classical philosophical approach. For an example of the more traditional approach, see *Leo Strauss: Political Philosopher and Jewish Thinker*, ed. Kenneth L. Deutsch and Walter Nicgorski (New York: Rowman and Littlefield, 1994). See especially, Steven B. Smith's excellent essay, "Leo Strauss: Between Athens and Jerusalem," pp. 81–106. For an example of the multicultural approach, see Dennis Fischman's discussion of Marx as a Jewish thinker in *Political Theory in Exile: Karl Marx and the Jewish Question* (Amherst: University of Massachusetts Press, 1991).

2. In a letter of 7 September 1952 to Jaspers that was a part of their ongoing correspondence over her Rahel Varnhagan manuscript, in which Jaspers urged her to publish and offered her suggestions for revisions, and Arendt claimed she was not interested in publishing, she reveals her ideas about the relationship between religious and nonreligious Jews: "Judaism doesn't exist outside orthodoxy on the one hand or outside the Yiddish-speaking, folklore-producing Jewish people on the other. There are also people of Jewish background who are unaware of any Jewish substance in their lives in the sense of a tradition and who for certain social reasons and because they found themselves constituting a clique within society produced something like a 'Jewish type.' This type has nothing to do with what we understand under Judaism historically or with its genuine content. Here there is much that is positive, namely, all those things that I classify as pariah qualities and what Rahel called the 'true realities of life'—'love, trees, children, music.' In this type there is an extraordinary awareness of injustices; there is great generosity and lack of prejudice; and there is—more questionably but nonetheless demonstrably present—respect for the 'life of the mind.' Of all these things only the last one can still be shown to have a link with originally and specifically Jewish substance" (*Correspondence* 199–200). In *The Origins of Totalitarianism*, Arendt described the transformation of the objective fact of Judaism into the subjective character trait of "Jewishness." Membership in a religion that was often regarded by anti-Semitic European Christians as a "crime" became a state of being, a character trait that was an "inherent" part of individual Jews, which anti-Semites could consider ineradicable. "As far as the Jews were

concerned, the transformation of the 'crime' of Judaism into the fashionable 'vice' of Jewishness was dangerous in the extreme.... A crime ... is met with punishment; a vice can only be exterminated" (Arendt, *Anti-Semitism: Part One of the Origins of Totalitarianism* (New York: Harcourt Brace Jovanovich), p. 87).

3. Yosef Hayim Yerushalmi, *Freud's Moses: Judaism Terminable and Interminable* (New Haven, Conn.: Yale University Press, 1991). Additional references follow in parentheses, indicated by Yerushalmi and page numbers.

4. Yosef Hayim Yerushalmi, *Zakhor: Jewish History and Jewish Memory* (New York: Schoken, 1989), p. xxiii. Additional references follow in parentheses, indicated by *Zakhor* and page numbers.

5. The Hebrew Bible will be referred to throughout as the Bible, rather than the "Old Testament." "Old Testament" is the Christian version of the Hebrew Bible, and carries the implication that the New Testament has absorbed the old into it and is both preemptive of and continuous with the Old. Neither is the case. See Robert Alter, *The Art of Biblical Narrative* (New York: Basic, 1981), p. ix.

6. In *Back to the Sources: Reading the Classic Jewish Texts*, ed. Barry Holtz (New York: Touchstone Books, Simon and Shuster, 1984). Additional references to this anthology will be identified by the specific author being cited in the text, and the page reference following in parentheses, identified by "Holtz."

7. Robert Alter, *The Art of Biblical Narrative* (New York: Basic, 1981), p. 25. Additional references are identified in parentheses by "Alter" and page number.

8. "Hannah Arendt's Pariah and The Old Testament," unpublished manuscript, originally presented at the Annual Meetings of the American Political Science Association, 1992, Chicago, Illinois.

9. "The destruction of the first Temple in Jerusalem in 586 b.c.e. and the exile to Babylon were traumatic events in Jewish history and threatened the continued existence of Judaism. The temple had been the religious and political center of Judaism. Upon his return from Babylon, Ezra determined to reconstruct the life of the Jews, and renewed, so to speak, the covenant with the Book that was in danger of being forgotten. Ezra's great accomplishment was to finally reestablish the centrality of the Book, the written Torah, as the basis for the entire life of the people." Susan Handelman, *The Slayers of Moses:*

The Emergence of Rabbinic Interpretation in Modern Literary Theory (Albany: State University of New York Press, 1982), p. 43.

10. As Susan Handelman notes:

> According to Rabbinic tradition, even principles of interpretation were given at Sinai, and whatever is drawn from the text by application of these principles is not an addition, but a latent aspect of the text which is revealed in its relevant time and place. Moreover, whatever is deduced by common human reasoning is given the same authority and status as that which is derived from the divinely given hermeneutic principles.... The boundaries between text and interpretation are fluid in a way which is difficult for us to imagine for a sacred text. (41)

11. Handelman, op. cit., p. 38.

12. From the Yom Kippur Musaf Service, *Mahzor for Rosh Hashanah and Yom Kippur,* ed. Rabbi Jules Harlow (New York: Rabbinical Assembly, 1972), p. 559.

13. Handelman, op. cit., p. 49.

14. Handelman, op. cit. p. 103.

15. "The *peshat* method ... should perhaps be glossed in English as the direct, *contextual* mode of exegesis, not 'plain' or 'literal,' which it often is not. The *derash* method is the acontextual approach because it disregards the contradicting of the historical, literary and linguistic conditions in which the text first came to us" (Holtz 226).

16. Amos Funkenstein, *Perceptions of Jewish History* (Berkeley: University of California Press, 1993).

17. See the essays on "Zionism and the Jewish State," in *The Jew as Pariah,* ed. Feldman, op. cit.

18. Funkenstein was University Professor and Koret Professor of History at the University of California, Berkeley. His volume, *Perceptions of Jewish History* was selected as a Centennial Book, one of a few books chosen by the University of California Press to represent "the Press's finest publishing and bookmaking traditions as we celebrate the beginning of our second century."

19. Certain things are easier than others. Allowing women into minyans is a "big deal," and usually a controversial issue in Conservative congregations. The ordination of women rabbis was a "big deal," and took some four thousand years to implement. But other matters of law are indeed changed in response to contemporary needs, without much

uproar. The question of *eruv*, or where to place the boundary around the "household," which has been reinterpreted to include entire communities in the ghettos of Eastern Europe, and often around entire urban centers in contemporary times, beyond which an observant Jew must not "carry" anything—not even an infant daughter or son—on Shabbat, is not quite as big a deal as the ordination of women rabbis, although it remains a significant issue for many Orthodox Jews. This is not unlike the historical tendency of the United States Constitution to embody and reflect, but not legislate or mandate change. When social changes have for the most part occurred and become practice without the explicit sanction of law, a constitutional amendment can be fairly unproblematically passed and ratified. In the absence of the general acceptance of change, passing a constitutional amendment is nearly impossible. Proclaiming the goal of change is tantamount to insuring resistance. When American women were actually voting in all the western states and territories, a federal suffrage amendment was passed. Ten years after the judicially mandated desegregation of public places, a civil rights bill was enacted. When women are in fact treated equally under the law politically, economically, and socially, an Equal Rights Amendment will be passed.

CHAPTER 8. GREEK AND HEBREW: THE STRUCTURE OF THINKING

1. Thorlief Boman, *Hebrew Thought Compared with Greek* (New York: Norton, 1960). Also referred to in this chapter is Max Kadushin, *The Rabbinic Mind* (New York: Bloch, 1952). Two contemporary sources have been consulted: Susan Handelman, *The Slayers of Moses: The Emergence of Rabbinic Interpretation in Modern Liberary Theory* (Albany: State University of New York Press, 1982) and Dennis Fischman, *Political Discourse in Exile Karl Marx and the Jewish Question* (Amherst: University of Massachusetts Press, 1992).

2. Dennis Fischman, for example, notes that "Boman's typology fails to allow for historical change. His concepts 'Hebrew' and 'Greek' reside in some timeless and universal dimension of thought, as in reality languages can do only when they are dead. Boman locates the two modes within a world of ideas and thinkers in which the Hebrew and Greek exist as opposing essences, always have and always will, even (one suspects) if there had never been any Jews or Greeks to instantiate them" (45). That is, perhaps Boman compares Hebrew and Greek thought by means of a Greek method of analysis.

3. Personal correspondence with Elisabeth Young-Bruehl.

4. Boman's stated project is admirable: "If Israelite thinking is to be characterized, it is obvious first to call it dynamic, vigorous, passionate, and sometimes quite explosive in kind; correspondingly Greek thinking is static, peaceful, moderate, and harmonious in kind.... From that viewpoint Greek mental activity appears harmonious, prudent, moderate and peaceful; to the person to whom the Greek kind of thinking occurs plainly as ideal, Hebrew thinking and its manner of expression appear exaggerated, immoderate, discordent, and in bad taste. Putting aside the negative, the biased, and the unjust, we intend to understand both peoples positiviely from within" (27).

5. Understanding for the Greeks is associated with light and vision; for the Hebrews it is associated with hearing and the belief that truth cannot be seen, or captured in terms of plastic images. Handelman contends that "this [Hebrew] tension between presence and absence is expressed more readily through voice than vision. Vision, appearance is fullness, complete presence of the thing; sound is a more subtle mode of presence, a moving vibration that both is and is not there. Sound creates patterns but not static presences.... Stability is attained through repetition."

"Perhaps one can ... understand the Biblical ban on images in this light. The Jewish idea of the invisible God culminates in the confession of faith, 'Hear O Israel!' In the account of the revelation at Sinai the Biblical text relates, 'And all the people saw the thunderings and the lightnings and the voice of the horn and the mountain smoking' (Exod. 20:15). Comments Rashi, the famous Jewish medieval commentator, 'They saw that which should be heard which is impossible to see in another place.' The revelation was to see what *is heard*, a voice not an image. The invisible is manifested through sound and the divine word, does not become 'fulfilled' or hypostatized into a present being. Revelation is not appearance" (Handelman, op. cit., pp. 34–35).

6. "Rabbinic value concepts are inseparable from normal, everyday, moment-to-moment experience. They are mental habits that are become second nature, more correctly in view of their organic characters, part of nature" (Kadushin 31).

7. Perhaps not surprisingly, given my project in this book, I am reminded of Margaret Canovan's description of the difficulty of describing Hannah Arendt's thought: "In themselves, too, Arendt's books invite misunderstanding, for they are often condensed and allusive. Their form is symphonic rather than sequential, interweaving and developing themes rather than presenting an argument." *Hannah*

Arendt: A Reinterpretation of her Political Thought (Cambridge: Cambridge University Press, 1992), p. 3.

8. I thank Rabbi Judy Shanks for the observation that insistence on an explicitly male God, indicated by sole use of the male generic, *is* idolatry.

9. I use the gender-neutral *person* self-consciously, more as a gesture of hope than a reflection of historical accuracy. Nothing in the Jewish tradition suggests that women can be or have been respected as interpreters. Jewish feminist theory often begins with that contradiction.

CHAPTER 9. TOWARD UNDERSTANDING ARENDT AS A JEWISH THINKER

1. See my "On Needing Both Marx and Arendt: Alienation and the Flight from Inwardness," *Political Theory* 17, 3 (August 1989): 432–48.

2. Margaret Canovan, *Hannah Arendt: A Reinterpretation of Her Political Thought* New York: Cambridge University Press, 1992. Page references follow in parentheses in the text.

3. In the next chapter I discuss Socrates as more worldly than Canovan sometimes presents him, and indeed, as Arendt's "best hope" for a worldly philosopher.

4. Hannah Arendt, "Civil Disobedience," in *Crises of the Republic* (New York: Harcourt Brace Jovanovich, 1972), p. 62ff.

5. Hannah Arendt, *The Life of the Mind: One/Thinking, Two/Willing.* (New York: Harcourt Brace Jovanovich, 1978). Page references appear in parentheses in text with the title *Thinking.*

6. Hannah Arendt, Karl Jaspers, *Correspondence, 1926–1969,* ed. Lotte Kohler and Hans Saner (New York: Harcourt Brace Jovanovich, 1992). (L.50, 12/17/46, p. 70). Arendt was cognizant of the importance of her membership in the Jewish community for her political identity. She did not believe that Jews could ever be assimilated Europeans, although she was more idealistic, and more conflicted about American Jews. "After being denied membership of the German nation, Arendt found in America a refuge not only from persecution but also from pressures toward communal togetherness in politics. She discovered with great relief that the United States was not a nation-state in the European sense of linking political unity with national homogeneity. In that country, with its many different ethnic groups held together by a Constitution that predated the great age of nationalism, it was possible to enjoy 'the freedom of becoming a citizen without having to pay the price of assimilation'" (Canovan 244).

7. Hannah Arendt, *Men in Dark Times* (New York: Harcourt Brace Jovanovich, 1968), pp. 17–18.

8. Hannah Arendt, *The Human Condition* (Chicago: University of Chicago Press, 1958), p. 170.

9. Ibid, p. 171.

10. *Correspondence*, pp. 47–48. L. 42, 9 July 1946, Arendt to Jaspers:

> Regarding the Heidegger note, your assumption about the Husserl letter is completely correct. I knew that this letter was a circular, and that many people have excused it for that reason. It always seemed to me that at the moment Heidegger was obliged to put his name to this document, he should have resigned. However foolish he may have been, he was capable of understanding that.... In other words, although I never had any professional or personal attachment to old Husserl, I mean to maintain solidarity with him in this one case. And because I know that this letter and this signature almost killed him, I can't but regard Heidegger as a potential murderer.

And p. 142, L. 93, Arendt to Jaspers, 19 September 1949, referring to Heidegger:

> What you call impurity I would call lack of character—but in the sense that he literally has none.... This living in Todtnauberg, grumbling about civilzation and writing *Sein* with a "y," is really a kind of mouse hole he has crawled back into because he rightly assumes that the only people he'll have to see there are the pilgrims who come full of admiration for him. Nobody is likely to climb 1,200 meters to make a scene. And if somebody did do it, he would lie a blue streak and take for granted that nobody will call him a liar to his face. He probably thought he could buy himself loose from the world this way at the lowest possible price, fast-talk himself out of everything unpleasant, and do nothing but philosophize. And then, of course, this whole intricate and childish dishonesty has quickly crept into his philosophizing.

11. John H. Schaar has suggested that Arendt's real target in *Eichmann in Jerusalem* should have been Heidegger, a worthier foil than Eichmann for her argument. Eichmann was a working-class nobody compared to Germany's Philosopher, who was the one who should really have been able to think, and to have been held accountable for his political choices. Accusing Eichmann of not thinking amounts to a failure of nerve as well as class bias on Arendt's part. The real problem was that the professional thinkers, and Heidegger most notably, failed to think. (Personal conversation with John H. Schaar.)

12. Hannah Arendt, "What is Existenz Philosophy?"*Partisan Review* 13, 1 (Winter 1946): 34–56, see especially, pp. 46; and "Martin Heidegger at Eighty," in *Heidegger and Modern Philosophy*, ed. M. Murray (New Haven, Conn.: Yale University Press, 1978 [1971]), pp. 293–303.

13. Canovan observes that the discrepency of the two accounts of Heidegger reflected Arendt's ongoing conflict about the nature of philosophy.

> In [the] essay on German "Existenz Philosophy" published in the *Partisan Review* in 1946 she gave a hostile and slighting account of Heidegger, comparing his philosophy unfavourably with that of Karl Jaspers, her other teacher, who had always opposed Nazism.... Apparently Jaspers, who had behaved so much better politically, was also the better philosopher, so that philosophy and politics seemed to be in harmony. We cannot tell how far this position satisfied Arendt at the time. All that is certain is that within a few years of the publication of the essay on "Existenz Philosophy" she came to see things very differently. Her bitterness against Heidegger did not survive reunion with him during her visit to Europe in 1949–50. Avidly reading his later writings, she once more saw him as the transcendent philosophical genius of the time, and was consequently faced once more with the problem of how such profundity in philosophy could coexist with such stupidity or perversity in politics. (Canovan 254–55)

14. Just such a volume has recently appeared, in the form of Elzbieta Ettinger's sloppy, exploitative *Hannah Arendt, Martin Heidegger* (New Haven, Conn.: Yale University Press, 1995).

15. Refer to Canovan's book, especially chapter 7, "Philosophy and Politics," pp. 253–74, for a fuller and very enlightening discussion.

16. *Between Past and Future* (New York: Viking, 1968). Page references appear in parentheses, along with "T. and P." in the text that follows.

CHAPTER 10. THE PARIAH AND PARVENU IN *THINKING*

1. Hannah Arendt, *The Life of the Mind: One/Thinking, Two/Willing* (New York: Harcourt Brace Jovanovich, 1978), p. 3. Page references appear in parentheses in the text with the title, *Thinking*.

2. Arendt (1966) is citing Hans Jonas, "The Nobility of Sight," in *The Phenomenon of Life*.

3. Jennifer Ring, "On Needing Both Marx and Arendt: Alienation and the Flight from Inwardness," *Political Theory* 17, 3 (August 1989): 432–48.

4. "Her statement that life is 'given' to us upon conditions has a religious flavor which reminds us that her earliest intellectual enthusiasm was for Kierkegaard, that she wrote her first book on St. Augustine, and that after the Holocaust she told a Jewish friend that she had never doubted the existence of God" (Canovan 104). See also Elisabeth Young-Bruehl, *Hannah Arendt: For Love of the World* (New Haven, Conn.: Yale University Press, 1982), pp. 36, 74–75. "She was so taken with [Kierkegaard's] work that she had decided to make theology her major field of study...."

5. Jennifer Ring, "The Pariah as Hero: Hannah Arendt's Political Actor," *Political Theory* 19, 3 (August 1991): 433–52.

6. "An ancient Roman court decreed that Jews could no longer teach the Torah. This court sentenced to death rabbis who chose to ignore the decree. The Torah was more precious than life itself for these rabbis, our teachers.... Rabbi Akiba also chose to continue teaching in spite of the decree. When they led him to the executioner, it was time for reciting the *Sh'ma*. With iron combs they scraped away his skin as he recited *Sh'ma Yisrael*, freely accepting the yoke of God's kingship. 'Even now?' his disciples asked. His reply: 'All my life I have been troubled by a verse: "Love the Lord your God with all your heart and with all your soul," which means even if He take your life. I often wondered if I would ever be able to fulfill that obligation. And now I can.' He left the world while uttering, 'The Lord is One'" (Yom Kippur Musaf Service, *Mahzor for Rosh Hashanah and Yom Kippur*, ed. Rabbi Jules Harlow [New York: Rabbinical Assembly, 1972], p. 557).

And Socrates, in the *Apology*: "It would be very strange conduct on my part if I were to desert my station now from fear of death or of any other thing when the god has commanded me—as I am persuaded that he has done—to spend my life in searching for wisdom, and in examining myself and others.... For to fear death, my friends, is only to think that we know what we do not know. For no one knows whether death may not be the greatest good that can happen to man. But men fear it as if they knew quite well that it was the greatest of evils. And what is this but that shameful ignorance of thinking that we know what we do not know?" (*Apology*, XVII 29, p. 35). "I do not care a straw for death; but ... I do care very much indeed about not doing anything unjust or impious (XX 32, p. 39). And finally, to Crito, who, as Socrates is about to drink the poison, asks how he may best serve his teacher: "Simply by doing what I always tell you, Crito. Take care of your own selves, and you will serve me and mine and yourselves in all that you do, even though you make no promises now. But if you are careless of your own selves, and will not follow the path of life which we have pointed out in our conversations both today and at other times, all your promises now, however profuse and earnest they are, will be of no avail" (*Crito*, LXIV 115, p. 67), in Plato, *Euthyphro, Apology, Crito*, trans. Robert D. Cumming (New York: Bobbs Merrill, Library of Liberal Arts, 1956).

7. See Hanna Fenichel Pitken, "Conformism, Housekeeping, and the Attack of the Blob: The Origins of Hannah Arendt's Concept of the Social" in Honig, *Feminist Interpretations of Hannah Arendt*, op. cit.

8. Exod. 23:19, Exod. 32:26, and Deut. 14:21.

CHAPTER 11. JEWISH THEMES IN POLITICAL ACTION AND HISTORY

1. Hannah Arendt, *The Human Condition* (Chicago: University of Chicago Press, 1958). Citations appear in text in parentheses, with page reference and HC).

2. Jennifer Ring, "The Pariah as Hero: Hannah Arendt's Political Actor," *Political Theory* 19, 3 (August 1991): 433–52.

3. "The *polis* was supposed to multiply the occasions to win "immortal fame," that is, to multiply the chances for everybody to distinguish himself, to show in deed and word who he was in his unique distinctness. One, if not the chief, reason for the incredible development of gift and genius in Athens ... was to make the extraordinary an ordinary occurrence of everyday life" (HC 197).

4. For example, from *Totalitarianism*: "To this aversion of the intellectual elite for official historiography, to its conviction that history, which was a forgery anyway, might as well be the playground of crackpots, must be added the terrible, demoralizing fascination in the possibility that gigantic lies and monstrous falsehoods can eventually be established as unquestioned facts, that man may be free to change his own past at will, and that the difference between truth and falsehood may cease to be objective and become a mere matter of power and cleverness, of pressure and infinite repetition.... Simple forgeries from the

viewpoint of scholarship appeared to receive the sanction of history itself when the whole marching reality of the movements stood behind them and pretended to draw from them the necessary inspiration for action." Hannah Arendt, 1951.

5. Hannah Arendt, *Between Past and Future* (New York: The Viking Press, 1954). Citations follow in the text in parentheses, with page reference and BPF.

6. See discussion in chapter 9 of Margaret Canovan's *Hannah Arendt: A Reinterpretation of her Political Thought.*

7. This, of course, was a subject of which Arendt had intimate knowledge.

8. Hannah Arendt, *The Origins of Totalitarianism, Volume 1, Anti-Semitism* (New York: Harcourt Brace Jovanovich, 1968), p. 77. Citations follow in the text in parentheses with page number and A-S.

9. Hannah Arendt, *The Jew as Pariah*, ed. Ron Feldman (New York: Grove, 1978), pp. 60–61. Citations follow immediately in text with page references in parentheses.

10. See Elisabeth Young-Bruehl's excellent discussion of this incident in Arendt's life. *Hannah Arendt: For Love of the World* (New Haven, Conn.: Yale University Press, 1982), pp. 152–55.

11. "The Concept of History" first appeared in *Review of Politics* 20, 4 (October 1958): 570–90, entitled "The Modern Concept of History." It was reprinted in *Between Past and Future*. "On Humanity in Dark Times" was Arendt's acceptance speech for the Lessing Prize in 1959. It is reprinted in *Men in Dark Times.*

12. "All things that owe their existence to men, such as works, deeds, and words, are perishable, infected, as it were, by the mortality of their authors. However, if mortals succeeded in endowing their works, deeds, and words with some permanence and in arresting their perishability, then these things would, to a degree at least, enter and be at home in the world of everlastingness, and the mortals themselves would find their place in the cosmos, where everything is immortal except men. The human capacity to achieve this was remembrance" (BPF 43).

13. "That living-ness is God's foremost quality informs the dietary and other ritual laws of the Torah. Blood, the paramount symbol of life, may not be eaten. While animal flesh is permitted for human consumption, the blood is not. It must be returned to God. . . . Animals

that themselves consume the blood of other animals may not be eaten by the Israelites. Nor may a kid be boiled in the milk of its mother. The flesh of the young goat may not be cooked in a secondary symbol of life, milk." Edward L. Greenstein, in Barry Holtz, *Back to the Sources*. (New York: Simon and Shuster, 1992), pp. 92–93.

14. In Hannah Arendt, *Men in Dark Times* (New York: Harcourt Brace Jovanovich, 1968 [1955]). Citations appear in the text in parentheses with page reference and MDT.

CHAPTER 12. CONCLUSION

1. Numbers XXIV:5. The prophet Balaam is commanded by the Moabite King Balak to curse the Jews. He makes three attempts, but each time "Balaam saw that it pleased the Lord to bless Israel" (XXIV:1), and his curses were turned into blessings, the most eloquent of which was the final one, "How goodly are your tents, O Jacob." Balek was infuriated, and dismissed Balaam, whose parting gesture was to reveal the fate in store for Moab.

2. I believe that Marx himself also refused to codify when he insisted in the preface to *Capital I* that he would not "write recipes for the cookery books of the future." His followers made up for lost time, in supplying the missing codifications of his theory.

3. Hannah Arendt, *The Human Condition* (Chicago: University of Chicago Press, 1958), pp. 177–78.

4. This of course, is not to say that some Jews, like any other people, are incapable of taking the law into their own hands, professing to "know" what God intends. Recent tragic events in Israel bear this out only too vividly. I mean this discussion to make the point that Jews taking Talmudic or Biblical law into their own hands are no more "Jewish" than any other outlaw or murderer. In the same way, Christian fundamentalists who believe that murdering homosexuals is what God commands, or that destroying the lives of women seeking abortions, or doctors willing to perform them, is ordained by God, are not acting like Christians, either.

5. Or as I was once asked by an elder statesman of the Jewish community of Columbia, South Carolina, who had reference to Arendt, "What was the name of the lady philosopher?"

6. In a recent *New York Times* interview with Henry Roth, Roth is quoted as ascribing his sixty-year-long writer's block to self-loathing,

and the sense that Judaism during the mid-twentieth century meant weakness. Reviewer Jonathan Rosen reports: "Roth suffered terribly during the years he could not write. He was filled with shame and self-loathing, wounded by a childhood of abuse and a young adulthood that was, in his mind, degenerate. He identified Judaism with weakness and cowardice and sought to purge it from his life, becoming a Communist and losing himself in manual labor. . . . Israel's victory in the 1967 war awakened Roth's pride in being a Jew and shattered the hold of Communism on his imagination. Roth's life became emblematic. He seems to stand outside the pantheon of familiar American Jewish writers—Bellow, Malamud, the other Roth—but in some ways he may be the most representative." "Bookend," Jonathan Rosen, *The New York Times Book Review*, 10 December 1995, p. 47.

SELECTED BIBLIOGRAPHY

Abel, Lionel. "New York City: A Remembrance," *Dissent* vol. 8, no. 3 (Summer 1961).

———. "The Aesthetics of Evil: Hannah Arendt on Eichmann and the Jews," *Partisan Review* vol. 30, no. 1 (Spring 1963).

Alter, Robert. *The Art of Biblical Narrative* (New York: Basic Books, 1981).

Alvarez, A. "It Did Not Happen Everywhere," *New Statesman*, 11 October, 1963, pp. 488, 489.

Arendt, Hannah. *Between Past and Future: Eight Exercises in Political Thought* (New York: Viking, 1968).

———. *Crises of The Republic* (New York: Harcourt Brace Jovanovich, 1972).

———. *Eichmann in Jerusalem: A Report on The Banality of Evil* (New York: Penguin, 1963).

———. "Martin Heidegger at Eighty" (1971), in *Heidegger and Modern Philosophy*, ed. M. Murray (New Haven, Conn.: Yale University Press, 1978).

———. *The Human Condition* (Chicago: University of Chicago Press, 1958).

———. *The Jew as Pariah*, ed. Ron Feldman (New York: Grove Press, 1978).

———. *The Life of the Mind: One/Thinking, Two/Willing* (New York: Harcourt Brace Jovanovich, 1978).

———. *Men in Dark Times* (New York: Harcourt Brace Jovanovich, 1968).

———. *On Revolution* (New York: Viking, 1962).

———. *The Origins of Totalitarianism* (New York: Harcourt Brace Jovanovich, 1968).

———. *Rahel Varnhagen: The Life of a Jewish Women* (New York: Harcourt Brace Jovanovich, 1974).

———. "A Reporter at Large: Eichmann in Jerusalem," *New Yorker* (16 February 1963): 40–113; (23 February 1963): 40–111; (2 March 1963): 40–91; (9 March 1963): 48–131; (16 March 1963): 58–134.

———. "Social Science Techniques and the Study of Concentration Camps," *Jewish Social Studies* vol. 12, no. 1 (1950).

———. "Thinking and Moral Considerations: A Lecture," *Social Research* vol. 38, no. 3 (Autumn 1971).

———. "What Is Existenz Philosophy?" *Partisan Review* vol. 18, no. 1 (Winter 1946).

———, and Karl Jaspers. *Correspondence*, ed. Lotte Kohler and Hans Saner, trans. Robert Kimber and Rita Kimber (New York: Harcourt Brace Jovanovich, 1991).

Asian Women United of California. *Making Waves: An Anthology by and about Asian American Women* (Boston: Beacon, 1989).

Barnouw, Dagmar. *Visible Spaces: Hannah Arendt and the German-Jewish Experience* (Baltimore: Johns Hopkins University Press, 1990).

Bazon, Jeanette M. "Hannah Arendt: Personal Reflections," *Response* vol. 30, no. 1 (1980).

Baskin, Judith R., ed. *Women of the Word: Jewish Women and Jewish Writing* (Detroit, Mich.: Wayne State University Press, 1994).

Bauer, Yehuda. *Jews For Sale: Nazi-Jewish Negotiations, 1933–1945* (New Haven, Conn.: Yale University Press, 1994).

Beatty, Joseph. "Thinking and Moral Considerations: Socrates and Arendt's Eichmann," *Journal of Value Inquiry* vol. 10, no. 1 (1976).

Beiner, Ronald, ed. *Hannah Arendt's Lectures on Kant's Political Philosophy* (Chicago: University of Chicago Press, 1982).

Bell, Daniel. "The Alphabet of Justice: Reflections on Eichmann in Jerusalem," *Partisan Review* vol. 30, no. 3 (Fall 1963).

Benhabib, Seyla. "Feminist Theory and Hannah Arendt's Concept of Public Space," *History of the Human Sciences* vol. 6, no. 2 (1993).

Berman, Aaron. *Nazism, The Jews and American Zionism, 1933–1948* (Detroit, Mich.: Wayne State University Press, 1990).

Bernstein, Richard. *Hannah Arendt and the Jewish Question* (Cambridge: MIT Press, 1996).

Biale, David. *Eros and the Jews* (New York: Basic, 1992).

Biale, Rachel. *Women and Jewish Law: An Exploration of Women's Issues in Halakhic Sources* (New York: Schoken, 1984).

Bloom, Alexander. *The New York Intellectuals and Their World* (New York: Oxford University Press, 1986).

Boehm, Eric H., ed. *We Survived* (Santa Barbara, Calif.: Clio, 1966).

Boman, Thorlief. *Hebrew Thought Compared to Greek* (New York: Norton, 1960).

Boyarin, Daniel. *Judaism and Gender: An Autobiography of the Jewish Man* (forthcoming).

Bradshaw, Leah. *Acting and Thinking: The Political Thought of Hannah Arendt* (Toronto: University of Toronto Press, 1989).

Breines, Paul. *Tough Jews: Political Fantasies and the Moral Dilemma of American Jewry* (New York: Basic, 1990).

Brightman, Carol. *Writing Dangerously: Mary McCarthy and Her World* (New York: Clarkson Potter, 1992).

———, ed. *Between Friends: The Correspondence of Hannah Arendt and Mary McCarthy, 1949–1975* (New York: Harcourt Brace Jovanovich, 1995).

Buber, Martin. *On Judaism*, ed. Nature Glazer (New York: Schoken, 1972).

Butler, Judith, and Joan W. Scott. *Feminists Theorize the Political* (New York: Routledge, 1992).

Canovan, Margaret. "Friendship, Truth, and Politics: Hannah Arendt and Toleration." In *Justifying Toleration: Conceptual and Historical Perspectives,* ed. Susan Mendes (Cambridge: Cambridge University Press, 1988).

———. *Hannah Arendt: A Reinterpretation of Her Political Thought* (Cambridge: Cambridge University Press, 1992).

———. *The Political Thought of Hannah Arendt* (New York: Harcourt Brace Jovanovich, 1974).

———. "Socrates or Heideger? Hannah Arendt's Reflections on Philosophy and Politics," *Social Research* vol. 51, no. 1 (Spring 1990).

Chodorow, Nancy. *The Reproduction of Mothering* (Berkeley: University of California Press, 1978).

Collins, Patricia Hill. *Black Feminist Thought: Knowledge, Consciousness, and the Politics of Empowerment* (New York: Routledge, 1990).

Cooney, Terry. *The Rise of the New York Intellectuals: Partisan Review and Its Circle* (Madison: University of Wisconsin Press, 1986).

Court of Appeal: The Black Community Speaks out on the Racial and Sexual Politics of Thomas V. Hill (New York: Ballantine, 1992).

Cuddihy, John. Murray *The Ordeal of Civility* (New York: Delta Books, 1974).

Cutting-Gray, Joanne. "Hannah Arendt, Feminism, and the Politics of Alterity: What Will We Lose if We Win?" *Hypatia* vol. 8, no. 1 (Winter 1993).

Davis, Angela. *Women, Race and Class* (New York: Vintage, 1983).

Deutsch, Kenneth L., and Walter Nicgorski, eds. *Leo Strauss: Political Philosopher and Jewish Thinker* (New York: Rowan and Littlefield, 1994).

Dietz, Mary G. "Feminist Receptions of Hannah Arendt." In *Feminist Interpretations of Hannah Arendt*, ed. Bonnie Honig (University Park: Pennsylvania State University Press, 1995).

———. "Hannah Arendt and Feminist Politics." In *Feminist Interpretations and Political Theory*, ed. Mary Lyndon Shanley and Carole Pateman (University Park: Pennsylvania State University Press, 1992).

Dinnerstein, Dorothy. *The Mermaid and the Minotaur* (New York: Colophon, 1977).

Disch, Lisa J. *Hannah Arendt and the Limits of Philosophy* (Ithaca, N.Y.: Cornell University Press, 1994).

Dossa, Shiraz. *The Public Realm and the Public Self: The Political Theory of Hannah Arendt* (Waterloo: Wilfred Laurier University Press, 1989).

Eliot, Gil. *Twentieth Century Book of the Dead* (New York: Scribner, 1972).

Elshtain, Jean Bethke. *Meditations on Modern Political Thought: Masculine and Feminine Themes from Luther to Arendt* (University Park: Pennsylvania State University Press, 1992).

Ettinger, Elzbieta. *Hannah Arendt, Martin Heideger* (New Haven, Conn.: Yale University Press, 1995).

Fackenheim, Emil L. *Encounters Between Judaism and Modern Philosophy: A Preface to Future Jewish Thought* (New York: Basic, 1973).

Fischman, Dennis. *Political Theory in Exile: Karl Marx and the Jewish Question* (Amherst: University of Massachusetts Press, 1991).

Forman, Frieda, Ethel Raicus, Sarah Silberstein Swartz, and Margie Wolfe, eds. *Found Treasures: Stories by Yiddish Women Writers* (Toronto: Second Story, 1994).

Friedmann, Georges. *The End of the Jewish People?* Trans. Eric Mosbacher (Garden City, N.Y.: Doubleday, 1967).

Freud, Sigmund. *Civilization and Its Discontents*, Trans. James Strachey (New York: Norton, 1961).

Funkenstein, Amos. *Perceptions of Jewish History* (Berkeley: University of California Press, 1993).

Gates, Henry Louis, Jr. "Annals of Race: Thirteen Ways of Looking at a Black Man," *The New Yorker* vol. 71, no. 33 (23 October 1995).

Gillian, Rose. "Love and the State: Varnhagen, Luxemburg and Arendt." In *The Broken Middle: Out of Our Ancient Society* (Oxford: Blackwell, 1992).

Gilman, Sander. *Jewish Self-Hatred* (Baltimore: Johns Hopkins University Press, 1986).

Glenn, Evelyn Nakano. *Issei, Nisei, War Bride: Three Generations of Japanese American Women in Domestic Service* (Philadelphia: Temple University Press 1986).

Glenn, Susan A. *Daughters of the Shtetl: Life and Labor in the Immigrant Generation* (Ithaca, N.Y.: Cornell University Press, 1990).

Handelman, Susan. *The Slayers of Moses: The Emergence of Rabbinic Interpretation in Modern Literary Theory* (Albany: State University of New York Press, 1982).

Hansen, Karen V. "Feminist Conceptions of Public and Private: A Critical Analysis," *Berkeley Journal of Sociology* vol. 32, no. 1 (1987).

Harlow, Rabbi Jules, ed. *Mahzor for Rosh Hashanah and Yom Kippur* (New York: Rabbinical Assembly, 1972).

Hartsock, Nancy. *Money, Sex and Power: Toward a Feminist Historical Materialism* (Boston: Northeastern University Press, 1985).

Hausner, Gideon. *Justice in Jerusalem* (New York: Schocken, 1974).

Hay, Malcolm. *Europe and the Jews: The Pressure of Christendom on the People of Israel for 1900 Years* (Boston: Beacon, 1960).

Heilbut, Anthony. *Exiled in Paradise* (New York: Viking, 1983).

Hertz, Deborah. "Hannah Arendt's Rahel Varnhagen," In *German Women in the Nineteenth Century: A Social History*, ed. John C. Fout (New York: Holmes and Meier, 1984).

Heschel, Abraham J. *The Prophets II* (New York: Harper and Rowe, 1975).

Heschel, Susannah. *On Being a Jewish Feminist: A Reader* (New York: Schoken, 1983).

Hilberg, Raul. *The Destruction of the European Jews* (Chicago: Quadrangle Books, 1967).

———. *Documents of Destruction: Germany and Jewry* (Chicago: Quadrangle Books, 1971).

Hill, Melvin A. *Hannah Arendt: The Recovery of the Public World* (New York: St. Martin, 1979).

Hinchman, Lewis P., and Sandra K. Hinchman, eds. *Hannah Arendt: Critical Essays* (Albany: State University of New York Press, 1994).

Holtz, Barry, ed. *Back to the Sources: Reading the Classic Jewish Texts* (New York: Simon and Schuster, 1984).

Honig, Bonnie, ed. *Feminist Interpretations of Hannah Arendt* (University Park: Pennsylvania State University Press, 1995).

hooks, bell. *Ain't I a Women* (Boston: South End, 1981).

———. *Talking Back: Thinking Feminist, Thinking Black* (Boston: South End, 1989).

Horowitz, Rabbi Dr. L. *Midrash Rabba* (London: Soncino, 1961).

Howe, Irving. "Mid-Century Turning Point: An Intellectual Memoir," *Mainstream* (June–July 1975).

———. "*The New Yorker* and Hannah Arendt," *Commentary* vol. 36, no. 4 (1963).

———. "More on Eichmann," *Partisan Review* vol. 31, no. 2 (Spring 1964).

Howe, Irving. *World of Our Fathers* (New York: Harcourt Brace Jovanovich, 1976).

Hyman, Paula. *Gender and Assimilation in Modern Jewish History: The Roles and Representation of Women* (Seattle: University of Washington Press, 1995).

Isaac, Jeffrey C. "Oasis in the Desert: Hannah Arendt on Democratic Politics," *American Political Science Review* vol. 88, no. 1 (March 1994).

Isaac, Jules. *The Teaching of Contempt: Christian Roots of Anti-Semitism*, trans. H. Weaver (New York: Holt, Rhinehart and Winston, 1969).

Jacoby, Russell. *The Last Intellectuals: American Culture in the Age of Academe* (New York: Basic, 1987).

Jaspers, Karl. *The Great Philosophers* (New York: Harcourt Brace Jovanovich, 1985).

Jay, Martin, and Leon Botstein. "Hannah Arendt: Opposing Views," *Partisan Review* vol. 95, no. 3 (Summer 1978).

Jonas, Hans. "Hannah Arendt 1906–1975" *Social Research* vol. 43, no. 2 (1976).

Jones, Jacqueline. *Labor of Love, Labor of Sorrow: Black Women, Work, and the Family from Slavery to the Present* (New York: Basic, 1985).

Jones, Kathleen B. *Compassionate Authority: Democracy and the Representation of Women* (New York: Routledge, 1993).

Jordan, June. *Technical Difficulties* (New York: Vintage, 1994).

Kadushin, Max. *The Rabbinic Mind* (New York: Bloch, 1952).

Kaplan, Gisella T., and Clive S. Kessler, eds. *Hannah Arendt: Thinking, Judging, and Freedom* (Sydney: Allen and Unwin, 1989).

Kaplan, Marion A. *The Making of the Jewish Middle Class: Women, Family, and Identity in Imperial Germany* (New York: Oxford University Press, 1991).

Kateb, George. "Hannah Arendt: Alienation and America," *Raritan* vol. 3, no. 1 (1983).

———. *Hannah Arendt, Politics, Conscience, Evil* (Totowa, N.J.: Rowman and Allenhead, 1984).

Kazin, Alfred. "In Every Voice, in Every Ban," *New Republic* vol. 110, no. 2 (10 January 1944).

Keller, Evelyn, and Christine Grontkowski. "The Mind's Eye." In *Discovering Reality*, ed. Sandra Harding and Merrill B. Hintikka (Dordrecht, Holland: D. Reidel, 1983).

Keohane, N. O., M. Z. Rosaldo, and B. C. Gelpi, eds. *Feminist Theory: A Critique of Ideology* (Chicago: University of Chicago Press, 1982).

Klawiter, Maren. "Using Arendt and Heidegger to Consider Feminist Thinking on Women and Reproductive/Infertility Technologies," *Hypatia* vol. 5, no. 3 (Fall 1990).

Kohn, Jerome. *Hannah Arendt: Essays in Understanding, 1930–1954* (New York: Harcourt Brace, 1994).

Lane, Ann. "The Feminism of Hannah Arendt," *Democracy* vol. 3, no. 3 (Summer 1983).

Lang, Berel. "Hannah Arendt and the Politics of Evil," *Judaism* vol. 37, no. 3 (1988).

Levin, Nora. *The Holocaust: The Destruction of European Jewry 1933–1945* (New York: Schocken, 1973).

Littel, Franklin H. *The Crucifiction of the Jews* (New York: Harper and Row, 1974).

Loewenstein, Rudolph M. *Christians and Jews: A Psychoanalytic Study* (New York: International Universities Press, 1951).

McCarthy, Mary. "The Hue and Cry," *Partisan Review* vol. 31, no. 1 (Winter 1964).

———. "Saying Good-bye to Hannah," *New York Review of Books* vol. 22, no. 21–22 (22 January 1976).

MacCannell, Juliet Flower. "Facing Fascism: A Feminine Politics of Jouissance," *Topoi* vol. 12 (1993).

MacDonald, Dwight. "More on Eichmann," *Partisan Review* vol. 31, no. 2 (Spring 1964).

Mayer, Jill, and Jane Abramson. *Strange Justice: The Selling of Clarence Thomas* (Boston: Houghton Mifflin, 1994).

Meiselman, Moshe. *Jewish Women and Jewish Law* (New York: KTAV Publishing House, 1978).

Miller, Randall, and Alan Woll. *Ethnic and Racial Images in American Film and Television* (New York: Garland, 1987).

Miller, Stuart Creighton. *The Unwelcome Immigrant* (Berkeley: University of California Press, 1969).

Minnich, Elizabeth Kamarck. "Hannah Arendt: Thinking as We Are." In *Teachers and Artists Write about Their Work on Women*, ed. Carol Ascherm, Louise DeSalvo, and Sara Ruddick (Boston: Beacon, 1984).

Mitchell, Juliet. *Psychoanalysis and Feminism* (New York: Pantheon, 1974).

Morrison, Toni. *Race-ing Justice, En-Gendering Power: Essays on Anita Hill, Clarence Thomas, and the Construction of Social Reality* (New York: Pantheon, 1992).

Mosse, George L. *German Jews Beyond Judaism* (Bloomington: Indiana University Press, 1985).

———. *Nationalism and Sexuality: Middle-Class Morality and Sexual Norms in Modern Europe* (Madison: University of Wisconsin Press, 1985).

Murray, Michael, ed. *Heidegger and Modern Philosophy, Critical Essays* (New Haven, Conn.: Yale University Press, 1978).

Nye, Andrea. *Philosophia: The Thought of Rosa Luxemburg, Simone Weil, and Hannah Arendt* (New York: Routledge, 1994).

O'Brien, Mary. *The Politics of Reproduction* (Boston: Routledge and Kegan Paul, 1981).

Okin, Susan Moller. *Women in Western Political Thought* (Princeton, N.J.: Princeton University Press, 1979).

Ozick, Cynthia. *Metaphor and Memory* (New York: Knopf, 1989).

Phillips, Anne. *Engendering Democracy* (Cambridge: Polity, 1991).

Phillips, William. "How Partisan Review Began," *Commentary* vol 49, no. 4 (December 1976).

Phillips, William. "More on Eichmann," *Partisan Review* vol. 30, no. 1 (Winter 1964).

Pitkin, Hanna. "Conformism, Housekeeping, and the Attack of the Blob: The Origins of Hannah Arendt's Concept of the Social." In *Feminist Interpretations of Hannah Arendt*, ed. Bonnie Honig (University Park: Pennsylvania State University Press, 1995).

———. "Justice: On Relating Private and Public," *Political Theory* vol. 9, no. 3 (August 1981).

Plaskow, Judith. *Standing Again at Sinai: Judaism from a Feminist Perspective* (New York: Harper Collins, 1990).

Plato, *Socrates' Euthyphro, Apology, Crito*, ed. Robert D.Cumming (New York: Bobbs Merrill, 1956).

Podhoretz, Norman. "Hannah Arendt on Eichmann: A Study in the Perversity of Brilliance," *Commentary* vol. 36, no. 3 (September 1963).

———. *Making It* (New York: Harper and Row, 1980 [1967]).

Poliakov, Leon. *Harvest of Hate* (Syracuse: Syracuse University Press, 1954).

Porat, Dina. *The Blue and Yellow Stars of David: The Zionist Leadership in Palestine and the Holocaust, 1939–1945* (Cambridge: Harvard University Press, 1990).

Rich, Adrienne. *On Lies, Secrets and Silence: Selected Prose, 1966–1978* (New York: Norton, 1979).

Ring, Jennifer. *Modern Political Theory and Contemporary Feminism: A Dialectical Analysis* (Albany: State University of New York Press, 1991).

———. "On Needing Both Marx and Arendt: Alienation and the Flight from Inwardness," *Political Theory* vol. 17, no. 3 (August 1989).

———. "The Pariah as Hero: Hannah Arendt's Political Actor," *Political Theory* vol. 19, no. 3 (August 1991).

Robinson, Jacob. *And the Crooked Shall be Made Straight* (Philadelphia: Jewish Publication Society, 1965).

Rose, Paul Lawrence. *Revolutionary Anti-Semitism in Germany: From Kent to Wagner* (Princeton, N.J.: Princeton University Press, 1990).

Rosen, Jonathan. "Bookend," *The New York Times Book Review* (10 December 1995), p. 47.

Rubenstein, Richard L. *After Auschwitz* (Indianapolis, Ind.: Bobbs Merrill, 1966).

———. *The Holocaust and the American Future* (New York: Harper and Rowe, 1975).

Saxonhouse, Arlene W. *Women in the History of Political Thought, Ancient Greece to Machiavelli* (New York: Praeger, 1985).

Schechter, Solomon. *Aspects of Rabbinic Theology* (Woodstock, Vt.: Jewish Lights Publishing,1993).

Segev, Tom. *The Seventh Million: The Israelis and the Holocaust*, trans. Haim Watzman (New York: Hill and Wang, 1993).

Shanley, Mary Lyndon, and Carole Pateman, eds. *Feminist Interpretations and Political Theory* (University Park: Pennsylvania State University Press, 1991).

Shklar, Judith N. "Hannah Arendt as Pariah," *Partisan Review* vol. 50, no. 1 (Winter 1983).

Skoller, Eleanor Honig. *The In-Between of Writing: Experience and Experiment in Drabble, Duras, and Arendt* (Ann Arbor: University of Michigan Press, 1993).

Syrkin, Marie. "Miss Arendt Surveys the Holocaust," *Jewish Frontier* (May 1963).

Teubal, Savina, J. *Sarah The Priestess: The First Matriarch of Genesis* (Athens: Ohio University Press, 1984).

Tredennick, Hugh, ed. *The Last Days of Socrates* (New York: Penguin, 1969).

Trunk, Isaac. *Judenrat: The Jewish Councils in Eastern Europe under Nazi Occupation* (New York: Macmillan, 1972).

Wald, Alan. *The New York Intellectuals: The Rise and Decline of the Anti-Stalinist Left from the 1930s to the 1980s* (Chapel Hill: University of North Carolina Press, 1987).

Walker, Alice. *The Same River Twice: Honoring the Difficult* (New York: Scribner, 1996).

Wolin, Richard, ed. *The Heidegger Controversy: A Critical Reader* (New York: Columbia University Press, 1991).

Yaeger, Patricia. *Honey-Mad Women: Emancipatory Strategies in Women's Writing* (New York: Columbia University Press, 1988).

Yahil, Leni. *The Holocaust: The Fate of European Jewry* (New York: Oxford University Press, 1990).

Yerushalmi, Yosef Hayim. *Freud's Moses: Judaism Terminable and Interminable* (New Haven, Conn.: Yale University Press, 1991).

———. *Zakhor: Jewish History and Jewish Memory* (New York: Schoken, 1989).

Young-Bruehl, Elisabeth. *Hannah Arendt: For Love of the World* (New Haven, Conn.: Yale University Press, 1982).

INDEX

Abel, Lionel, 27–30, 96, 138, 163
Abraham, 285
Adenauer, Chancellor Konrad, on the Holocaust, 76
Afro-American racial stereotypes, 11
Aggada (narrative commentary), 186
Akiba, Rabbi, 180, 252
Alcabiades, 245
Aleichem, Sholem, 147–148
Allen, Woody, 130
Alter, Robert, *The Art Of Biblical Narrative*, 177–178
American Joint Distribution Committee (JDC), 56
anti-semitism, 10–11, 60–61, 112–119, 129
   before the Holocaust, 60–61
   and homophobia, 10–11
   sexual component in, 10–11, 112–119, 129
Arendt, Hannah
   Between Past and Future, 19–20, 41, 259, 263, 283; quoted, 260, 262
   "Collective Responsibility," essay in, 217
   "The Concept Of History," essay in, quoted, 264–270
   "The Crisis in Culture," essay in, quoted, 273
   "Concern With Politics in Recent European Philosophical Thought," 224
   correspondence with Gertrude Jaspers, 3; Karl Jaspers, 3, 26, 160–161, 218, 222; Mary McCarthy, 151–152; Gershom Sholem, 7
   and Adolph Eichmann, 31
   Eichmann In Jerusalem, 21–37, 39, 80–88, 103, 106–112, 119–131, 162–163, 213–217, 231, 285, 288
   and Leo Baeck, 24, 162–163
   and "the banality of evil," 23–24
   Dagmar Barnouw on, 107; quoted, 24–25, 162–163
   criticisms of, by Lionel Abel, 27–30, 107; Daniel Bell, 30, 35–36; Norman Podhoretz, 27–28; Gershom Sholem, 27, 29–32, 163, 169
   defended by Alfred Kazin, 28; Dwight Macdonald, 27–28, 35–37; Mary McCarthy, 27–30, 34
   effect of controversy on Arendt's thought, 21–22
   and Nathan Glazer and Daniel Patrick Moynihan, *Beyond The Melting Pot*, 107
   and Raul Hilberg's *The Destruction Of The European Jews*, 27–28, 33, 39, 109–110
   and Jewish leadership (*Judenräte*), 23–24, 26, 28, 34, 80–88

Arendt, Hannah *continued*
and William Phillips, 29
why upsetting to Jewish men,
22–24, 103–108, 110–112,
119–131, 285–286
and gender, 157, 166–171, 284–288
The Human Condition, 3, 20, 41,
213, 229, 254, 260, 282;
quoted, 256–258, 268, 283–284
as Jewish thinking, 255–268,
282
influenced by Aristotle, 3, 41,
216; Augustine, 41, 216;
Camus, 42; Duns Scotus,
41; Heidegger, 3, 41, 158–159, 216, 219, 220–225,
229, 233–235, 238, 241–242;
Jaspers, 3, 41, 216, 219–221;
Jesus, 216–217; Kant, 3, 41,
216, 219; Lazare, 219; Luxemburg, 219; Machiavelli,
216; Judah Magnes, 219;
Marx, 216, 219; Plato, 41,
220–221, 234, 241–243;
Socrates, 3, 29, 41, 160–166,
216–217, 219–221, 229, 238,
241–248, 250–252, 277–278;
Vico, 41; Weber, 216
and Jewish identity, 158–171,
218–219, 222–234, 261–263,
275–284
as a Jewish thinker, 19–20, 160,
174, 213–229, 231–284
The Life Of The Mind (v.1,
Thinking), 3, 6, 19, 41, 160,
183, 205, 213–225, 229,
231–251, 255; quoted, 22,
231–237, 240–248
Canovan on, 216–221, 224–225,
232, 242, 261
"Martin Heidegger at Eighty,"
222; quoted, 223–224
Men in Dark Times, 19, 41

"On Humanity in Dark Times,"
essay in, 263, 273, 279;
quoted, 218–219, 270–272
and pariahs, 238–252, 258–260
and parvenus, 6–7
On Revolution, 41, 218
The Origins Of Totalitarianism
on assimilation, 168
Alexander Bloom on, 105
and Alfred Kazin, 105
and "The New York Intellectuals," 28–29, 40, 103–106,
151, 153, 155
and "radical evil," 104–107
Alan Wald on, 104
and plurality, 218–233
*Rahel Varnhagen: The Life Of a
Jewish Woman*, 2–3, 41
Karl Jaspers on, 3
"Thinking and Moral Considerations," quoted, 22, 163–164
"Truth and Politics," 22, 225–228
"We Refugees," 261–262
"What Is Existenz Philosophy?,"
222, 225; quoted, 223

Ba'al Shem Tov, 187
Baeck, Leo, 24, 162
Barnouw, Dagmar, 24–25, 162–163
Bauer, Jehudah, *Jews For Sale: Nazi-
Jewish Negotiations, 1933–
1945*, quoted, 47, 58–63,
68, 70
Begin, Menachim, leader of *Herut*,
77–78; opposed to negotiations with Germany, 77;
and the "Kastner Trial," 82
Bell, Daniel, 30, 94; quoted, 35–36,
102
Bellow, Saul, 130
Ben Gurion, David, 19, 34, 49,
50, 53, 55, 67; quoted, 52,
54–57, 77, 85, 100, 111
and the "Final Solution," 58

and the "Kastner Trial," 81–84
and negotiations with Germany, 71, 75–80
and parachuting Jewish troops into occupied Europe, 65
as Prime Minister, 75–80
On "Trucks For Blood," 69
Bergen Belsen, 74
Berkeley Free Speech Movement, 259
Bettelheim, Bruno, 126
Between Past and Future, 19–20, 41, 259–263, 283
Biale, David, *Eros and the Jews*, 139; quoted, 128–131
Bible, The (Torah), 177–179, 186, 188, 206, 209–211, 277, 282
Handelman on, 206
Birkenau, 64
Bloom, Alexander, *Prodigal Sons: The New York Intellectuals and Their World*, quoted, 44, 92–95, 99–102, 104, 107–108, 133, 135–137
Bloom, Harold, 276; quoted, 174–175
Blucher, Heinrich, husband of Hannah Arendt, 104
Boman, Thorlief, *Hebrew Thought Compared With Greek*, 20, 195–202, 206–207, 211, 233, 243, 246
and Hannah Arendt, 195
Boyarin, Daniel, *Judaism and Gender: An Autobiography of the Jewish Man*, 139, 148, 286; quoted, 119–126
Brand, Hansi, widow of Joel, 79–80
Brand, Joel, associate of Kastner, 68–71
Breines, Paul, *Tough Jews: Political Fantasies and the Moral Dilemma of American Jewry*, 121, 130, 139; quoted, 123–127, 134, 153

Buber, Martin, on trying Eichmann, 85

Camus, Albert, 42
Canovan, Margaret, *Hannah Arendt: A Reinterpretation Of Her Political Thought*, 216–221, 224–225, 242; quoted, 216–217, 219, 221, 224–225, 238
Char, Rene, 260–262; quoted, 260–261
Christian Thinking, 190, 195, 198–200, 216, 219
Arendt on, 266–267
Funkenstein on, 190
Churchill, Winston, and the bombing of death camps, 64
Cicero, 264; quoted, 273
Clemenceau, Georges, 217, 219
"Collective Responsibility," 217
Commentary, 26–27, 91, 96
"Concept Of History, The," 264–270
"Concern with Politics in Recent European Philosophical Thought," 224
Cooney, Terry, *The Rise Of the New York Intellectuals: Partisan Review and Its Circle*, quoted, 92–93, 101, 137–138
"Crossing Delancey," 130
Cuddihy, John Murray, *The Ordeal Of Civility*, quoted, 168

Davidowicz, Lucy, 126, 151
Davis, Angela, *Women, Race, and Class*, 14
De Leon, Moses Ben Shem Tov, 187
Derash, commentaries on the Bible, 187
Diaspora (Jewish), 72
Dissent, 26–27

Dobkin, Eliyahu, 51, 53–54;
  quoted, 72
  and parachuting Jewish troops
    into occupied Europe, 65
Dreyfus case, 219
Duns Scotus, 41

Eden, Anthony, quoted, 49
  and the bombing of the death
    camps, 64
  and the Holocaust, 46, 48
Eichmann, Adolf
  and Arendt, 31
  negotiations with Zionists, 61–63
  on trial in Jerusalem, 84–89
Eichmann In Jerusalem, 21–37, 39,
  80–88, 103, 106–112, 119–
  131, 162–163, 213–217, 231,
  285, 288
Einstein, Albert, 99
ethnicity, 3–4, 9, 37–42, 158–171,
  214–215, 234, 261, 275–284

Farrell, James T., 136
Fausto-Sterling, Anne, 16
Feldman, Ron, *The Jew As Pariah*,
  41
Feminism
  Black Feminism, 11–14, 140
    Angela Davis, 14
    Anita Hill, 11
    bell hooks, 11; quoted, 14–15
  Jewish Feminism, 139–150
    and David Biale, 139
    and Daniel Boyarin, 139
    and Paul Brienes, 139
    and the education of Jewish
      girls, 148–150
    Susannah Heschel, 141
    Marian Kaplan, 149–150, 168–
      169
    Irena Klepfisz, 146–147
    and Moshe Meiselman, 141–142
    and George Mosse, 139
    Cynthia Ozick, 140, 143, 145–146

  role of Yiddish and Hebrew,
    146–148
  Sandra Harding, 16–17
  Nancy Hartsock, 17
  Evelyn Fox Keller, 16
  Catharine MacKinnon, 16
  Anne Fausto Sterling, 16
Freud, Sigmund, 199
  Civilization and Its Discontents, 41
  The Interpretation Of Dreams,
    123–124
  as a Jewish writer, 176
  and sexuality, 121–122; quoted,
    125, 153

Gemara, 186
German thinking, 216
gender, 1–2, 37–42
  and Arendt, 157–160, 166–171,
    284–288
  and assimilation, 131–139
  bias, 13–15, 17, 110–131, 285–
    286
  and Jewish Feminism, 139–150
Gilligan, Carol, *In a Different Voice*,
  15–16; quoted, 15
Glazer, Nathan, and Daniel
  Patrick Moynihan, *Beyond
  the Melting Pot*, 107
Gold, Mike, editor of *The New
  Masses*, 137–138
Goldman, Emma, 130, 151
Goldman, Nahum, president of
  the World Zionist Organization during the Eichmann
  trial, 85
Golomb, Eliahu, leader of
  Haganah, quoted, 65–66
Greek (Western) thinking, 174,
  195–202, 204, 207, 215–216,
  233–236, 239–240, 248,
  251–252, 256–259, 264,
  266–267, 278
  Boman on, 195–201, 204, 206–
    207, 243, 246

Funkenstein on, 190–191
Handelman on, 210
Greunbaum, Yitzhak, leader of JAE, 50, 53, 55–57; quoted, 72
and bombing of the death camps, 64
and "Trucks for Blood," 69, 71
Gruenwald, Michael, accuser of Rudolf Kastner, 71, 80–83

Haavara (transfer of Jews from under nazi dominance), 59–63, 84
and the AJC, 61
and Eichmann, 61–63
and Gestapo, 61
and the Jewish Agency, 61–62
and the Nazis, 61–63
Halakha (Jewish legal commentary), 186, 193
Handelman, Susan, *The Slayers of Moses: The Emergence of Rabbinic Interpretation in Modern Literary Theory*, 181–183, 206, 210
Harding, Sandra, 16–17
Hardwicke, Elizabeth, 152
Harlow, Rabbi Jules, *Mahzor for Rosh Hashanah and Yom Kippur*, 181–182
Hartsock, Nancy, "The Feminist Standpoint," quoted, 17
Hassidism, 187
Hausner, Israeli Attorney General Gideon, quoted, 86–87
"Heartbreak Kid, The," 130
Hegel, G. W. F., 192, 257
Philosophy Of History, 283–284
Heidegger, Martin, 3, 41, 158–159, 216, 219, 220–225, 229, 233, 235, 238, 241–242
Heilbut, Anthony, *Exiled in Paradise*, Arendt quoted in, 151

Heraclitus, 196
Herodotus, 264
Herut party of Israel, led by Begin, 77, 82
Herzl, Theodor, 125
Heschel, Susannah, ed., *On Being a Jewish Feminist: A Reader*, quoted, 141, 144–145
Heshin, Israeli Justice Salman, quoted, 84
Himmler, Heinrich, on sexuality and race, quoted, 117–118
Hill, Anita, 11
Hilberg, Raul, *The Destruction of the European Jews*, 27–28, 33, 39, 43–44, 109–110, 151, 154–155
Histadrut (General Federation of Jewish Workers in Palestine), 50, 55–56
Hitler, Adolf, 49, 117
Mein Kampf, 59, 100
in debate over negotiations to save Jews, 62
Holocaust
attitude toward by "The New York Intellectuals," 10; Zionists, 10, 46, 71–75
and Konrad Adenauer, 76
in Eichmann trial, 85–89
and Anthony Eden, 46, 48
and Adolf Hitler, 49
and JAE, 50
and *Mapai*, 50
and Moshe Shertok, 49
and Rabbi Weissmandel, 48
and Chaim Weizmann, 49
Holtz, Barry, ed., *Back to the Sources: Reading the Classic Jewish Texts*, 177, 181, 183–187
Homer, 264
Hook, Sidney, "Tragedy of German Jewry," 99–100
hooks, bell, 11, quoted, 15

Howe, Irving, *World Of Our Fathers*, quoted, 93, 101, 108–109, 133, 135, 167
Hungarian Revolution, 259
Human Condition, The, 3, 20, 41, 213, 229, 254–258, 260, 268, 282–284

Israel
  and the Holocaust, 71–75
  and negotiations with Germany, 71, 75–80
  Begin, opposed to, 77–78
  Rimalt, quoted on, 177
  party politics of the Eichmann trial, 75–89

Jacob, 208–209
Jacoby, Russell, *The Last Intellectuals: American Culture in the Age of Academe*, quoted, 92–93
Jaspers, Karl, 3, 26, 41, 160–161, 216, 219, 220–221, 225
"Jazz Singer The," 130
Jesus, 216–217
Jewish Agency Executive (JAE), 50, 55–57
  and Eliyahu Dobkin, 51
  and Yitzhak Gruenbaum, 50
  and *Haavara*, 61
  and Meyer Schapira, 51
  and Moshe Shertok, 51
  and "Trucks for Blood," 68
Jewish historicism, 188–193, 207, 263–274
  Funkenstein on, 188–193, 207, 264
  Yerushalmi on, 188–193, 207, 264
Jewish identity, 3–4, 9, 37–42, 158–171, 175, 214–215, 234, 261, 275–284
Jewish mysticism, Hassidism, Kabbalism, *Zohar*, 187

Jewish thinking, 174–193, 195–211, 213–229, 231–284
  Alter on, 177–178
  and see Arendt and Jewish identity, 158–171, 214–215, 275–278; Arendt as a Jewish thinker, 19–20, 160, 174, 213–229, 231–274
  The Bible, 177–179, 186, 188, 206, 209–211, 253–254, 276, 283
  Alter, Holtz, and Rosenberg on, 177–178, 181
  Bloom on, 175–176, 276
  Boman on, 195–201, 204, 206–207, 243, 246
  defined, 201, 205–211
  and *Eichmann in Jerusalem*, 213–215
  Freud as a Jewish writer, 176
  Handelman on, 207, 210
  Hebrew thought compared with Greek thought, 20, 195–211, 213–236, 239–240, 248, 256–259, 266–267, 278
    Boman on, 195–201, 204, 206–207, 243, 246
    Heraclitus, 196
    Plato, 196, 198
  historicism and, 188–193, 207, 263–264
    Funkenstein on, 188–193, 207, 264
    Yerushalmi on, 188–193, 207, 264
  The Human Condition as, 213
  Jewish identity and, 158, 171, 175, 214–215, 276–284
  Kabbalism, 187
  Kadushin on, 20, 202–205
  Kafka as a Jewish writer, 176
  Midrash, 177, 185–188
    Derash and *Peshat*, 187
    Holtz on, 185–187
    Rashi, 186

Mishnah, 186
mysticism, 187
Rabbinic thought, 201–211
Talmud, 177, 179–186, 188, 210–211, 252–254, 270, 277, 282
  Akiba, 180
  Holtz on, 181, 184–185
Johnson, Lyndon, 162
Joint Rescue Committee, 55
Jonas, Hans, 235
Judaism, 4–7, 9, 42
  and male dominance, 11–14

Kabbalism and *Zohar*, 187
Kadushin, Max, *The Rabbinic Mind*, 20, 202–205, 209, 277; quoted 202–204
Kafka, Franz, as a Jewish writer, 176
Kant, Immanuel, 3, 41, 216, 219, 222
Kaplan, Marian, *The Making of the Jewish Middle Class*, 168–169; quoted, 149–150
Kastner, Rudolf, 67–84
  head, Hungarian Rescue Committee and "Trucks For Blood," 67–71
  the "Kastner trial," 80–84
  assassinated, 83
"Kastner trial," the, 80–84, 153
  and Ben Gurion, 81
  and Gruenwald, 80
  and the *Judenräte*, 80–84
  and Tamir, 81
Kazin, Alfred, 28, 96
  "In Every Voice, in Every Ban," *New Republic*, 100; quoted 101, 104
Keller, Evelyn Fox, 16
Kirshenbaum, Rabbi David, 130
Klepfisz, Irena, 130
  Introduction to *Found Treasures: Stories by Yiddish Women Writers*, quoted, 146–147

Klinger, Chaika, Hungarian underground fighter, quoted, 72
Kohlberg, Lawrence, 15–16
Kurtz, Ya'acov, quoted, 53

Lazare, Bernard, 219
Lessing, G. E., 271–272
Life of the Mind, The (v.1, *Thinking*), 3, 6, 19, 22, 41, 160, 183, 205, 213–225, 229, 231–251, 255
Luria, Isaac, 187
Luxemburg, Rosa, 151, 219
"Lying in Politics," 162

Macdonald, Dwight, 27, 28, 30, 35, 96, 98; quoted, 36–37, 104
Machiavelli, Niccolo, 216
MacKinnon, Catharine, 16
Magnes, Judah, 219
Mailer, Norman, reviews Mary McCarthy's *The Group* as a "lady book," 152
Maimonides, Moses, 187, 192; quoted on women and Judaism, 142
Mapai party (Israel), 19, 34, 50, 55, 57, 111
  and Ben Gurion, leader, 50
  and the "Kastner trial," 82
  and negotiations with Germany, 71–80
"Martin Heidegger at Eighty," 222–224
Marx, Karl, 17, 134, 191, 203, 216, 219, 265, 268–269, 277
masculinity
  Boyarin on, 119–126, 139, 286
  Breiner on, 121–127, 134, 139
  and *Eichmann in Jerusalem*, 126–128
  and Jewish identity, 115–118, 153–154, 286–287
  Arendt, 126, 151–152

masculinity *continued*
  Biale on, 128–131, 139
  and Marx, 134, 138
  Mosse on, 112–118, 121, 127, 130, 139
  and sexism, 151–156, 170, 284–285
  and Leon Trotsky, 134
  and Yiddish *versus* Hebrew, 146–148
Mason, Jackie, 130
Meir, Golda, 66
Meiselman, Moshe, *Jewish Women in Jewish Law*, quoted, 141–142
Men in Dark Times, 19, 41
  "On Humanity in Dark Times," essay in, 218–219, 263, 270–273, 279
Midrash, 177, 180, 185–187
  Aggada and *Halakha*, 186
  Derash and *Peshat*, 187
  and Rashi, 186
Mishnah, 186
Montaigne, Michel, 176
Montgomery (Alabama) bus boycott, 259
Moses, 181
  and religious imagery, 208–209
Mosse, George, *Nationalism and Sexuality: Middle-Class Morality and Sexual Norms in Modern Europe*, 101, 127, 130, 139; quoted, 112–118, 121
McCarthy, Mary, 27–30, 34–37, 136–137, 151–152
McCarthyism, *see* "The New York Intellectuals," 101, 103–104, 106, 108

New Leader, The, 99–100
New Republic, The, 26–27
"New York Intellectuals, The"
  Abel, Lionel, 27–30, 96, 107, 163
  and assimilation, 91–101, 153–156, 159, 167

Bell, Daniel, 30, 35–36, 94, 102
Bloom, Alexander on, 44, 92–95, 99–103
and *Commentary*, 26–27, 91, 96, 167
Cooney, Terry on, 92–94, 101, 137–138
guilt for ignoring plight of European Jews, 101, 108
Howe, Irving, 93, 101, 108–109, 133, 135, 167
Hook, Sidney, 99–100
Russell Jacoby on, 92–93
and Jewish identity, 19, 91–98
Kazin, Alfred, 28, 44, 96, 100–101, 104–105
and McCarthyism, 101, 103–104, 106, 108
Macdonald, Dwight, 96, 98, 104
The Origins of Totalitarianism, reaction to, 103–106
and *The Partisan Review*, 26–27, 91, 96, 99, 101, 105–106
Phillips, William, 29, 94, 96–97, 137
Podhoretz, Norman, 27–28
Rahv, Philip, 94, 97
Rosenberg, Harold, 96
  and sexism, 151–156
and Stalinism, 101, 106, 138
and Trotsky, Leon, and Trotskyism, 134–135
Trilling, Lionel, 94–96
Wald, Allen on, 98, 104
Warshaw, Robert, 133
Wilson, Edmund, 96
New York Review of Books, The, 152
"Norma Rae," 130

On Revolution, 41, 218
Origins of Totalitarianism, The, 28–29, 40, 103–107, 151, 153, 155, 168
Ozick, Cynthia, "Notes toward Finding the Right Question," quoted, 140, 143, 145–146

Palgi, Joel, paratrooper associate of Hanna Senesh, quoted, 75
pariahs, 238–252, 258–260
Parmenides, 271
Partisan Review, The, 26–27, 96–97, 99, 101, 105–106, 111, 128, 134–139, 151–152
Passover service (seder), 262–263
Peretz, I. L., 147
Peshat, commentaries on the Bible, 187
Phillips, William, 29, 94, 96, 97, 137
Philo of Alexandria, 224, 233–234, 237
Pinkerton, Lowell C., American Consul in Jerusalem, on bombing of death camps, 64
Plato, 41, 96, 198–199, 204, 220–221, 234, 241–243, 271, 273
Podhoretz, Norman, 27–28
Pomerantz, Venia, and "Trucks for Blood," 68
Porat, Dina, *The Blue and Yellow Stars of David: The Zionist Leadership in Palestine and the Holocaust, 1939–1945*, quoted, 45–50, 52–56, 58, 64–69, 72–73
Proust, Marcel, 176

Rahel Varnhagen: The Life of a Jewish Woman, 2–3, 41
Rahv, Philip, 94, 96–97, 136–137
Rashi, 186
Remez, David, Leader of *Histadrut*, 50; quoted, 72
rescue of Jews from Nazi-dominated Europe, debates on bombing of death camps, 59
  and Ben Gurion, 64
  and Churchill, 64
  and Eden, 64
  and JAE, 64
  paratroopers to occupied territory, 63, 65–67
  and Ben Gurion, 65
  and Dobkin, 65
  and Golomb, 65–66
  and Meir, 66
  and Palgi, 75
  and Rott, 66
  and Senesh, 66–67
  and Shertok, 65
  "Trucks for Blood," 59, 61–71
  and Ben Gurion, 69
  and Joel Brand, 68–71
  and Eichmann, 68–71
  and Gruenbaum, 69, 71
  and JAE, 68
  and Kastner, 67–71
  and Pomerantz, 68
Rich, Adrienne, 130
Rimalt, Elimelech, member of the Knesset, quoted, 76
Rosenberg, Harold, 96; quoted, 138
Rosenberg, Joel, in B. Holtz, ed., *Back to the Sources*, 178
Roth, Philip, 124, 130
Rott, Egon, Jewish rebel leader in Slovakia, quoted, 66

Sarah, 285
Schapira, Meyer (JAE), 51
Segev, Tom, *The Seventh Million: The Israelis and the Holocaust*, 44–45, 58, 63, 67, 69, 72; quoted, 44, 52, 54, 60, 62, 65–66, 73–76, 78–83, 85–86
Senesh, Hanna, Jewish paratrooper and hero, 66–67, 75; quoted, 67
Sforim, Mendele Mokher, 147
Shertok, Moshe (later Sharett), JAE, 49, 51, 58
  and bombing of death camps, 64
  and paratroopers to occupied Europe, 65

Sholem, Gershom, 27, 29–32, 37, 163, 169
Singer, I. B., 124, 148
Socrates, 3, 20, 41, 160–161, 163, 166, 219–221, 229, 238, 241–242, 248–252, 278
   Jaspers on, 166
   as pariah, 242–247, 251–252
   quoted, 164–165, 216–217, 225
Sophocles, quoted by Aristotle, 13
S. S. Struma incident, 53
Syrkin, Marie, 27, 29, 32–34, 37, 151, 163

Talmud, 177, 179–186, 188, 210–211, 252–254, 270, 277
   Akiba, 180
   Handelman quoted on, 181–183
   Rabbi Haninah Ben Tradyon, quoted, 182
   Holtz, quoted on, 181, 183–184
Tamir, Shmuel, attorney for Gruenwald, 81–83
   quoted on Ben Gurion, 83
Thales, 246
"Thinking and Moral Considerations," 22, 163–164
Thomas, Justice Clarence, 13
Totalitarianism, 4, 219–220
Tradyon, Rabbi Haninah Ben, 181–182
Trilling, Lionel, 94–96; quoted, 95–96
Trotsky, Leon, 134–135
Trunk, Isaiah, 126
"Truth and Politics," 22, 225–228; quoted, 22, 226–228

Universalism (or Objectivism), 5, 9
   versus tribalism, 35–42

Vico, Giambattista, 41

Wald, Allen, *The New York Intellectuals: The Rise and Decline of the Anit-Stalinist Left, from the 1930's to the 1980's*, 98; quoted, 104
Warshaw, Robert, quoted, 133
"Way We Were The," 130
"We Refugees," 261–262
Weber, Max, 216
Weissmandel, Rabbi Michael Dov-Beer, quoted, 48
Weizmann, Chaim, president World Zionist Organization, 49, 51
Weininger, Otto, *Sex and Character*, 117
"What Is Existenz Philosophy?," 222–223, 225
Wilson, Edmund, 96, 136; quoted, 137
Wise, Rabbi Stephen, chair, American Jewish Congress, 61

Xenophon, *Anabasis*, 258

Yerushalmi, Yosef Hayim, *Freud's Moses: Judaism Terminable and Interminable*, quoted 175; *Zakhor: Jewish History and Jewish Memory*, with an Introduction by Harold Bloom, 175, 188–193, 264, 267; quoted, 189
Young-Bruehl, Elisabeth, quoted, 21
Youngman, Henny, 130

Zionists
   and *Eichmann in Jerusalem*, 18–19, 34
   and *Haavara*, 59–63
   and the Holocaust, 45, 71–80
   intervention to rescue Jews from Europe, 18, 19, 34, 57, 64–71